# The Identification of English Pressed Glass 1842-1908

Jenny Thompson

*Published by:*
Mrs. Jenny Thompson

*Printed by:*
Dixon Printing Co. Ltd., Kendal, Cumbria.



ISBN 0 9515491 0 3

*Front Cover Pictures:*
Taken from the *"Encyclopaedia of Practical Cookery"* published in the reign of Queen Victoria.

*Back Cover Picture:*
Sowerby & Co. Pattern Book c1879 gold colour.

# Foreword

Unlike most other items of Victorian glass, pressed glass can nearly always be precisely identified either by Patent Office Design Registry marks, or by the maker's trademarks, which could easily be incorporated into the iron moulds. It is this aspect of pressed glass that makes it a fascinating subject for a collector, and although some of the rarer objects, such as the Derbyshire 'Winged Sphinx' paperweight, fetch high prices, the majority of pieces are within the price range of collectors of modest means.

Jenny Thompson's book is to be welcomed as providing a concise, clear and comprehensive guide to the identification of pressed glass objects, with an analysis of the characteristic designs of the individual firms as well as details of the actual registrations. The publication of some of the original drawings from the Patent Office Design Registers is a new feature, not included in previous volumes on the subject. These drawings are especially fascinating as they show exactly what was registered, sometimes merely the shape, sometimes just a pattern which was then applied to a number of different articles. This book will undoubtedly be an invaluable tool for the keen collector of pressed glass.

Mrs. Barbara Morris
March 1989

# Acknowledgements

I owe many thanks to the Ceramics department of the Victoria and Albert Museum when Mr. John Mallet was Keeper, and especially to Ann Eatwell, for all the help given to me over the many years that I was studying the registrations. I thank the Trustees of the Victoria and Albert Museum for their photographs of pressed glass in the Museum.

I am very grateful to Mrs. Barbara Morris for her encouragement and help in many ways and always for her sound advice; to Nicolas Powell for his photographs, and to all those who valiantly coped with my handwriting and typed sheets of numbers.

I must acknowledge the custody of the Design Registers and the Representations by the Public Record Office and thank them gratefully for permission to publish these lists and for their cooperation.

The cover to this book is from the Victorian "*Encyclopaedia of Practical Cookery*". In lieu of an author my reference goes to Messrs. Ring and Brymer, Caterers then and today, who assisted in the original volume.

Finally this book is for Martin with my very best love and thanks, for all his splendid help, and for our family.

I hope all lovers of pressed glass will find it useful.

Jenny Thompson.
July 1989

# References

1) The Design Registrations and Representations.

2) *English Pressed Glass.* Raymond Slack

3) *Glass Circle Paper No. 4,* March 1980. Roger Dodsworth.

4) *History of the Homeland.* Henry Hamilton.

5) *Sowerby Gateshead Glass.* Simon Cottle.

6) *Victorian Table Glass & Ornaments.* Barbara Morris

# The Identification of Victorian and Edwardian Pressed Glass up to 1908

Pressed glass belongs to that golden age of Victorian industrial and commercial expansion which came in with the aftermath of the Industrial Revolution.

One of the main characteristics of that time was the greatly increased use of power driven machinery and therefore, the expansion of the factory system as opposed to the workshop, in which previously it was usual for the worker to own his own tools and work was on a much smaller scale. With costly machinery this was no longer possible so the industrialist owned the machinery and directed his workforce. This led to a further feature of the period, that of industrial concentration and considerable urbanization.

The population of Birmingham was 144,000 in 1831 and 233,000 in 1851 and that of Manchester and Salford for the same years was 238,000 and 401,000. People poured into the towns from the countryside as streets of Victorian houses bear witness.

At that time Britain stood unique in the world, confident of supplying any goods required and sure that she would be able to meet any foreign competition. There was great industrial and commercial prosperity and with it a new and ever increasing middle class. Indeed, there were several divisions within that class and because the Victorians crammed their houses with objects and decoration, these people desired for themselves what had been the prerogative in the 18th century of the gentry, merchant, clerical, banking and legal professions.

In the bigger houses it was necessary to have two or three large dinner services, three dessert services and dozens of glasses to cope with ale, water, sherry, wine, port and brandy apart from those for custard and syllabubs. Then there were the decanters, carafes, finger bowls, ice plates, chutney, marmalade and jam jars, comports, sweetmeat dishes and so on. Some of these items were made in silver and porcelain, but those in glass were usually cut or engraved and came from Ireland, where there was no glass tax, and the first class glass houses of Stourbridge, Birmingham and London, with names such as Richardson's, Thomas Webb, Bacchus, James Powell and Apsley Pellatt.

With the upsurge in the profits of steel, coal, railways, cotton, wool and commerce this new flourishing middle class market with its varied echelons wanted similar pieces but at a lower cost.

Pressed glass provided an answer; the tax on glass was repealed by 1845 which lessened the price and it could be made in vast quantities in moulds. Just before 1845, the excise duty on glass yielded some £600,000 but the remission of the duty meant an increase in production of glass for both home use and export.

The earliest British pressed glass was probably made about 1836 in the Birmingham area, although as early as 1831, mindful of American competition, Apsley Pellatt took out a patent for a new way of assembling moulds.

The Pottery Gazette of February 1st 1886 describes the making of pressed glass as follows:

### "THE POTTERY GAZETTE" — February 1st 1886

"In glass making as in other industries many ingenious tools, etc. have at different times been invented with a view to replace hand labour. To obviate hand-blowing, for instance, a process of shaping with press and iron moulds was substituted. The beneficial results of this invention are incalculable. It placed manufacturers in a position to make regular and cheap wares while skilled labour became no longer necessary. The simplicity of the operation of pressing glass was such that in a short time men could be trained to perform the work. It does not require much knowledge to train men to gather glass, drop it into a mould and cut off sufficient quantity. The glass now being in the iron mould, a plunger is made to press the plastic mass, and in solidifying, by cooling, the objects retain the form of the mould and the plunger. Next came improvements in combining the different pieces of moulds, improvements in presses and in tools for holding the pieces while being fine-polished."

The process was not without hazards as an observer called George Dodd, writing in the 1840's put it: "If the quantity of glass be too large, the over plus gives considerable trouble, if too little the article is spoiled. If the die and plunger be too hot the glass will adhere to them, if too cold the surface of the glass becomes cloudy and imperfect" — As a method even the pressing of glass had to be controlled properly.

Not only was the glass needed for the home market, but most of the big firms had offices in Europe, in fact, pressed glass was destined for all over the world. In 1888, Sowerby's stated in the Pottery Gazette that their pressed and cut glass was suitable to be sent to the Colonies and India — in the days of a vast Empire there was no limit to what could be achieved. Indeed, an early report of about 1830 to the Commissioners of Excise stated that "our correspondent in New York advised us that the market for flint glass in that city is destroyed by importations from Newcastle and almost entirely from the Gateshead works. The exports of flint glass from the Tyne are immense". Later on this became a two-way business with the Pottery Gazette sagely commenting in April 1878 "Some months ago, we drew attention to the quantity of American pressed glass now in England and pointed out the necessity of our manufacturers giving the matter their attention. The warning we are happy to state will have a good effect not only in the present but on the future trade of England." Likewise, at the International Health Exhibition of 1884, the Pottery Gazette reviewing Sowerby's wares said "their fancy glass should have been in the art gallery but being of such a cheap and popular character we suppose they were inadmissable." Much of the glass was of very high quality, when made by the best firms, with an astonishing variety of colour, pattern and decoration.

The amazing variety of pressed glass in every way, from colour, shape, utilitarian and decorative items, ranging from poor quality to the superb, makes the collecting of the glass especially fascinating. The Sowerby Pattern book of 1882 advertises these colours: "opal, turquoise, gold, jet, venetian in several colours, giallo, blanc de lait, malachite and patent ivory Queen's ware." The Sowerby colours deserve explanation as for their vitro-porcelain wares they used gem terminology "opal, turquoise, gold, jet" all jewels in their own right. The opal in this context was white while the jet was black, but the confusion arises with their "blanc de lait" which because of the true definition of the opaque vitro-porcelain wares was meant to be opalescent like watery bluish milk. Yet in the Pattern book of 1882, "blanc de lait" is advertised as "decorated, opaque, stained, blanc de lait" — so it may be that "blanc de lait" could be opalescent but when decorated and opaque then literally it became 'milk white' glass. The malachite in blue and green looked like marble as did the purple, streaked glass and some of the ivory Queen's ware resembled carved ivory with raised decoration. Each firm had its own specialities, such as Sowerby's ivory Queen's ware and Davidson's blue and primrose pearline though certain colours, like opalescent, amber, clear blue, clear green, opaque white, opaque turquoise and marble wares were made by many of the firms, but the marbled glass items came mainly from the North Eastern glass houses.

Collections can be made in so many permutations that it is hard to suggest any one way. Anyone interested in social history can form a series of domestic items like the enormous sugar bowls, or tiny cream jugs, custard cups and many different salts, both flint and coloured. The colours of pressed glass are so varied a whole collection could be formed from the malachite and marbled pieces, Sowerby's

OF

# FANCY GOODS

Manufactured in Glass by

## Sowerbys Ellison Glass Works,

Limited,

Gateshead-on-Tyne,

England.

*Opal, Turquoise, Gold, Jet, Venetian in several colours.*

*Giallo, Blanc-de-lait, Malachite.*

Patent Ivory Queens Ware.

DECORATED OPAQUE STAINED BLANC DE LAIT,

and new

TORTOISE SHELL WARE.

| | |
|---|---|
| OFFICES AND SHOW ROOMS. | LONDON; *6, Coleman Street, City, E.C.* |
| | GATESHEAD ON TYNE. |
| | BIRMINGHAM; *10, Broad Street.* |
| | PARIS; *52, Rue d'Hauteville.* |
| | HAMBURG; *49, Gr Reichen Strasse,* |

JUNE, 1882, BOOK IX.

Patent Queen's Ivory ware, or Davidson's Pearline. Some of these pieces are so elegant and attractive, along with the Sowerby nursery character ones that they are far removed from the popular concept of cheap moulded glass, the attention to detail being superb.

The most collectable pieces are probably the John Derbyshire famous paper weights "Lion after Landseer", Greyhound, Britannia, Punch and Judy (no design registration) and Winged Sphinx. The latter is, so far, the most valuable and sought after of the group, and one of the rarest pieces of pressed glass. Then there are all the pre-1884 pieces of glass with their distinctive Victorian diamond registration marks and the post-January 1884 ones with their numbers on the side or base. Some people just collect trade marked items; with the peacock's head of Sowerby, the lion rising from a mural crown of Davidson and the two lion crests of Greener. Equally, the commemorative and Royal occasion pieces form a pattern of historical events. One of the best and rarest pieces is the Greener "Marquis of Lorne" item, especially in marbled glass, like malachite and the "Gladstone for the Million" plates are still seen often enough to stir the imagination, along with John Bright "Peace and Plenty".

In fact so much pressed glass was made that it should be easy to decide and form a collection as rare, or simple, plain or colourful, as the individual wants. Naturally being originally made for a mass market, a considerable quantity of the glass found today bears the scars of use, and misuse, and therefore is chipped. The only maxim is to buy the best that is available and affordable. Prices are going up all the time as the glass gets rarer.

Identification is all important. From the registration marks and the pattern books of the glass houses and also just by looking, an amazing amount of visual information can be absorbed and stored up. There is satisfaction in knowing what individual pieces are and indeed recognition is paramount in the valuation of any piece.

For the purposes of discussing the design registrations, as the registrations are essential for identification, it is best to divide the principal factories making pressed glass into groups, those from the North East and those from Manchester. There are, of course, a number of lesser known factories.

The most notable firms in the 1880's were from the North East. They are Greener, Davidson, Sowerby, Edward Moore and also W.H. Heppell which name has to be included because of the firm's connection with George Davidson, but the first three names are the most important ones.

The Sowerby name is probably the best known of the North Eastern firms. The family had been engaged in the glass industry long before the invention of the machinery needed for pressed glass. George Sowerby owned a glass works in Pipewellgate, Gateshead in the early 1800's and was followed by his son John as owner in 1844, — it was during John Sowerby's lifetime that the famous Ellison Glass Works became the focus of the pressed glass industry, for certainly Sowerby's was the most prolific, imaginative and artistic of the firms. In 1850 Sowerby took on Samuel Neville, his former manager of the old Gateshead Stamped Glass Works and together they leased land from Cuthbert Ellison for the purpose of building a new glass house. This was in East Street, Gateshead and the new factory was known as "Sowerby & Neville" in the early 1850s. By the mid 1860s they had purchased the land outright and were set to become the largest manufacturers of pressed flint glass in the country.

In 1871 Neville left the company to start up on his own and Sowerby's reverted to being a family concern as Sowerby & Co. John Sowerby's son, John George Sowerby, managed the Works from the early 1870s on, and inherited the firm on his father's death in 1879.

In 1882, the firm became 'Sowerby's Ellison Glass Works Ltd.', the title by which it is best known today and by then the firm was the largest pressed glass manufacturer in the world.

Sowerby
1876-c1930

George Davidson of the Teams Glass Works was the second best known of the firms from the North East. The firm was founded in 1867, also in Gateshead, and quickly became renowned for the manufacture of pressed glass. Apart from the already present demand, this was due to the energy and creativity of George Davidson, the founder of the Works. Starting with only a small workforce he succeeded in building an expanding major glass house over the following two decades. George Davidson died on February 22nd, 1891 aged 68, the day after his horse fell while he was driving home from Newcastle. It was a sad loss for the firm, though his son, Thomas was equally capable and succeeded him.

Despite the devastating fire of January 1881, which would have crippled lesser firms, new buildings commenced and production was able to forge ahead by the end of the year.

In December 1889 the firm's best known line in glass, the blue and primrose pearline was patented by Thomas Davidson, George's son. However, accounts of this new, special glass were reported in the Pottery Gazette as early as March 1889 so it was suitably advertised prior to the patent.

"Messrs. George Davidson & Co. have just secured provisional protection for a new fancy glass to which they have given the name of 'Pearline'. The base is in a rich blue and the edge is of a paler colour, to which the name of Pearline is most appropriate".

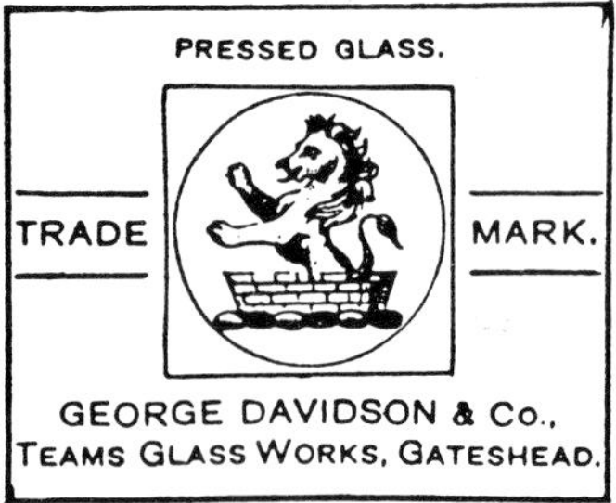


George Davidson
1880-c1890

Essentially, George Davidson & Co. was a family firm at the top, and also succeeding generations of employees worked at the factory well into the twentieth century. At British Trade Fairs in the 1930's, the wares of both Sowerby and Davidson were admired and bought by Queen Mary and other Royal visitors.

The third firm of Angus & Greener of the Wear Flint Glass Works, Sunderland made some of the earliest registrations for pressed glass in the North East. Little is known about John Angus, but Henry Greener who was born in 1820 at Deptford came from a glass making family. He was apprenticed at the age of twelve to John Price, glass manufacturers at Pipewellgate. He became the firm's traveller and in his twenties he was employed in similar circumstances by Sowerby's the top Tyneside glass house.

In 1858 he returned to Sunderland and entered into partnership with James Angus as owners of the Wear Flint Glass Works. In 1869, following the death of John Angus, the firm traded as Henry Greener from mid 1869-84, then Greener & Co., from 1885 on, proprietors of the Wear Flint Glass Works, Sunderland.

Henry Greener
1st Trade Mark
1875-c1885

All three of these firms had their own distinctive trade marks: in 1876 Henry Greener registered his first trade mark — a demi-rampant lion, balancing a star on one paw. After 1886, the lion is similar, but is holding an axe between his paws. George Davidson also used a lion crest, the torso rising from a mural crown. This mark was used for about ten years between 1880 and 1890. Sowerby & Co. had a crest trade mark of a peacock's head and that was registered in 1876. They were registering a large number of designs from the 1870's on, and even small pieces might have both the crest and registration date mark.

It is interesting to see in the Trade Marks advertisement of 1886 that Sowerby Ltd., and George Davidson & Co. are ranked with such pottery and porcelain marks as Crown Derby, George Jones, Minton, Worcester and also with Baccarat glass.

Greener & Co.
2nd Trade Mark
c1885-1900

The Fourth firm Edward Moore & Co., of South Shields, was a medium sized glass works producing both pressed and blown glassware. The firm was established by 1860 and had three furnaces in working order by 1865. Edward Moore's business did well and in 1869 he exhibited at the Netherlands International Exhibition of Domestic Economy (held in Amsterdam) and won a silver medal.

# EXTRACTS FROM REPORTS

BY

# HER MAJESTY'S SECRETARIES OF EMBASSY & LEGATION

ON THE

## Manufactures, Commerce, &c.,

OF THE COUNTRIES IN WHICH THEY RESIDE.

---

PRESENTED TO BOTH HOUSES OF PARLIAMENT BY COMMAND OF HER MAJESTY,
MAY, 1870.

---

NETHERLANDS.—**Report by the Hon. T. J. Hovell Thurlow** *on the International Exhibition of Domestic Economy, held at Amsterdam, in 1869.—(Page 306.)*

*January 7th, 1870.*

MESSRS. E. MOORE & CO., of the Tyne Flint Glass Works, South Shields, for Cheap Glass. This firm was established in 1860; has a very large home demand for its manufactures, which are distinguished for cheapness, durability, and beauty of design, and exports very largely to every part of the world. Its collection of Glass at Amsterdam was much admired by the Dutch, and it is to be hoped that the firm will reap, in a practical shape, advantage from their appreciation.

Despite a catastrophe in the late summer of 1881, when the largest cone at the Works fell with a resounding crash, Edward Moore was back in business by 1882 with many orders and able to provide competition for the Tyneside firms nearby. In 1888 Moore bought the moulds of Joseph Webb of Coalbourne Hill Glassworks at Stourbridge. The executors trading as "Jane Webb, Joseph Hammond & Henry Fitzroy Webb" continued to trade to 1888, and as would be expected from a Stourbridge firm, produced excellent quality pressed glass, so it was felt that the Moore acquisition of these moulds could only be advantageous.

Chiefly Edward Moore is best known for the registrations of 1887 and 1888. These are of importance for their classical design, reminiscent of eighteenth century silver, but produced at a time when other firms were experimenting with new shapes and colours.

On 14th February 1884, John Walsh Walsh of the Soho Vesta Glass Works, Birmingham, registered the 'arch topped, rolled over pillar, known as the "Queen Anne" and applied to glass'. Many of the Edward Moore registrations for 1887 and 1888 elaborated on this theme and the firm produced a series of sets of glass with pillars, curving gadroons and twists to the handles. These pieces look very handsome though they appear somewhat heavy for today's taste.

The fifth firm of W.H. Heppell, Newcastle Flint Glass Works, Newcastle is included because of the firm's unusual designs registered over ten years only, and because of the affiliation with George Davidson & Co., who in the mid 1880's bought the Heppell moulds and patterns after the firm foreclosed.

Before that in 1874, W.H. Heppell took over an existing glass works in Forth Street, Newcastle, which had been one of the most flourishing with five furnaces working in its heyday.

The Heppell family were reasonably well known in Gateshead where they had an iron foundry and it seems reasonable to suppose that moulds for the making of pressed glass were supplied from there to the new factory. In 1880, the firm was advertising in the Pottery Gazette their "blown, pressed flint, opal and marble, glass".

The registered designs were novel enough for George Davidson to want to buy up the Heppell moulds when the firm closed its doors in 1884, and certainly Heppell pieces should be in any collection for their originality.

The second group of glass houses consist of firms which were Manchester based. With good communications and access to the port of Liverpool, this group was just as important as those firms of the North East though less is known about the start of the firms and their owners.

The firms in this group are Molineux & Co., who first registered in 1846 and then became Molineaux, Webb & Co., Kirby Street, Manchester from 1864 and finally Molineaux, Webb & Co. Ltd. from 1890.

Their main rivals in Manchester were Percival & Yates who registered their first item in 1847, then as Percival, Yates & Vickers, and finally, Percival, Vickers & Co. Ltd., in 1867. Both firms produced excellent domestic wares as did James Derbyshire & Brother of Hulme, Manchester. In 1870 the firm became J. J. & T. Derbyshire and James Derbyshire & Sons in 1876. This firm produced some of the best quality services made in pressed glass.

John Derbyshire broke away from his brother and set up his own glasshouse in 1873 from Regent Road Flint Glass Works. He registered his first item in that year. By 1877, the works were known as the Regent Flint Glass Co. Apart from the very fine domestic pieces in 1873, John Derbyshire is known chiefly for his handsome paperweights of 1874 which, though they were registered as paperweights, were probably meant to be used as chimney piece ornaments. He too had a trade mark consisting of the letters JD and an anchor. His registered paperweights are probably the best known pieces of pressed glass, and his work is really in a superior class of its own.

Burtles, Tate & Co., Poland Street Glass Works, Manchester started in the 1850s but did not register a design until 1870. In the early 1880s the firm had a second glass house in Bolton known as the Victoria Glass Works. This was closed when they opened another works near the original one in Poland Street.

The firm is known for its flower holders both in blown and pressed glass. Several of their pressed glass items equal both Sowerby and Davidson in design and colour and they also manufactured good domestic items as the Pottery Gazette advertisements show.

In 1891 the firm's new "Topas opalescent" ware was described as a 'striking imitation of the old Venetian Topas'. In reality, it was similar to the Davidson Pearline of 1889, although the Burtles, Tate & Co. pieces are considerably harder to find today.

These firms form a tapestry of design, form, colour and pattern for Queen Victoria's reign and into the Edwardian era. Like a good weave, the colours and patterns intermingle and are dependant on each other. Each firm complements the other and it is necessary to take each firm separately to see how the registrations compare, and what the differences are.

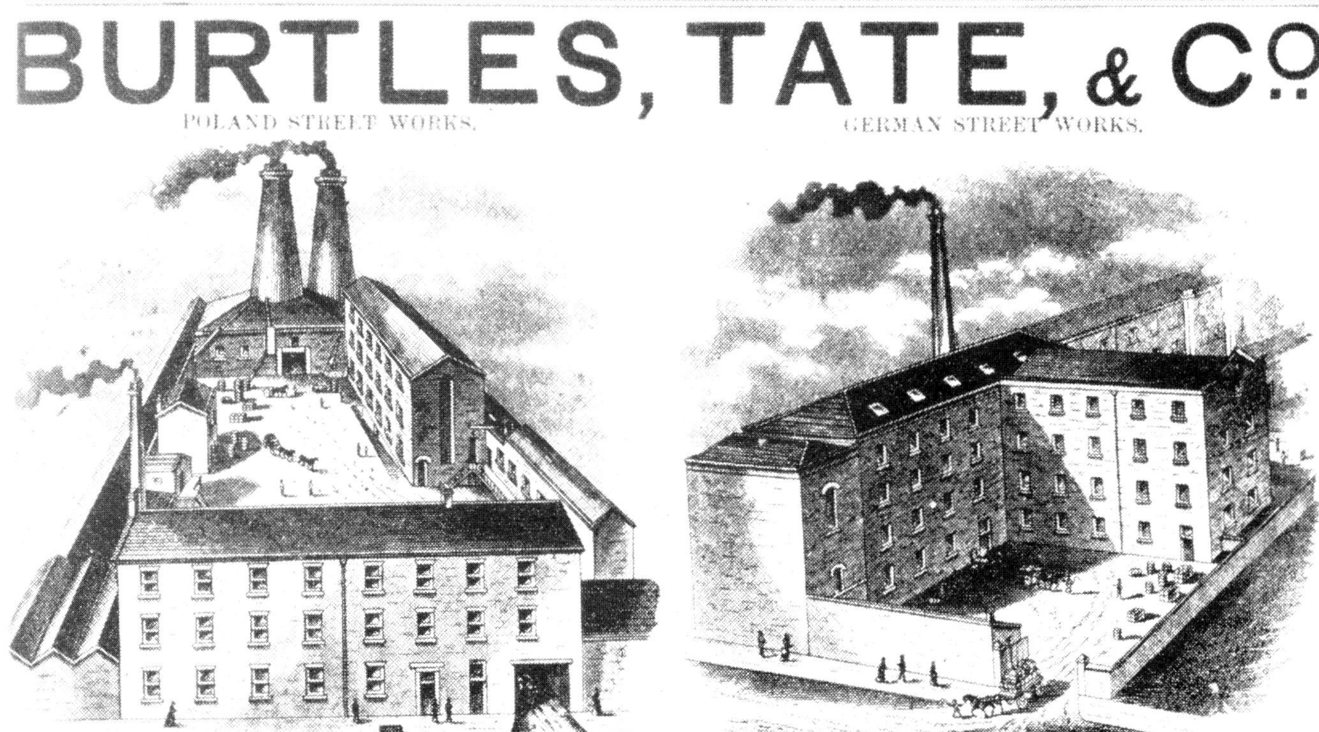

# Greener

231430

31 July 1869

Design for "Gladstone" Plate showing detail even to raised dots.

176239

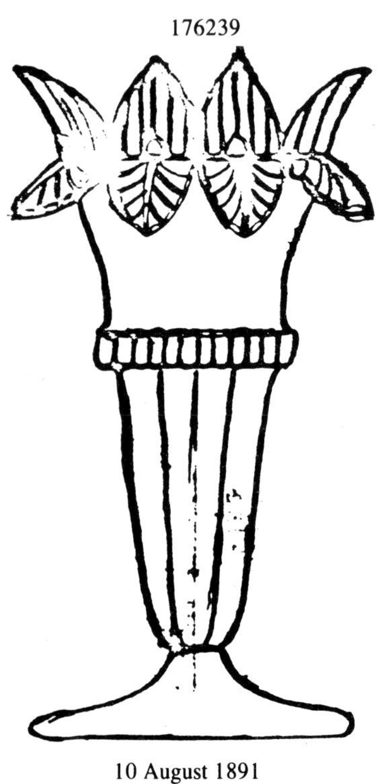

10 August 1891

The firm of Greener, Wear Flint Glassworks, Sunderland was first Angus & Greener, Henry Greener 1869-1884, and Greener & Co. from 1885 onwards. The first registration was in 1858, then there was a gap until ten items were registered between 1866 and 1869, mainly sugar basins with a few decanters. The pattern for the sugar basin of June 1867 is also found on plates of many sizes, dishes, cream jugs, as well as for the original registered sugar basin. It is in frosted glass and has a lozenge pattern with small dots and a ribbed edge. The sugar basin is large by today's standards, but is extremely elegant and compares happily with earlier glass for both style and design.

On July 31st 1869, under Henry Greener, the firm registered designs for a circular glass plate, or stand, to commemorate Gladstone's appointment as Prime Minister — "Gladstone for the Million". Next a lustre candlestick and later in that year, a sugar basin to acknowledge the work of the Anglo-American Philanthropist, George Peabody. In 1876 they produced the vine and grapes decoration for a pierced dessert service, mainly to be found in opaque turquoise blue, milk-white and also in jet black. The registration is for the rim alone, as the diamond registration mark is found on other pieces with a different pattern. It is worth comparing them with the similar coloured plates of Sowerby. In June 1878, Greener registered a design for plates, butter dishes, spoon holders, sugar basins and cream jugs, and those which are commemorative, have medallion portraits of H.R.H. Princess Louise and her husband, the Marquis of Lorne to celebrate their visit to Halifax, Nova Scotia in November of 1878. The butter dish has portraits of the couple and a cartouche with the words "Marquis and Marchioness of Lorne landed Halifax N.S., 25th November 1878". In between the medallions are raised national floral emblems. The knob to the butter cover is a replica of the coronet of a Marquis and on the inside of the butter dish cover is Greener's first trade mark. It is one of the most striking pieces of pressed glass, especially in pale green marble, which is the colour best known for this particular piece, although it was made both in clear and coloured glass. As well that year the firm registered a glass plate and sugar basin with a portrait head of Benjamin Disraeli, Lord Beaconsfield, on it to commemorate the Congress of Berlin.

From then on to 1884, there is a remarkable change in policy as most of the entries (apart from 1881 when there was a design for ornamenting table glass) are for pavement lights and slabs of glass, probably necessary, but very dull. In fact, there is hardly anything of note in the design registrations until the pattern of the Silver Wedding plate for the Prince and Princess of Wales in 1888. In 1888 also, two patterns were registered with an aesthetic Japanese influence. It was at that time that the design for a rustic handle was registered; hence, baskets can be found in several colours, amongst them, a clear blue, amber and a smokey palest amethyst. Most of them have three registrations on them, not two, one for the handle, and two for the patterns of March and April 1888. The design for the patterns are very alike and motifs from one are incorporated in the other. It is as if two designs were needed to make up one elaborate pattern and as the patterns are typically aesthetic, it is an important piece. That same year, there is a bowl with shell shapes and chain decoration and a plate with cornucopia, flowers and fruit. The design of 10th August 1891 continues the naturalistic trend and is for a vase with a top formed by a double row of stylised leaves with the top row upright and the bottom row curving downwards. The registration is for the top alone as this piece may be found as a night-light holder in plain and coloured glass, but still with the same leaf rim. The leaf shape reappears in the same form in the pattern of 6th September 1893. However, in 1890 there is a chariot with gadroons and in 1893 a wheelbarrow with gadroons. It is interesting to compare them with the simple wagon and cradle shapes of W.H. Heppell ten years earlier. Both those of

Heppell & Greener are found in large and small sizes and certainly the smaller ones must have made delightful salt cellars.

Throughout the 1890s and into the 1900s Greener & Co. produced many designs imitating the contemporary, brilliant cut glass. Some are very elaborate and there is one swirly Art Nouveau pattern in September 1898. Few other firms attempted to produce these complex designs in the registrations apart from George Davidson & Co. It is impossible not to think of Greener and Davidson together, as their work was complementary, especially earlier on.

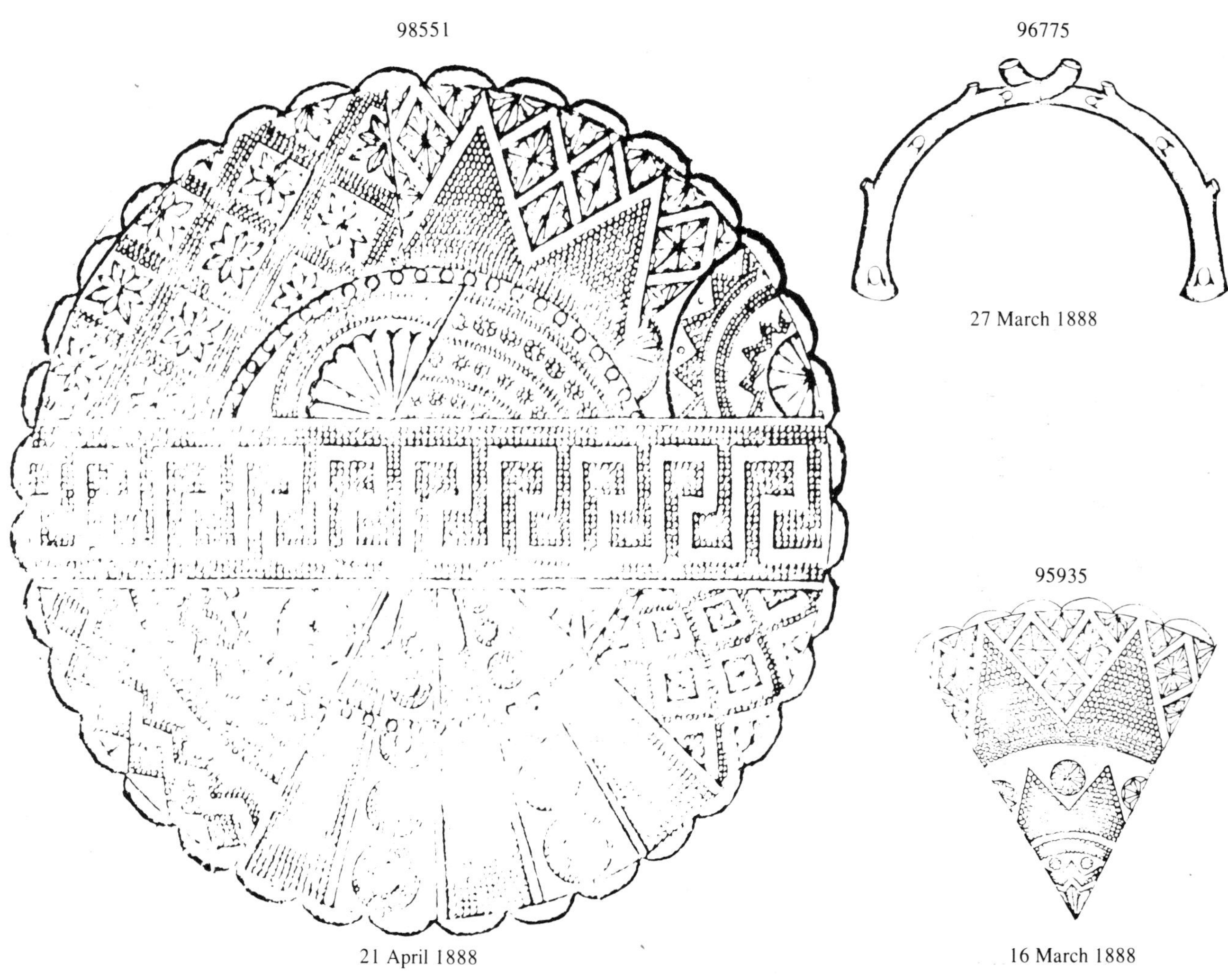


These three Registered Numbers may appear on those baskets which have this design.

197704

Shows early imitation cut glass.

81160

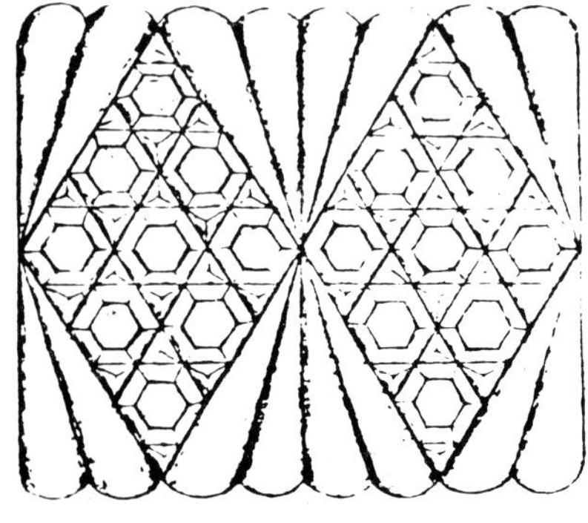

Shows gadroons similar to those of Edward Moore.

15 September 1887

150277

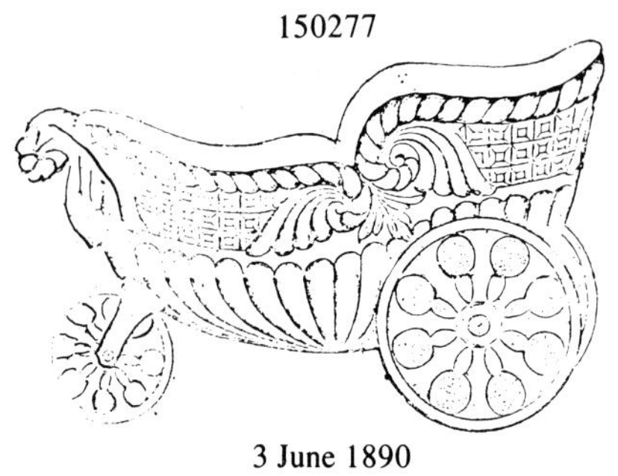

3 June 1890

## Angus & Greener, Sunderland. Registrations

| *Registration* No. | *Date* | *Year* | *Parcel* No. | *Design* |
|---|---|---|---|---|
| 117501 | 21 December | 1858 | 6 | Dish |
| 197703 | 24 May | 1866 | 1 | Bottom of decanter |
| 197704 | 24 May | | 1 | Decanter |
| 200233 | 25 August | | 6 | Dish or butter float |
| 205812 | 26 January | 1867 | 4 | Decanter and stopper |
| 209161 | 26 June | | 8 | Sugar basin (lozenge pattern) |
| 214357/8 | 26 November | | 9 | Sugar basin foot & sugar basin |
| 217728 | 1 April | 1868 | 7 | Salt cellar |
| 218561 | 4 May | | 6 | Sugar basin |
| 221689 | 17 September | | 5 | Sugar basin |
| 228782 | 20 April | 1869 | 9 | Sugar basin |

## Henry Greener, The Wear Flint Glass Works, Sunderland.

| | | | | |
|---|---|---|---|---|
| 231430 | 31 July | 1869 | 8 | Design for a circular glass plate or stand (Gladstone) |
| 231927 | 12 August | | 8 | Lustre candlestick |
| 236921 | 7 December | | 7 | Sugar basin (Peabody) |
| 238105 | 14 January | 1870 | 11 | Glass basket |
| 247081 | 10 November | | 11 | Sugar basin (Friedrich) |
| 250723 | 2 March | 1871 | 8 | Glass plate |
| 268734 | 10 December | 1872 | 7 | Dessert dish |
| 284695 | 27 August | 1874 | 9 | Plate |
| 302199 | 29 July | 1876 | 6 | A dessert service (vine and grapes) |
| 322393 | 8 June | 1878 | 11 | (Glass plate) |
| 325547 | 31 August | | 8 | A sugar basin showing both sides (Lord Beaconsfield) |
| 330470 | 18 December | | 10 | A slab of glass for reflecting daylight |
| 337416 | 22 July | 1879 | 7 | A slab of glass |
| 338015 | 8 August | | 12 | A pavement light |
| 340104 | 19 September | | 19 | A tile made from a mixture of glasses |
| 359361 | 8 December | 1880 | 14 | Drinking cup (tankard shape E. Hanlan, the oarsman) |
| 362328 | 1 March | 1881 | 12 | For a "circular glass light" |
| 364187 | 21 April | | 13 | |
| 366032 | 14 June | | 9 | Design for ornamenting basins, cream jugs, butter dishes and covers, plates and all other descriptions of table glass |
| 366408 | 24 June | | 10 | Pressed glass light |
| 374475 | 7 December | | 17 | |
| 378022/3 | 4 March | 1882 | 10 | A base or pavement light |
| 381481 | 25 May | | 12 | |
| 383640 | 19 July | | 6 | |
| 394098 | 12 February | 1883 | 9 | |
| 396305 | 31 March | | 9 | (Slab of glass) |
| 397604 | 1 May | | 16 | (Slab of glass) |
| 406944 | 14 November | | 12 | (Slab of glass) |

## Henry Greener, The Wear Flint Glass Works, Sunderland and 5 Farringdon Road, London.

| *Registration* No. | *Date* | *Year* | *Design* |
|---|---|---|---|
| 14390 | 3 October | 1884 | Ornamental design for glasses for pavement lights, floor lights, etc. |

## Greener & Co., Sunderland

| | | | |
|---|---|---|---|
| 38582 | 23 November | 1885 | Shape for a glass mould |
| 48352 | 5 May | 1886 | Shape of glass dish |
| 71736 | 9 April | 1887 | Design for the ornamentation of glass |
| 81160 | 15 September | | Pattern of table glass |
| 88120 | 26 November | | Pattern and shape of a dish (centenary) |
| 91449 | 11 January | 1888 | Pattern of a plate (Silver Wedding) |
| 94543 | 25 February | | |
| 95935 | 16 March | | (Partly imit. cut. Part of pattern included in 98551) |
| 96775/6 | 27 March | | (Rustic handle) |
| 98551 | 21 April | | (Japanese influence) |
| 103434 | 11 July | | (Dish) |
| 103975 | 17 July | | |
| 108018/9 | 14 September | | |
| 109461/2 | 29 September | | (Decoration candle holder, 62 imit. cut) |
| 113896 | 15 November | | (Shell and chain effect) |
| 115743 | 14 December | | (Fruit and flowers with "peace and plenty" in words) |
| 121985 | 23 March | 1889 | |
| 128882 to 84 | 17 July | | (Patterns) |
| 138051 | 14 November | | (Patterns) |
| 150277 | 3 June | 1890 | (Chariot with gadroons) |
| 150401 | 5 June | | (Pattern imit. cut mostly) |
| 160244 | 3 November | | (Patterns) |
| 163075 | 16 December | | (Mostly imit. cut) |
| 176239 | 10 August | 1891 | (Vase, naturalistic top) |
| 182002 | 30 October | | (Pattern, mostly imit. cut) |
| 196641 | 10 August | 1892 | (Pattern, mostly imit. cut) |
| 210371 | 10 April | 1893 | (Fancy, rustic) |
| 215154 | 18 July | | |
| 217749 | 6 September | | (Free design, acanthus etc.) |
| 218710 | 20 September | | (Wheelbarrow with gadroons) |
| 223742 | 11 December | | (Pattern) |
| 234231 | 14 June | 1894 | (Imit. cut) |
| 241930 | 10 October | | (Imit. cut) |
| 258156 | 15 July | 1895 | (Imit. cut with star pattern and lines forming diamonds) |
| 262018 | 16 September | | (Imit. difficult cut) |
| 276977 | 1 June | 1896 | (Imit. cut. Base diamonds and squares - sides shell or fans pattern) |
| 284639 | 23 September | | (Elab. imit. cut) |
| 304505 | 3 September | 1897 | (Elab. imit. cut) |
| 325194 | 9 September | 1898 | (Interesting free design Art Nouveau) |
| 325539 | 15 September | | (Very elab. imit. cut) |
| 343063 | 11 August | 1899 | (Very elab. imit. cut) |
| 360332 | 14 July | 1900 | (Fan shaped edge with gadroons. Imit. cut) |
| 378765 | 27 August | 1901 | (Elab. imit. cut similar to 343063) |
| 388197 | 6 March | 1902 | (Tumbler shape) |
| 465892 | 26 September | 1905 | (Elab. imit. cut) |
| 514796 | 31 October | 1907 | (Bowl, imit. cut) |

Imit. cut = Imitation cut glass Elab. = elaborate

Descriptions not in brackets are as described in the Design Register or on the Representation drawing itself. Other descriptions in brackets are from the look of the drawings and are observation. This applies to all the factories.

218710

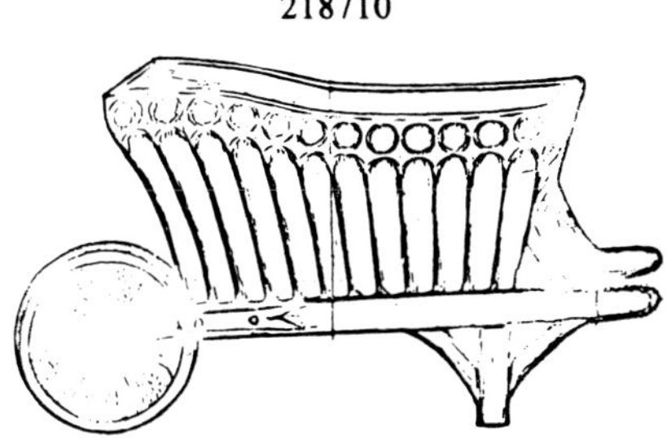

325194

343063

# George Davidson & Co.

153858

2 August 1890

Between 1877 and 1878 this firm registered only four items, tumblers being the most interesting in 1878. For ten subsequent years there were no registrations for shape or design, but in 1888 appeared the very good Thomas Davidson pattern of 31st March and then in 1890 they registered the well known hobnail pattern, imitating cut glass. In 1891, there was an elaborate pattern of flower shapes formed by triangles which is not very different from the one of Sowerby of 1889 and in 1893 the flower trough with stylised shells round it. It is a pretty pattern and is often seen in pearline, both blue and primrose. From the 1st August 1894 until February 1908 there were fifteen registrations of patterns, mostly imitating cut glass and they are really very good. The articles, bowls, dishes, jugs and so on are sometimes very like the real thing with diamond and hobnail effects. They turn up in clear glass, coloured glass and in pearline. Pearline as the name implies, has a rim of opalescent glass, the glass itself being in pale blue and primrose yellow, which were the two registered colours, and less often, palest grey, like a moon beam. The primrose yellow must not be confused with vaseline glass which is a completely different type of glass. Though the firm did not register as much as Sowerby they were very prolific in the late 19th and early 20th centuries; earlier, between 1880-1890 they used their trade mark of a lion rising from a mural crown and many pieces have just this. Despite the bad fire in the factory in 1881 the use of the trade mark may be the reason for the lack of registrations in the 1880s, but the need for a luxurious looking glass, albeit pressed, in the late 1890s and 1900s more than made up for lack of registrations in the 1880s and the patterns for imitation cut glass were certainly rich looking, though the glass itself does not have the same feel of quality as the earlier pieces.

Advertised in the Pottery Gazette several years prior to registration.

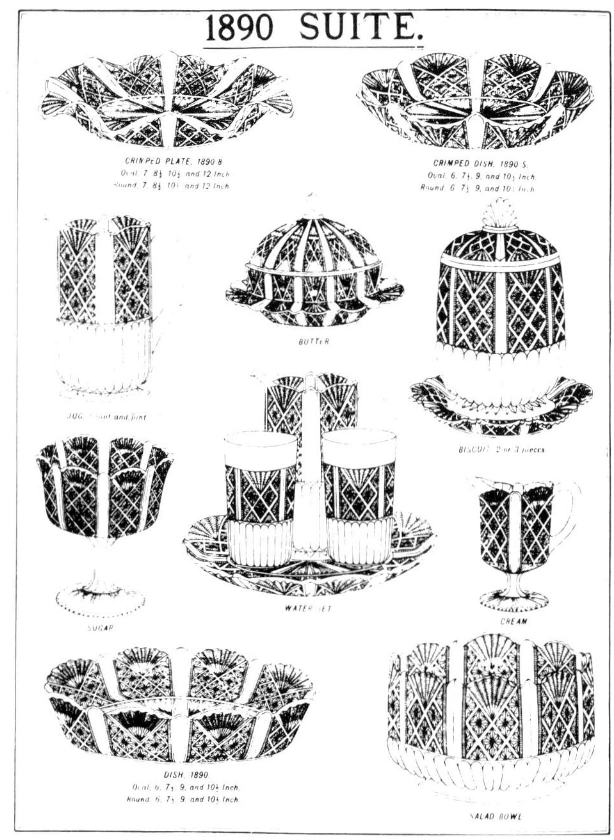

**George Davidson & Co., Teams Glass Works, Gateshead-on-Tyne. Registrations.**

| *Registration* No. | *Date* | *Year* | *Parcel* No. | *Design* |
|---|---|---|---|---|
| 306884 | 16 January | 1877 | 8 | Vase |
| 308104 | 28 February | | 15 | Vase |
| 326775/6 | 23 September | 1878 | 6 | Glass Tumblers |

| | | | | |
|---|---|---|---|---|
| 96945 | 31 March | 1888 | | Thomas Davidson (imit. cut) |
| 123198 | 10 April | 1889 | | |
| 126694 | 5 June | | | (Swirling leaf pattern) |
| 130641 to 43 | 13 August | | | 41 (Jelly mould shape) |
| 153858 | 2 August | 1890 | | (Pattern similar to hobnail imit. cut) |
| 176566 | 15 August | 1891 | | (Elaborate pattern imit. cut of flower shapes, formed by triangles) |
| 193365 | 1 June | 1892 | | (Pattern imit. cut) |
| 207909 | 20 February | 1893 | | (House shape) |
| 212684 | 25 May | | | (Basket shape. Pattern of stylised shells) |
| 217752 | 6 September | | | (Imit. cut) |
| 224171 | 19 December | | | (Pattern of dots within a form similar to Greek key pattern) |
| 237038 | 1 August | 1894 | | (Some imit. cut, overlapping circular pattern) |
| 254027 | 1 May | 1895 | | (Imit. cut) |
| 285342 | 2 October | 1896 | | (Imit. cut, star centre) |
| 303519 | 18 August | 1897 | | (Imit. cut) |
| 320124 | 10 June | 1898 | | (Imit. cut in sections) |
| 340825 | 5 July | 1899 | | (Relatively simple imit. cut, linear radiating pattern) |
| 360167 | 13 July | 1900 | | (Imit. cut radiating pattern from centre) |
| 413701 | 14 July | 1903 | | (Imit. cut with pattern of eight petal shapes) |
| 436804 | 12 July | 1904 | | |
| 444604 | 5 November | | | (Elab. imit. cut star centre) |
| 464621 | 11 September | 1905 | | (Elab. imit. cut diamond and ribbing pattern) |
| 486298 | 1 September | 1906 | | (Imit. cut) |
| 512560 | 25 September | 1907 | | |
| 514848 | 1 November | | | (Imit. cut, daisy flower pattern on base area) |
| 520674 | 25 February | 1908 | | (Elab. imit. cut. Clear separation of motifs) |

306884

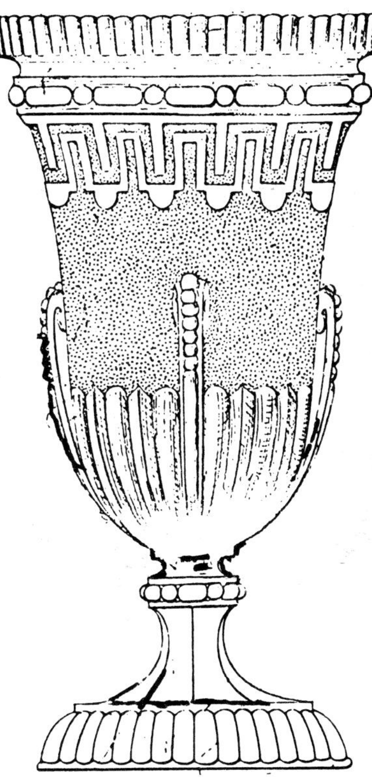

176566

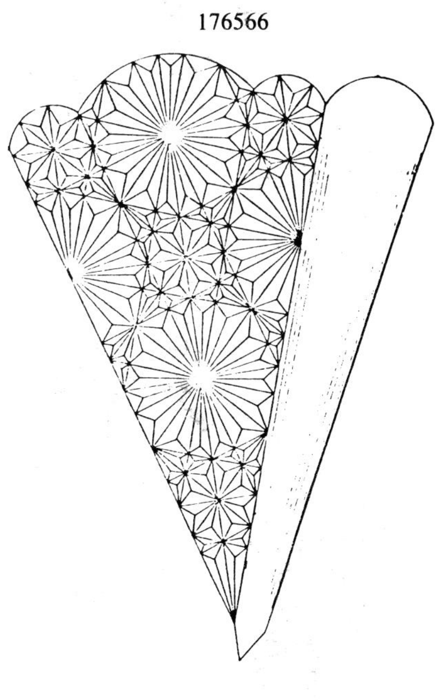

207909

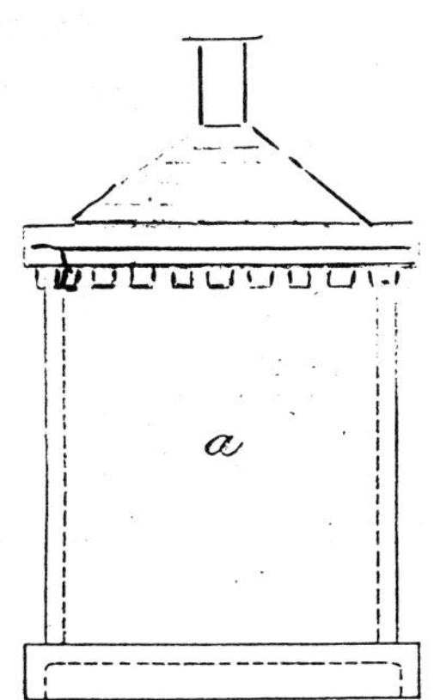

284672

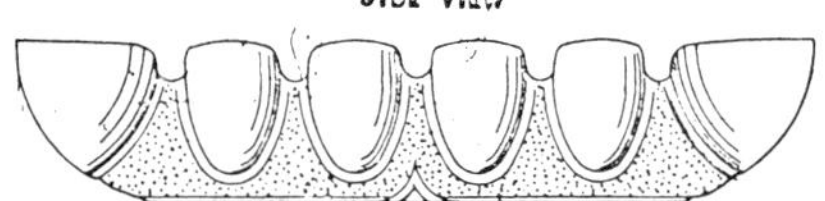


# W.H. Heppell, Newcastle Flint Glass Works, Forth Street, Newcastle-upon-Tyne

This firm registered some fifteen items between 1874 and 1882. In February 1880, there is the coal scuttle shape and in the June of that year, the coal truck wagon shape as used in the collieries. They are in many sizes, the biggest probably being meant for sugar and the smallest as a salt cellar. There is a barrow shape and in 1881 a cradle one. These items are novelties. The 1882 Dolphin series, however, is heavy and not very attractive, but it did reflect the then current popularity of dolphins as a decorative motif. After the firm gave up in the mid-1880s George Davidson's firm acquired the Heppell moulds and patterns and some of these were later produced by Davidson's.

**William Henry Heppell & Co., Newcastle Flint Glass Works, Forth Street, Newcastle-upon-Tyne. Registrations.**

| *Registration* No. | *Date* | *Year* | *Parcel* No. | *Design* |
|---|---|---|---|---|
| 284672 | 26 August | 1874 | 5 | Dish (inverted thumb nail pattern round sides) |
| 295362 | 23 October | 1875 | 3 | Butter dish and flower stand combined |
| 295919 | 13 November | | 4 | Plate or bowl |
| 338286 | 14 August | 1879 | 13 | Tile |
| 338287 | 14 August | | 13 | Slide or top light |
| 346543 | 17 February | 1880 | 9 | (Coal scuttle shape) |
| 351191 | 19 June | | 16 | (Wagon shape) |
| 354935 | 7 September | | 1 | |
| 359806 | 18 December | | 15 | (Wagon shape?) |
| 370524 | 26 September | 1881 | 1 | (Indistinct cradle shape?) |
| 372860 | 7 November | | 3 | (Plate) |
| 374437 | 6 December | | 13 | |
| 390584 to 86 | 24 November | 1882 | 17 | (Dolphin series) |

Advertisement in Pottery Gazette, December 1880.

TYNE FLINT GLASS WORKS

SOUTH SHIELDS,

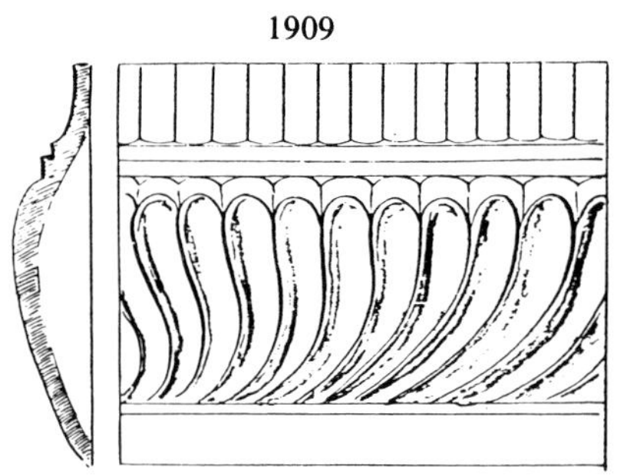


Pattern of John Walsh Walsh of 14 February 1884 which influenced firms such as Edward Moore.

# Edward Moore & Co., Tyne Flint Glass Works, South Shields

The earliest registrations are in June 1861 and are for patterns. One is an oval thumb nail pattern and the other a more complicated one of petal and crescent shapes. This pattern has been used on a decanter and it is a handsome looking piece, imitating cut glass. Apart from 1868, when there is a registration for a glass gas globe, there are no more registrations until October 1886. The pattern of the October piece is the first of the gadroon ones and was probably done for a gas globe initially. There were many of these registrations in 1887 for glass shades in bowl shapes with various patterns, such as the hobnail one of April 13th, and at that time there were several patterns registered for tumblers.

As mentioned earlier, the principal registrations are for September 1887 and for March 1888 when the firm registered classical designs with gadroons and pillars for bowls, covered bowls and jugs. Most of these bowls are in plain glass, but they were made also in an opaque caramel colour. This shade, however, is extremely rare and is not often seen. Edward Moore produced marbled glass like that of the Sowerby malachite items and also a clear emerald green. It is interesting to note as well that in the November of 1887, Sowerby's registered a sugar basin with small pillars and gadroons to the base, whilst in September 1887 Henry Greener registered a pretty pattern for table glass incorporating fan shaped gadroons. George Davidson & Co. made a fine sugar and cream set with pillars in August 1889. They come in clear glass but are often seen in pearline as well. It seems that the first registration of a new style or type of decoration was always followed swiftly by a similar one, from one or other of the glass firms, but the name Edward Moore is closely associated with the word 'gadroons'.

The last registrations are in 1889 and the most interesting one is that of September 18th, which is for a bowl imitating basket work and is reminiscent of Sowerby's many baskets. Sadly, there are no further registrations after the disastrous fire of 1891, although the firm continued to operate until the 20th century.

BISCUIT BOXES. ICE PAILS & VASES
c 1870

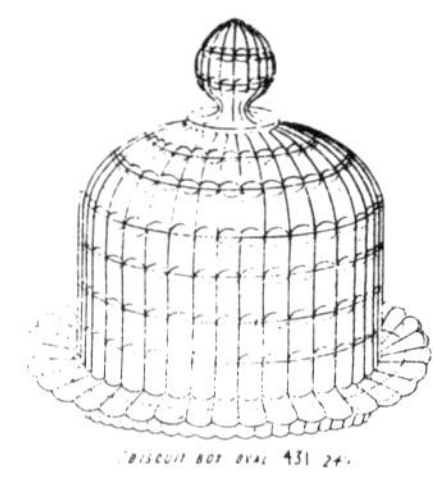

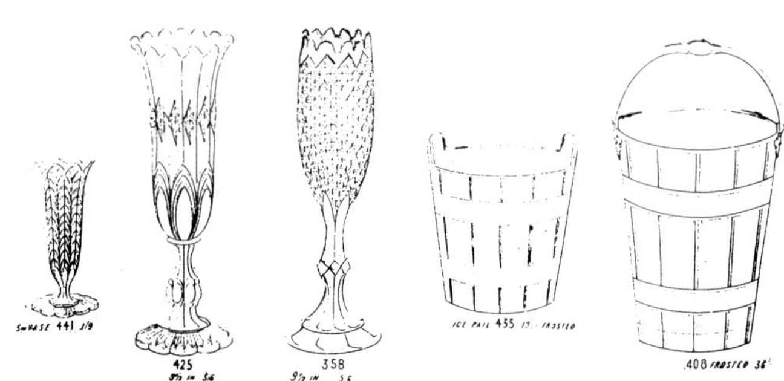

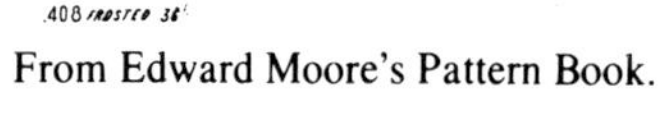

TERMS, &c.

Payment received in Cash only; less five per cent. discount, at one month from date of Invoice.

The Goods are delivered to the Carriers in South Shields; the Carriage from thence is payable by the Purchaser.

No allowance is made for Breakage.

Packages are charged:—Hogsheads, 6/- each; Large and middle size Tierces, 5/- each; Smaller Tierces, 3/6 each; Casks, 2/6 each.

Empty Packages, can only be allowed for, if returned *in good condition* Carriage Paid, within one month from date of Invoice, addressed in full, EDWARD MOORE AND Co., TYNE FLINT GLASS WORKS, SOUTH SHIELDS; with the name of the *Sender* added. They must also be advised to us by post.

From Edward Moore's Pattern Book.

**Edward Moore & Co., Tyne Flint Glass Works, South Shields.**
**Registrations.**

| *Registration* No. | *Date* | *Year* | *Parcel* No. | *Design* |
|---|---|---|---|---|
| 141573 | 27 June | 1861 | 1 | (Pattern) |
| 141642 | 29 June | | 4 | (Pattern) |
| 217207 | 5 March | 1868 | 11 | Pressed glass gas globe |

| | | | | |
|---|---|---|---|---|
| 58275 | 7 October | 1886 | | Pattern (all over gadroon pattern) |
| 63543 | 15 December | | | Shape and pattern of gas moon or shade (similar to above) |
| 65339 | 14 January | 1887 | | Shape and pattern of pressed glass gas shade (bowl shape with horizontal ridging) |
| 67425 | 7 February | | | Shape and pattern of pressed glass gas shade (similar to above) |
| 68249 | 18 February | | | Shape and pattern of pressed glass lamp shade (similar to above) |
| 71753 | 12 April | | | Shape and pattern of an oval covered dish (with gadroons) |
| 71816 | 13 April | | | Shape and pattern of a gas shade (bowl shape with hobnail pattern) |
| 72815 | 28 April | | | Pattern for a pressed glass shade (bowl shape) |
| 72884 | 29 April | | | Pattern for a pressed glass shade (bowl shape with serrated rim and pattern of circles) |
| 75015/6 | 8 June | | | Pattern (tumblers) |
| 75091/2 | 9 June | | | Pattern (tumblers) |
| 76878 to 80 | 13 July | | | Shape (oval, lobed) |
| 76935 | 14 July | | | Pattern (gadroon base to tumbler shape) |
| 77341 | 25 July | | | Pattern (tumbler shape with facets) |
| 80012 | 1 September | | | Shape and pattern (swirling gadroons on bowl shape) |
| 80013 | 1 September | | | Shape and pattern (jug and covered bowls with pillars and gadroons. Twisted handles) |
| 81959 | 24 September | | | Shape and pattern (similar to 71816) |
| 82606 | 30 September | | | Shape and pattern (similar to 80013 but more elaborate) |
| 83773 | 12 October | | | Shape (jug and covered bowls in oval and lobed shape. Twisted handles) |
| 88124 | 29 November | | | Shape (similar to above) |
| 88125 | 29 November | | | Pattern (tumbler) |
| 88730 | 5 December | | | Shape (similar to 88124) |
| 92045 | 23 January | 1888 | | Shape (imit. cut quatre foil shape. Twisted handles) |
| 94820 | 1 March | | | (Set of covered bowls and jug with gadroons on bowls and covers. Twisted handle to jug) |
| 95625 | 12 March | | | (Tazza shape) |
| 95775 | 14 March | | | (Swirling gadroons. Twisted handle) |
| 107316 | 5 September | | | (Double shell light) |
| 109612 | 2 October | | | (Imit. cut dish with clear lobes) |
| 120437 | 26 February | 1889 | | (Comport shape. Elaborate imit. cut with plain swags) |
| 129933 | 31 July | | | |
| 132189 | 31 August | | | (Fluted hat) |
| 133560 | 18 September | | | (Bowl imit. basket work with twisted handles) |
| 139589 | 4 December | | | (Bowl shape - circular raised pattern) |
| 141068 | 24 December | | | (Bowl shape with ivy or vine leaf and tendrils) |

217207

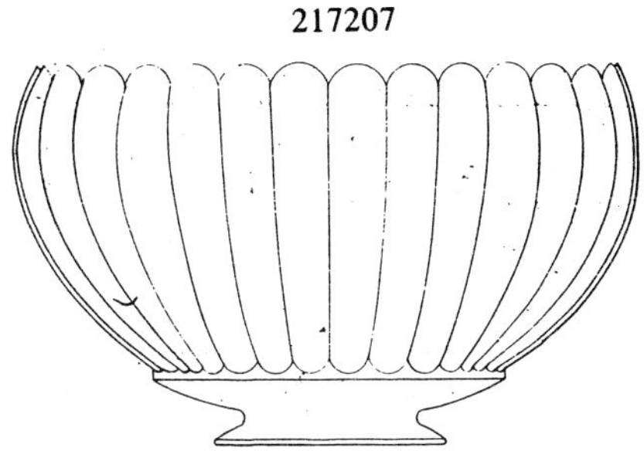

80012

Side View:

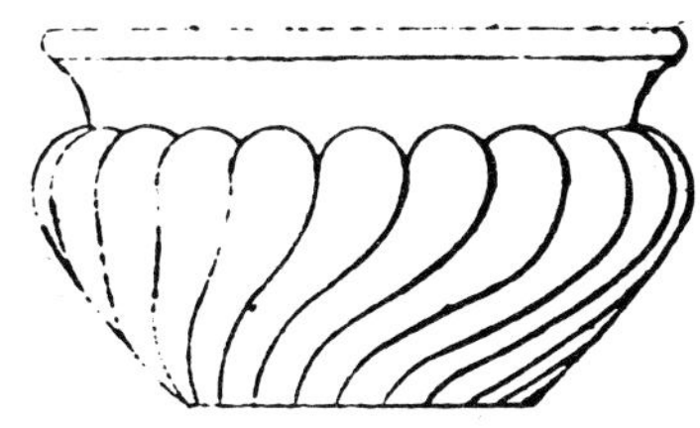

Underside View:

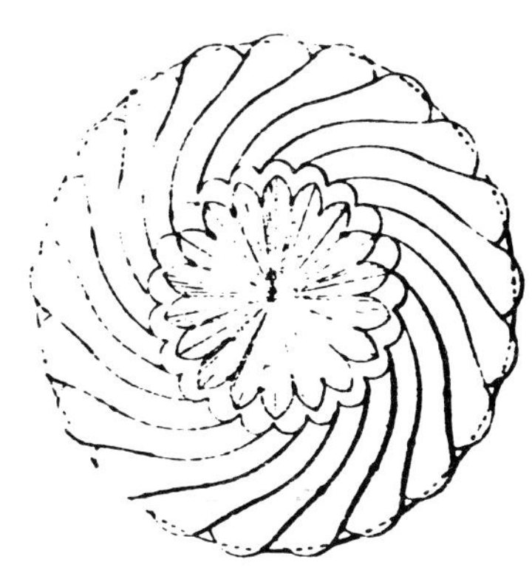

133560

Elevation.

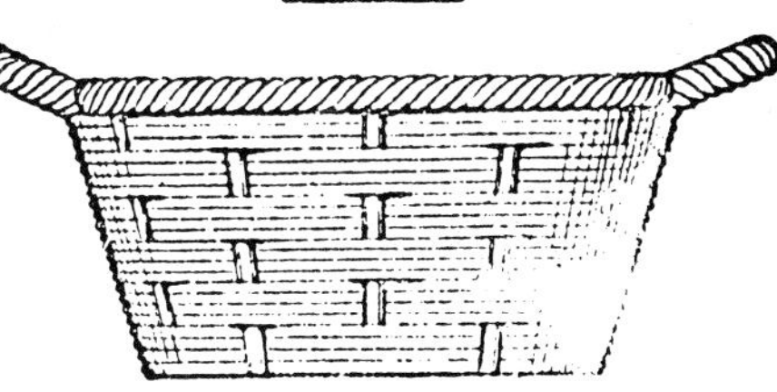

Plan.

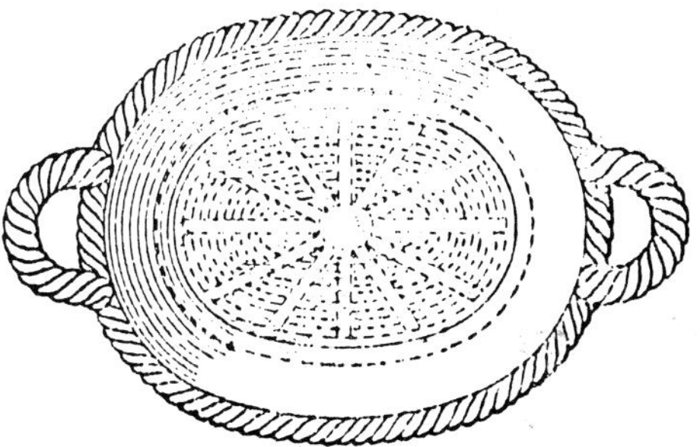

## Edward Moore & Co.

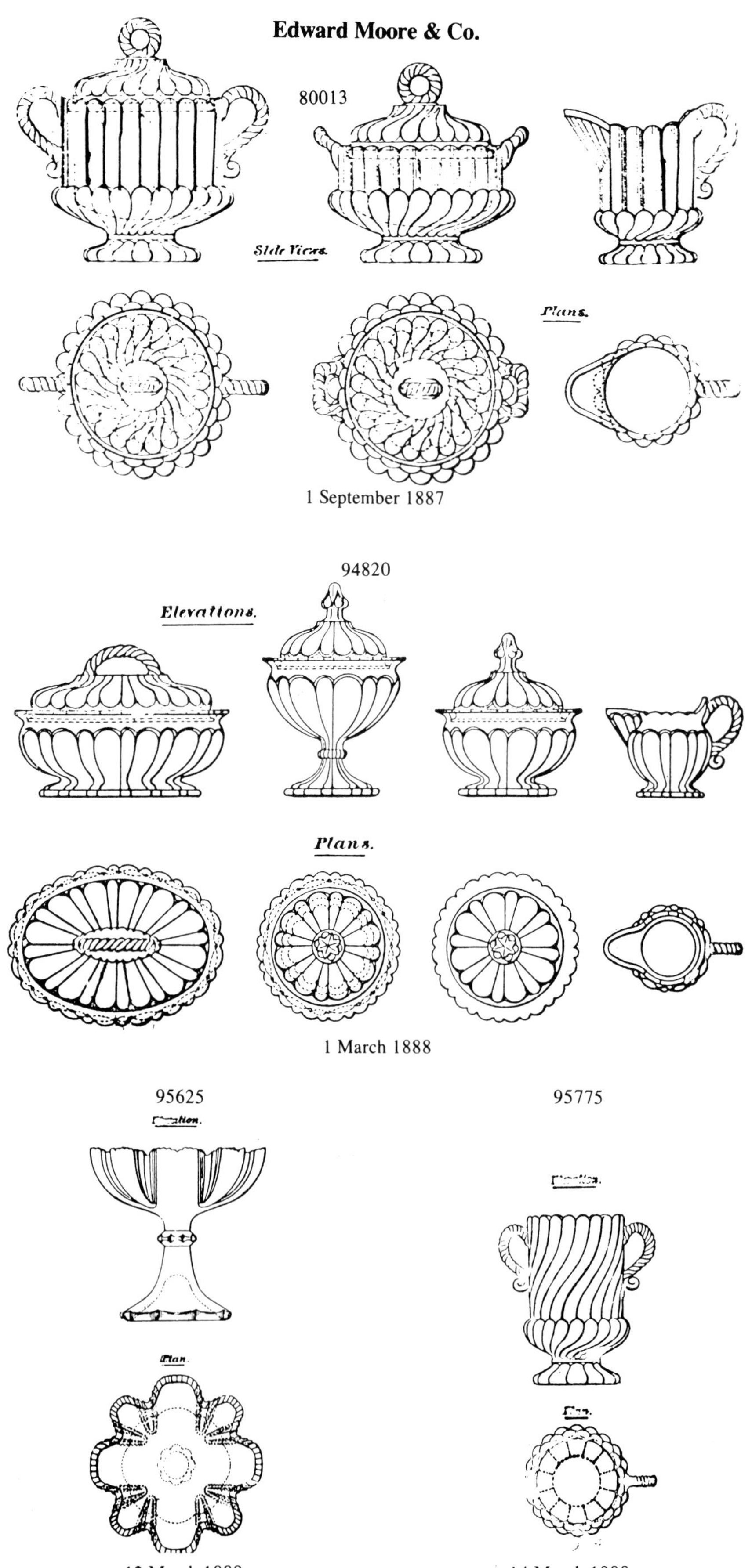


80013

1 September 1887

94820

1 March 1888

95625

12 March 1888

95775

14 March 1888

# Sowerby & Co., Ellison Glass Works, Gateshead-on-Tyne.

## In 1882 Sowerby's Ellison Glass Works Limited

Sowerby & Co first registered a design in 1872, there were to be nine that year, 1873 had two, 1874 six, but by 1877 over sixty registrations. The pieces registered were various, ranging from a covered dish, decanters and bowl (these were the first items in 1872) through the gamut of sugars, butters, ice pails, sweetmeats, baskets, vases, celery vases, flower troughs, spill vases and so on to cater for the Victorian taste. The imagination was as prolific as the output and there are some delightful articles considering these were meant to be the day to day pieces of the ordinary home. For instance, some of the celery vases were made so that they could be upturned and a dish balanced on top to form a comport.

One of the first Sowerby items to be registered in February 1872.

Sowerby's pattern books show in detail the decoration of the majority of their special pieces and also which of the items were registered. It is possible that they started to register more and more designs when they realized the success of the vitro-porcelain ware, which being opaque, gave the glass a substance similar to porcelain. It was pretty and delicate but did not look fragile.

The 1870s and 1880s were the important years. In 1877, and 1878, the most prolific years, there is a spill vase with basket work effect, a flower pot with figures and fan decoration, another vase with bullrush motif, items with angular bar shaped handles, many candlesticks and the inevitable butters and large sugars shaped like comports. It is not until later that the design of the sugars alters and they become stemless. 1879 was another important year with the plate with the design of geese and a scalloped edge, another with peacock feathers as well as different round and square vases. The 'new bowl' was in that year which is probably the best known of the Sowerby wares. It has upright ends shaped like hair combs and though the registration was just for the shape of the bowl, it is found in Queen's Ivory ware with a decoration of raised blossoms to simulate carved ivory. These pieces are typically 'aesthetic' with many of the motifs inspired by the art of Japan. In 1883 they patented the most unusual pyramid shaped glass cheese stand, in 1884 a glass post pillar money box and in 1886 a fan picture frame and the pattern and shape of a boat stand. The latter can be compared to other firm's flower trough boats of a few years earlier and that of 1888, albeit gondola shape, to John Walsh Walsh's registration in January 1887 of a boat with a space for a lamp in the centre.

393638

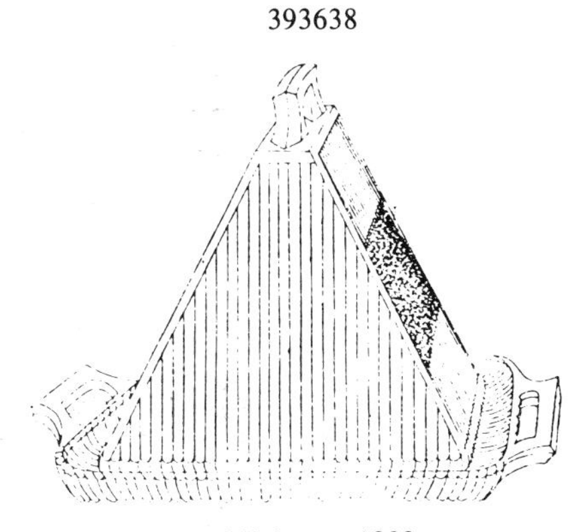

3 February 1883

Sowerby's is not as well known for their commemorative wares as Henry Greener and Greener & Co. but they produced a striking Golden Jubilee plate in 1887 with a portrait of the Queen in the centre and a rim of national emblems. There was a similar plate for the Diamond Jubilee, and also a plate and bowl commemorating the Scottish poet, Robert Burns.

The unusual items are interesting because they are rare but the charm of Sowerby glass lies in the enormous range of decoration and colour. There are the frosted angular sugars and cream jugs, with the clear glass ribbed ones, the frosted ice pails, the basket weave spill vases and hanging vases, and the flower troughs some with Nursery Rhyme and Kate Greenaway type figures. Many of the Nursery Rhyme pieces were taken from designs in the children's books by Walter Crane. These include Little Bo-peep, Jack Horner and Oranges and Lemons. Then there were country scene figures like the apple pickers or pieces with peacock, parrot, swan or bee patterns. The list is long and the pieces with patent office design registry marks often have the peacock's head trademark as well. Apart from clear glass there are many colours, some of which have been mentioned, as well there was an amber and a ruby with a hint of orange in the depths. Later on, in the mid 1920s they did iridescent orange items ('carnival glass') using the earlier moulds so that the glass continues the Victorian shape.

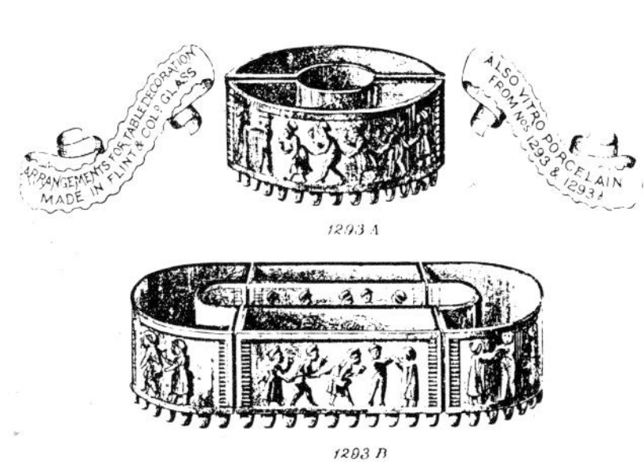

Taken from drawings by Walter Crane.
See black and white photograph number 31 for Lavender's Blue.

These colours are all very distinctive and in addition there are some rare aesthetic colours which are not often found. Sowerby glass is the collectors' joy for the quality of decoration and for the range of shape and colour.

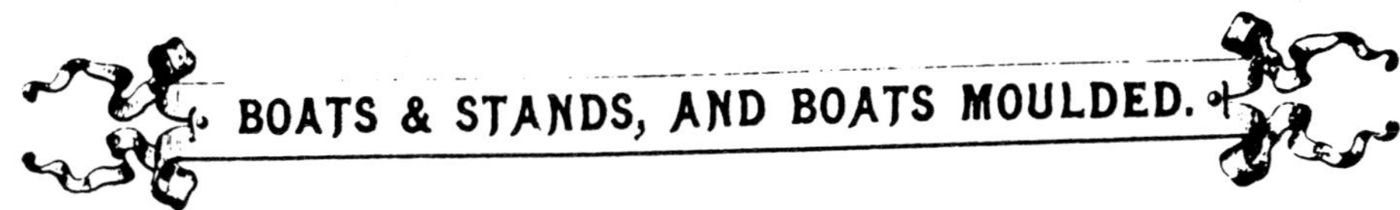


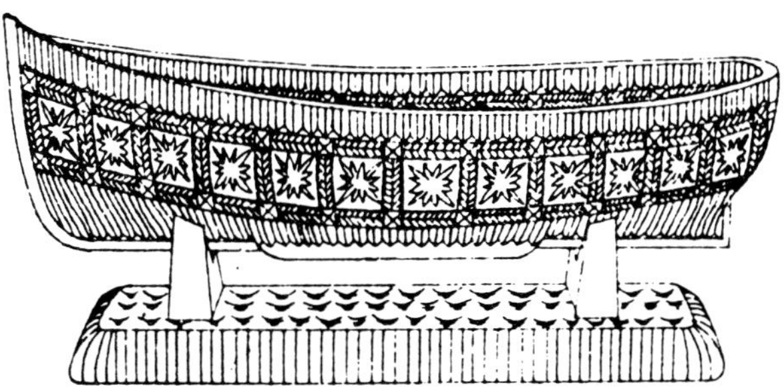

1874 *3 Sizes*
*10, 12, 15 Inches and Stands.*

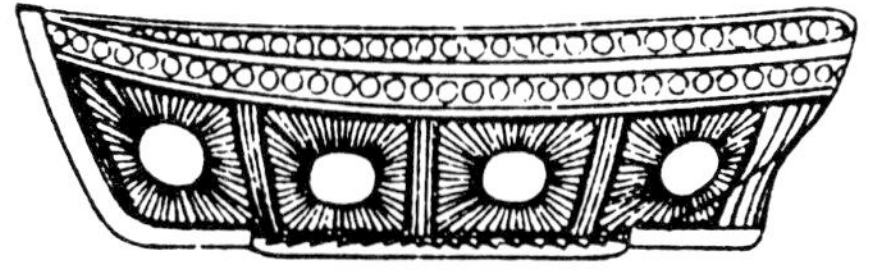

1921
*5 Inch.*

One Stand fits all Boats.

1874
*4½ Inch.*
*4 Sizes.*

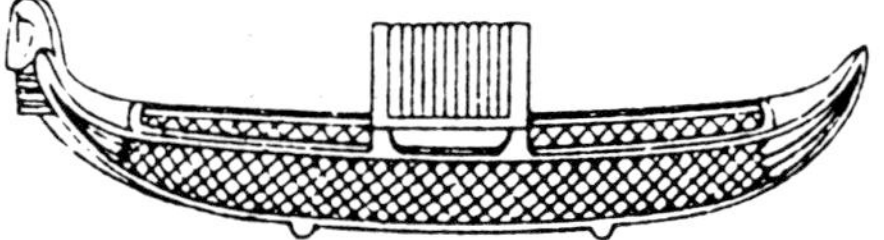

1972
***Moulded**, 8 and 10 Inch.*
*Two Sizes, no Cabin to Largest Size.*

From Sowerby's Pattern Book 1880s.

39414

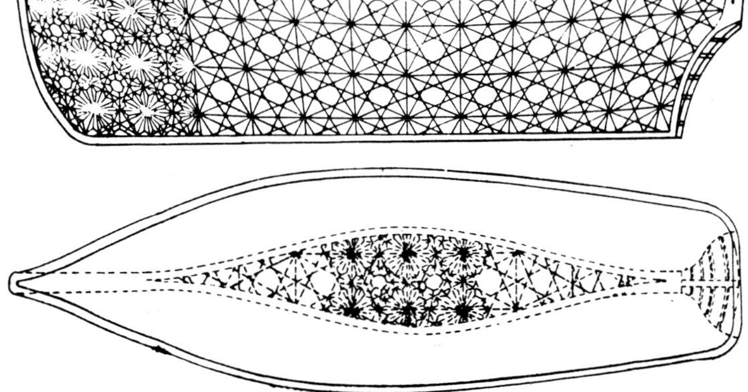

Edward Bolton 11 December 1885.

The best known of the registered glass boats.

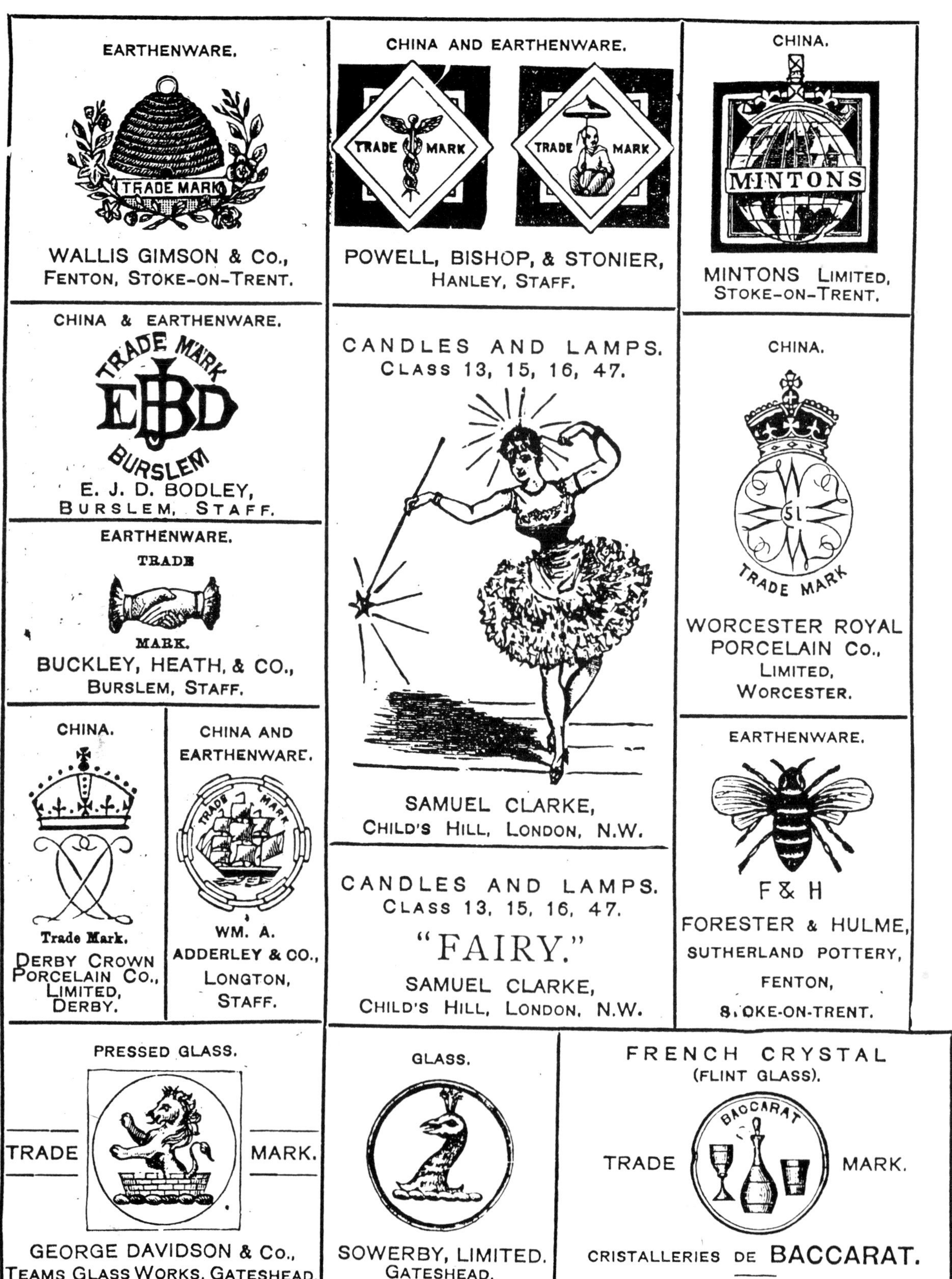


Pottery Gazette advertisement of 1 May 1889, showing the trade marks of Sowerby & Co. with George Davidson & Co. in the company of such firms as Worcester Royal Porcelain Co. Ltd. and Mintons Ltd.

SOWERBY & CO. GATESHEAD-ON-TYNE.

VITRO-PORCELAIN.

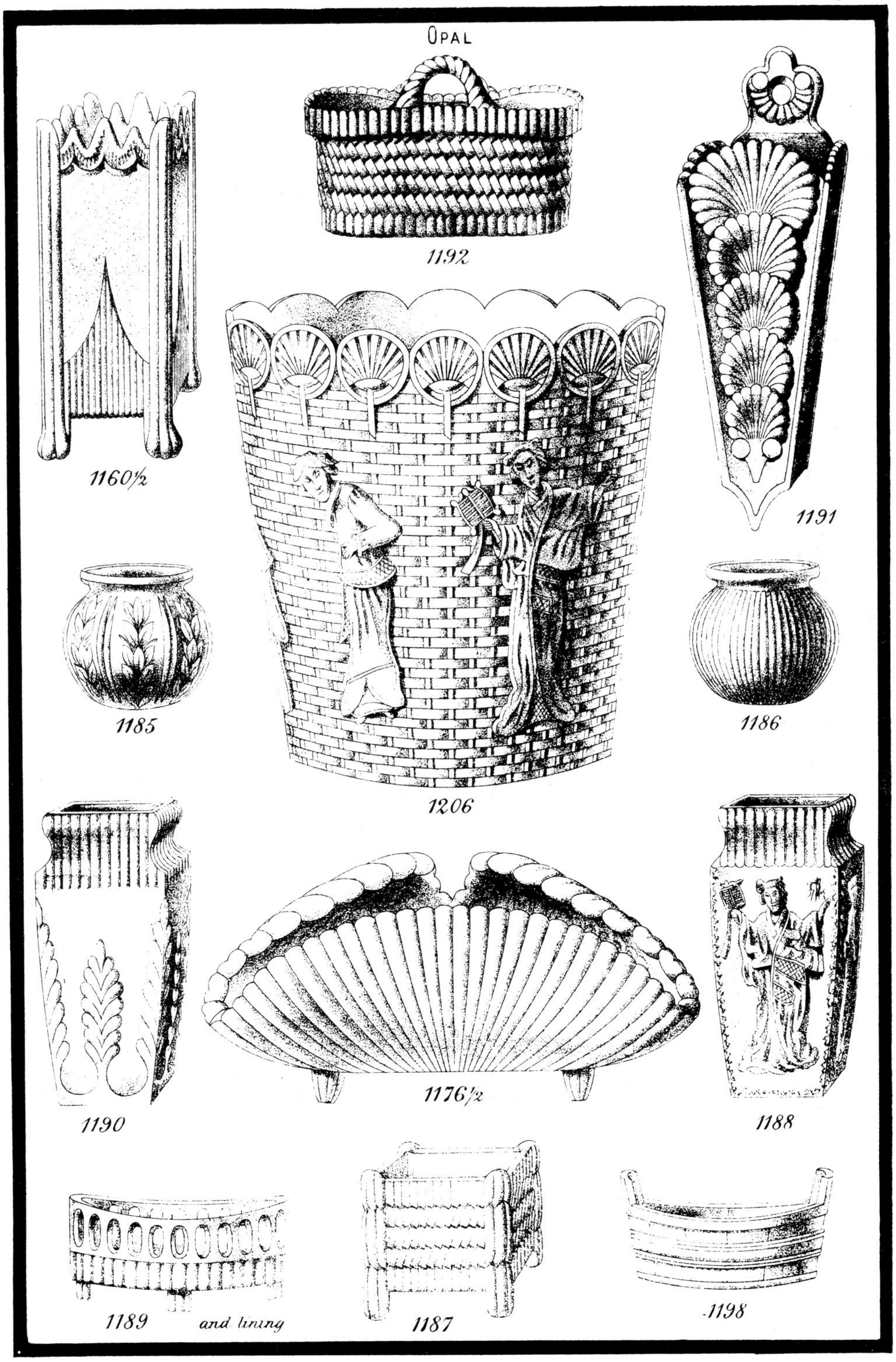

9

OPAL

1160½ 1192 1191

1206

1185 1186

1190 1176½ 1188

1189 and lining 1187 1198

Pattern Book c1879.

From Sowerby's Pattern Book 1880s showing Pattern Book numbers.

# SOWERBY & CO. GATESHEAD-ON-TYNE.

## Jet Goods.

6

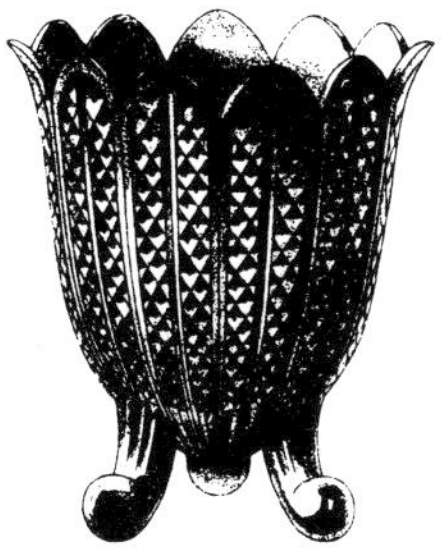

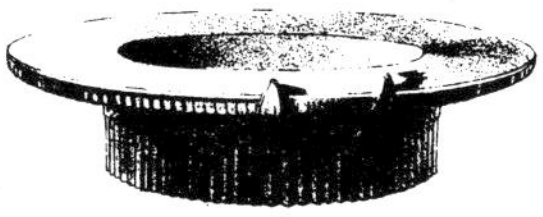

1132

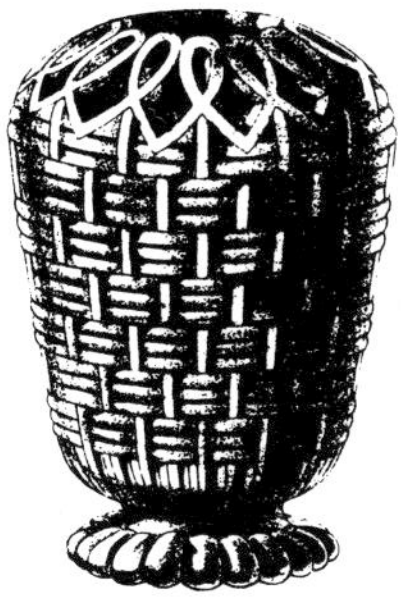

1151½

1152

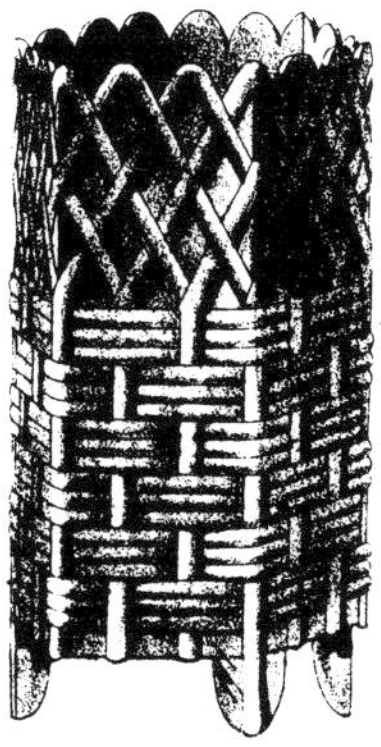

1166

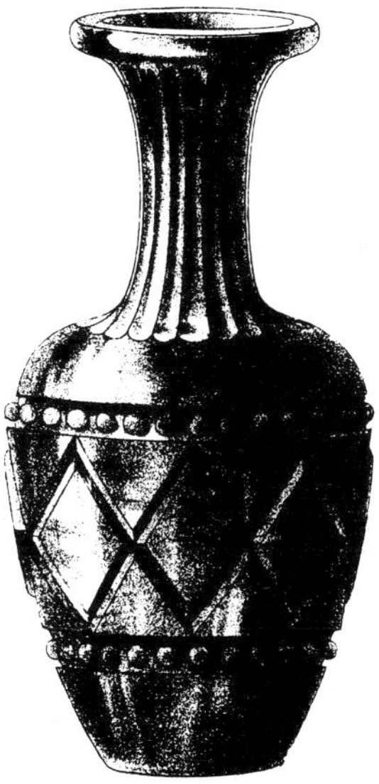

1061

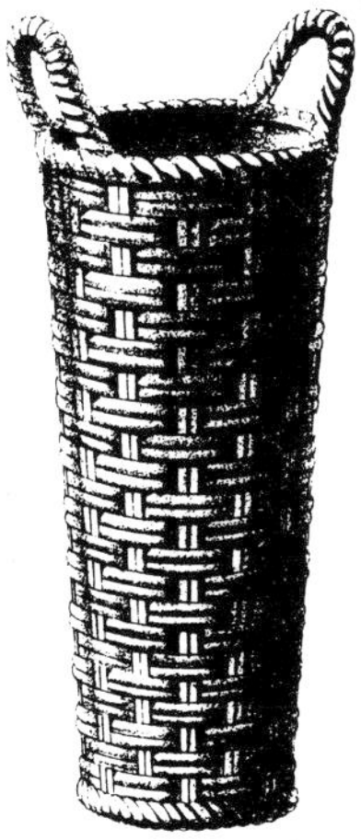

1102

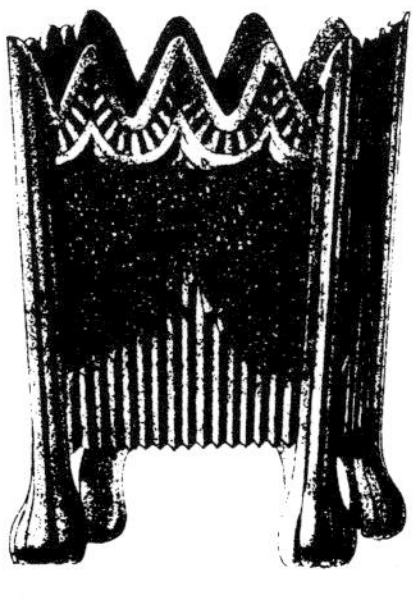

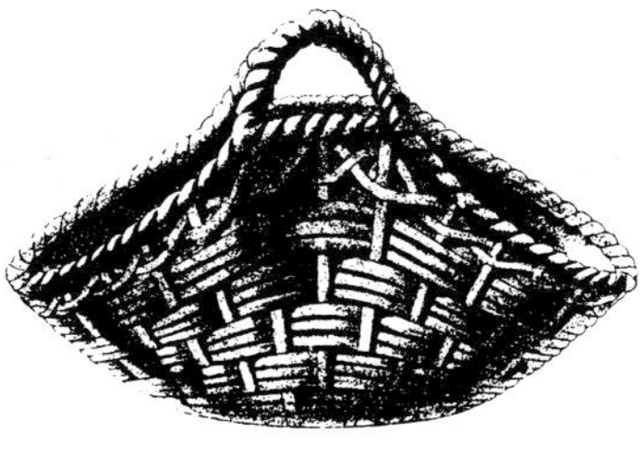

1157

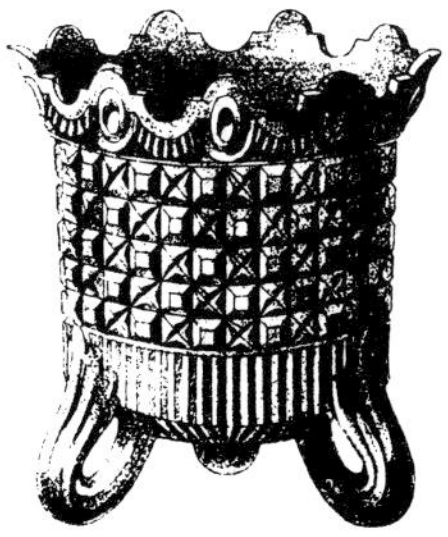

1160

1154½

Pattern Book c1879.

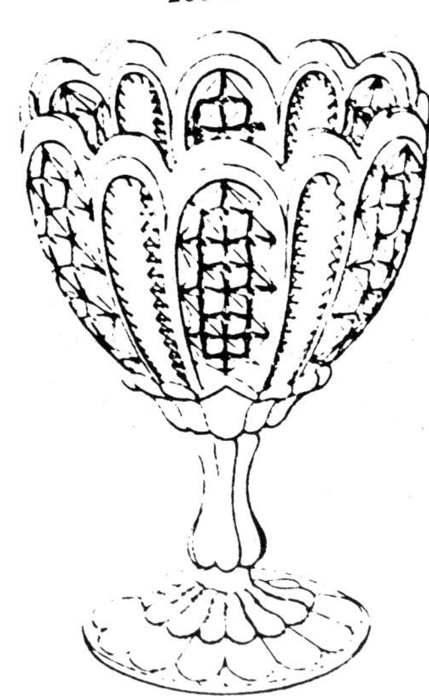

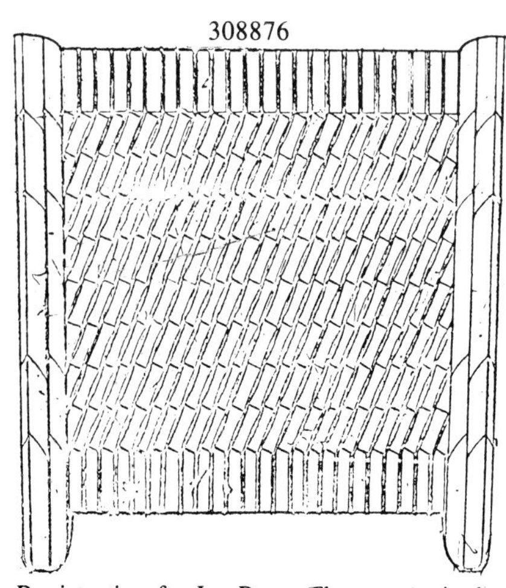


Registration for Ice Bowl. The pattern is the same as for 13 February 1877.

**Sowerby & Co., Ellison Glass Works, Gateshead-on-Tyne. Registrations**

| *Registration* No. | *Date* | *Year* | *Parcel* No. | *Design* |
|---|---|---|---|---|
| 260183 to 86 | 2 February | 1872 | 1 | (Covered dish, decanters and bowl) |
| 260404/5 | 12 February | | 6 | (Sugars) |
| 260802 | 29 February | | 5 | (Butter) |
| 267742/3 | 7 November | | 7 | |
| 273866 | 20 June | 1873 | 13 | Plate |
| 274743 | 31 July | | 5 | |
| 279876 | 15 January | 1874 | 6 | (Sugar) |
| 281933 | 22 April | | 8 | (Sugar) |
| 282663/4 | 1 June | | 8 | (Ice plate and Plate) |
| 284431 | 17 August | | 5 | (Dish and cover) |
| 285016 | 10 September | | 6 | (Tumbler shape) |
| 288210 | 1 January | 1875 | 2 | |
| 290778 | 19 April | | 5 | (Basket) |
| 291873/4 | 5 June | | 9 | Butter dish and Ice Pail |
| 294376 to 79 | 10 September | | 6 | 78 (Bowl)<br>79 (Dish and cover) |
| 295444 | 28 October | | 4 | Dish |
| 297041/2 | 17 December | | 16 | Sugar and sweetmeat. Suite of glass (rope handle) |
| 298870 to 76 | 6 March | 1876 | 3 | 72 (Elaborate sugar)<br>73 (Bowl)<br>74 (Covered dish)<br>75 (Pail)<br>76 (Jug) |
| 299050 to 54 | 9 March | | 7 | 51 and 52 (Covered dish)<br>53 and 54 (Sugars) |
| 299424 to 26 | 27 March | | 13 | 24 and 25 (Vases)<br>26 (Covered dish) |
| 299473 | 28 March | | 7 | (Handled vase) |
| 300419/20 | 8 May | | 6 | 19 (Vase)<br>20 (Basket) |
| 300748 | 24 May | | 5 | Basket (woven effect) |
| 300940 | 29 May | | 19 | |
| 301312 | 20 June | | 1 | Flower trough |
| 301326/7 | 21 June | | 1 | (Covered dish and vase) |
| 302114/5 | 24 July | | 13 | Glass butter middle and glass butter |
| 302804/5 | 18 August | | 10 | Plate and Celery vase |
| 304363 to 66 | 16 October | | 8 | 63-65 Vases<br>66 Plate |
| 305209 | 15 November | | 4 | (Vase) |
| 306887 | 16 January | 1877 | 11 | Salt |
| 307686 to 96 | 13 February | | 8 | 86 (Finger plate or small vase)<br>87 and 89 (Bowls)<br>90 and 91 (Covered vase shapes)<br>92 and 94 (Bowls)<br>93 (Vase)<br>95 and 96 (Sugars) |
| 307957/8 | 23 February | | 8 | (Candlestick and fluted bowl) |
| 308122/3 | 1 March | | 5 | (Straight handled bowl and dish) |
| 308414 | 13 March | | 10 | (Spill vase, basket effect) |
| 308495 | 15 March | | 1 | (Vase similar to above) |
| 308644 | 19 March | | 5 | Flower pot (figures and fans) |
| 308713 to 15 | 22 March | | 12 | (Bullrush motif) |
| 308776 | 23 March | | 7 | (Vase woven effect) |
| 308876 | 29 March | | 4 | Glass Ice Bowl |
| 310595 to 97 | 31 May | | 9 | 95 and 96 (Angular bar shape handles) |
| 314265 to 85 | 18 September | | 7 | 65-82 Vases<br>83 and 84 Baskets<br>(83 Gladstone Bag shape) |

**Sowerby & Co. (continued)**

| *Registration* No. | *Date* | *Year* | *Parcel* No. | *Design* |
|---|---|---|---|---|
| 315664 to 74 | 29 October | 1877 | 6 | 64 Bowl |
| | | | | 65-70 Vases |
| | | | | 71 Sugar basin |
| | | | | 72 Handled vase |
| | | | | 73 Basket |
| 316490 to 92 | 20 November | | 4 | 90 Glass plate |
| | | | | 91 and 92 Baskets |
| 317233/4 | 17 December | | 12 | 33 Candlestick |
| | | | | 34 Jug |
| 317277 to 80 | 19 December | | 1 | 77 Candlestick |
| | | | | 78 Sugar basin |
| | | | | 79 and 80 Butters |
| 318789 to 95 | 20 February | 1878 | 3 | 89 Covered sugar |
| | | | | 90 Candlestick |
| | | | | 91 Butter |
| | | | | 92 Inkstand |
| | | | | 93 Sugar |
| | | | | 94 Stand |
| | | | | 95 Covered sugar |
| 319585 to 89 | 20 March | | 7 | 85 Vase |
| | | | | 86 Biscuit jar |
| | | | | 87 Glass plate |
| | | | | 88 Two-handled basket |
| | | | | 89 Round vase |
| 319619/20 | 22 March | | 8 | Vase and Basket |
| 321368 to 79 | 14 May | | 9 | 68 Butter |
| | | | | 69 Sugar box |
| | | | | 70 Butter with sunk handle |
| | | | | 71 Basket |
| | | | | 72 and 73 Vases |
| | | | | 74 Two-handled basket |
| | | | | 75-8 Vases |
| | | | | 79 Basket |
| 322819 to 25 | 25 June | | 10 | 19 Sugar basin |
| | | | | 20 Butter |
| | | | | 21 Salt |
| | | | | 22 Vase |
| | | | | 23 Vase |
| | | | | 24 Butter |
| | | | | 25 Salt |
| 323400 | 8 July | | 9 | Basket |
| 324321/2 | 29 July | | 4 | (Vases) |
| 324929 to 32 | 12 August | | 6 | 29 Flower vase |
| | | | | 30 Round salt |
| | | | | 31 Round vase |
| | | | | 32 Four-footed dish |
| 325096 to 101 | 16 August | | 11 | 96 Butter |
| | | | | 97 Three-footed salver |
| | | | | 98 Round sugar |
| | | | | 99 Round trinket stand |
| | | | | 100 Round vase |
| | | | | 101 Round vase |
| 325534 | 30 August | | 16 | Comport |
| 328740 to 51 | 4 November | | 10 | 40 Biscuit box |
| | | | | 41 Vase |
| | | | | 42 Sugar |
| | | | | 43 Sugar |
| | | | | 44 Vase |
| | | | | 45 Vase |
| | | | | 46 Basket |
| | | | | 47 Jug |
| | | | | 48 Water Bottle |
| | | | | 49 Round sugar |
| | | | | 50 Butter |
| | | | | 51 Round dish |

314283

18 September 1877

319589

321371

These drawings are taken from the Pattern Book in lieu of the representations.

## Sowerby & Co. (continued)

| *Registration* No. | *Date* | *Year* | *Parcel* No. | *Design* |
|---|---|---|---|---|
| 328919 | 7 November | 1878 | 17 | Candlestick |
| 329376 | 20 November | | 11 | Candlestick |
| 330348 to 52 | 13 December | | 16 | 48 Double vase |
| | | | | 49 Dish |
| | | | | 50 Dish |
| | | | | 51 Candlestick |
| | | | | 52 Double vase |
| 330604 | 23 December | | 2 | New pattern vase |
| 330964 | 8 January | 1879 | 10 | Round handled sweetmeat |
| 332051 to 54 | 8 February | | 8 | 51 Round vase on four feet |
| | | | | 52 Three-square vase |
| | | | | 53 Butter |
| | | | | 54 Dish |
| 332195 | 12 February | | 17 | Dish |
| 333167 to 73 | 10 March | | 9 | 67 Plate and butter dish |
| | | | | 68 Round sugar and cover |
| | | | | 69 Round butter with two handles |
| | | | | 70 Mustard and cover |
| | | | | 71 Basket |
| | | | | 72 Vase |
| | | | | 73 Tea caddy |
| 333424 to 29 | 17 March | | 11 | 24 Butter |
| | | | | 25 Dish on feet |
| | | | | 26 Plate |
| | | | | 27 Trinket stand |
| | | | | 28 Vase |
| | | | | 29 Vase (trinket) |
| 334634 to 43 | 28 April | | 7 | 34 Plate (new design geese & scalloped edge) |
| | | | | 35 Round vase |
| | | | | 36-42 Vases |
| | | | | 43 Mustard |
| 335969 to 72 | 6 June | | 10 | 69 New vase |
| | | | | 70 Butter |
| | | | | 71 Flower pot |
| | | | | 72 New bowl (sometimes found decorated to simulate carved ivory) |
| 336594/5 | 30 June | | 14 | 94 Plate |
| | | | | 95 Double vase |
| 337409 to 15 | 22 July | | 6 | 09 Carafe |
| | | | | 10 Square plate |
| | | | | 11 Plate |
| | | | | 12 Hanging vase |
| | | | | 13 Two handled bowl |
| | | | | 14 Double vase |
| | | | | 15 Vase |
| 337623 to 27 | 29 July | | 13 | 23-25 Vases |
| | | | | 26 Handled sweetmeat |
| | | | | 27 Sugar |
| 338294 to 98 | 14 August | | 15 | 94 Sugar |
| | | | | 95 Basket |
| | | | | 96 Vase, three swans |
| | | | | 97 Basket |
| | | | | 98 Double hanging vase |
| 339194 to 200 | 4 September | | 7 | 94 Sugar and cover |
| | | | | 95 Sugar (three feet) |
| | | | | 96 Dish |
| | | | | 97 Basket |
| | | | | 98 Vase |
| | | | | 99 Square dish on four feet |
| | | | | 200 Candlestick with perforations |

335972

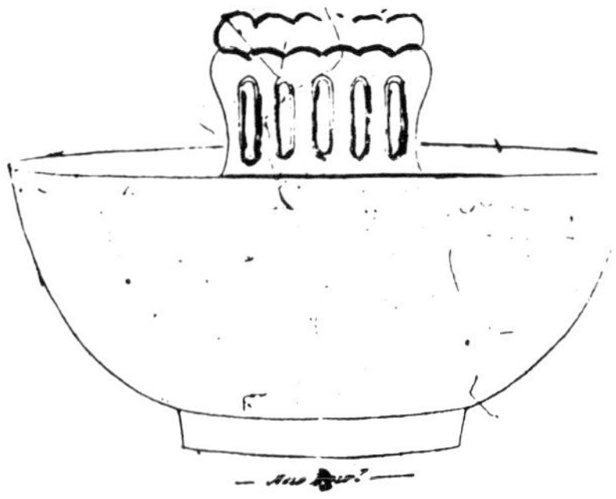

"New bowl". Most often seen in Patent Ivory Queen's Ware with raised decoration of blossoms.

338296

**Sowerby & Co. (continued)**

| *Registration* No. | *Date* | *Year* | *Parcel* No. | *Design* |
|---|---|---|---|---|
| 339498 to 502 | 12 September | 1879 | 13 | 498 Butter and cover<br>499 Sugar<br>500 Butter and cover<br>501 Celery vase<br>502 Jelly dish |
| 340002 to 06 | 18 September | | 13 | 02 Basket<br>03 Bowl<br>04 Sugar<br>05 Square vase<br>06 Handled jelly |
| 340254 | 23 September | | 13 | New decoration for pressed glass |
| 343724 to 31 | 2 December | | 21 | 24 Round butter and cover<br>25 Butter<br>26 Two handled plate<br>27-31 Vases |
| 345042 to 44 | 9 January | 1880 | 11 | 42 Round vase<br>43 Square trinket<br>44 Square sugar |
| 350083 to 93 | 24 May | | 8 | 83 Bowl<br>84 Sugar<br>85 Vase<br>86 Dish<br>87 Handled dish<br>88 Basket<br>89-90 Bowls<br>91-92 (Trinkets or similar with handles)<br>93 Butter |
| 352133 to 37 | 13 July | | 11 | (Vases) |
| 352840 to 45 | 26 July | | 10 | 40-41 New sugar<br>42 New butter<br>43 New shape dish<br>44 New shape basket<br>45 New shape sugar |
| 355154 to 58 | 14 September | | 1 | 54 Candlestick (bedroom shape)<br>55 Butter<br>56-58 Dishes |
| 355627 to 29 | 24 September | | 9 | 27 Butter<br>28 Sugar<br>29 Vase |
| 362734 to 44 | 11 March | 1881 | 2 | 34-36 Sugars (36 upright churn shape)<br>37 Round salt<br>38 Mustard<br>39 Sugar<br>40 Salt<br>41 Candlestick<br>42 Dish<br>43 Butter<br>44 Sugar |
| 363048/9 | 19 March | | 11 | 48 Basket<br>49 Sweetmeat |
| 364167 | 20 April | | 9 | Butter |
| 365165 | 19 May | | 9 | Sugar |
| 370370 to 79 | 21 September | | 16 | 70-71 Sugars<br>72 and 75 Butters with hollow for ice<br>73 and 74 Butters (round)<br>76 Celery vase<br>77 and 79 Sugars (not on stems, bowl shape)<br>78 Sweetmeat (has handles, scalloped rim) |

352844

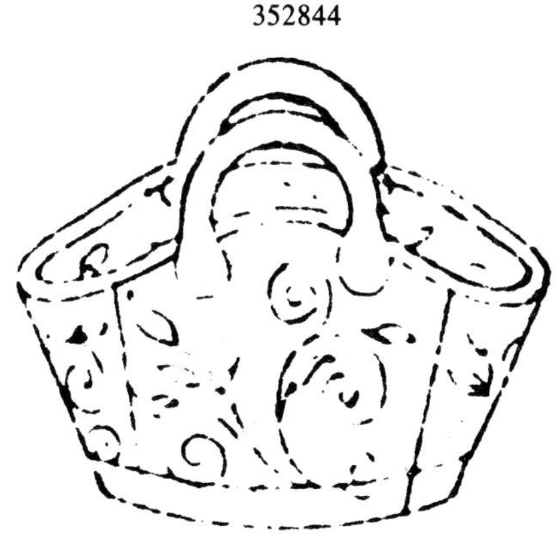

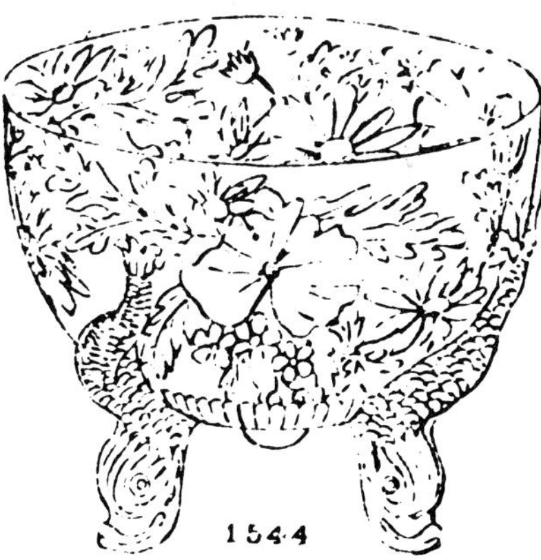


"Dolphin Bowl". In Sowerby Pattern Book of 1882, trade marked but not registered.

6481

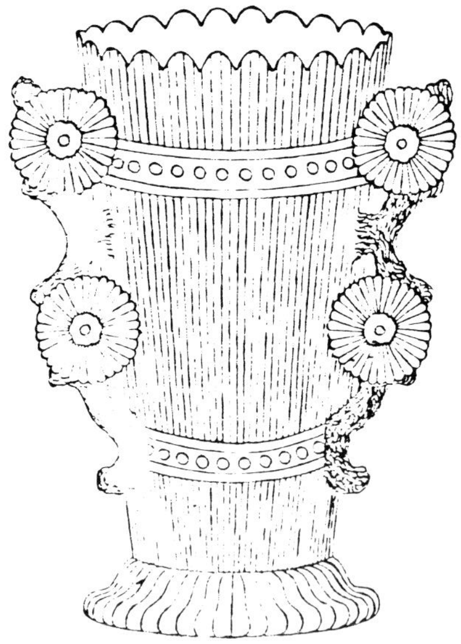

19937

48909

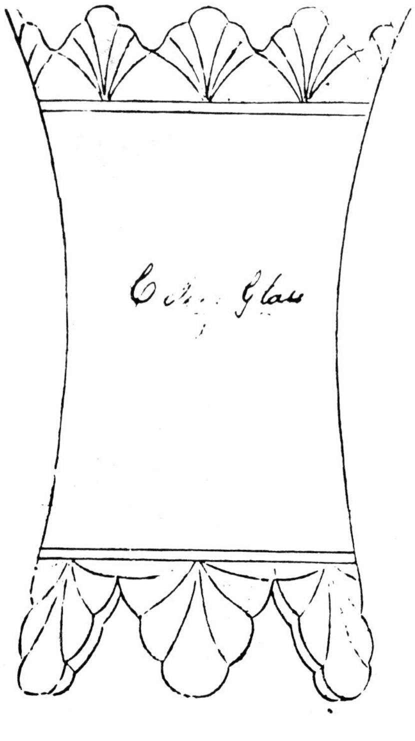

| *Registration* No. | *Date* | *Year* | *Parcel* No. | *Design* |
|---|---|---|---|---|
| 374682 to 86 | 14 December | 1881 | 6 | 82 Comport<br>83 Dish (square)<br>84 Sugar<br>85 and 86 Salts |
| 374774 to 78 | 15 December | | 10 | 74 Toast Rack<br>75 and 77 Sugars<br>76 and 78 Salts |
| **Sowerby's Ellison Glass Works Limited.** | | | | |
| 376905 | 9 February | 1882 | 20 | Glass picture frame |
| 380132 to 34 | 28 April | | 13 | 32 Dish<br>33 and 34 Sugars |
| 384453 to 55 | 9 August | | 14 | 53 Bowl<br>54 Sugar<br>55 Photo frame |
| 385624/5 | 29 August | | 13 | 24 Butter<br>25 Sugar |
| 388896 | 25 October | | 16 | Dish |
| 393638 to 43 | 3 February | 1883 | 11 | 38 Cheese stand (pyramid shape)<br>39 and 41 Sugars (41 not on stem)<br>40 Pillar butter & cover<br>42 Bowl<br>43 Butter |
| --- | | | | |
| 4833 | 7 April | 1884 | | Pattern |
| 5849 | 29 April | | | Pattern and shape |
| 6481 | 8 May | | | Pattern and shape of flower vase (twig handles with flowers on twig) |
| 7978/9 | 5 June | | | Butter dish and cover, shape and pattern (78 vertical all over ribbing, 79 horizontal ribbing) |
| 10966/7 | 11 August | | | 66 Pattern and shape<br>67 Sugar basin, shape and ornamentation |
| 13563 | 19 September | | | Handle of jug made at the side instead of at the back opposite the lip |
| 13792 | 24 September | | | Shape of glass post pillar money-box manufacturered in one piece |
| 19937 | 6 January | 1885 | | Pattern of sugar basin |
| 20775 | 21 January | | | Pattern of water jug (middle band of imit. cut) |
| 21284 | 31 January | | | Pattern of glass dish |
| 24953 | 13 April | | | Shape of butter dish |
| 30244 | 22 July | | | Pattern of a sugar |
| 32253 | 27 August | | | Pattern of dish (imit. cut) |
| 37110/11 | 4 November | | | 10 Shape of sugar<br>11 Pattern of sugar (fruit pattern) |
| 39062 to 64 | 3 December | | | Pattern of sugar (62 not on stem) |
| 42947 | 10 February | 1886 | | Pattern of dish |
| 44659 | 11 March | | | Shape of dish |
| 45759 | 25 March | | | Pattern of sugar (scroll band in middle) |
| 47514 | 21 April | | | Pattern and shape of pressed glass fan picture frame |
| 48228 | 4 May | | | Pattern and shape of butter (fan shaped lid) |
| 48909/10 | 11 May | | | 09 Shape of celery (scalloped top and feet)<br>10 Shape of sweetmeat (shell shape on shell feet) |
| 50071 | 1 June | | | Pattern of butter |
| 52434 | 13 July | | | Pattern and shape of boat stand |

## Sowerby's Ellison Glass Works Ltd. (continued)

| *Registration No.* | *Date* | *Year* | *Design* |
|---|---|---|---|
| 54314 to 16 | 18 August | 1886 | 14 Shape and design of moulded glass sugar basin (star burst pattern with plain glass bands criss-crossing)<br>15 and 16 Shape of moulded glass jelly dish |
| 56961 to 66 | 23 September | | Shape and pattern of sugar.<br>61 (with stem)<br>62 (stemless, basket weave pattern)<br>63 (with stem, imit. cut) |
| 64086 | 22 December | | Pattern of sugar (sun pattern) |
| 64106 | 23 December | | Pattern of butter (with vertical ribbing) |
| 68846 | 1 March | 1887 | Pattern of dish (similarities to 64086) |
| 77881 | 2 August | | Pattern and shape of butter (leaf pattern) |
| 77967 | 3 August | | Pattern and shape of biscuit (imit. cut with flutes) |
| 78084 | 3 August | | Pattern and shape of sugar and cover (free pattern with dots) |
| 78551 | 11 August | | Pattern of sugar (free pattern with dots) |
| 78704 | 13 August | | Pattern of sugar (imit. cut) |
| 80530 | 10 September | | Pattern of sugar basin in glass (imit. cut) |
| 83777 | 7 October | | Pattern and shape of an advertising plate in pressed glass |
| 84001 | 15 October | | Pattern of sugar (imit. cut in squares bordered by plain glass) |
| 84218 | 18 October | | Pattern of dish (imit. cut) |
| 84747 | 21 October | | Pattern of butter (vine pattern) |
| 85870 | 1 November | | Shape of comportier and dish (shown with leaf pattern to dish) |
| 87058 | 15 November | | Pattern and shape of shoe (with bow, fluted side and toe) |
| 87776/7 | 24 November | | 76 Pattern of sugar (gadroons on base)<br>77 Pattern of salt (hexagonal with mitres) |
| 91431/2 | 14 January | 1888 | 31 Pattern of dish (imit. cut)<br>32 Pattern of sugar (imit. cut and mitres) |
| 95300 | 7 March | | (Gondola shape with imit. cut) |
| 95894 | 16 March | | |
| 98215/6 | 18 April | | (Imit. cut coal bucket and an anvil) |
| 99715 | 9 May | | (Elaborate imit. cut) |
| 106892 | 30 August | | (Vase and pattern) |
| 106938 | 31 August | | (Elaborate imit. cut) |
| 111269/70 | 17 October | | 69 (All pillars star shaped)<br>70 (Flower shape with six petals) |
| 113560 | 13 November | | (Imit. cut. Engraved?) |
| 114044 | 17 November | | (Candle holder) |
| 117569 | 17 January | 1889 | |
| 120229 | 23 February | | (Cup) |
| 122393 | 30 March | | (Swan sitting on bowl) |
| 126940 | 11 June | | (Elaborate imit. cut) |
| 133053 | 11 September | | (Jug shape) |
| 133909 | 24 September | | (Jug shape) |
| 139808 | 6 December | | |
| 141080 | 27 December | | (Imit. cut flower shapes) |
| 142675 | 22 January | 1890 | (Basket shape) |
| 165559 | 30 January | 1891 | |
| 173059 | 18 June | | (Mostly imit. cut)(Sowerby & Co., Lemington Glass Works, Newcastle-on-Tyne) |

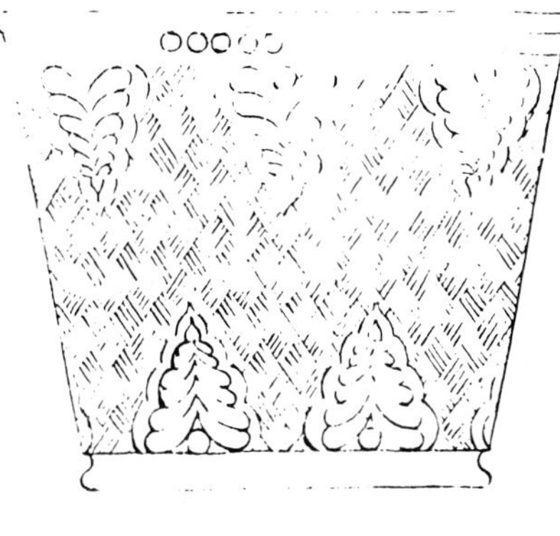

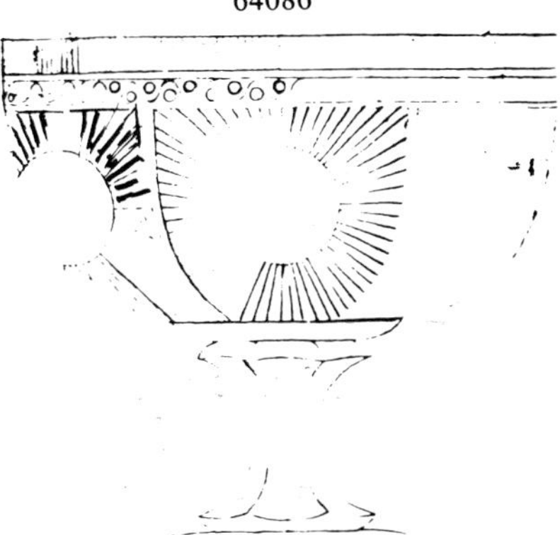

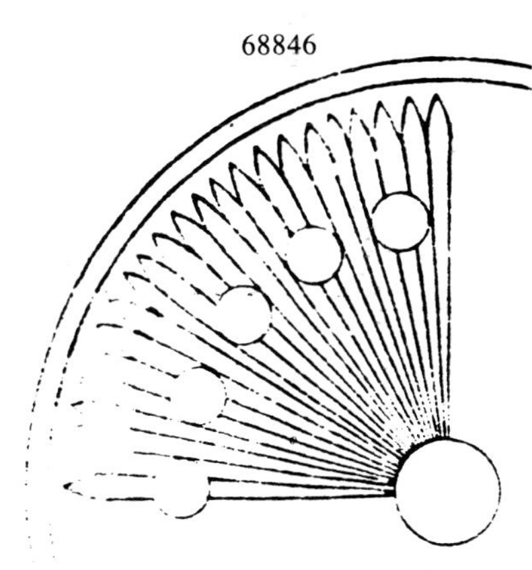


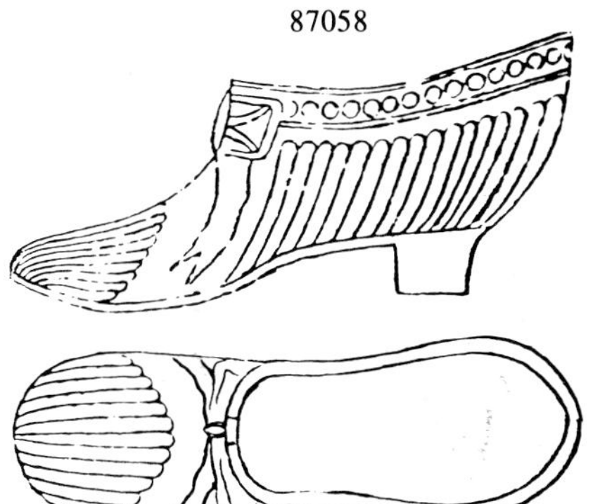

87776

24 November 1887
Gadroons similar to Edward Moore.

## Sowerby's Ellison Glass Works Ltd. (continued)

| *Registration No.* | *Date* | *Year* | *Design* |
|---|---|---|---|
| 189324 | 16 March | 1892 | (Imit. cut) |
| 215082 | 15 July | 1893 | (Angular, tumbler design) |
| 217199 | 25 August | | (Angular, dish) |
| 238352 | 23 August | 1894 | (Tumbler with twisted pillar base) |

## George Sowerby Ltd, Lemington Glassworks, Newcastle-upon-Tyne

| | | | |
|---|---|---|---|
| 358727 | 13 June | 1900 | (Tumbler shape) |
| 363130 | 8 September | | (Similar) |
| 374792 | 1 June | 1901 | |

99715

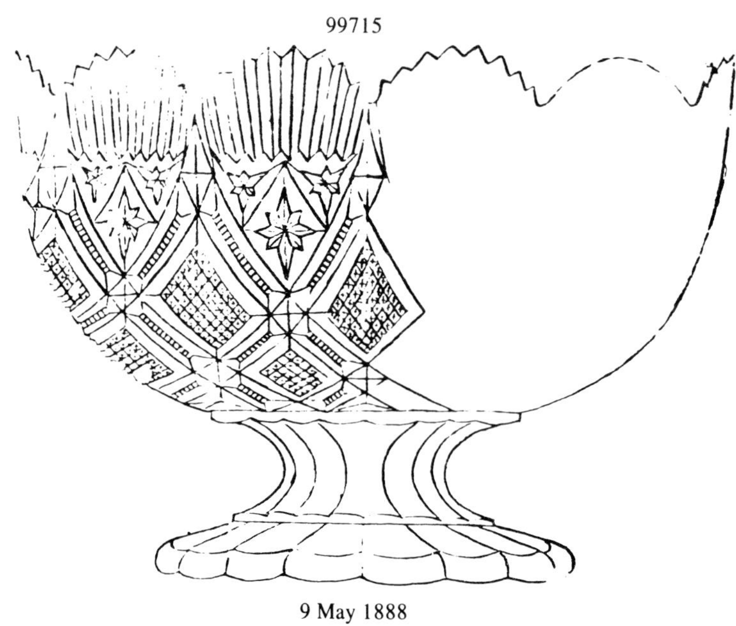

9 May 1888

141080

27 December 1889
Not unlike pattern of G. Davidson & Co. of August 1891.

# Burtles, Tate & Co., Poland Street, Manchester.

Burtles, Tate & Co., Poland Street first registered in 1870 a design for ornamenting glass. The second registration in October 1871 was of a hand, registered as a chimney piece ornament. There is not much between then and 1885 when there were several registrations of flower stands and holders. The best known in pressed glass are January 8th 1885, a swan flower holder, not unlike the one in Sowerby's pattern book, June 29th, a flower boat and on December 28th 1886, an elephant flower holder. All three can be found in opal glass and remind one very much of Sowerby pieces. In 1887 there is a shoe flower holder, which again can be compared to one of Sowerby's of about that time. At the end of the century the electric light shade patterns are pretty, but the best pieces were definitely mid-1880s because of their resemblance to Sowerby.

64234

28 December 1886

65455

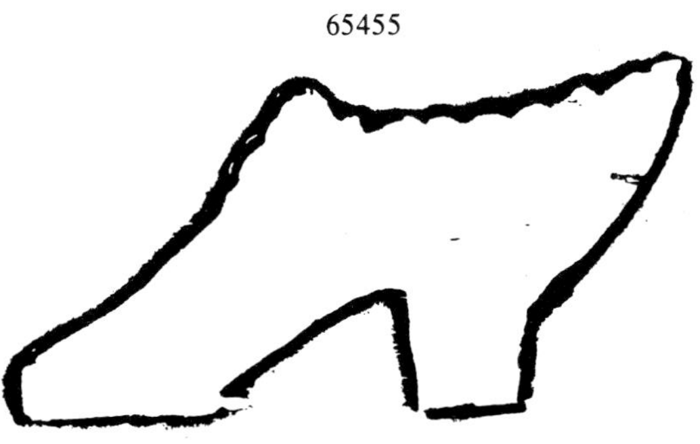

17 January 1887

475286

501822

## Burtles, Tate & Co., Poland Street Glass Works, Manchester. Registrations

| *Registration* No. | *Date* | *Year* | *Parcel* No. | *Design* |
|---|---|---|---|---|
| 239136 | 24 February | 1870 | 9 | Design for ornamenting glass (vertical columns) |
| 256336 | 3 October | 1871 | 4 | Design for Chimney Piece ornament (hand) |
| 262193 | 23 April | 1872 | 5 | Ornamental glass |
| 351062 | 17 June | 1880 | 19 | (Crimped edge: glass vessel) |
| 399313 | 12 June | 1883 | 14 | (Glass vase and stand) |

| | | | | |
|---|---|---|---|---|
| 3613/4 | 14 March | 1884 | | Ornamental design applicable for patterns |
| 20085/6 | 8 January | 1885 | | 85 Design for glass flower holder or bracket<br>86 Design for glass flower holder (swan) |
| 20972 | 24 January | | | Shape and pattern of flower stand |
| 21108 to 10 | 28 January | | | Pattern and shape of flower stand (crimped edge) |
| 21326/7 | 2 February | | | Shape and pattern of flower stand (similar) |
| 21328/9 | | | | Shape and pattern of flower stand (29 slender stem - turned over crimped top) |
| 24100 | 20 March | | | Shape and pattern of flower stand |
| 26480 | 7 May | | | Shape of glass shell |
| 29106 | 29 June | | | Pattern of flower boat |
| 34196 | 26 September | | | Pattern and shape of glass flower vase |
| 39807 | 18 December | | | Pattern and shape of flower bracket |
| 44445 | 8 March | 1886 | | Pattern and shape of flower boat |
| 64234 | 28 December | | | Pattern and shape of flower holder (elephant) |
| 65455 | 17 January | 1887 | | Pattern and shape of new flower holder (shoe) |
| 98578 | 23 April | 1888 | | Design for a glass sugar basin (imit. cut) |
| 109531 | 1 October | | | |
| 117556/7 | 14 January | 1889 | | Design for flower vase (56 naturalistic tree trunk shape) |
| 120808 | 4 March | | | Design for flower vase (ostrich shape) |
| 142985 | 28 January | 1890 | | Design for electric light globe |
| 148661 | 30 April | | | Whisky vase |
| 166178 | 10 February | 1891 | | (Triple flower vase on short stem) |
| 216088 | 3 August | 1893 | | Design for glass dish (simple imit. cut) |
| 316413 | 24 March | 1898 | | |
| 336261 | 6 April | 1899 | | Design for electric light shade (leaf pattern) |
| 339343 | 8 June | | | Design for electric light shade (oak leaves and acorns) |
| 351372 | 5 January | 1900 | | Design for electric light shade (shell pattern) |
| 386616/7 | 3 February | 1902 | | (Spiral rods) |
| 388857 | 20 March | | | (Elab. patterned vase) |
| 391814 | 3 June | | | Design for a perforated division of a dish |
| 403657 | 17 January | 1903 | | Design for electric shade |
| 406300 | 5 March | | | Design for cover for bird glass |
| 427524 | 25 February | 1904 | | Design for arm of flower stand (spiral rod shape) |
| 474329 | 20 February | 1906 | | Design for railway carriage lamp glass (classical leaf motifs) |
| 475286 | 7 March | | | Design for salad bowl (imit. cut) |
| 501821/2 | 11 May | 1907 | | Designs for salt cellar and ink-pot (as if set in a book for the base) |
| 502044 | 15 May | | | Design for flower vase |
| 510504 | 29 August | | | Design for salt cellar - (scuttle shape) |

510504

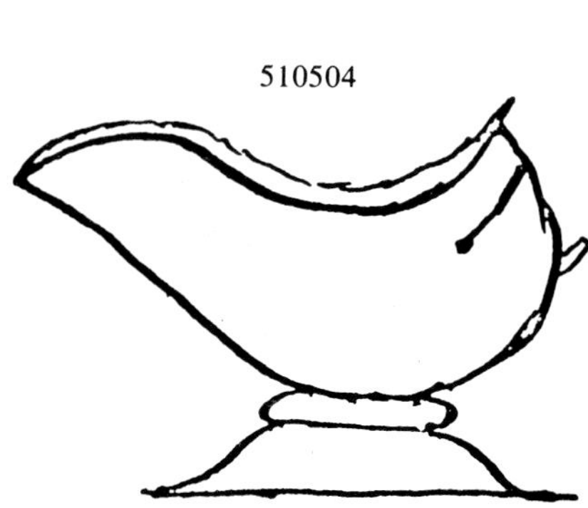

# James Derbyshire & Brother, Hulme, Manchester.

189321

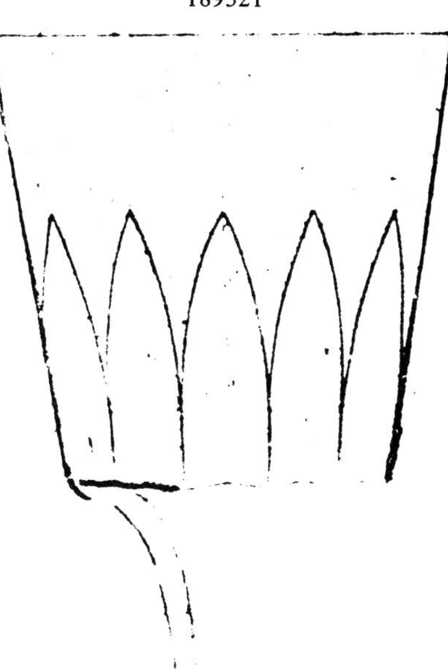

25 August 1865

The fourth Manchester firm, James Derbyshire & Brother of Hulme, registered thirteen items between 1864 and 1869, namely five goblets, two butter coolers, pressed basin moons (the description given in the register), a gas moon, a celery stand, a plain barrel shaped tumbler, a dish imitating cut glass and ornamental designs for a set, to consist of sugar basin, cream jug and butter dish, equally imitating cut glass. The designs of 1865 for the celery stand and gas moon have the Greek key pattern like the Molineux & Webb comport of 1864, though the James Derbyshire celery is more elaborate and heavy looking.

In 1870 the firm registered as J.J. & T. Derbyshire. Both in 1870 and 1872 there are ornamental designs for a Breakfast set. The 1868 design for a set of sugar basin, cream jug and butter dish is an elaborate one imitating cut glass with faceted diamond shapes, set in petal swags. The pattern is continuous around the bowl. The dish which follows in the records is similar. The Breakfast set pattern for sugar basin, butter dish, cream jug and vase of 1870 has a scroll border with a diamond shaped pattern spaced at equal distance round the bowl of the sugar basin and butter dish cover. For the butter lid there are four diamond cartouches round the centre of the domed lid. The pattern is much simpler than that of 1868, though there is a resemblance. The 1872 set consists of designs for sugar basin, cream jug, butter dish and cover, flower vase and celery, round and oval dishes and a comport. The design is classical and different with star centres and vertical lines to give the impression of columns. There is a scroll border and a fine ribbed edge to the pieces. Most of these James Derbyshire sets were of the highest quality and sadly are difficult to find. In 1872 too, there are such diverse registrations as a hand, quite plain with a jewelled wrist, a Roman vase, and a dolphin comport, which is a couple of years earlier than the Percival, Vicker's dolphin stand. The dolphins form the base of the comport. The dish top has a most attractive shell pattern. By 1876 the firm became James Derbyshire & Sons. These early Derbyshire registrations set a standard by which later registrations should be judged.

242570

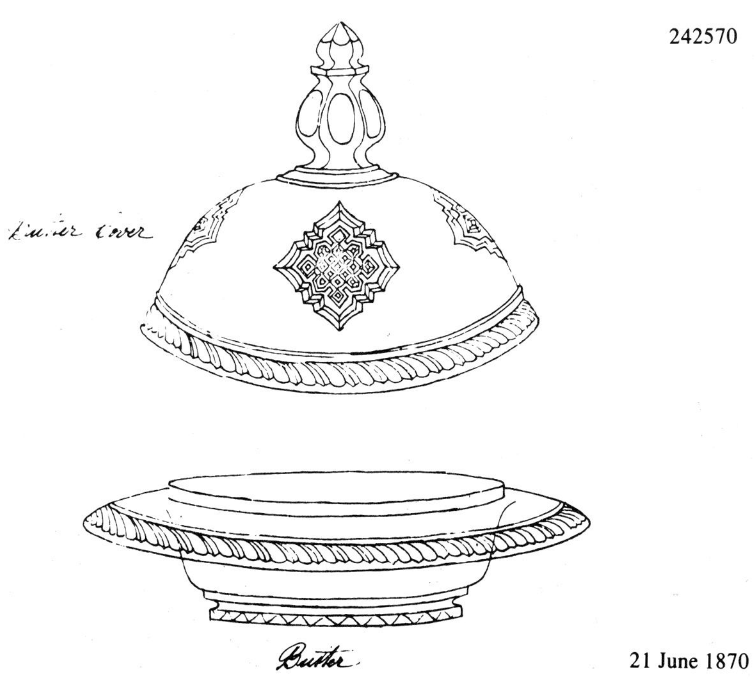


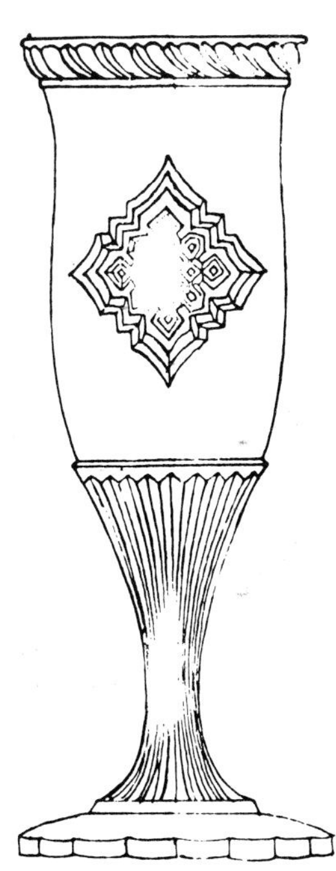

21 June 1870

198277

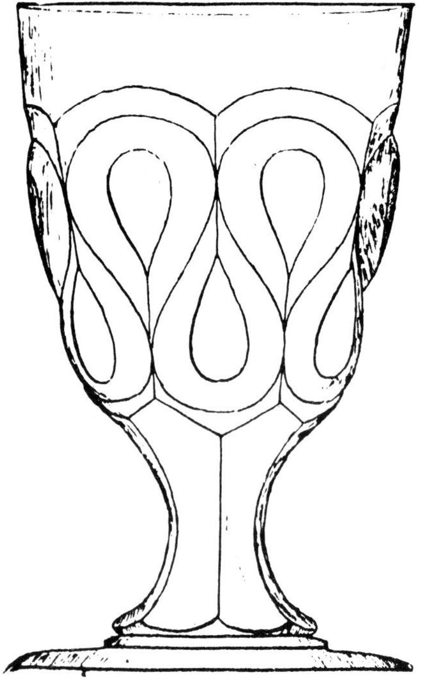

## James Derbyshire & Brother, Hulme, Manchester. Registrations

| *Registration* No. | *Date* | *Year* | *Parcel* No. | *Design* |
|---|---|---|---|---|
| 175421 | 14 June | 1864 | 4 | Goblet |
| 180699 | 2 November | | 4 | Butter cooler |
| 182248 | 10 December | | 7 | Pressed basin moons |
| 186847 | 16 May | 1865 | 4 | Celery stand |
| 189066 | 15 August | | 4 | Gas moon |
| 189321 | 25 August | | 6 | Goblet |
| 189705 | 12 September | | 2 | Goblet |
| 193419 | 14 December | | 5 | Plain barrel shape tumbler |
| 198277 | 16 June | 1866 | 4 | Goblet |
| 206304 | 25 February | 1867 | 5 | Butter cooler |
| 218988 | 29 May | 1868 | 11 | Ornamental designs for set; sugar basin, cream jug and butter dish |
| 227410 | 22 February | 1869 | 12 | Ornamental design dish (imit. cut) |
| 228612 | 13 April | | 7 | Goblet |

## J.J. & T. Derbyshire

| | | | | |
|---|---|---|---|---|
| 242570 | 21 June | 1870 | 3 | Ornamental design for a breakfast set |
| 251012 | 15 March | 1871 | 9 | (Ornamental design) |
| 261445 | 25 March | 1872 | 5 | Bridgewater & British Union Glass Works, Manchester. (Pattern) |
| 262680 | 11 May | | 9 | (Hand) |
| 267727 | 6 November | | 11 | Roman vase |
| 268739 | 11 December | | 4 | The dolphin comport |
| 268810 | 14 December | | 8 | Breakfast set |

## James Derbyshire & Sons, Trentham Street, Chester Road, Hulme

| | | | |
|---|---|---|---|
| 305541 | 28 November | 1876 | 10 |

186847

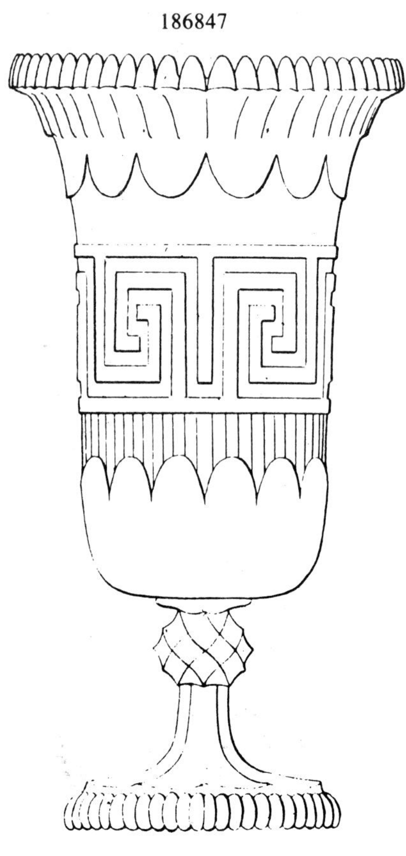

218988

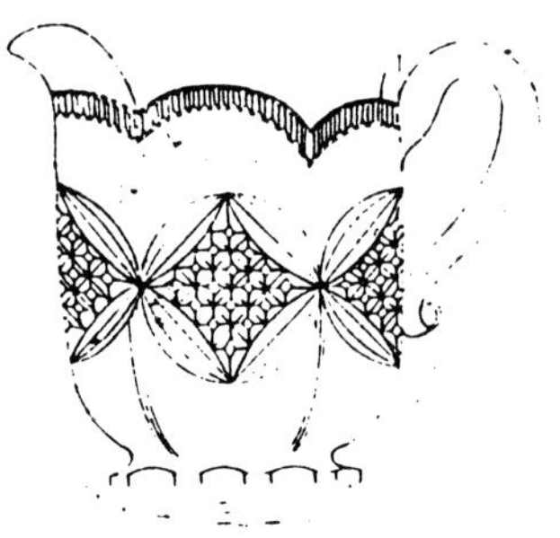

# John Derbyshire, Regent Road Flint Glass Works, Salford, Manchester.

In 1873 John Derbyshire produced a fine "sugar, cream and service in glass" in the pineapple pattern. Between the oval shaped diamond pattern, like the body of a pineapple, are leaf shapes similar to the top of the fruit. At that time too, he registered a couple of goblets with an oval figure of eight pattern. They are somewhat similar to those registered in 1866 when the firm was James Derbyshire & Brother. In 1874 came the now best known registrations; a glass hand holding a naturalistic vase with bullrushes; the most sought after of all, the lion paperweight after Landseer; a greyhound for "paperweight and jar cover" and the figure of Britannia. About a year later John Derbyshire produced two more figures in the shape of Punch and Judy. These were marked with his trademark and can be found in both frosted and clear glass. In 1875 also there was a Conservatory vase and "Lady's Boot" spill holder. This is one of the earliest shoe shapes, Sowerby's was over ten years later. Glass shoes with streamers, bows or buckles, like the boat troughs and swan shapes were a popular theme. In 1876 John Derbyshire registered a winged sphinx paperweight (Molineaux, Webb & Co did a sphinx in 1875) a swan vase, "spell" glass, and finally a tobacco jar with lid. The lion, greyhound and Britannia paperweights all have a distinctive ridged plinth as do some of the Newfoundland dog paperweights (which are mostly unmarked) that are attributed to John Derbyshire. The dog in question is similar to the one that was painted by Landseer in a painting known as "A Distinguished Member of the Humane Society", and then used as a model for porcelain plaques and such like. The plinth for the winged sphinx is completely different and has a pattern of scroll motifs. The last registration in 1877 is in the name of "The Regent Flint Glass Co." Apart from the patents John Derbyshire marked some of his glass with an anchor and his initials, the lion for instance has both registration and personal mark. A. Ruch & Co., of 12 Lawrence Pountney Lane, London, also used an anchor as a trademark in the 1890s and therefore if the pieces were registered they have a set of numbers to identify them, whereas Derbyshire pieces are prior to the 1884 registered numbers and have the diamond shaped mark.

The whole point of the Patent Office design registrations is that if the letters and numbers are clear in the diamond shaped marks up to 1884, a definite day, month, year and parcel number can be given for the item registered. So often the marks are indistinct and it is no good hazarding a guess at the unformed letter or number without checking the item's description against the possibilities and eliminating the unlikely ones. The parcel number is very important as an added clue if the marks are not clear, and there are also registered drawings of the objects so it should be possible to say what factory it cannot be, even if it is difficult to ascertain the exact date of the piece. The same applies to the numbers given after 1884. As with jigsaws, there is only one answer, but when the pieces fit together it is very satisfying and rewarding and for the collector the search for certain colours, pieces and patterns, is very special.

280197

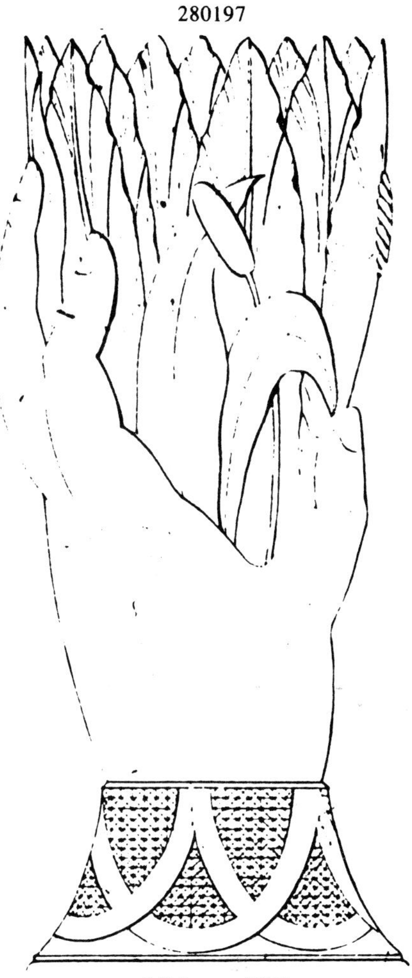

3 February 1874

300300

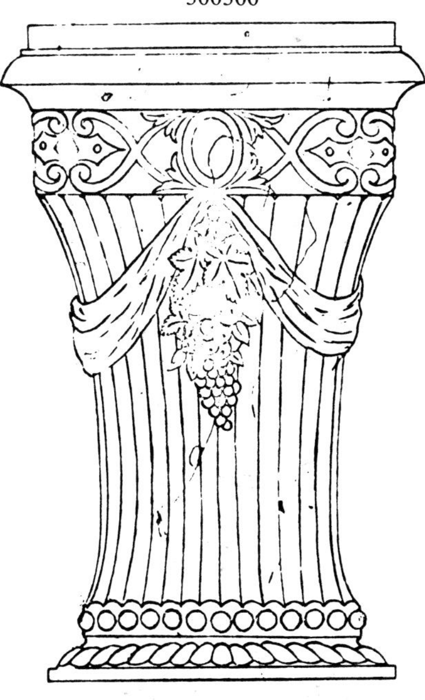

28 April 1876

274962

## John Derbyshire, Regent Road Flint Glass Works, Salford

| *Registration* No. | *Date* | *Year* | *Parcel* No. | *Design* |
|---|---|---|---|---|
| 274961 to 63 | 8 August | 1873 | 7 | 61 Sugar, cream and service in glass (pineapple pattern)<br>62 and 63 Goblet and service in glass (oval pattern) |
| 275756 | 2 September | | 9 | Piano foot |
| 279532 | 6 January | 1874 | 6 | Sugar basin and cream ewer |
| 280197 | 3 February | | 5 | Glass hand and vase |
| 282260 | 12 May | | 6 | Piano foot |
| 283406 | 3 July | | 4 | Lion after Landseer for a paperweight |
| 285175 | 11 September | | 5 | Greyhound |
| 287495 | 26 November | | 5 | Britannia - same figure but different sides |
| 293356 | 5 August | 1875 | 8 | Conservatory vase |
| 296643 | 6 December | | 7 | Lady's boot. Spill holder |
| 299022/3 | 9 March | 1876 | 4 | 22 Winged sphinx. Paperweight<br>23 Swan vase |
| 300300 | 28 April | | 2 | Spell glass |
| 300655 | 17 May | | 9 | Tobacco jar with lid |

## Regent Flint Glass Co., Regent Road

| | | | | |
|---|---|---|---|---|
| 308667 | 21 March | 1877 | 4 | Preserve jar |
| 309902 | 4 May | | 4 | Bull's head piano foot |

279532

299022

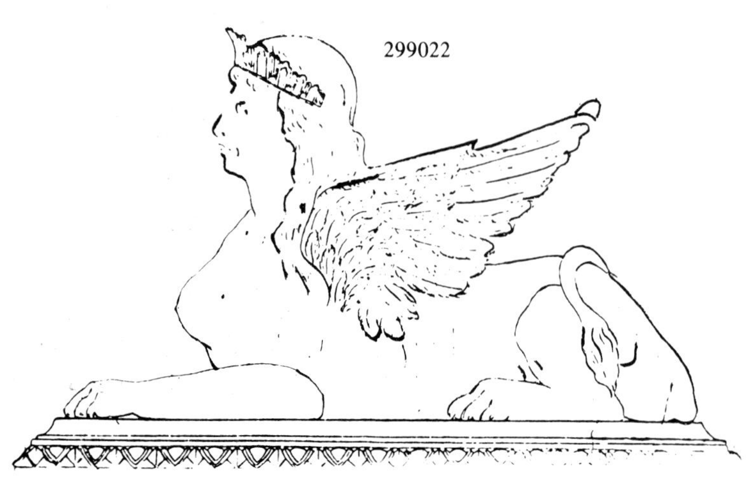

# Molineux & Co., Manchester

The second area to be considered for pressed glass firms is that of Manchester. Molineux & Co. of Manchester registered their first design on 7 December 1846 for a decanter — they were one of the earliest of the main firms to register. The firm as Molineux & Webb (then Molineaux, Webb & Co. from 1864 to 1890) registered some sixty designs, but it was not until 1865 that the spelling changed to Molineaux. It was in 1864 that they registered a comport, or raised dish, with the well known Greek key pattern. It is interesting to compare the celery glass of 1865, which equally has the Greek key pattern with that of the heavier James Derbyshire celery glass for the same year. The pattern is carried through into 1866 with a cream jug. The domestic items of the 1860s and 1870s are of a certain quality; simple and in good taste. In 1870 some of the designs have a look of Davidson with panelled designs of plain glass next to diamond ones and there is a butter with the Greek key motif back again. In 1874 and 1875 there are some mundane registrations for railway carriage glass roof lamps, but later in 1875 there is an unusual pressed glass sphinx which is worth comparing with the year later, winged sphinx of John Derbyshire. They also did a pressed glass 'dolphin' pillar that year which was one of the earliest although Percival, Vickers & Co. Limited registered a naturalistic flower holder in 1874 with a dolphin stand. In 1882 W.H. Heppell did their dolphin series; in 1884 Davidson showed a dolphin base candlestick in their pattern book and Sowerby's made a dolphin bowl. This bowl has blossom decoration on it and has three dolphins for feet. The bowl is found in many colours and is very striking to look at. It is illustrated in the Sowerby pattern book of 1882, but the bowls were made for many years after, and into the twentieth century, so it is not always easy to date them. Dolphins were a popular theme in Victorian glassware, along with swans and the more aesthetic peacock.

Molineaux, Webb & Co., unlike Davidson and Greener, registered only a few designs imitating cut glass early on, but their pattern books show that they produced many other types of glass. Not all is for pressed glass, but for high quality cut and engraved glass, normally associated with Stourbridge. There are pages of claret jugs and thin fine wine glasses. The largest section of the designs is of decanters, followed by sugar basins and cream jugs, carafes and tumblers, water jugs, goblets and celeries with smaller sections on butters, marmalades, comports and so on. Some of these patterns were for moulded glass in imitation of cut glass as shown in the advertisements of the early 1880s in the Pottery Gazette. In the 1890s there are two interesting registrations, one in 1895 showing a service of glass with a scale design and in 1896 a typical Art Nouveau design similar to the Greener one.

186462

1 May 1865
Celery glass can be compared with that registered by James Derbyshire & Brother.

293100

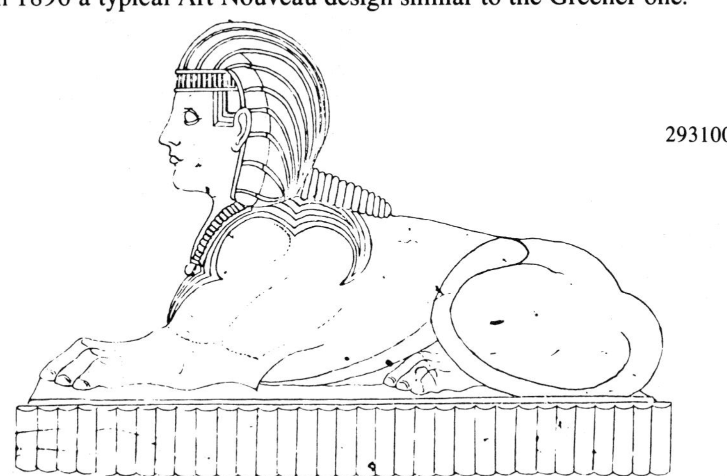

26 July 1875
Glass Sphinx. Again comparisons may be made with the later "Winged Sphinx" of John Derbyshire.

178045

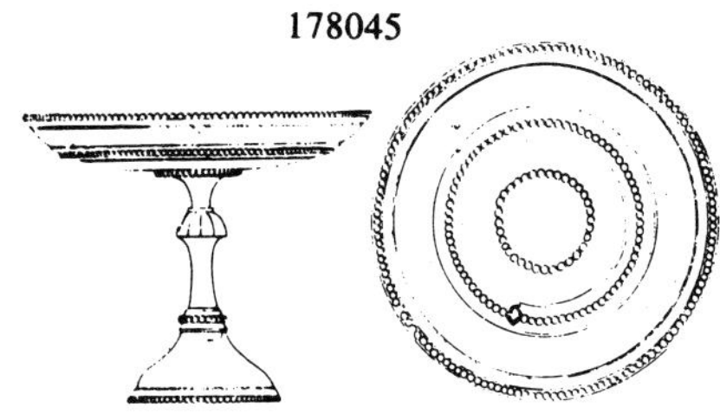
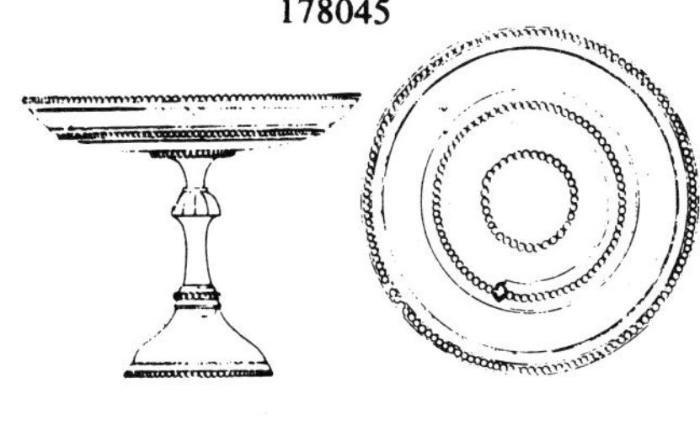

178046

Both the above have the same registration lozenge.

195262

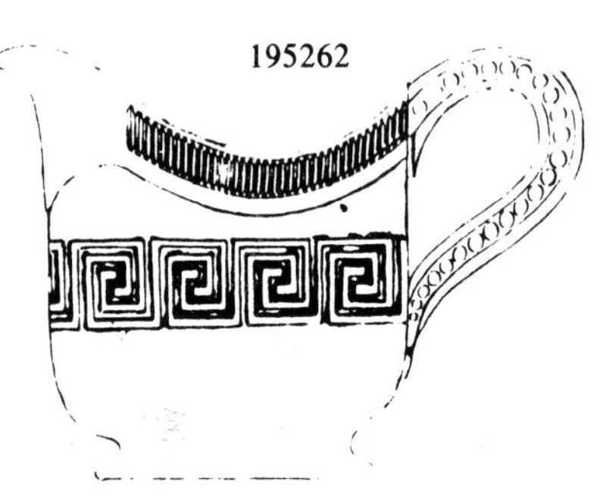

209086

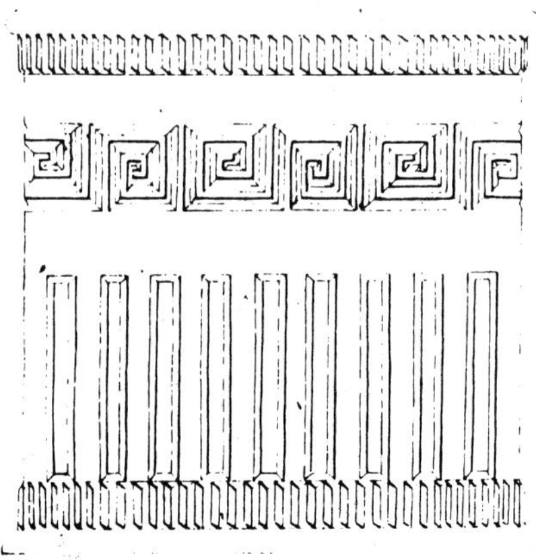

**Molineux & Co., Manchester. Registrations**

| *Registration* No. | *Date* | *Year* | *Parcel* No. | *Design* | |
|---|---|---|---|---|---|
| 38643 | 7 December | 1846 | 2 | Decanter | |

**Molineux & Webb, Kirby Street, Manchester**

| | | | | | |
|---|---|---|---|---|---|
| 178045/6 | 27 August | 1864 | 4 | Comport or raised dish | |

**Molineaux, Webb & Co.**

| | | | | | |
|---|---|---|---|---|---|
| 182483 | 22 December | 1864 | 6 | Dish | |
| 186462/3 | 1 May | 1865 | 8 | 62 Celery glass<br>63 Sugar basin | Registered as Molineux, Webb & Co. |
| 186808 | 12 May | | 6 | Dish | |
| 187182/3 | 29 May | | 8 | Cream jug & dish | |
| 190755 to 58 | 4 October | | 4 | 55 Cover of butter dish<br>56 Stand of butter dish<br>57 Butter dish<br>58 Cover of butter dish | |
| 191555 | 31 October | | 8 | Glass dish | |
| 194616 to 18 | 18 January | 1866 | 6 | 16 Basin<br>17 Cream jug<br>18 Celery | |
| 194685 | 20 January | | 2 | Marmalade | |
| 194825 | 30 January | | 7 | Marmalade | |
| 195262 | 15 February | | 2 | Cream jug | |
| 209086 | 24 June | 1867 | 3 | Ornamental design for a glass biscuit jar | |
| 210199 | 10 August | | 3 | Dish — ornamental design | |
| 210484 | 26 August | | 5 | Ornamental design for a basin or butter cover | |
| 210941/2 | 10 September | | 4 | Cream jug and basin, ornamental design | |
| 215734 | 13 January | 1868 | 1 | Ornamental design for a comport or elevated dish | |
| 216348 | 31 January | | 9 | Ornamental design for a comport or elevated dish | |
| 216632 | 8 February | | 4 | Ornamental design for an inkstand and cover | |
| 219769 | 11 July | | 4 | Ornamental design for a celery glass | |
| 220898/9 | 20 August | | 6 | Ornamental designs for a cream glass and basin glass | |
| 220900 | 20 August | | 6 | Ornamental design for a sardine glass | |
| 226916/7 | 1 February | 1869 | 12 | Ornamental designs for a dish and celery glass | |
| 228202 | 27 March | | 1 | Ornamental design for a butter | |
| 237741 | 3 January | 1870 | 3 | Ornamental design for a dish | |
| 239084 | 22 February | | 4 | Ornamental design for a glass tumbler | |
| 240217 | 2 April | | 4 | Ornamental design for a butter | |
| 241961 | 26 May | | 6 | Ornamental design for a comport | |
| 242968 to 70 | 6 July | | 2 | Ornamental designs for two butters and a biscuit jar | |
| 247463/4 | 18 November | | 2 | Butter dishes | |
| 249600 | 17 January | 1871 | 7 | Dish | |
| 249808 to 10 | 24 January | | 3 | 08 Butter dish<br>09 Cream jug<br>10 Basin | |
| 280493 to 95 | 14 February | 1874 | 10 | Glass railway carriage roof lamps | |
| 289283 | 12 February | 1875 | 9 | Roof lamp for railway carriages | |
| 289645 to 47 | 26 February | | 4 | Butters | |
| 293100 | 26 July | | 3 | A pressed glass sphinx | |
| 295133 | 16 October | | 10 | A pressed glass dolphin pillar | |

## Molineaux, Webb & Co., (continued)

| *Registration* No. | *Date* | *Year* | *Parcel* No. | *Design* |
|---|---|---|---|---|
| 315429 | 17 October | 1877 | 2 | Pressed glass dish |
| 316776 | 3 December | | 2 | Pressed glass dish |
| 316862 | 6 December | | 3 | Pressed glass dish |
| 340206 | 23 September | 1879 | 2 | A pressed glass dish |
| 344911 | 5 January | 1880 | 2 | Design for a pressed glass butter |
| 344960 | 7 January | | 2 | Design for a pressed glass basin (star on foot of bowl and base) |
| 345166 to 68 | 14 January | | 2 | Pressed butter dishes |
| 370618/9 | 28 September | 1881 | 3 | 18 Cream jug (star on base)<br>19 Basin (star on foot) |
| 371262 | 12 October | | 5 | A pressed glass pickle dish |
| 375281 | 2 January | 1882 | 1 | Pressed glass dish (star on base) |

| | | | | |
|---|---|---|---|---|
| 23040/1 | 5 March | 1885 | | Pattern and shape |
| 23333 to 38 | 10 March | | | Pattern and shape |
| 23378 | 11 March | | | Pattern and shape |
| 29780/1 | 14 July | | | Pattern and shape |
| 31844 | 21 August | | | Shape and pattern |
| 70422 | 23 March | 1887 | | Shape |
| 71528 | 6 April | | | Pattern |
| 134908 | 5 October | 1889 | | (Imit. cut) |

## Molineaux, Webb & Co. Ltd.

| | | | | |
|---|---|---|---|---|
| 143153 | 28 January | 1890 | | (Imit. cut) |
| 144779 | 25 February | | | (Free pattern) |
| 158948 | 15 October | | | |
| 164521 | 12 January | 1891 | | |
| 201225 | 21 October | 1892 | | (Tumbler) |
| 209414 | 17 March | 1893 | | (Imit. cut service) |
| 217651 | 4 September | | | (Barrel) |
| 220471 to 73 | 14 October | | | (Liquor holder) |
| 233768 | 11 June | 1894 | | (Horse shoe shape) |
| 251393 | 15 March | 1895 | | (Scale design suite) |
| 269113 | 15 January | 1896 | | (Vase. Free design - similar to Greener 325194 in 1898) |
| 271700 | 26 February | | | (Dish as above) |
| 338590 | 20 May | 1899 | | |
| 352198 | 20 January | 1900 | | (Imit. cut with gadroons) |
| 388595 | 15 March | 1902 | | (Lamp shade imit. cut) |
| 391285 | 21 May | | | (Lamp shade imit. cut) |

271700

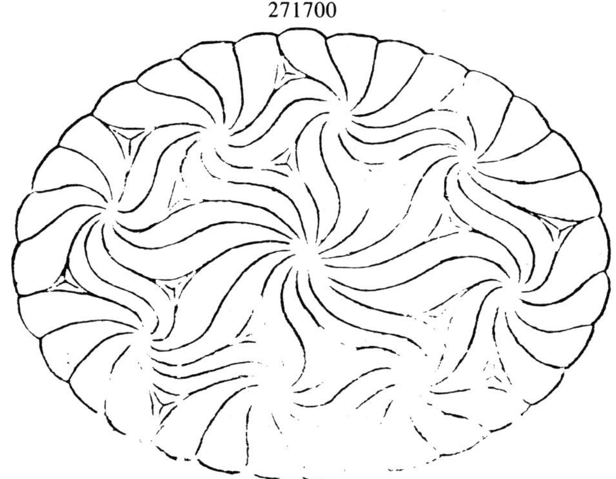

210484

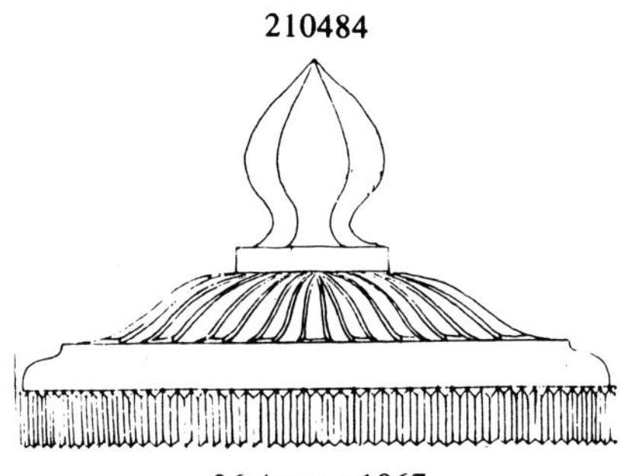

26 August 1867

210941

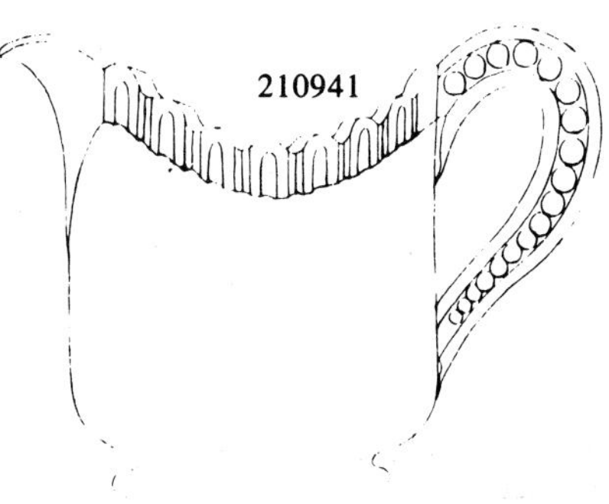

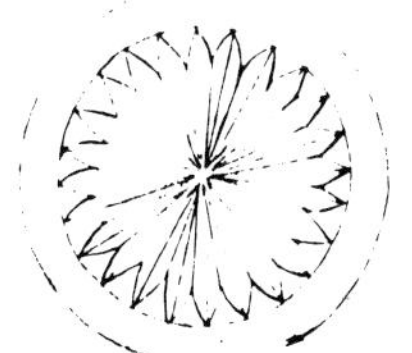

10 September 1867

220900

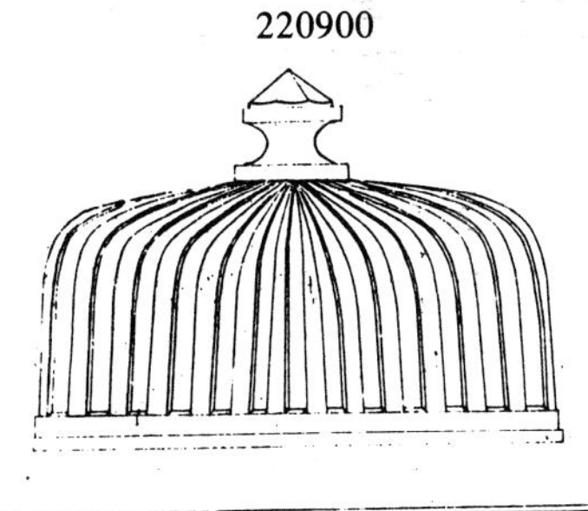

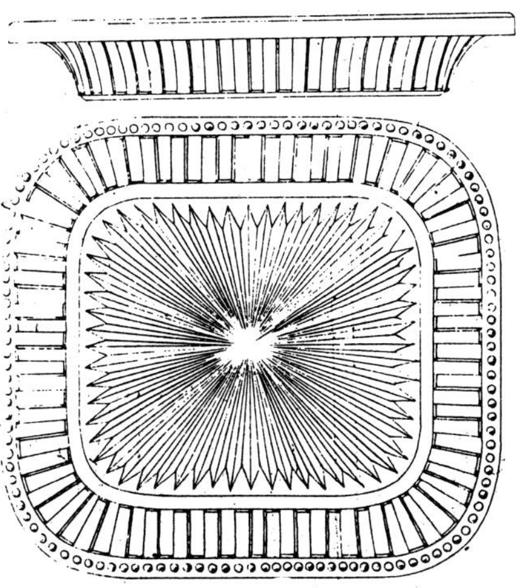

20 August 1868

6658

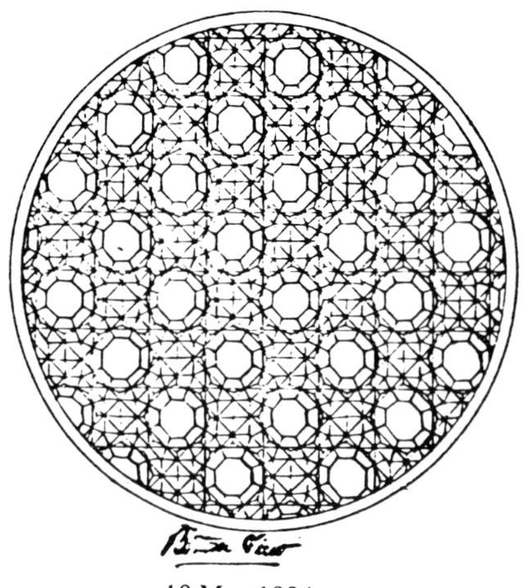

10 May 1884

# Percival, Yates & Vickers Jersey Street, Manchester

Percival, Yates & Vickers of Jersey Street, Manchester as Percival & Yates registered their first item in 1847, three months after Molineux & Co., which was for an unexciting bottle. In June and November of that year they registered a salt cellar, a decanter, a match box and dish and in 1848 their first sugar basin. In 1865 there are four domestic items, a sugar and cream jug, comport and butter dish. Nothing is registered in 1866 but from 1867, when the firm became Percival, Vickers & Co. Ltd., there are registrations for every year to 1902 with the exceptions of 1875, 1877, 1879 and 1901. The firm registered a good many goblets and tumblers including in the 1880s all the usual domestic items of butters, cruets, marmalade jars and dishes. In 1884 the design for a round platter was in a pattern very similar to hobnail cutting. It is very like the Davidson registered one of 1890. In the mid 1880s and 1890s there were several patterns imitating cut glass, though one of the earliest pieces is the celery glass of December 1868. One of the best registrations is in 1891 when there was a set of glass with vertical and horizontal parallel mitres and this pattern occurs a few times. Some of the earlier glass had a distinctive frosted look with patterns of clear stars or diamond and leaf shapes. It is good quality colourless pressed glass, and it is relatively easy to find.

13 March 1891

217227

6 March 1868

One of the early leaf patterns (see photograph).

**Percival & Yates, The British and Foreign Flint Glass Works, Manchester. Registrations**

| *Registration* No. | *Date* | *Year* | *Parcel* No. | *Design* |
|---|---|---|---|---|
| 42296 | 25 March | 1847 | 3 | Bottle |
| 43655 | 17 June | | 1 | Bottle |
| 43850 | 30 June | | 6 | Salt cellar |
| 46788/9 | 5 November | | 2 | 88 Decanter (address given as Jersey St., Manchester)<br>89 Match box |
| 47344 | 27 November | | 2 | Dish |
| 49779 | 11 February | 1848 | 2 | Sugar basin |

183353

**Percival, Yates & Vickers, Jersey Street, Manchester**

| | | | | |
|---|---|---|---|---|
| 183352/3 | 18 January | 1865 | 1 | Sugar and cream (large star pattern grouped round middle) |
| 185030 | 21 March | | 6 | Comport (similar) |
| 189121/2 | 18 August | | 4 | Butter dish (sunburst pattern on base, ribbed rim) |

**Percival, Vickers & Co. Limited**

| | | | | |
|---|---|---|---|---|
| 209574/5 | 16 July | 1867 | 2 | (Bowl and oval dish elaborate pattern imit. cut) |
| 217227 | 6 March | 1868 | 7 | (Decoration leaf pattern) |
| 223322 | 23 October | | 4 | (Goblet pattern of circles) |
| 225440 | 14 December | | 6 | (Ornamental design tankard) |
| 225673 | 21 December | | 4 | Celery (imit. cut) |
| 228889 | 26 April | 1869 | 5 | (Pattern imit. cut) |
| 234517 | 16 October | | 3 | (Goblet imit. cut similar to above) |
| 235821 | 6 November | | 3 | (Tumbler) |
| 237550 | 23 December | | 8 | (Tumbler) |
| 240010 | 26 March | 1870 | 8 | (Goblet) |
| 243554 | 1 August | | 1 | (Flower vase on stem) |
| 253067 | 7 June | 1871 | 5 | (Pattern imit. cut with clear oval vertical bands) |
| 256264 | 30 September | | 10 | (Pattern - tumbler) |
| 258445 | 7 December | | 5 | (Pattern - tumbler) |
| 262405 | 2 May | 1872 | 7 | (Goblet) |
| 263032 | 30 May | | 7 | |
| 263314 | 11 June | | 4 | Piano foot |
| 269194 | 23 December | | 3 | (Goblet) |
| 269694 | 15 January | 1873 | 4 | (Tumbler shape) |
| 272685 to 88 | 7 May | | 2 | (Ornamental designs - plates) |
| 278266 | 13 November | | 8 | Butter cover |
| 284031 | 29 July | 1874 | 8 | (Naturalistic flower holder. Dolphin stand) |
| 301579 | 30 June | 1876 | 7 | A butter middle |
| 319090 | 1 March | 1878 | 8 | Pressed dish |
| 351024 | 17 June | 1880 | 3 | Glass tumbler |
| 352870 | 27 July | | 9 | Celery stand. Shape only registered |
| 357730 | 5 November | | 5 | Piano foot |
| 372018 | 22 October | 1881 | 15 | Finger bowl (triangular) |
| 378495 | 17 March | 1882 | 4 | (Dish and cover concentric ribbing) |
| 381436 | 25 May | | 1 | Oblong dish |
| 390615 | 27 November | | 1 | Design for oblong dish in glass (hobnail pattern on base) |
| 394205 | 14 February | 1883 | 11 | Half pint tumbler |
| 397022 | 17 April | | 3 | (Oblong dish - hobnail pattern on base) |
| 402690 | 24 August | | 2 | Tumbler |
| 406456 | 2 November | | 12 | Jelly glass (mould) |

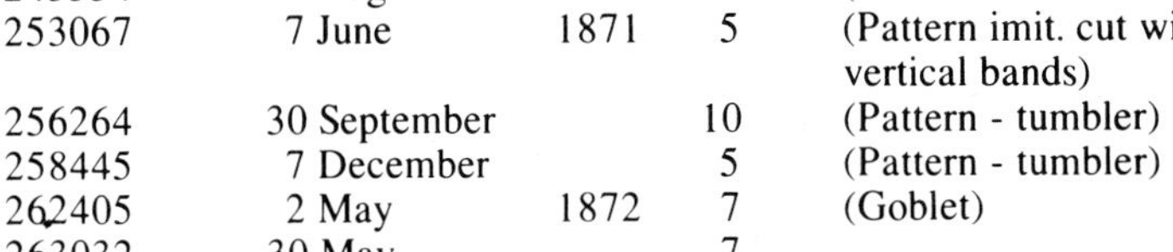

209574

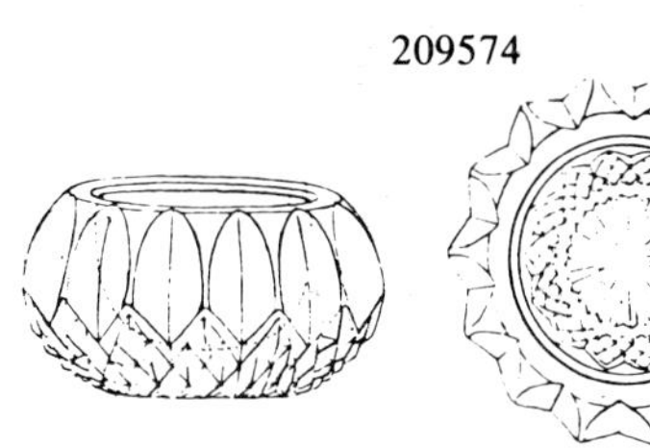

284031

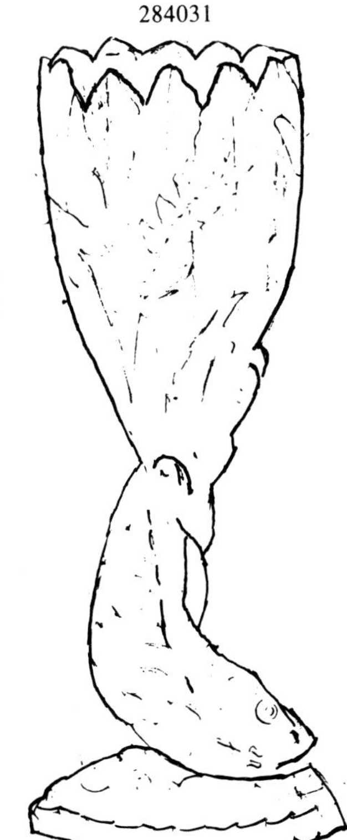

# Percival, Vickers & Co. Limited

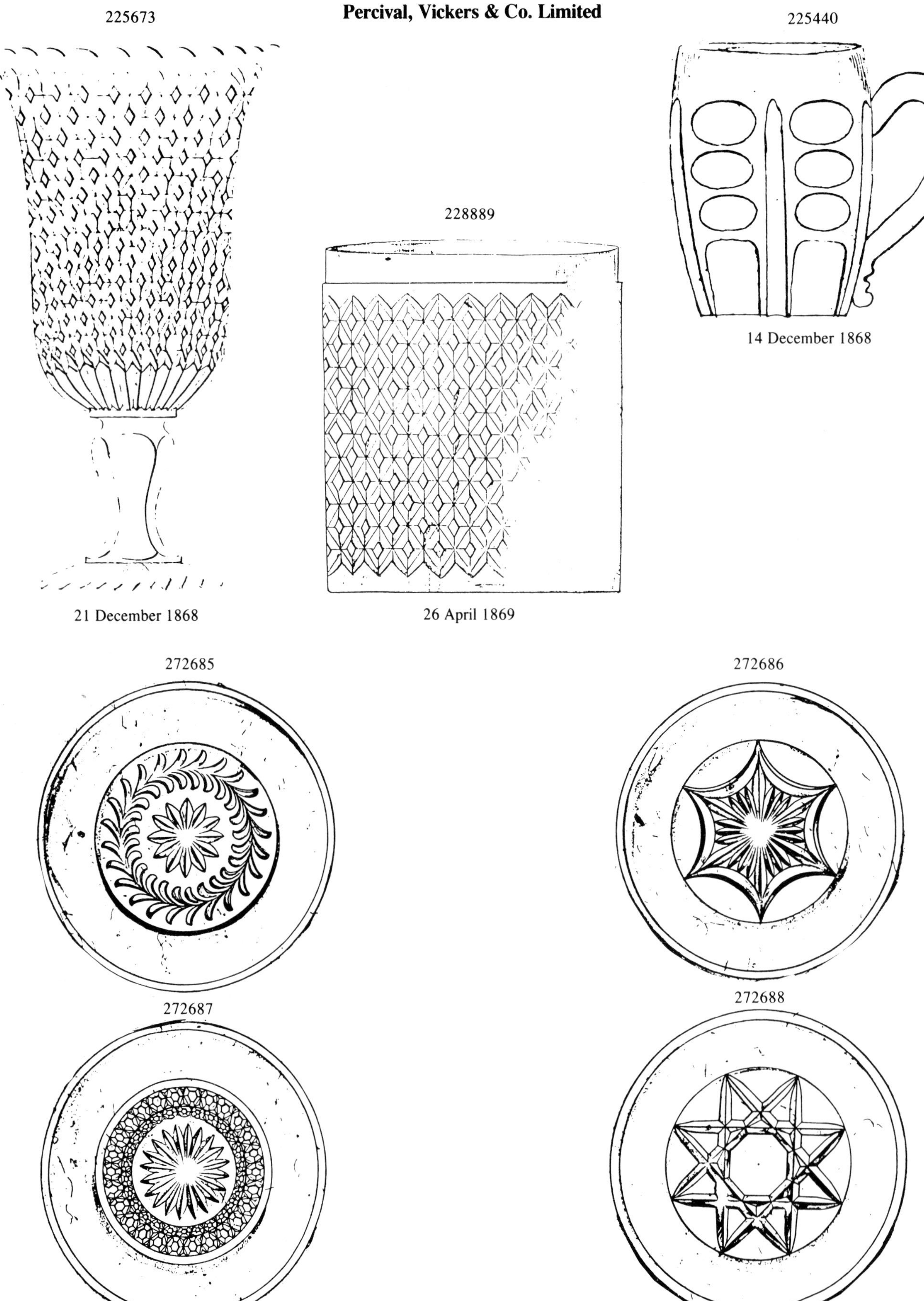

225673

21 December 1868

228889

26 April 1869

225440

14 December 1868

272685

272686

272687

272688

7 May 1873

**Percival, Vickers & Co., Ltd. (continued)**

| *Registration No.* | *Date* | *Year* | *Design* |
|---|---|---|---|
| 1415 | 7 February | 1884 | Pattern for pressed glass ware |
| 6658 | 10 May | | Design for round platter in moulded glass (imit. cut similar to hobnail) |
| 15332 | 18 October | | Shape and pattern in pressed glass (imit. cut similar to above) |
| 18749 | 10 December | | Railway and other lamps - pressed scalloped band on glass |
| 20355 | 14 January | 1885 | Pattern for pressed butter trencher (imit. cut) |
| 20936 | 22 January | | Design for pressed glass marmalade (imit. cut) |
| 27553 | 28 May | | Pattern for moulded marmalade |
| 29145 | 1 July | | Design for pressed glass butter (imit. cut) |
| 35293 | 10 October | | Design for pressed glass cruets (imit. cut) |
| 40484 | 1 January | 1886 | Pressed glass cruet (imit. cut & plain glass) |
| 45942 | 26 March | | Moulded glass marmalade or biscuit jar (imit. cut) |
| 53468 | 3 August | | Moulded glass tumbler |
| 56047 | 11 September | | Pattern for pressed glass dish |
| 60108 | 29 October | | Design for pressed glass pillar or lamp stand (in form of lighthouse) |
| 71869 | 14 April | 1887 | Pattern of a moulded cruet |
| 75942 | 29 June | | Pattern for moulded glass marmalade (with vertical mitres) |
| 80632 | 12 September | | Pattern of a pressed glass celery vase (imit. cut) |
| 93905 | 18 February | 1888 | (Dish, pattern with octagons and squares) |
| 115077 | 28 November | | (Dish oval and two triangular shaped dishes for jam and marmalade. All have vertical mitres) |
| 126869 | 8 June | 1889 | (Imit. cut) |
| 134907 | 5 October | | (Bowls, sugar and cream imit. cut with squares of plain glass) |
| 159189 | 16 October | 1890 | Jam dish (plain vertical mitres) |
| 168130 | 13 March | 1891 | Set of glass (vertical and horizontal parallel mitres) |
| 173044 | 18 June | | (Imit. cut) |
| 189247 | 15 March | 1892 | Marmalade (imit. cut) |
| 189344 | 16 March | | Marmalade |
| 192876 | 21 May | | Improved shape of glass retort |
| 193694/5 | 9 June | | |
| 193821 | 14 June | | (Imit. cut) |
| 194638 | 27 June | | Cruet bottle |
| 196639 | 10 August | | Celery glass (imit. cut with clear glass vertical bands) |
| 211617 | 3 May | 1893 | Jam dish (imit. cut) |
| 213381 | 10 June | | (Imit. cut) |
| 233766 | 11 June | 1894 | Moulded jam dish (imit. cut base, plain plinth) |
| 254406 | 7 May | 1895 | Electric light shade (imit. cut) |
| 268968 | 13 January | 1896 | (Imit. cut) |
| 275802 | 7 May | | (Simple imit. cut) |
| 287653 | 4 November | | (Hobnail imit. cut moulded glass dish) |
| 292506 | 23 January | 1897 | Moulded glass jam stand (imit. cut round upper half, octagonal shape) |
| 305840 | 20 September | | Moulded glass electric shade (imit. cut) |
| 314494 | 18 February | 1898 | Glass spirit jar |
| 319151 | 19 May | | Butter dish, moulded glass (imit. cut) |
| 323997 | 20 August | | |
| 336510 | 12 April | 1899 | (Moulded sugar and cream jug elab. imit. cut and classical shape for cream jug) |
| 361366 | 3 August | 1900 | Design for electric shade in moulded glass (shade has pattern of over-lapping leaves) |
| 390019 | 22 April | 1902 | Design for moulded glass dish (imit. cut upper half of dish) |

45942

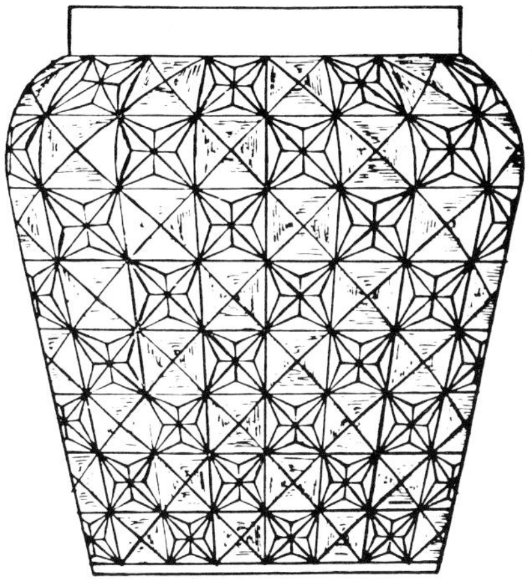

80632

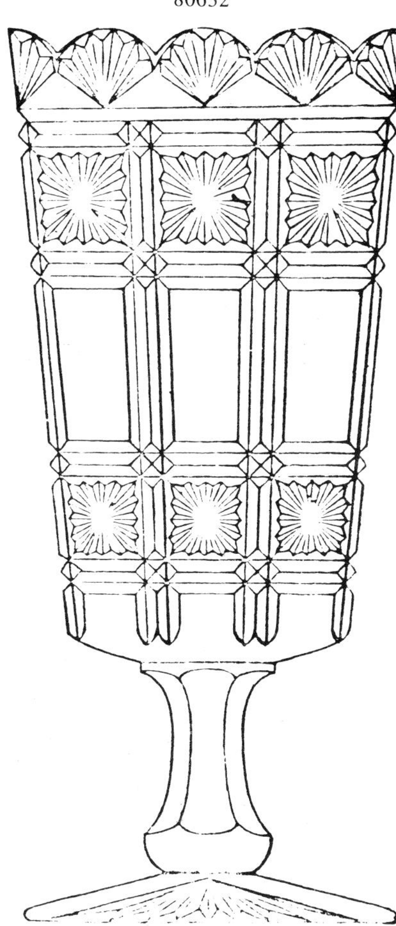

75942

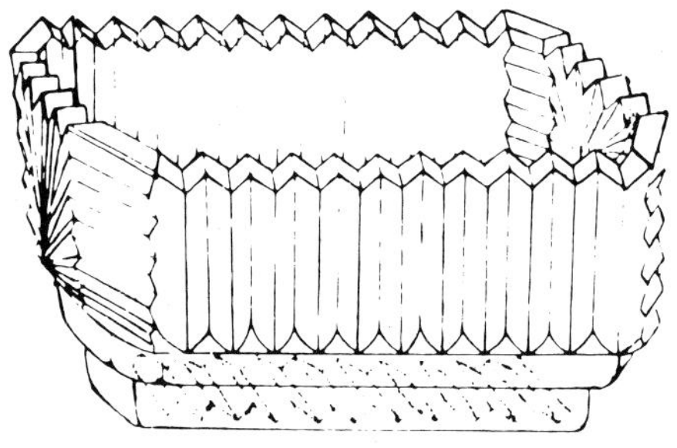

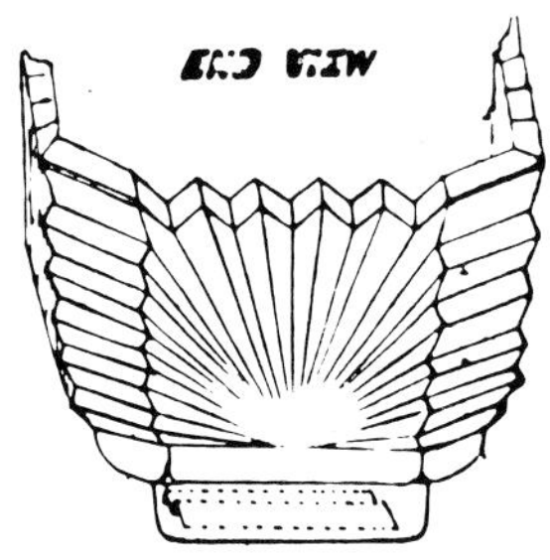

29 June 1887

268968

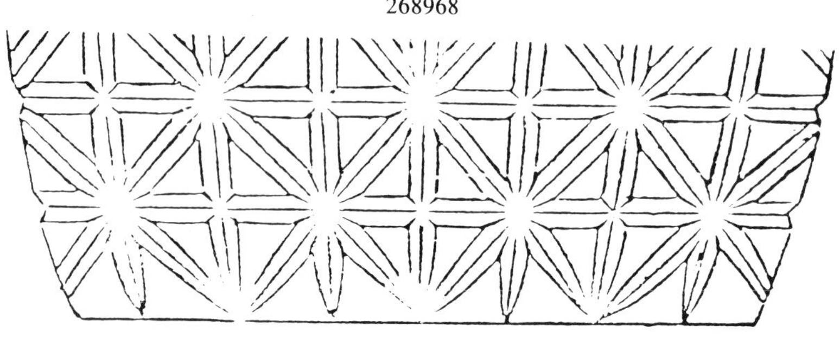

13 January 1896

(See photograph of three celery vases)

305840

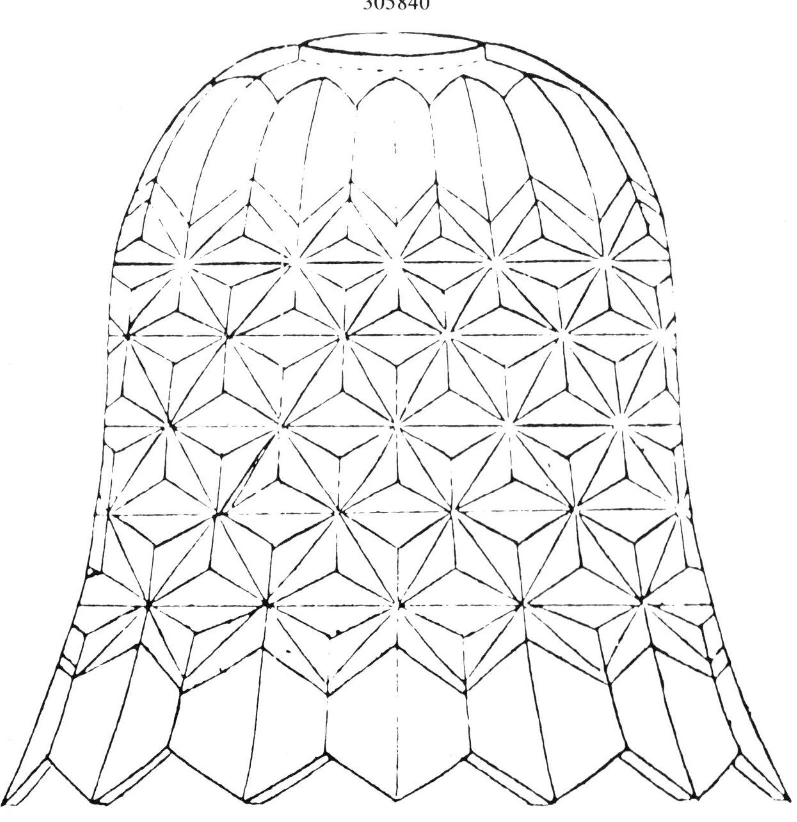

20 September 1897

71869

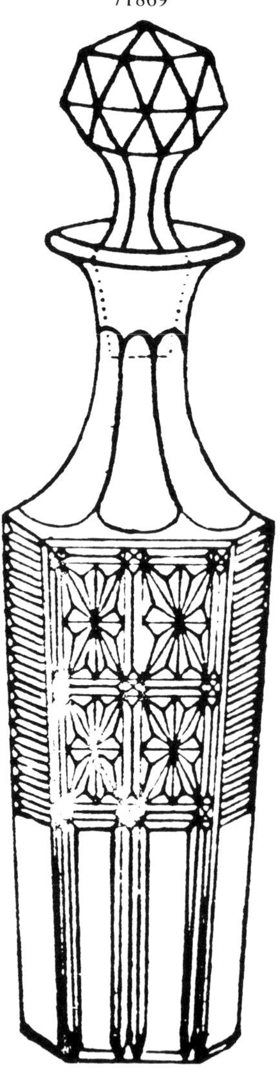

14 April 1887

GOLD MEDAL.

NEWCASTLE EXHIBITION, 1887.

GOLD MEDAL.

NEWCASTLE EXHIBITION, 1887.

# SPECIMEN PAGES

OF

# 1889 Catalogue

OF

# PRESSED GLASS

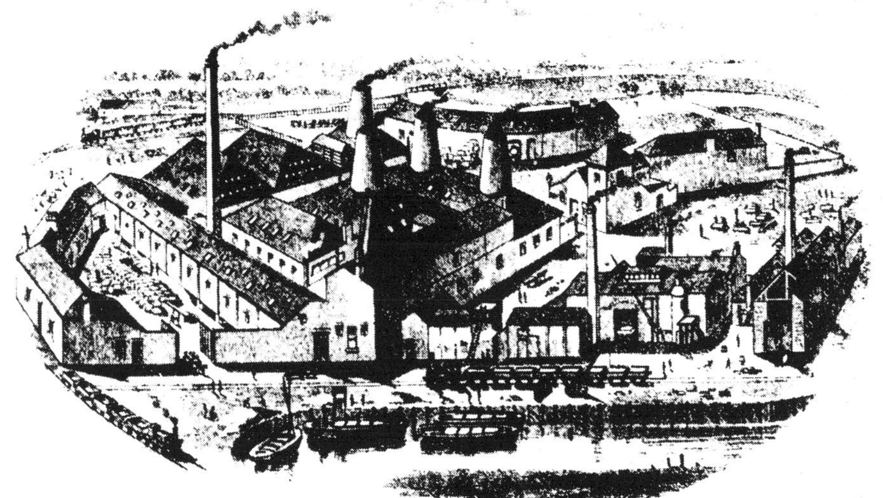

MANUFACTURED BY

## GEO. DAVIDSON & CO.,

## Teams Glass Works,

## GATESHEAD-ON-TYNE.

OFFICES WHERE SAMPLES MAY BE SEEN:—

LONDON:— 23, Thavies Inn, Holborn, E.C.

MANCHESTER:— 15, Booth Street, Piccadilly.

# INDEX OF BLACK AND WHITE PHOTOGRAPHS

1. John Derbyshire. 3 July 1874.
   Lion paperweight after Landseer.
   (Trustees of the Victoria & Albert Museum)

2. Henry Greener. 14 June 1881.
3. G. Davidson c1885. In catalogue of 1885.
4. Percival, Vickers & Co. Ltd. 13 January 1896
   2, 3, 4 Celery vases.
   (Trustees of the Victoria & Albert Museum)

5. G. Davidson & Co. 14 July 1903.
   Tea caddy.

6. Sowerby & Co. 13 February 1877.
   Salt cellar. Shows both registration and trade marks.
   Registration for basket weave pattern.

7. Sowerby & Co. 29 October 1877 trade mark on lid and bowl.
   Covered sugar. Frosted and plain glass.

8. Angus & Greener. 26 June 1867.
   Sugar basin. Frosted and plain glass.

9. Heavy cut glass bowl on stand to be compared with moulded piece by Percival, Vickers & Co., Ltd. Probably from a Manchester firm and likely to be Percival, Vickers & Co., Ltd.

10. Percival, Vickers & Co. Ltd. 16 July 1867.
    Comport, showing how good imitation cut glass could be.
    (Trustees of the Victoria & Albert Museum)

11. Percival, Vickers & Co. Ltd. 26 April 1869.
12. Sowerby & Co. 1 June 1874.
13. George Davidson & Co. c1885.
    Trade Marked.
    Three biscuit barrels.

14. Percival, Vickers & Co. Ltd. 6 March 1868.
    Comport and sugar bowl in frosted and plain glass.
    See registration drawings. (Private Collection)

15. Sowerby & Co. 4 November 1878 and trade mark.
    Cream jug. Patent Ivory Queen's Ware.

16. Sowerby & Co. c1879 trade marked.
    Swan flower holder. Patent Ivory Queen's Ware.

17. Sowerby & Co. 4 November 1878 and trade mark.
    Cream jug. Patent Ivory Queen's Ware. Registration was for the four feet and possibly the rim.

18. Sowerby & Co. 6 June 1879. Trade marked.
    "New Bowl". Patent Ivory Queen's Ware.

19. Henry Greener. 31 July 1869.
    Sugar bowl. Lettered "Gladstone for the Million".
    (Private collection)

20. G. Davidson & Co. c1885 trade marked.
    Dish. Daisy pattern and lettering "Give us this day", etc.

21. Edward Moore. 7 October 1886.
    Covered butter.
    (Trustees of the Victoria & Albert Museum)

22. Jane Webb & Joseph Hammond trading as the Executors of the late Joseph Webb. 16 April 1873.
    Dish. Frosted with clear shell feet. A piece of Stourbridge pressed glass. Edward Moore bought up this firm's moulds in 1888.

23. G. Davidson & Co. c1890 trade marked.
    Covered butter. 'Twig' knop similar to basket handle of 15 August 1891.

24. Molineux, Webb & Co. 1 May 1865.
    Sugar bowl. Frosted and clear glass.
25. Angus & Greener. 26 June 1867.
    Raised dish. Frosted and clear glass.
    (24, 25 Trustees of the Victoria & Albert Museum)

26. Sowerby's Ellison Glass Works Ltd. 15 November 1887 and trade mark. Shoe.

27. Sowerby's Ellison Glass Works Ltd. c1888 trade marked.
    Shoe.

28. Unmarked c1890.
    Shoe. Probably Sowerby's. Amber glass.

29. Sowerby & Co. c1880 trade marked.
    Opal. "Elizabeth, Elspeth, Betsy and Bess".
30. Opal. "Crosspatch".
31. Turquoise. "Lavender's Blue".
    29, 30, 31 Three vitro-porcelain pieces showing nursery rhyme characters from designs by Walter Crane.

32. W. H. Heppell & Co. 6 December 1881.
    Sugar bowl in opal. Shell shape.

33. Sowerby & Co. 17 December 1875.
    Cream jug in jet with "rope" handle.

34. Percival, Yates & Vickers. 18 August 1865.
    Covered butter dish in frosted glass.

35. Greener & Co. 14 December 1888.
    Dish lettered "Peace and Plenty".

36. Sowerby's Ellison Glass Works Ltd. 1 March 1887.
    Dish.
37. Sowerby's Ellison Glass Works Ltd. 22 December 1886.
    Small Boat.
    36, 37 Two similar patterns. Trade marked.

38. Edward Bolton. 11 December 1885.
    Flower trough made as a boat. One of the best known of the boat shapes.

39. Sowerby & Co. 20 February 1878 and trade mark.
    Bowl in frosted and plain glass.

40. Sowerby's Ellison Glass Works Ltd. 10 February 1886.
    Boat flower trough.

41. Molineux & Webb. 27 August 1864.
    Comport in frosted glass with clear glass "Greek Key" motif.

42. Edward Moore. 7 October 1886.
Comport.

43. Sowerby & Co. c1880 trade marked.
Half-pint tumbler.

44. No mark, manufacturer not known. c 1865.
Tumbler with heavy base.

45. Percival, Yates & Vickers. 18 January 1865.
Sugar bowl in frosted and clear glass.

46. Sowerby's Ellison Glass Works Ltd. 1 March 1887.
Plate incorporating pattern of 22 December 1886.
(Trustees of the Victoria & Albert Museum)

47. Sowerby's Ellison Glass Works Ltd.
Plate for Golden Jubilee of Queen Victoria.
(Trustees of the Victoria & Albert Museum)

48. The Rochester Tumbler Co., Pittsburgh, Pennsylvania, U.S.A.
13 February 1880.
Showing lozenge mark clearly.

49. G. Davidson & Co. c1885 trade marked.
Basket in amber glass.

50. G. Davidson & Co. 15 August 1891.
Two baskets in amber and clear glass with
rustic handles.

51. Sowerby & Co. 20 February 1878.
Inkstand in roughened and clear glass.

52. G. Davidson & Co. c1888 trade marked.
Small comport.

53. Henry Greener. 14 June 1881 and first trade mark.
Comport.

54. Sowerby & Co. 1 June 1874.
Toast rack. Registration appears on other different pieces and was probably for distinctive "bobble" rim.

55. *Top Row*
Sowerby's Ellison Glass Works Ltd.
3 Custard cups. 1st c1885, 2nd c1890, 3rd registered
11 March 1881. All three trade marked.

*Row Two*
Sowerby's Ellison Glass Works Ltd.
2 Custard cups registered 23 February 1889 and
11 March 1881. Trade marked.
G. Davidson & Co. c1885.
1 Large tot glass "Only a Thimble Full".

*Row Three*
Sowerby & Co.
Basket 13 February 1877 and trade mark.
Small tot glass c1880 trade marked.

*Row Four*
Sowerby & Co. c1880 trade marked.
Hexagonal salt cellar. In pattern book of 1882.

Percival, Vickers & Co. Ltd. 29 June 1887.
Salt cellar.

*Bottom Row*
G. Davidson & Co. 15 August 1891.
Salt cellar.

Henry Greener. First trade mark c1880
Small salt cellar.

56. Possibly Greener & Co. c1880
Three unmarked small ornamental lions after John Derbyshire's famous lion paperweight. In clear, amber and bright blue glass.

57. Greener & Co. 20 September 1893.
Wheelbarrow salt cellar/ornament.

58. W. H. Heppell & Co. 19 June 1880.
Colliery truck salt cellar/ornament.

59. Sowerby's Ellison Glass Works Ltd. c1885 trade marked.
Biscuit barrel with fern decoration.

1

2
3
4

6

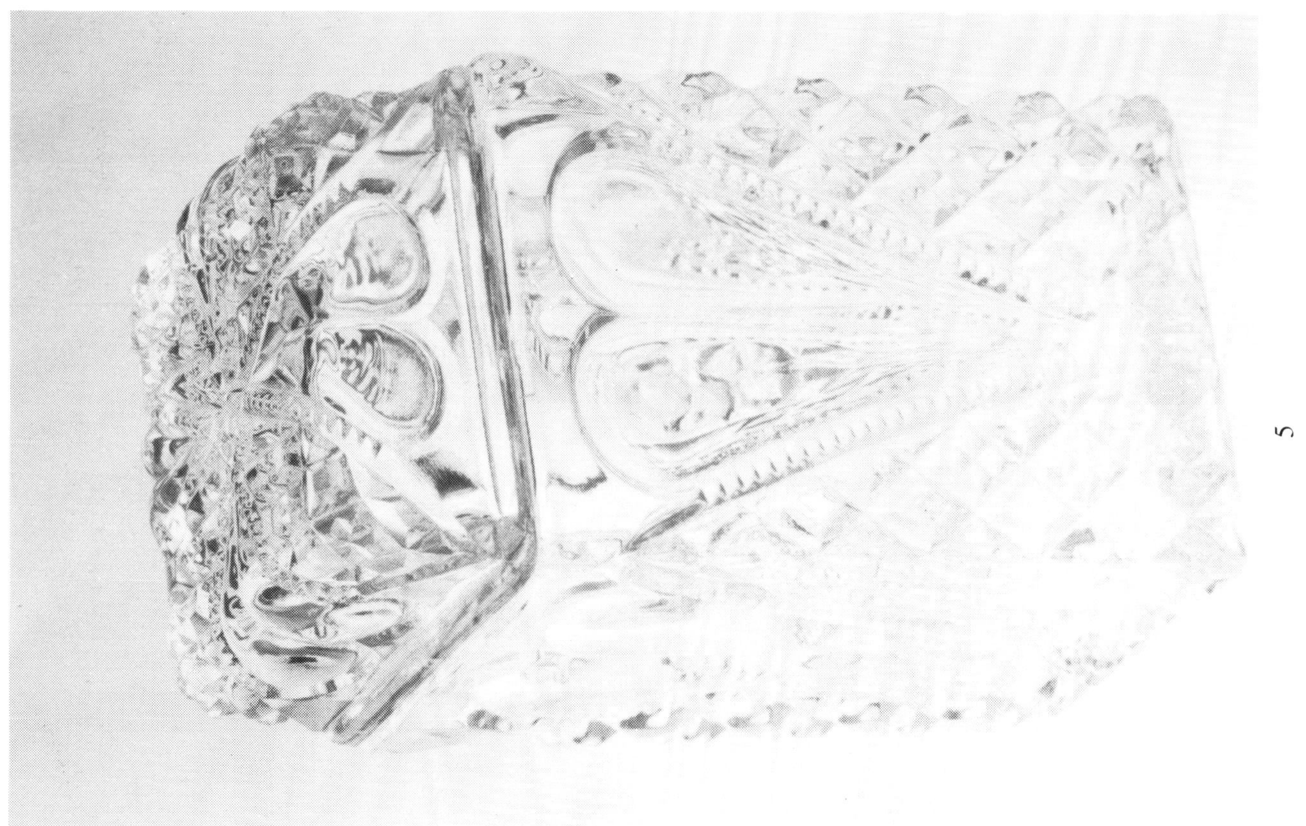

5

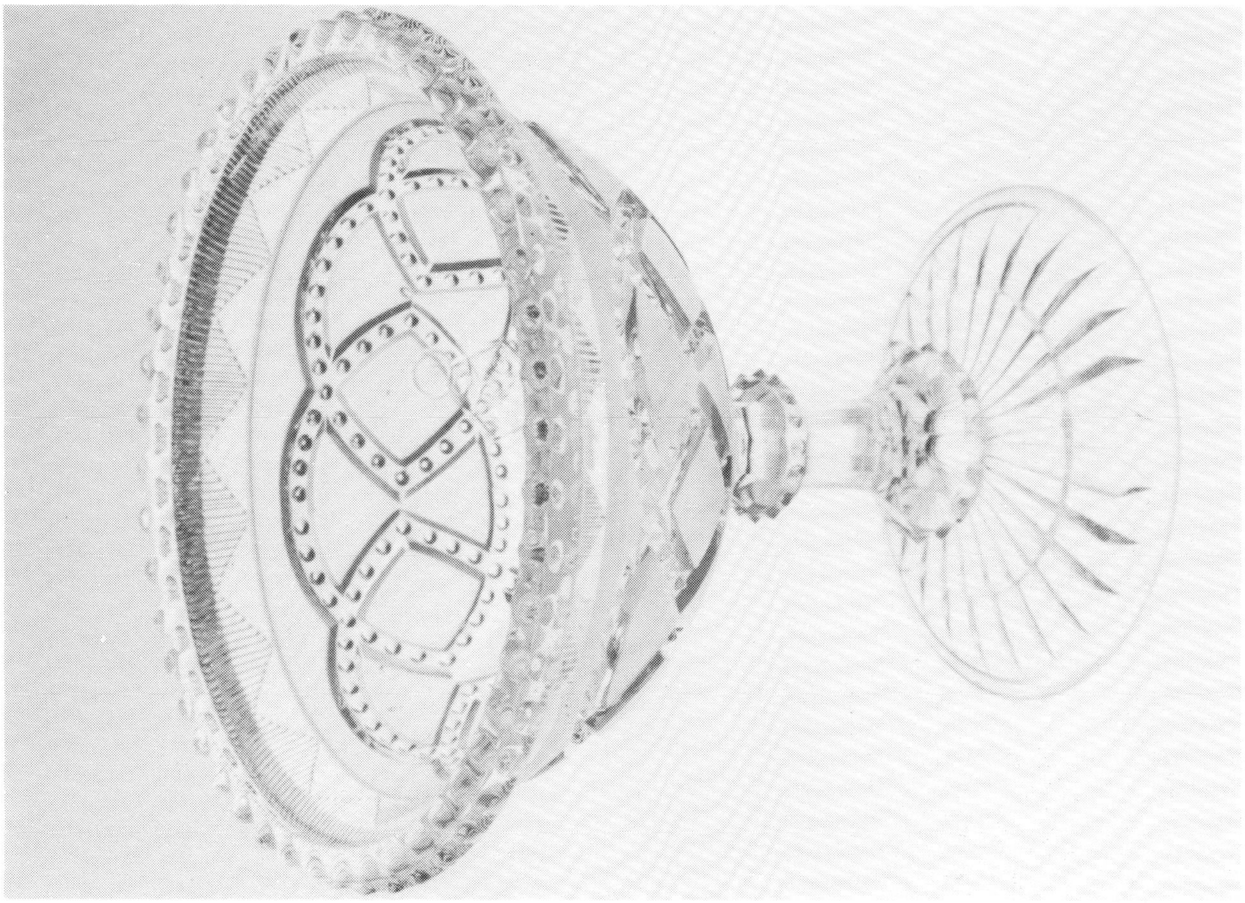

8

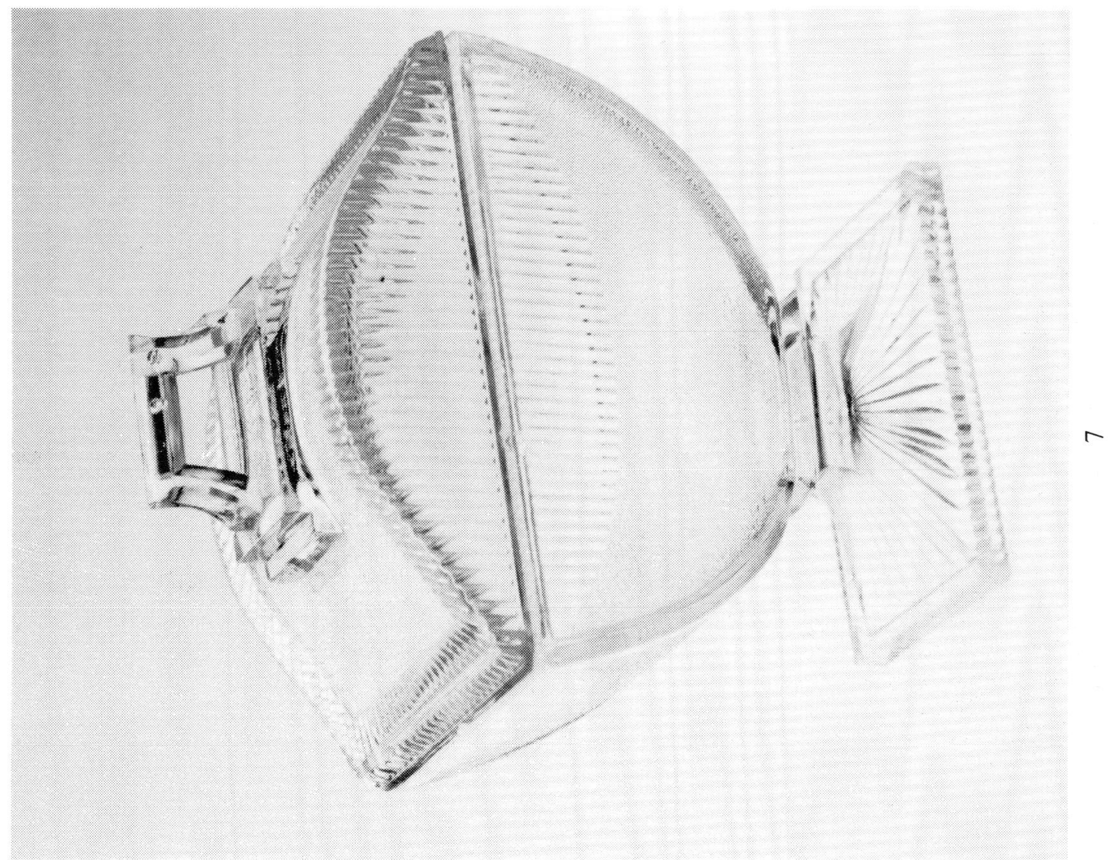

7

9

10

11 12 13

14

15 16 17

19

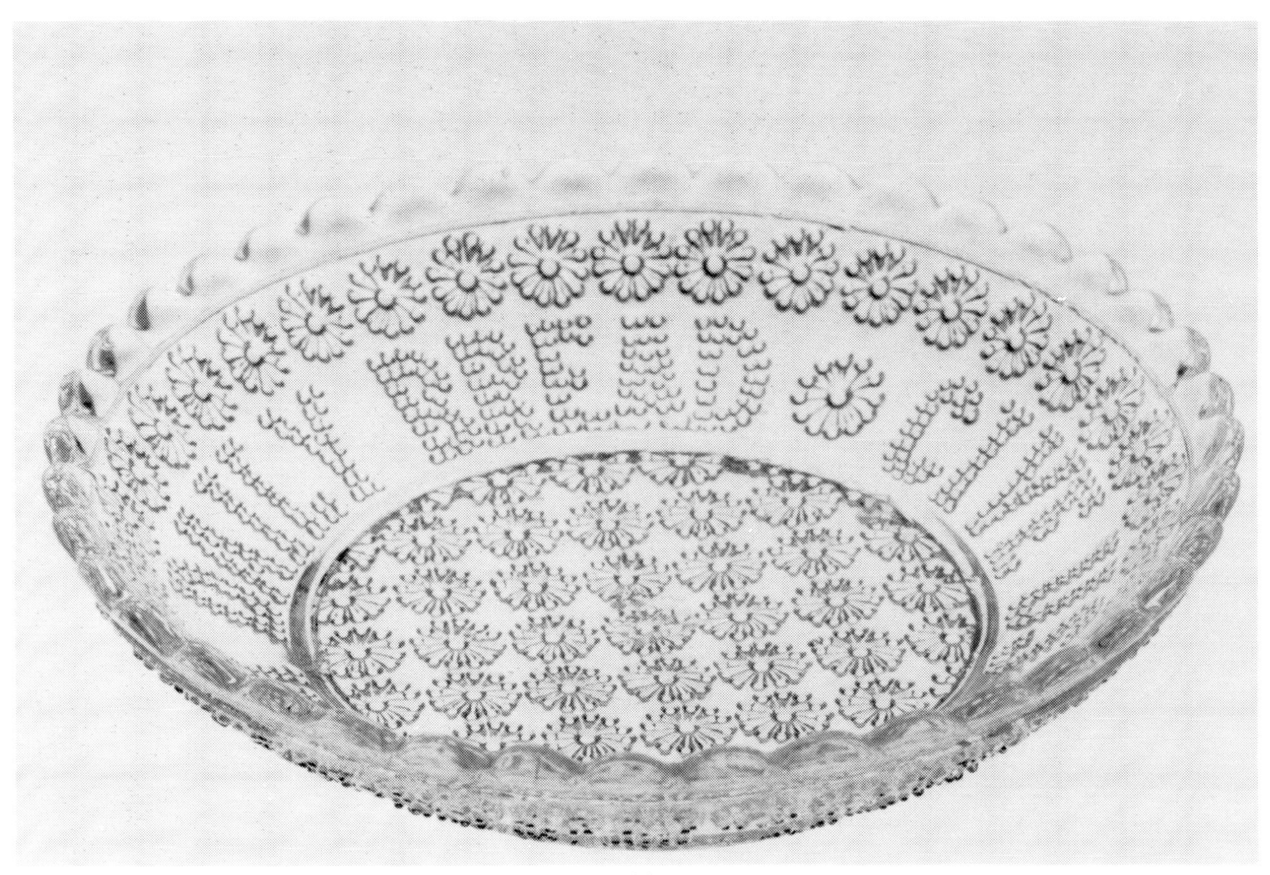

20

21

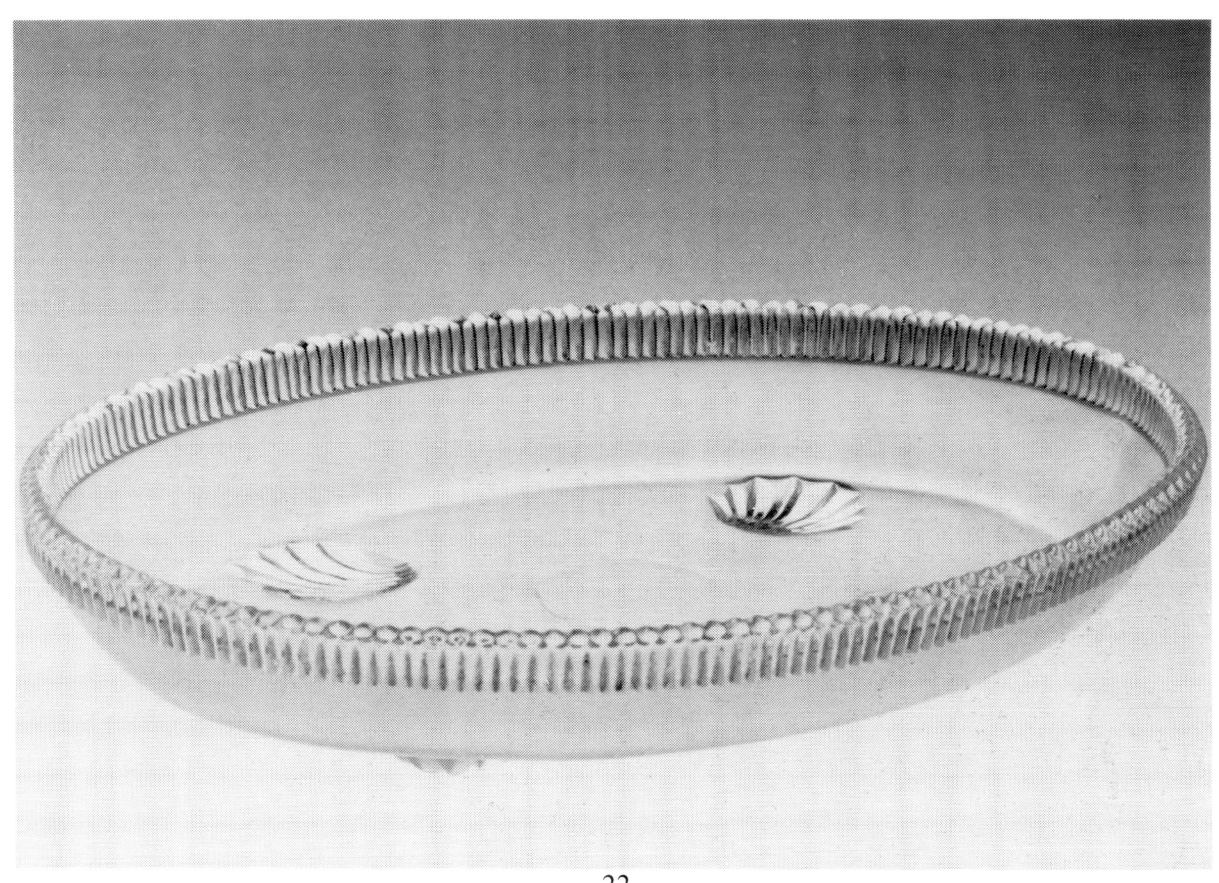

22

23

24 25

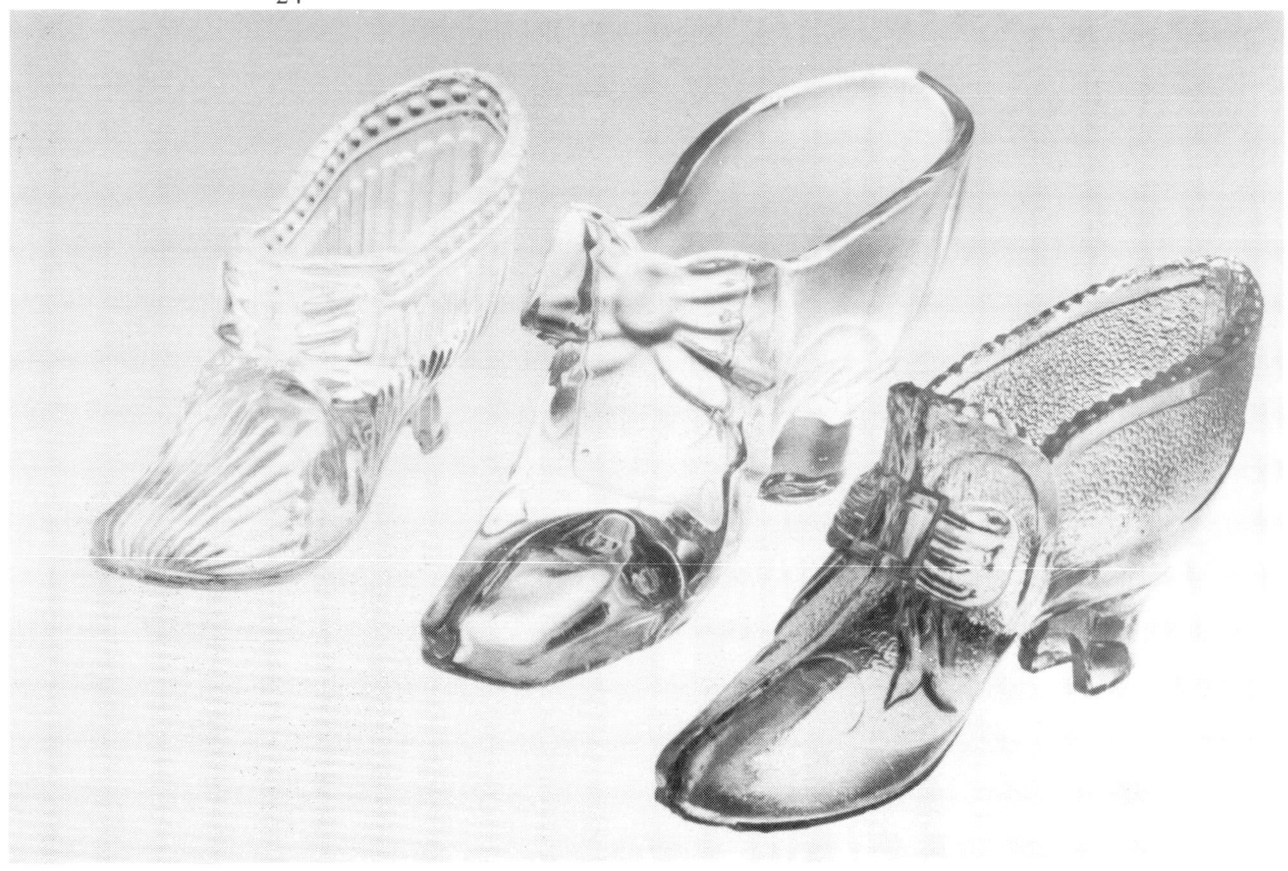

26 27 28

29
30
31

32

33

34

35

36

37

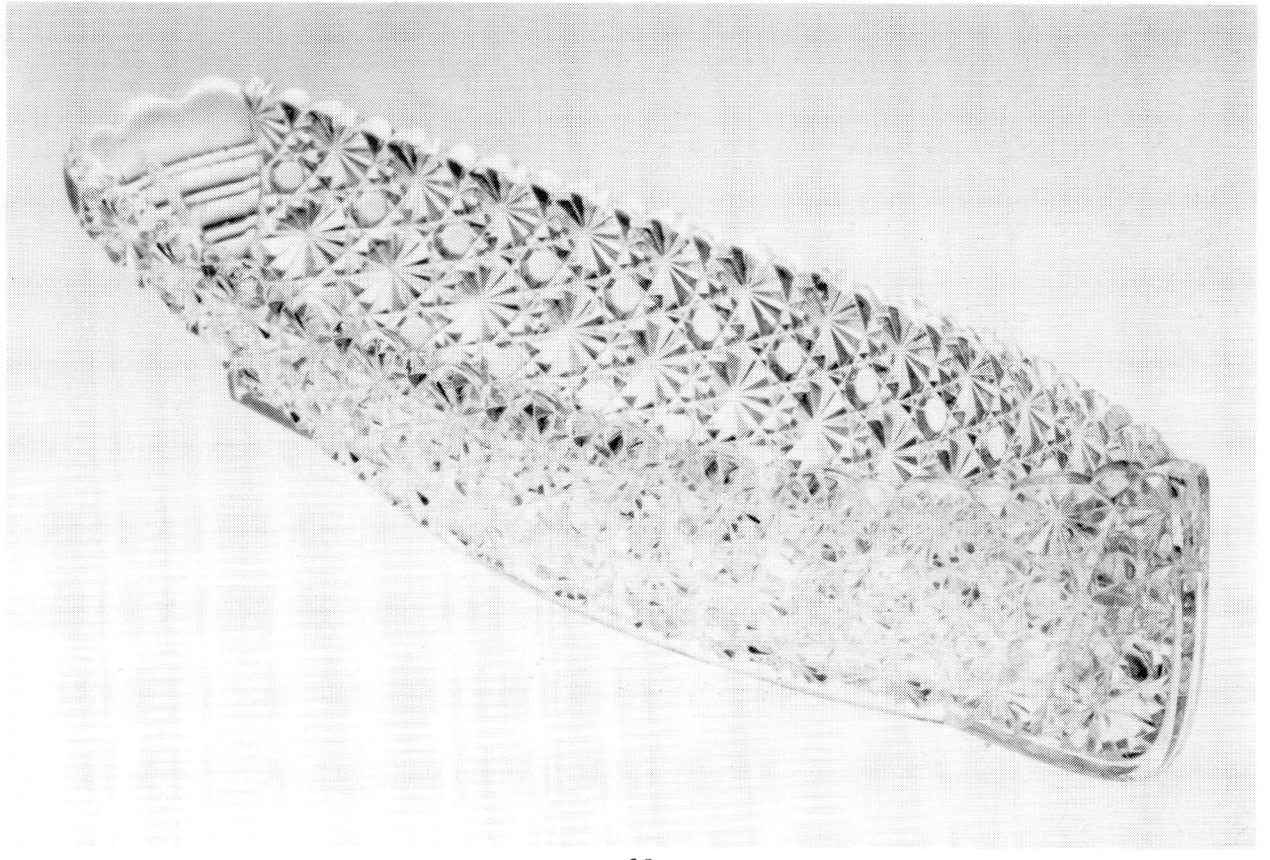

38

39

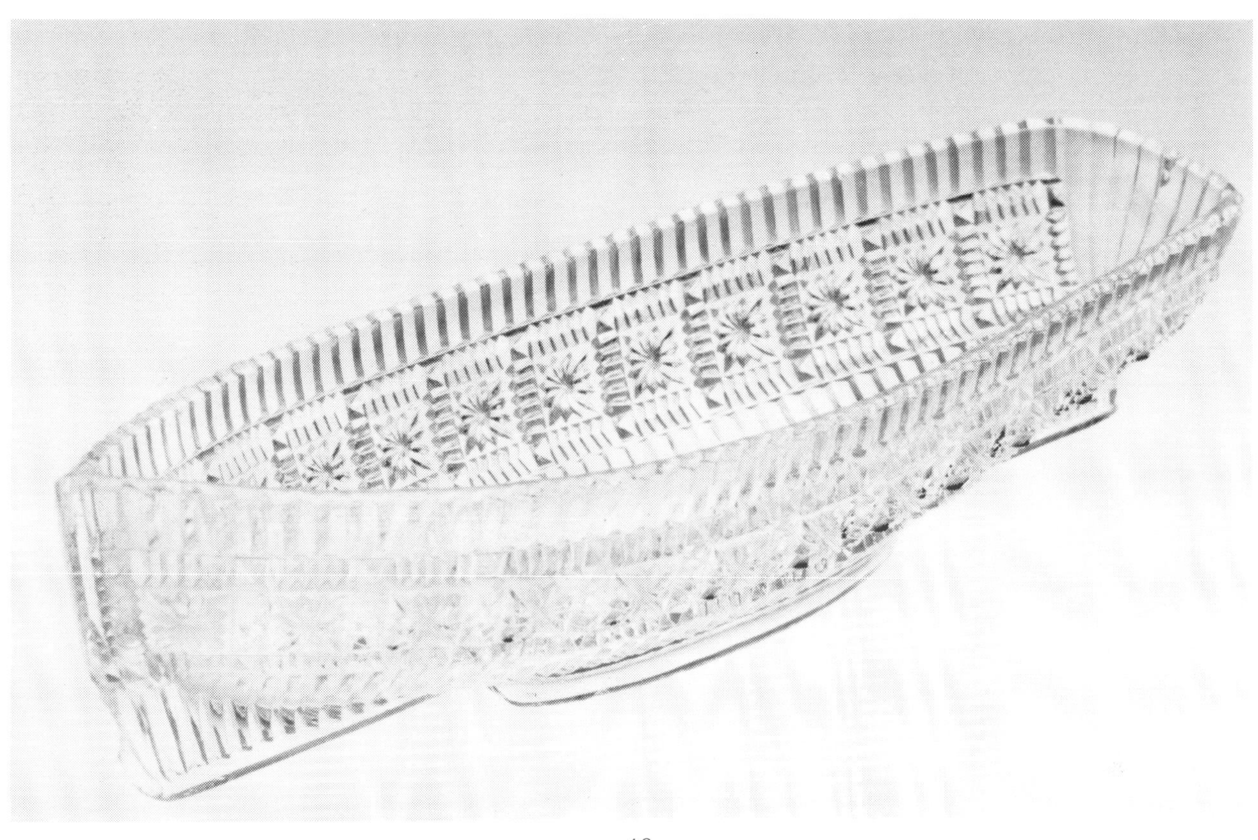

40

41

42

43

44

45

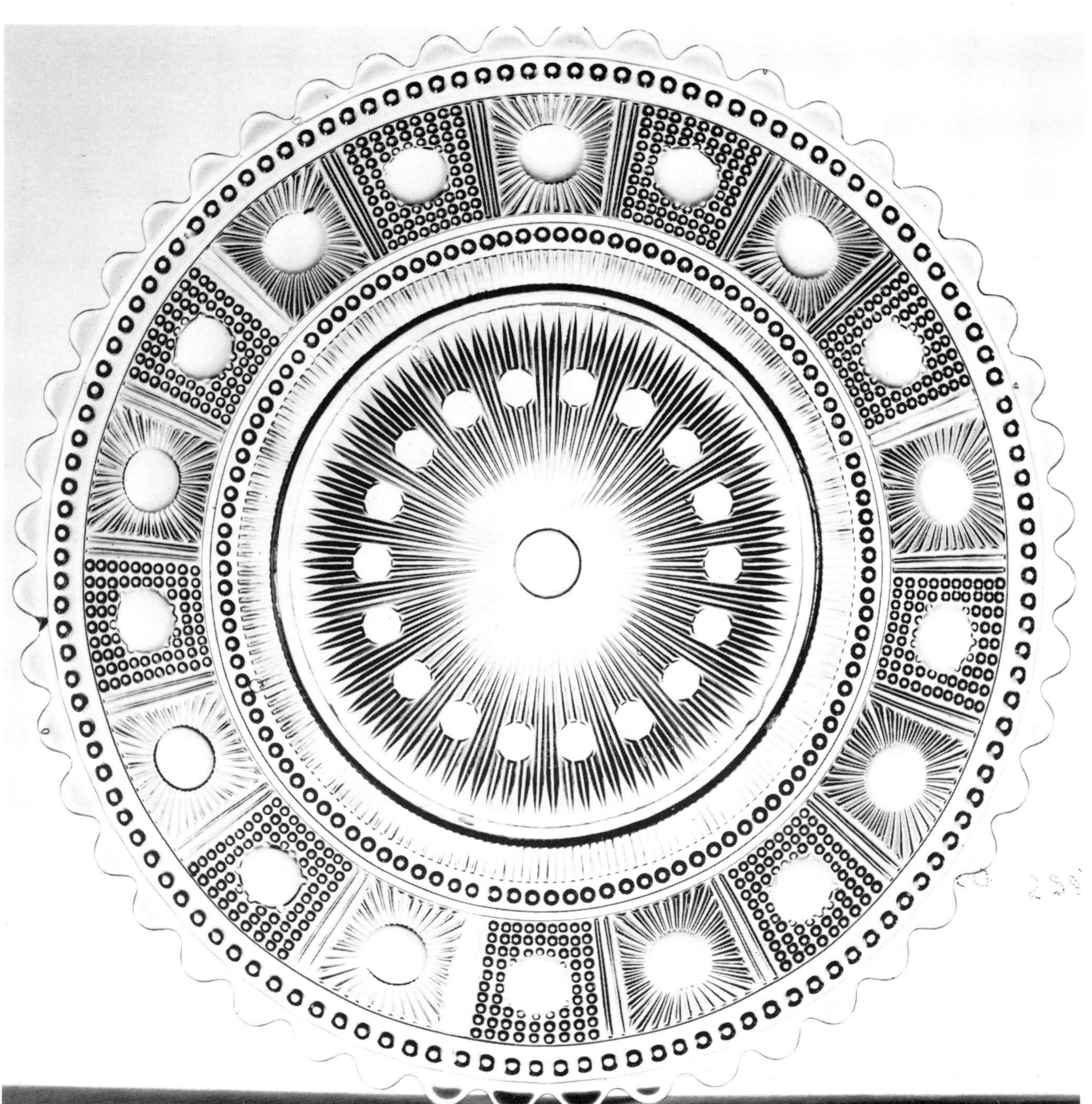

46

47

49

48

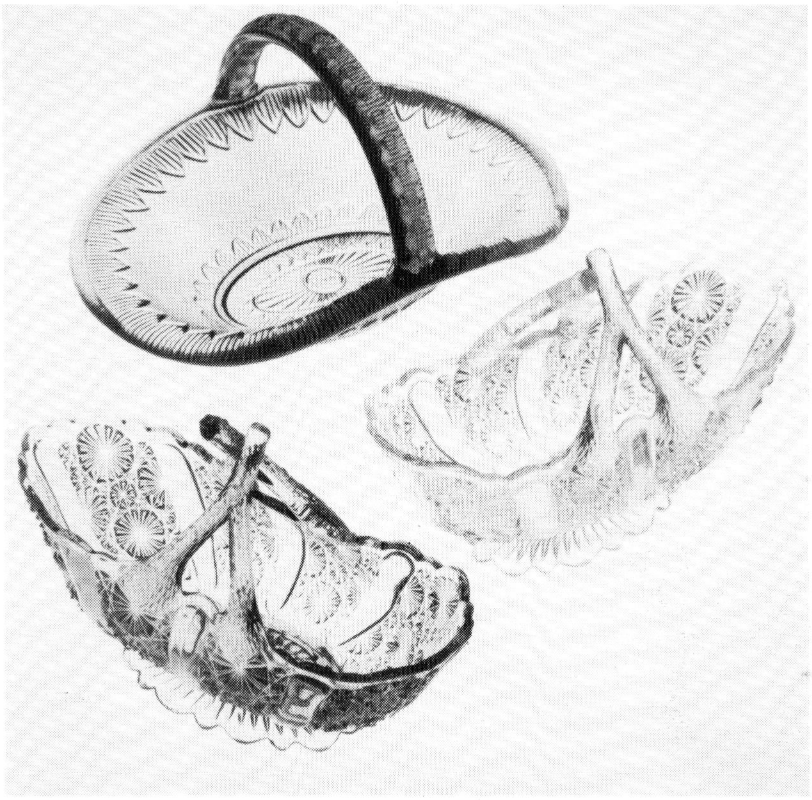

50

51

52 53

54

55

56

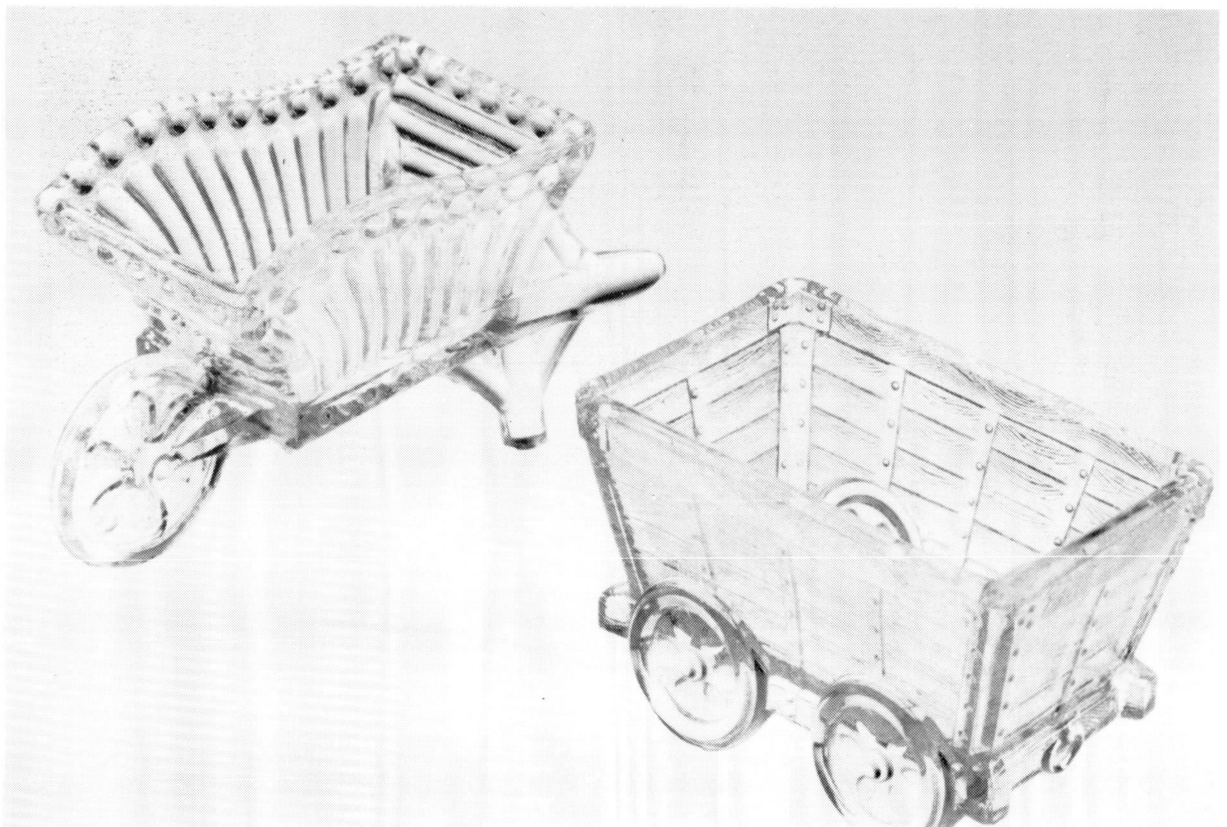

57 58

59

# INDEX OF COLOUR PHOTOGRAPHS

1. Sowerby's Ellison Glass Works Ltd. Trade marked. Dolphin bowl, in pattern book of 1882. This bowl in amber was probably late 19th century. These bowls were made well into the 20th century and much depends on the colour of the glass.
2. Sowerby's Ellison Glass Works Ltd. c1910 trade marked. Sugar bowl in ruby coloured glass.
3. Sowerby's Ellison Glass Works Ltd. Mid 1920s trade marked. Sugar bowl in iridescent orange coloured glass ("Carnival" glass). Albeit earlier moulds were used so the glass looks older.
4. Unmarked. c1880. Blue marble obelisk. Probably from Tyneside and possibly Edward Moore & Co.
5. Sowerby & Co. c1880 trade marked. Flower trough in blue malachite.
6. Sowerby & Co. 20 March 1878 and trade marked. Basket in pale purple marble.
7. Sowerby & Co. c1880 trade marked. Salt cellar in purple marble.
8. Henry Greener. c1880. First Greener trade mark. Sugar bowl in amber. Probably made for the Christmas market.
9. G. Davidson & Co. c1889 trade marked. Posy vase in blue pearline — early piece of pearline.
10. G. Davidson & Co. c1888 trade marked. Jug with hobnail pattern in amber.
11. Greener & Co. 10 August 1891. Night light holder in amber.
12. G. Davidson & Co. 6 September 1893. Dish in primrose pearline.
13. Sowerby & Co. 1 June 1874. Basket with 'snake' handle in clear blue. The "bobble" rim is as on the toast rack No. 54 in black and white photographs.
14. G. Davidson & Co. c1893. Cream jug in primrose pearline.
15. G. Davidson & Co. c1891. Pair of posy baskets in blue pearline.
16. Greener & Co. 3 November 1890. Flower basket — copying the blue pearline of G. Davidson & Co. As 'Pearline' had been registered this would seem to be a deliberate infringement.
17. Davidson & Co. 25 May 1893. Trinket dish, star shaped in blue pearline.
18. Burtles, Tate & Co. 8 January 1885. Opalescent swan flower holder.
19. Thomas Davidson. 31 March 1888. Opalescent tumbler.
20. Burtles, Tate & Co. 29 June 1885. Opalescent flower trough.
21. Henry Greener. 8 June 1878. Although visit was in November 1878. Greener first trade mark on lid. "Marquis of Lorne" covered butter in pale green marble.
22. Edward Moore. c1880. Unmarked but in the Moore pattern book. Pair of flower vases in clear, bright green.
23. Greener & Co. c1885. Greener first trade mark. Cake basket in flint glass with rustic handle similar to the registration of 27 March 1888.

1

2 3

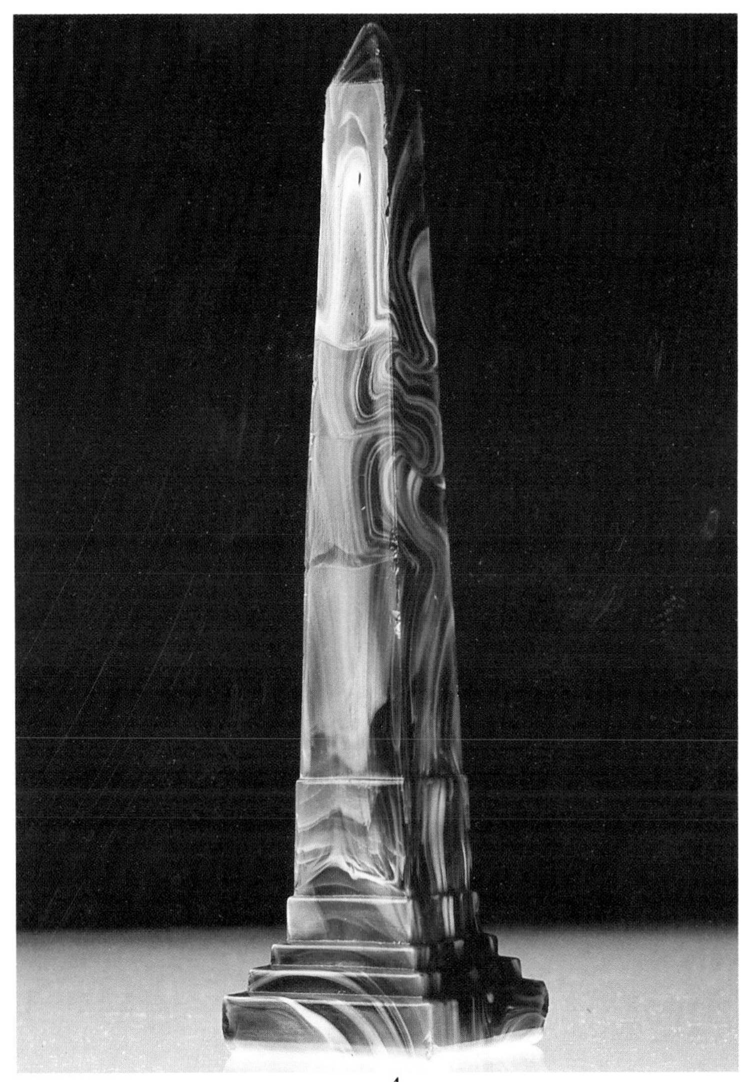

4

5

6 7

8

9

10

11

12

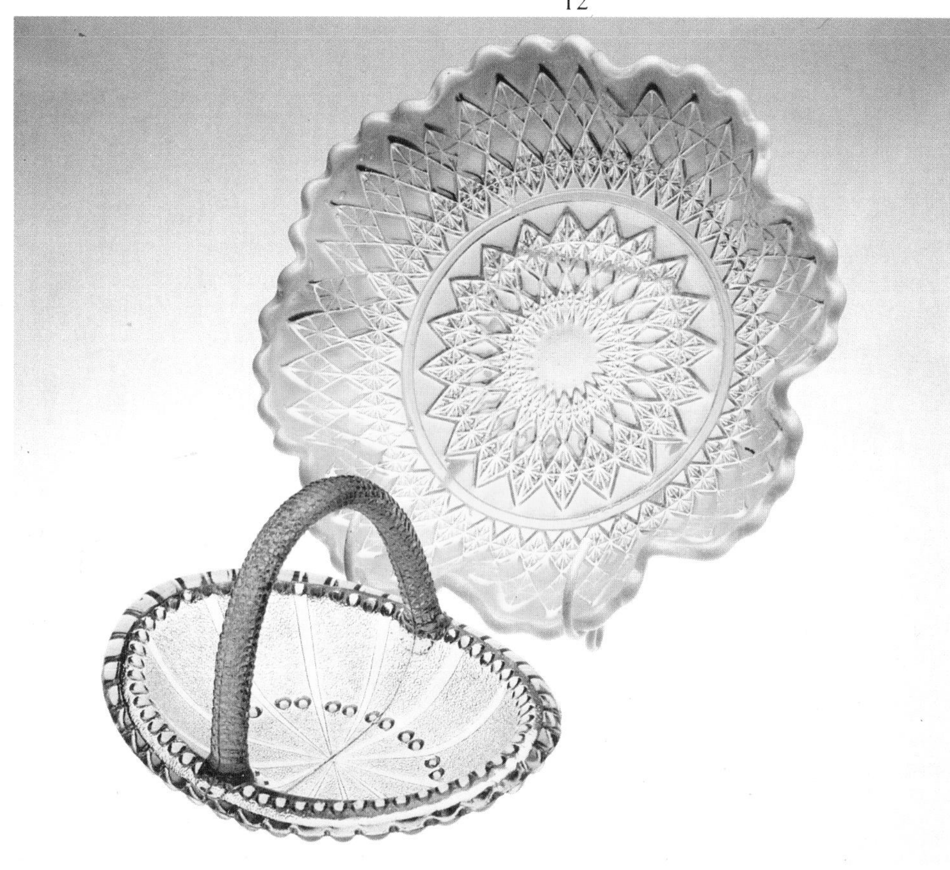

13

14

15

16

17

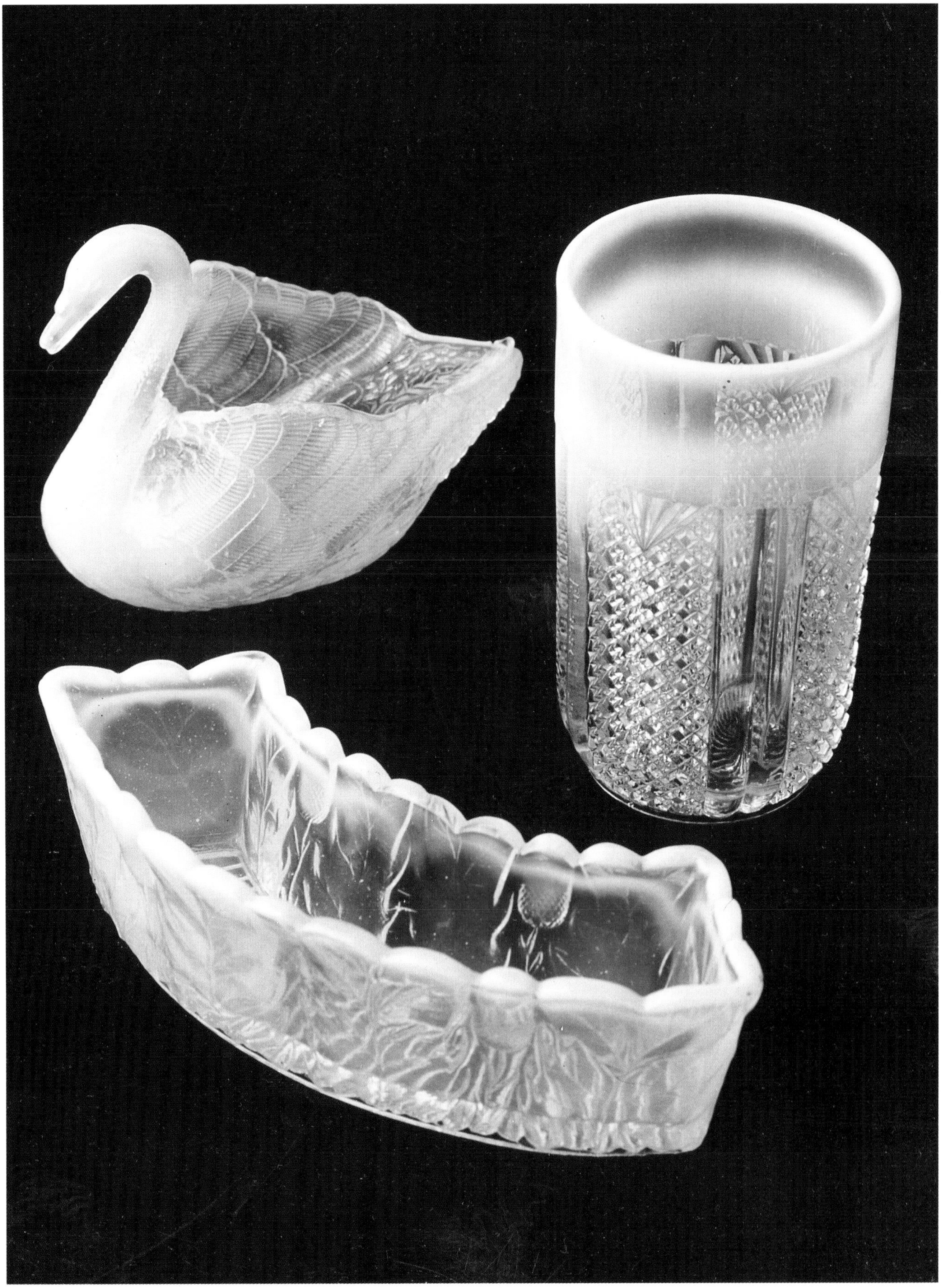

18

19

20

21

22

23

# Designs and Trade Marks: Registers and Representations

Information from the Public Record Office states:

*"Those records of the Patent Office and Industrial Property Department of the Board of Trade which have now been transferred to the Public Record Office include Registers and Representations of Designs and Trade Marks. A Representation of a Design gives a sample, drawing or photograph of the article, whilst the Registers give the registered number, the exact date of registration, type of design and the maker's name and address but not necessarily the name of the designer. Registered designs should carry either a diamond mark or the registered number. Trade Marks also have a registered number."*

**Ornamental Designs 1842-1883**

The Designs Act 1842 created thirteen classes of ornamental designs including all manufactured goods. It gave three years protection to the proprietors of ornamental designs of articles wholly or chiefly made of (1) metal, (2) wood, (3) glass or (4) earthenware, of (5) paper-hangings and (6) carpets, of (8) shawls, if not printed, and of (11) woven and printed fabrics of linen, cotton, wool, silk, hair or mixed material, if they were properly described as "furnitures" and if the repeat of the design was more than 12″ x 8″.

Nine months protection was given to (7) printed shawls, (9) printed yarns, threads and warps, and to (10) woven and printed fabrics of linen, cotton, wool, silk, hair or mixed material, not covered by the three years protection.

One year's protection was given to (12) woven fabrics not included in the previous two categories, and to (13) lace and any other manufactured ornamental substance or article not included elsewhere.

**Records**
BT 43: Ornamental Designs Act 1842: Representations
BT 44: Ornamental Designs Act 1842: Registers

The Patents, Designs and Trade Marks Act 1883 amalgamated the previous categories into which designs had been divided and registered the articles, both ornamental and useful, in a single numerical series, extending the protection to five years.

**Records**
BT 50: Patents Designs and Trade Marks Act 1883: Representations
BT 51: Patents Designs and Trade Marks Act 1883: Registers
BT 82: Representations of Trade Marks (in numerical sequence from 1876 to 1938)

---

Before 1884 if a firm registered several items on any one day, each object had the same registration date lozenge, although the Register gave each item an individual number. An example of this is the registration of three lots for 8th August 1873 by John Derbyshire. Both of the designs for the table glass were very different, but items of these designs would have had the same date lozenge, as the designs were entered on the same day.

# Registry Marks

Glass objects (particularly pressed glass objects) made between 1842 and 1883 sometimes bear a diamond shaped mark which indicates that they were registered at the Patent Office Design Registry. This mark can be used to determine the exact date of registration and, by consulting official records held by the Public Record Office, the name of the firm or person who registered the design. Glass objects were registered under Class III.

After 1883 a new series of registrations began which are indicated on the object by a serial number. These numerical registrations were not divided into classes but continued in straight sequence irrespective of material. Details of the numbers of the first registration in each year from 1884 to 1908 are given for glass.

1842-1867

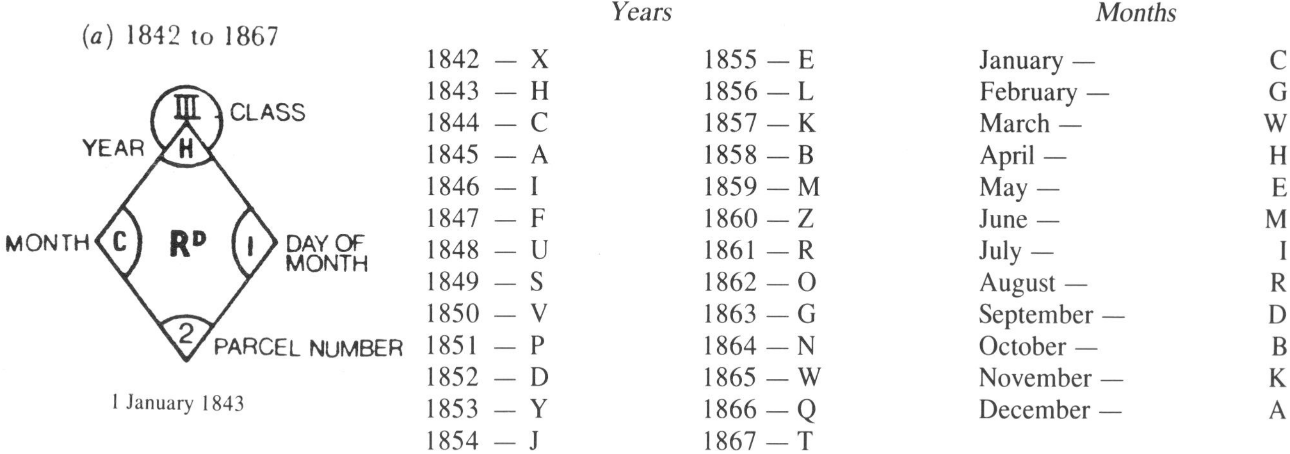


(*a*) 1842 to 1867

1 January 1843

| *Years* | | *Months* | |
|---|---|---|---|
| 1842 — X | 1855 — E | January — | C |
| 1843 — H | 1856 — L | February — | G |
| 1844 — C | 1857 — K | March — | W |
| 1845 — A | 1858 — B | April — | H |
| 1846 — I | 1859 — M | May — | E |
| 1847 — F | 1860 — Z | June — | M |
| 1848 — U | 1861 — R | July — | I |
| 1849 — S | 1862 — O | August — | R |
| 1850 — V | 1863 — G | September — | D |
| 1851 — P | 1864 — N | October — | B |
| 1852 — D | 1865 — W | November — | K |
| 1853 — Y | 1866 — Q | December — | A |
| 1854 — J | 1867 — T | | |

(R may be found as the month mark for 1—19 September 1857, and K for December 1860).

1868-1883

(*b*) 1868 to 1883

III
CLASS
DAY OF MONTH
1
PARCEL NUMBER
2
Rᴰ
H
YEAR
C
MONTH

1 January 1869

| *Years* | | *Months* | |
|---|---|---|---|
| 1868 — X | 1876 — V | January — | C |
| 1869 — H | 1877 — P | February — | G |
| 1870 — C | 1878 — D | March — | W |
| 1871 — A | 1879 — Y | April — | H |
| 1872 — I | 1880 — J | May — | E |
| 1873 — F | 1881 — E | June — | M |
| 1874 — U | 1882 — L | July — | I |
| 1875 — S | 1883 — K | August — | R |
| | | September — | D |
| | | October — | B |
| | | November — | K |
| | | December — | A |

(For 1—6 March 1878, G was used for the month and W for the year)

| Date of Deposit | No. of Parcel | No. of Design | Name of Proprietor | Address of Proprietor |
|---|---|---|---|---|
| 1842 Septr 1 | 4 | 1461 | Henry Cope Junr | Victoria St Pimlico London |
| 6 | 1 | 1480 | Rice Wm Harris | Birmingham |
| 14 | 1 | 1684 | Fredk Gye Junr | South Lambeth, Surrey |
| 28 | 4 | 1774 | Sir John Scott Lillie Knt | Kensington, Middlesex |
| Octr 27 | 6 | 2132 | Reeves & Sons | 150 Cheapside |
| 28 | 5 | 2136 | Alfred Ward | 74½ Quadrant, Regent St |
| Novr 19 | 3 | 2319 | Chance Brothers & Co | The Glass Wks near Birmingham |
| " | " | 2320 | do | do |
| " | " | 2321 | do | do |
| 28 | 2 | 2508 | Philip James [illegible] | 16 Bread St Hill Upper Thames St |
| 1843 Jany 25 | 7 | 4338 | Apsley Pellatt | Falcon Glass Wks Blackfriars |
| March 15 | 1 | 5857 | Rice, Williams, Harris | Islington Glass Wks Birmingham |
| April 24 | 5 | 6689 | Apsley Pellatt | Falcon Glass Wks Blackfriars |
| June 17 | 7 | 7359 | do | do |
| " | " | 7360 | do | do |
| Septr 8 | 8 | 9809 | Palmer & Co | Sutton St Clerkenwell |
| Octr 7 | 5 | 10385 | Thomas Taylor | 23 Milk St Cheapside |
| Novr 18 | 8 | 11638 | Apsley Pellatt | Falcon Glass Wks Holland St Blackfriars |
| Feby 27 | 8 | 16636 | John Webb Christy / Alfred Joy | [illegible], Westminster / Castle St Holborn |
| July 29 | 9 | 20397 | Alfred Joy | Castle St, Holborn |
| 30 | 3 | 20335 | Apsley Pellatt | Falcon Glass Works, Holland St Blackfy |
| 1845 April 1 | 4 | 27045 | Robert Waller Winfield | Cambridge Street Works Birmingham |
| 11 | 7 | 27232 | Crosse & Blackwell | Soho Square |
| May 10 | 2 | 27481 | Uriah Lane | 158 North St Brighton |
| 14 | 4 | 27509 | do | do |
| " | " | 27510 | do | do |
| " | " | 11 | do | do |
| " | " | 12 | do | do |
| " | " | 13 | do | do |
| 15 | 2 | 27515 | do | do |
| 23 | 3 | 27641 | Charles Heaton & Co | 23 & 25 Lime St City |

| Date of Deposit | No. of Parcel | No. of Design | Name of Proprietor | Address of Proprietor |
|---|---|---|---|---|
| 1845/6 June 7 | 7 | 28035 | Phillipson & Co | Budge Row London |
| July 9 | 3 | 28723 | Joseph Wingrave | 80 Saint Pauls Church Yard London |
| 17 | 5 | 28865 | Wilson & Southern | Wheeldon Works, Sheffield |
| August 12 | 3 | 29718 | Joseph Wingrave | 80 St Pauls Church Yard |
| 19 | 1 | 29847 | Apsley Pellatt | Falcon Glass Works, Holland St Southwark |
| 26 | 3 | 29930 | Charles Heaton & Co | [illegible] |
| September 23 | 6 | 30427 | Isaac Clifton | 9 Upper North Place, Grays Inn Road |
| [illegible] 6 | " | 31057 | Charles [illegible] | Curtain Road, Shoreditch |
| December 5 | 5 | 31721 | Aire & Calder | 10 Upper Thames Street |
| 9 | 2 | 31877 | The Aire & Calder Bottle Company | do |
| 24 | 1 | 32479 | William Binnion | Birmingham |
| " | 2 | 32480 | William Wray Woolcom Pigott | London |
| 31 | 3 | 32643 | William Binnion | Birmingham |
| 1846 January 12 | 3 | 32954 | Robert Waller Winfield | Cambridge Street Works, Birmingham |
| February 13 | 4 | 33765 | Crosse & Blackwell | Soho Square |
| 19 | 2 | 33917 | R. W. Winfield | Birmingham |
| March 20 | 4 | 34443 | Anthony Thatcher | The Yorkshire Bottle Company Ferry Bridge near Pontefract |
| 31 | 1 | 34522 | do | do |
| April 9 | 1 | 34577 | R. Torbock & Co | Bakers Row, Whitechapel London |
| 15 | 5 | 34601 | W. Binnion | Birmingham |
| May 9 | 4 | 34929 | William Binnion | do |
| 14 | 3 | 34943 | Anthony Thatcher | Yorkshire Bottle Co Ferry Bridge Pontefract |
| June 12 | 4 | 35283 | The Aire & Calder Bottle Company | 10 Upper Thames Street |
| 22 | 9 | 35385 | do | do |
| 26 | 3 | 35778 | Jonas Defries | Houndsditch |
| July 7 | 1 | 35925 | The Aire & Calder Bottle Co | 10 Uppr Thames Street |
| | | 6 | do | do |
| August 1 | 1 | 36441 | Rice Harris | Islington Glass & Alkali Works Birmingham |
| " | " | 2 | do | do |
| " | " | 3 | do | do |
| " | " | 4 | do | do |

| Date of Deposit | No of Parcel | No. of Design | Name of Proprietor | Address of Proprietor |
|---|---|---|---|---|
| 1846/7. August 1 | 1 | 36445 | Rice Harris | Islington Glass & Alkali Works Birmingham |
| " | " | 6 | do | do |
| 20 | 1 | 36925 | Anthony Thatcher | {The Yorkshire Bottle Compy Ferry Bridge near Pontefract Yorkshire} |
| 23 | 3 | 36987 | William [illegible] | Birmingham |
| 27 | 3 | 36997 | Anthony Thatcher | {Yorkshire Bottle Co. Ferry Bridge Nr. Pontefract, Yorkshire} |
| Sept. 3 | 4 | 37[illegible] | do | do |
| 8 | 1 | 37224 | do | do |
| October 7 | 4 | 37676 | Griffith & Stone Crown Glass Manufacturers | 32 Gt Guilford Street Southwark |
| 14 | 2 | 37706 | Samuel Chambers | 92 Aston St. Birmingham |
| Nov. 26 | 4 | 38329 | George Upton & Co | 24 Queens Row Pentonville Hill |
| Dec 7 | 2 | 38643 | Molineaux & Co | Manchester Flint Glass Manufacturers |
| 1847. January 2 | 5 | 39810 | Hammond Turner & Sons | Birmingham |
| 7 | 2 | 39960 | John Weeks Kincaird | 16 Great Trinity Lane Bread Street London |
| March 17 | 10 | 42071 | The Aire & Calder Bottle Compy | 10 Upper Thames Street |
| 25 | 3 | 42296 | Percival & Yates | The British & Foreign Flint Glass Works Manchester |
| April 12 | 3 | 42601 | Vincent Price | 33 Wardour St. in the County of Middlesex |
| 16 | 2 | 42631 | W.H. B & J Richardson | Wordsley near Stourbridge |
| " | " | 3 | do | do |
| May 10 | 6 | 43137 | The Aire & Calder Bottle Compy | 10 Upper Thames Street |
| " | " | 8 | do | do |
| 19 | 3 | 43243 | Arthur Young & Compy | Leadenhall Street |
| 31 | 4 | 43426 | The Aire & Calder Bottle Company | 10 Upper Thames Street |
| June 3 | 3 | 43469 | Felix Summerly | 13 Old Bond Street London |
| 17 | 1 | 43655 | Percival & Yates | Manchester |
| 22 | 1 | 43729 | John Cliff Junr | 32 Cheapside |
| 30 | 6 | 43850 | Percival & Yates | Manchester |
| July 5 | 4 | 43915 | John Dockree | {12½ Macclesfield St. South City Road} |
| 6 | 2 | 43924 | W.H. B & J. Richardson | {Wordsley near Stourbridge & at 3 Dyers Buildings Holborn London} |
| " | " | 5 | do | do |
| " | " | 6 | do | do |
| " | " | 7 | do | do |

| Date of Deposit | No of Parcel | No. of Design | Name of Proprietor | Address of Proprietor |
|---|---|---|---|---|
| 1847/8 July 17 | 3 | 44041 | Robert Best | Birmingham |
| 29 | 5 | 44616 | The Aire & Calder Bottle Compy | 10 Upper Thames Street |
| October 1 | 5 | 46131 | F. & C. Osler | Broad Street Birmingham |
| 12 | 3 | 46292 | The Aire & Calder Bottle Compy | 10 Upper Thames Street |
| 14 | 6 | 46306 | Charles Lloyd | {Newhall St. Birmingham & 28 Upper North Place, Grays Inn Road London} |
| Class I & III 20 | 5 | 46484 | Charles Rowley | {23 & 24 Newhall St. Birmingham and 19 Hadle St. Wood St. London} |
| - | - | - | | |
| 23 | 3 | 46519 | F & C. Osler | 44 Oxford St. London & Broad St. Birmingham |
| 25 | 2 | 46523 | John Fell Christy & Co | Stangate Glass Works Lambeth |
| 28 | 1 | 46662 | Alexis Soyer | The Reform Club Pall Mall |
| November 2 | 1 | 46748 | F. & C Osler | 44 Oxford St. London & Broad St. Birmingham |
| 5 | 2 | 46788 | Percival & Yates | Jersey Street Manchester |
| " | " | 9 | do | do |
| 27 | 2 | 47344 | do | do |
| December 9 | 5 | 47532 | Edmund Crosse & Thomas Blackwell | 21 Soho Square |
| 11 | 4 | 47601 | do | do |
| 28 | 2 | 48516 | Edmund Crosse and Thomas Blackwell | do |
| 1848 January 6 | 5 | 48718 | Joseph Barlow | 120 Long Acre London |
| 11 | 3 | 48858 | R. W. Winfield | Birmingham |
| 17 | 5 | 49021 | John Davis | near Stourbridge |
| 26 | 2 | 49205 | The Yorkshire Bottle Company | London Wall |
| February 7 | 5 | 49700 | Cornelius Bagnall and John Westwood | 73 Lambs Conduit Street |
| 11 | 2 | 49779 | Percival & Yates | Jersey Street Manchester |
| 22 | 7 | 50271 | John Combs & Son | 11 Bush Lane |
| 26 | 3 | 50369 | The Yorkshire Bottle Company | London Wall |
| " | 6 | 50378 | The Aire & Calder Bottle Compy | 10 Upper Thames Street |
| 28 | 2 | 50413 | Crosse & Blackwell | Soho Square |
| 29 | 6 | 50463 | Cornelius Bagnall & John Westwood | 73 Lambs Conduit St. London |
| March 2 | 4 | 50520 | The Aire & Calder Bottle Compy | 10 Upper Thames St |
| 18 | 4 | 50942 | Jonas Defries | Houndsditch |
| " | " | 3 | do | do |

| Date of Deposit | No of Parcel | No. of Design | Name of Proprietor | Address of Proprietor |
|---|---|---|---|---|
| 1848/9 | | | | |
| March 18 | 4 | 50944 | Jonas Defries | Houndsditch |
| 20 | 5 | 50988 | Henry Pershouse | Birmingham |
| 27 | 10 | 51199 | William Bennion | do |
| 30 | 2 | 51213 | Joseph Wingrave & Co | 80 St Pauls Church yard |
| May 10 | 3 | 51882 | Jonas Defries | Houndsditch |
| 25 | 1 | 52120 | Alexis Soyer | The Reform Club Pall Mall |
| 30 | 1 | 52158 | W H B & J Richardson | Wordsley Nr Stourbridge, Worcestershire |
| " | " | 9 | do | do |
| " | " | 52160 | do | do |
| June 1 | 6 | 52179 | do | do |
| 13 | 4 | 52328 | do | Wordsley, Worcestershire |
| " | " | 9 | do | do |
| July 3 | 2 | 52554 | Anthony Thatcher & The Yorkshire Bottle Company | Ferry Bridge Yorkshire |
| 21 | 4 | 53121 | Wm Bissett | 19 Kings Arch Place East St Walworth |
| August 2 | 6 | 53633 | John Wood and John Henry Weston | 27 Church St Lambeth, 1 Lant Place, Southwark Bridge Road |
| 17 | 2 | 53861 | do | do |
| 30 | 3 | 54128 | do | do |
| " | " | 9 | do | do |
| " | " | 54130 | do | do |
| " | " | 1 | do | do |
| September 7 | 3 | 54273 | George & Robert Macdonald | [illegible] Regent St London, [illegible] Dublin |
| " | 4 | 54274 | Joseph Guise | 73 Margaret St Wilmington Square |
| 23 | 5 | 54552 | Elton & Everton | 6 Princes St Lincolns Inn Fields |
| October 2 | 1 | 54614 | Joseph Green | Birmingham |
| 28 | 2 | 55052 | Westwood & Moore | The Bottle Works, Moor Lane Brierley Hill Staffordshire |
| 1849 January 4 | 6 | 57024 | do | do |
| 12 | 5 | 57319 | J. Wingrave & Co | 80 St Pauls Church yard |
| February 28 | 5 | 58596 | Westwood & Moore | Brierley Lane, Staffordshire |
| March 12 | 1 | 58852 | David Wilkinson | Manchester |
| April 2 | 7 | 59335 | Crosse & Blackwell | 21 Soho Square London |
| 18 | 1 | 59584 | Thomas Gammon | Birmingham |

| Date of Deposit | No of Parcel | No. of Design | Name of Proprietor | Address of Proprietor |
|---|---|---|---|---|
| 1849 | | | | |
| April 24 | 3 | 59686 | W H B & J Richardson | Wordsley near Stourbridge Worcestershire |
| May 8 | 2 | 59872 | R W Winfield | Birmingham |
| 22 | 2 | 60072 | Thomas Gammon | Birmingham |
| June 8 | 8 | 60692 | John Davis | Brettell Lane, Staffordshire |
| July 3 | 1 | 61,115 | F & C Osler | 44 Oxford St London & Broad St Birmingham |
| 5 | 6 | 61144 | R W Winfield | Birmingham |
| 18 | 4 | 61573 | David Wilkinson | Manchester |
| October 1 | 3 | 62740 | John Cliff Junr | 32 Cheapside |
| 12 | 6 | 62918 | Thomas Gammon | Birmingham |
| 13 | 2 | 62923 | W. H B & J Richardson | Wordsley near Stourbridge Worcestershire |
| 16 | 4 | 62989 | Westwood and Moore | The Bottle Works, Brierley Hill, Staffordshire |
| 17 | 6 | 63016 | Henry [illegible] | [illegible] Street St Pauls London [illegible] |
| Nov 5 | 5 | 63411 | Alfred Bird | Birmingham |
| 19 | 6 | 64172 | Badger Brothers & Co | Dudley |
| 21 | 3 | 64164 | Stott Walker Moore [illegible] and Bottle Company | Upper Thames Street London |
| 22 | 3 | 64340 | F & C Osler | Broad Street Birmingham, 44 Oxford Street London |
| 23 | 5 | 64359 | Crosse & Blackwell | Soho Square |

| Date of Deposit | No of Parcel | No. of Design | Name of Proprietor | Address of Proprietor |
|---|---|---|---|---|
| 1850 | | | | |
| January 31 | 4 | 66954 } 5 | William Rowe | 12 New Wharf Whitefriars |
| Feby 6 | 9 | 67167 | Henry Trinder | 75 Watling Street |
| 13 | 8 | 67467 } 8 | Sherwood & Co | Eccleston Flint Glass Works Nr St Helens Lancashire |
| 27 | 2 | 67781 | Rees, Emery, Napoleon Price | 32 Lombard Street |
| March 4 | 3 | 67831 } 2 | William Kidd | Saunders Cottage, New Road, Hammersmith |
| 11 | 11 | 68066 | Anthony Hinchcliffe of the Yorkshire Bottle Company | London Wall |
| 12 | 6 | 68073 | John R. Isaac | Liverpool |
| April 16 | 2 | 68834 | Price John McManus | 14 Wolcomb[?] Street Belgrave Square |
| 19 | 8 | 69046 | Wm Hancock & Rd Brown & R. Davis | 10 Cross St Islington, 72 Old Broad St City |
| May 23 | 4 | 69516 } 17 | George Sherwood & Co | Eccleston Flint Glass Works near St Helens Lancashire |
| 30 | 2 | 69601 | John Kilner | Dewsbury |
| 31 | 4 | 69607 | John Cliff Quince | 32 Cheapside London |
| June 29 | 3 | 70042 | Joseph Stacey [illegible] | High Street Southwark |
| July 11 | 3 | 70296 | F & C Osler | 44 Oxford St London & Broad St Birmingham |
| 17 | 4 | 70377 | Badger Brothers | Dudley |
| 19 | 5 | 70487 | Thomas Gates | 34 Rose Place Liverpool |
| 23 | 3 | 70609 | George Mosley | Paragon Row, George Rd Birmingham |
| 24 | 7 | 70622 | George J Green | Bond Street, Birmingham |
| August 7 | 5 | 71064 | Henry Pershouse | Birmingham |
| 16 | 3 | 71179 | John Kilner | Brick Hill Lane, Upper Thames Street |
| 17 | 3 | 71202 | do | do |
| Sept 18 | 3 | 71983 | do | Brick Hill Lane London |
| Octr 9 | 3 | 72397 | William Hodson[?] & Jonathan Richardson | Wordsley, Stourbridge, Worcestershire |
| 15 | 4 | 72500 | Crosse & Blackwell | Soho Square |
| [illegible] 25 | 6 | 73130 | J H Brown | 4 South Street Finsbury, Lond. |
| November 5 | 3 | 73334 | Thomas Gammon | Birmingham |
| [illegible] 9 | 2 | 73428 | Thomas Bragg | Birmingham |

| Date of Deposit | No of Parcel | No. of Design | Name of Proprietor | Address of Proprietor |
|---|---|---|---|---|
| 1850 | | | | |
| Nov 29 | 4 | 73917 | Jonas Defries | Houndsditch |
| Dec 11 | 2 | 74530 | John Cliff Quince | 32 Cheapside London |
| 1851 | | | | |
| Jany 11 | 3 | 75174 } 3 | W. H. B and J. Richardson | 73 Lambs Conduit Street and Wordsley Glass Works Stourbridge Worcester |
| 13 | 13 | 75738 | Eugene Rimmel | 39 Gerrard Street Soho London |
| 20 | 5 | 75885 | John Cliff Quince | 32 Cheapside, London |
| 22 | 8 | 75900 | Eliezer Edwards | Birmingham |
| Feby 11 | 9 | 76783 | George Lloyd & Thomas Summerfield | Park Glass Works Birmingham |
| March 29 | 6 | 77954 | Isaac Aldebert otherwise Hallmarke, Aldebert & Hallmarke | 57 Long Acre, London |
| April 1 | 6 | 78039 | Benjamin Black | 49 South Moulton Street |
| 2 | 3 | 78019 } 30 | Lloyd & Summerfield | Park Glass Works, Spring Hill, Birmingham |
| 17 | 7 | 78476 | Philip Benjamin | 105 Hatton Garden Holborn London |
| " | 8 | 78477 | Lloyd & Summerfield | Park Glass Works Spring Hill Birmingham |
| June 10 | 4 | 79180 | Henry David Green Truscott | 7 Coburg Road Old Kent Road |
| July 4 | 3 | 79537 | Frederic Pellatt | Falcon Glass Works London |
| 21 | 6 | 79749 | George Jos Green | Etna Flint Glass Works Birmingham |
| September 12 | 2 | 80554 | Davis Greathead & Green | Stourbridge |
| October 11 | 3 | 80929 | Joseph Webb | Coalbourn Hill Stourbridge |
| 21 | 2 | 81056 | Hancock Rixon & Dunt | Cockspur Street Pall Mall East |
| 24 | 3 | 81078 | Davis Greathead & Green | Brettell Lane, Staffordshire |
| " | 6 | 81081 | F & C Osler | Broad St Birmingham & 44 Oxford Street London |
| 31 | 4 | 81217 | Berens Blumberg & Co | St Pauls Churchyard London |

| Date of Deposit | No of Parcel | No. of Design | | Name of Proprietor | Address of Proprietor |
|---|---|---|---|---|---|
| 1851 | | | | | |
| Novr 18 | 7 | 81613 | 1 | W.H. B. & J. Richardson | Wordsley Stourbridge Worcestershire |
| Decr 26 | 2 | 82568 | 1 | Robert Lancaster | Bolton Lancashire |
| 1852 | | | | | |
| Jany 10 | 3 | 82737 | 1 | Thomas Gammon | Birmingham |
| Feby 9 | 1 | 83700 | 1 | Crosse & Blackwell | Soho Square |
| 14 | 3 | 83811 | 1 | George Twigg | Powell Street Birmingham |
| 16 | 4 | 83825 | 1 | Westwood and Moore | Glass Works Brierley Hill |
| March 3 | 4 | 84128 | 2 | Hancock Rixon and Dunt | Cockspur Street Pall Mall East |
| " | | 9 | | | — |
| 4 | 4 | 84136 | 1 | Archibald Henderson Ross and Robert Henderson Ross | Sunderland |
| " | 3 | 84137 | 2 | Jonas Defries | Houndsditch |
| " | " | 8 | | | |
| 5 | 4 | 84155 | 1 | George Twigg | Powell Street Birmingham |
| 10 | 4 | 84217 | 1 | Archibald Hilson Ross | Sunderland, Optician |
| 12 | 4 | 84228 | 2 | Hancock Rixon and Dunt | Cockspur Street Pall Mall East |
| " | " | 9 | | | |
| 17 | 4 | 84264 | 1 | Archibald Hilson Ross, Optician and Robert Henderson Ross, Miner | Sunderland |
| 18 | 5 | 84300 | 1 | Joseph W[illegible] | Coalbourn Hill Nr Stourbridge |
| 19 | 4 | 84308 | 1 | William [illegible] | 34 Queen St. Cheapside |
| 23 | 1 | 84386 | 1 | Joseph We[illegible] | Coalbourn Hill Stourbridge |
| April 6 | 1 | 84598 | 1 | John W[illegible] | Birmingham |
| " 14 | 4 | 84673 | 2 | John M[illegible] | 44 High Street Marylebone |
| " | " | 4 | | | — |
| 20 | 1 | 84816 | 1 | Twigg & Silvester | Powell Street Birmingham |
| May 1 | 2 | 84947 | 1 | Crosse & Blackwell | Soho Square |
| 11 | 5 | 85064 | 1 | A. Marion & Co | Regent Street |
| June 29 | 3 | 85540 | 1 | Jonas Defries | 137 Houndsditch |
| July 21 | 3 | 85790 | 1 | J. Bevan & Co | 7 Wilderness Row Clerkenwell |

| Deposit | Parcel | Design | | Name of Proprietor | Address of Proprietor |
|---|---|---|---|---|---|
| 1852 | | | | | |
| July 23 | 5 | 85806 to 85811 | 6 | William Churcher | 28 Thomas Street Oxford Street London |
| August 30 | 4 | 86391 | 1 | Alfred Hely | 13 Cannon Row, Westminster, Middlesex |
| Novr 3 | 3 | 87523 | 1 | William [illegible] | Old College Hoxton |
| 13 | 3 | 87656 | 1 | Dixley & Son | Stourbridge |
| 16 | 5 | 87723 | 1 | Howard Brothers | Woolwich Kent |
| Decr 9 | 2 | 88218 | 1 | King & Co | 50 Rupert St Haymarket London |
| 1853 | | | | | |
| Jany 28 | 8 | 89210 | 1 | Davis Greathead & Green | Stourbridge, Glass Manufacturers |
| Feby 5 | [illegible] | 89320 | 1 | Dixley & Son | Stourbridge |
| 14 | 6 | 89601 | 1 | John Cliffe Quince | 10 Upper Thames Street London |
| April 12 | 7 | 90767 | 1 | John Walsh Walsh | Soho & Vesta Glass Works Birmingham Heath Birmingham Warwickshire |
| May 17 | 3 | 91193 | 1 | Wood & Perkes | Worsbro Dale near Barnsley, Yorkshire |
| " | 6 | 91228 | 1 | Stott Walker | 10 Upper Thames Street London |
| 31 | 2 | 91284 to 5 | 2 | do | do do |
| June 9 | 2 | 91341 | 1 | Hodge & Roberts | London |
| 10 | 4 | 91381 | 1 | Robert Best | Birmingham |
| 23 | 2 | 91476 | 1 | Joseph Webb | Coalbourn Hill Stourbridge |
| July 9 | 1 | 91634 | 1 | John Walsh Walsh | Soho and Vesta Glass Works, Birmingham Heath, Birmingham, Warwickshire |
| 22 | 1 | 91764 | 1 | Blackwood & Co | 26 Long Acre London |
| August 19 | 3 | 92120 | 1 | Joseph Tylor and Son | Warwick Lane, Newgate Street, London |

| Date of Deposit | No of Parcel | No. of Design | | Name of Proprietor | Address of Proprietor |
|---|---|---|---|---|---|
| 1853 | | | | | |
| Octr. 3 | 4 | 92734 to 92755 | 22 | Chance Brothers & Co | the Glass Works near Birmingham |
| 13 | 4 | 92927 | 1 | W. Reichenbach | 33 Borough Road, Southwark |
| Novr. 5 | 4 | 93183 | 1 | J. Defries & Sons | 147 Houndsditch |
| 11 | 3 | 93320 | 1 | John Rothwell | Manchester |
| Decr. 14 | 6 | 93615 | 1 | Prices Patent Candle Compy. | Belmont Vauxhall |
| 17 | 1 | 93626 | 1 | Joseph Webb | Coalbourn Hill Stourbridge |
| 1854 | | | | | |
| Jany 9 | 5 | 94308 | 1 | Stell Walker | Horseshoe Wharf 10 Upper Thames Street |
| 21 | 4 | 94720 | 1 | Davis Greathead & Green | Stourbridge Worcestershire |
| Feb. | 2 | 94906 | 1 | W. Reichenbach | 33 Borough Road Southwark |
| 14 | 3 | 95036 | 1 | Benjamin Richardson | Wordsley near Stourbridge |
| 17 | 1 | 95065 | 1 | Wm. Reichenbach | 33 & 34 Borough Road Southwark |
| 22 | 6 | 95135 | 1 | William Blumner Tate | [illegible] Street Gosnell Street |
| Class III & IV March 3 | 2 | 95237 | 1 | Thomas Jackson | Strangeways Manchester |
| May 6 | 3 | 95745 | 1 | Blackwood & Co | Long Acre |
| 24 | 3 | 95928 | 1 | John S Willway | 29 St. Augustines Parade Bristol |
| June 3 | 3 | 96004 | 1 | Benjamin Richardson | Wordsley Glass Works nr. Stourbridge |
| 15 | 2 | 96036 | 1 | Joseph Webb | Coalbourn Hill, Stourbridge |
| July 27 | 2 | 96491 to 96493 | 3 | George Novra | 95a Regents Quadrant, London |
| August 2 | 3 | 96543 | 1 | Jonas Defries & Son | Houndsditch |
| 3 | 1 | 96544 | 1 | Joseph Webb | Coalbourn Hill Stourbridge |
| 22 | 1 | 96657 | 1 | George Novra | 95a Regents St. London |
| 26 | 2 | 96703 | 1 | Benjamin Richardson | Wordsley Nr. Stourbridge |

| Date of Deposit | No of Parcel | No. of Design | | Name of Proprietor | Address of Proprietor |
|---|---|---|---|---|---|
| 1854 | | | | | |
| August 30 | 1 | 96720 / 1 | 2 | Geo. Novra | 95a Regent St. London |
| Septr. 21 | 3 | 96898 | 1 | Jonas Defries & Sons | 147 Houndsditch |
| Octr. 7 | 2 | 97145 / 6 | 2 | Wm. Reichenbach | 33 Borough Road Southwark |
| 9 | 5 | 97161 | 1 | F. Kinsell & Co. | Hampton Wick Middlesex |
| 14 | 1 | 97190 | 1 | Thos. Turner | Redditch |
| " | 2 | 97191 | 1 | Davis Greathead & Green | Flint Glass Works Stourbridge |
| 17 | 5 | 97249 | 1 | Jonas Defries and Sons | 147 Houndsditch |
| 23 | 6 | 97346 | 1 | Benjamin Richardson | Wordsley Nr. Stourbridge |
| Novr. 16 | 2 | 98170 | 1 | do | do |
| 18 | 4 | 98201 | 1 | Joseph Webb | Coalbourn Hill Glass Works Stourbridge |
| 23 | 1 | 98238 | 1 | Wm. Reichenbach | 33 Borough Road Southwark |
| 1855 | | | | | |
| Class I & III Jany 29 | 7 | 99107 | 1 | Prices Patent Candle Compy. | Belmont Vauxhall |
| February 11 | 7 | 99344 | 1 | Cripps and Blackwell | 21 Soho Square |
| 22 | 5 | 99466 | 1 | Price's Patent Candle Co. | Belmont Vauxhall |
| Mar. 3 | 6 | 99572 | 1 | Charles Wellbourne [illegible] | Newgate Street, London |
| 11 | 3 | 99632 | 1 | Davis Greathead & Green | Stourbridge |
| April 10 | 4 | 99823 | 1 | John McLachlan | William Street High Street Lambeth |
| 12 | 4 | 99882 | 1 | John Walsh Walsh | Soho & Vesta Glass Works Birmingham |
| " | 5 | 99883 | 1 | Joseph Lane | Town Hall Buildings Manchester |
| June 9 | 5 | 100296 | 1 | F & C Osler | 44 Oxford St. London & Broad St. Birmingham |
| 14 | 2 | 100432 | 1 | Hodge & Roberts | London |
| 23 | 3 | 100549 | 1 | do do | do |
| August 1 | 2 | 100997 | 1 | James Tyson Nibbs | Bakewell, Derbyshire |
| " | 3 | 100998 | 1 | Davis Greathead & Green | Flint Glass Houses Stourbridge |

| Date of Deposit | No. of Parcel | No. of Design | Name of Proprietor | Address of Proprietor |
|---|---|---|---|---|
| 1855 | | | | |
| August 25 | 1 | 101235 | John Pinkerton | 75 Lambs Conduit Street London |
| Octr 22 | 4 | 102292 | John Smith | Stonecutter Street Farringdon Street City of London Glasscutter |
| " | | – | | |
| Novr 9 | 3 | 102519 | Alfred Tooth | 14 Mincing Lane City |
| 10 | 4 | 102537 | William Reichenbach | 33 Boro' Road Southwark |
| 12 | 3 | 102545 | Samuel Harraden | East Temple Chambers 2 Whitefriars St. Fleet St. London |
| " | " | – | | |
| 17 | 2 | 102701 | Henry Neve | 16 New Castle Street, Shoreditch |
| 21 | 3 | 102720 | Aubin Chappuis | 69 Fleet St and St. Mary Axe London |
| 1856 | | | | |
| Feby 9 | 3 | 103724 | Benjamin Richardson | Wordsley near Stourbridge |
| 11 | 4 | 103731 | Crosse and Blackwell | 21 Soho Square |
| 13 | 4 | 103739 | Jonas Defries & Sons | Houndsditch |
| March 25 | 6 | 104212 | Benjamin Richardson | Wordsley near Stourbridge Flint Glass Manufacturer |
| " | " | | | |
| April 5 | 3 | 104307 | William Reichenbach | 33 Boro Road Southwark |
| 17 | 3 | 104379 | Elizer Edwards | Birmingham |
| May 1 | 4 | 104614 | John Kilner | Brook's Wharf Lane 48 Upper Thames Street |
| 14 | 1 | 104728 | Wm Young | Queen Street Cheapside |
| June 23 | 2 | 105196 | Peter Robinson & Edward Bolton | Warrington Lancashire |
| " | " | | | |
| Septr 8 | 3 | 106216 | Benjamin Richardson | Wordsley Nr Stourbridge |
| 20 | 3 | 106366 | do | do do |
| Octr 1 | 6 | 106452 | William Reid | University Street |
| 7 | 4 | 106554 | Solomon Maw | 11 Aldersgate Street London |
| 8 | 4 | 106559 to 106562 | Louis Groux and Charles Francis Hayward | 9 Park Road Dalston |

| Deposit | Parcel | Design | Name of Proprietor | Address of Proprietor |
|---|---|---|---|---|
| 1856 | | | | |
| Octr 9 | 2 | 106571 | George Ensell & Co | Birmingham |
| Novr 5 | 2 | 106915 | John Pinkerton | 75 Lambs Conduit Street |
| 15 | 2 | 107070 | George Bell & Co | 2 Wellington Street in the Parish of Saint Lukes Middlesex |
| " | " | | | |
| 18 | 1 | 107566 | William England | 4 Turner Street, Suffolk Road Sheffield |
| " | " | – | | |
| Decr | | ~~[illegible]~~ | ~~Mayer Brothers & Elliott~~ | ~~Dale Hall Pottery Longport Staffordshire~~ |
| – | – | – | | |
| [illegible] 18 | 4 | 108055 | Andrew Brundish | Birmingham |
| 1857 | | | | |
| January 5 / I to XIII | 2 | 108485 to 6 | Owen Parry | 6 Charles Terrace Asylum Road Old Kent Road |
| 14 | 5 | 108575 | James Joseph Bastien | 1 Helmet Row Old Street Saint Lukes London |
| 30 | 4 | 108815 | James Lewis | 6 Bartletts Buildings Holborn London |
| Feby 10 | 8 | 108985 | B. Hurwitz | 9 Southampton Street, Strand |
| March 21 | 3 | 109434 | Joseph Webb | Coalbourn Hill Stourbridge |
| April 30 | 4 | 109830 | Elizer Edwards | Birmingham |
| May 14 | 3 | 109909 | Jonas Defries & Sons | Houndsditch |
| 16 | 7 | 109943 | Crosse and Blackwell | 21 Soho Square |
| June 9 | 2 | 110109 | Benjamin Richardson | Wordsley near Stourbridge |
| July 2 | 1 | 110293 | Powell & Hooten | Parade Works, Birmingham |
| August 20 | 2 | 110942 2 to 3 | James Couper & Sons | City Glass Works, Glasgow |
| 24 | 1 | 111017 | F & C Osler | 44 Oxford St London & Broad St Birmingham |

| Date of Deposit | No. of Parcel | No. of Design | Name of Proprietor | Address of Proprietor |
|---|---|---|---|---|
| 1857 | — | — | — | |
| Sept. 12 | 2 | 111228 | Frederick Simpson | Red Hill Surrey |
| Nov. 6 | 3 | 111878 | Benjamin Richardson | Wordsley near Stourbridge |
| 7 | 4 | 111901 | George Brown | York |
| 11 | 2 | 111917 | Hodge & Reed | 101 Hatton Garden London |
| Dec. 17 | 3 | 112427 | James Couper & Sons | City Glass Works Glasgow |
| 19 | 4 | 112467 | Ambrose Hall | Limerick |
| 21 | 1 | 112469 to 112470 | R. W. Winfield & Son | Birmingham |
| 1858 | | | | |
| Feb. 24 | 7 | 113105 to 113107 | Isaac Hawker Bedford | Birmingham |
| March 9 | 3 | 113179 | Nibbs & Hunt | Birmingham |
| 10 | 4 | 113236 | John Henry Weston and James Frederick Curtl trading under the title of Weston & Curtl | 16 Cross Street Newington Butts London |
| 20 | 7 | 113260 | W. H. Eschenbach | 33 & 34 Bore Road, Southwark |
| April 13 | 3 | 113410 | George Edward Ashton | 8 Winsley Street Oxford St. |
| 15 | 1 | 113422 | James Goodchild | 77 High Street, Borough in the County of Surrey |
| May 10 | 4 | 113685 | John Ix Long | 465 Duke St. Glasgow |
| 11 | 5 | 113728 | John Cunnington & Co. | of Liverpool |
| June 2 | 2 | 113907 | Powell and Ricketts | Bristol |
| 23 | 5 | 114047 | F. & C. Osler | Broad St. Birmingham and 44 Oxford St. London |
| 24 | 3 | 114071 | William Blamire Tate | 47 Seward St. Goswell St. |
| 29 | 2 | 114082 | Benjamin Richardson | Wordsley Flint Glass Works near Stourbridge |
| July 29 | 3 | 114531 | Matthew Wheelton | Sytch, Burslem Staffordshire Glass cutter |

| Deposit | Parcel | Design | Name of Proprietor | Address of Proprietor |
|---|---|---|---|---|
| 1858 | | | | |
| August 28 | 2 | 114989 | Joseph Webb | Coalbourne Hill Glass Works Stourbridge |
| Sept. 16 | 3 | 115551 to 115553 | Henry Emery | 58 Cheapside, London E.C |
| Oct. 27 | 2 | 116444 | David Jacobs | 33 Haymarket, London |
| Dec. 10 | 5 | 117336 | Edward Ashton | 90 Newman St. Oxford Street |
| 21 | 5 | 117501 | Angus & Greener | Wear Flint Glass Works, Sunderland |
| 1859 | | | | |
| Jany. 1 | 2 | 117763 | Tower & Arrol | 16 Dixon Street Glasgow |
| 4 | 5 | 117809 | Joseph Hutchin | St. Johns Lane Liverpool Biscuit Manufacturer |
| Feby. 11 | 5 | 118467 | Joseph Sedger | 3 Gomm Terrace Rotherhithe in the County of Surrey |
| 21 | 5 | 118630 | Mrs Eliza Hunt | 113 Aldersgate St. Boarding House Keeper |
| March 14 | 5 | 118804 | Robert Cogan | 4 Red Lion Square |
| May 20 | 6 | 119975 | Davis Greathead & Green | of the Flint Glass Works Stourbridge |
| 21 | 4 | 119980 | Finch Hill & Paraire | 1 St. Swithins Lane, King William Street |
| June 14 | 7 | 120332 | James Copcutt | 26 Kirby Street Hatton Garden |
| July 8 | 2 | 120613 | Thomas Dawkins | 4 Little Warner Street Clerkenwell London |
| September 22 | 5 | 122349 | William Leggatt Gilbert | St. Pauls Square Birmingham |
| 23 | 4 | 122368 to 122370 | Tucker and Son | 190 Strand |
| Octr. 26 | 6 | 123473 | J. & F. Lloyd & Co. | 77 Snow Hill London |
| Novr. 25 | 1 | 124288 | Clarke & Timmins | Birmingham |

| Date of Deposit | No. of Parcel | No. of Design | | Name of Proprietor | Address of Proprietor |
|---|---|---|---|---|---|
| 1860 | | | | | |
| Jan^y. 19 | √ 5 | 125806 | 1 | Weston Carel & Symons | 16 Cross St. Newington Butts and |
| " | " | — | | | 13 Old Fish Street Hill St Pauls E. C |
| Feby 4 | √ 7 | 126202 | 1 | Samuel Limobeer | 41 Clayton Street, Caledonian |
| " | " | — | | | Road Islington London |
| 28 | √ 3 | 126847 | 1 | Peter Peel | Birmingham |
| April 14 | √ 4 | 128002 | 1 | Francis Mordan | Goswell Road |
| 18 | √ 8 | 128066 | 1 | James Hinks | Birmingham |
| Septr 5 | √ 1 | 132703 | 1 | Wootton & Powell | Parade Works, Birmingham |
| 25 | √ 3 | 133418 | 1 | Francis Spark | 144 Oxford Street W |
| Nov. 10 | √ 7 | 135384 | 1 | George Benton of Birmingham and James Henry Stone of | |
| " | " | — | | Birmingham trading under the Firm of Benton & Stone | |
| 23 | √ 6 | 136029 | 1 | James Lewis | 6 Bartlett's Buildings and |
| " | " | — | | | 66 Oxford Street |
| 1861 | | | | | |
| Jan^y 3 | √ 2 | 137154 | | James Syson Nibbs | 31 Harford Street Birmingham |
| 26 | √ 2 | 137646 | 1 | James Hinks | Birmingham |
| Feby 12 | √ 4 | 138254 | 1 | George Mathieson | 126 Bothwell St, Glasgow |
| March 6 | √ 10 | 138724 | 1 | David Kinnyand Robert Brown | Union St Glasgow |
| 14 | √ 4 | 138947 | 1 | James Hinks | Birmingham |
| 20 | √ 10 | 139075 | 2 | S Defries & Sons | Houndsditch |
| " | " | 139076 | | | |
| 28 | √ 4 | 139266 | 1 | Weston Carel & Co | 16 Cross Street Newington Butts |
| Classes III & IV 30 | √ 1 | 139286 | 5 | J. & J. D. Cooke | 56 Wellington Street, Glasgow |
| do do " | " | to | | | |
| do do " | " | 139290 | | | |
| April 8 | √ 6 | 139493 | 1 | R. W. Winfield & Son | Birmingham |
| 24 | √ 2 | 140188 | 1 | Frederic Lewis | 6 Fleet Street Dublin |
| May 23 | √ 1 | 140932 | 1 | Edward Morris | Castle Street Reading |

| Date of Deposit | No. of Parcel | No. of Design | | Name of Proprietor | Address of Proprietor |
|---|---|---|---|---|---|
| 1861 | | | | | |
| June 5 | √ 7 | 141261 | 2 | Dobson & Pearce | 19 St James's Street, London. |
| " | " | 2 | | | |
| 27 | √ 1 | 141573 | 1 | Edward Moore & Compy | The Tyne Flint Glass Works, South Shields |
| " | | — | | | |
| 29 | √ 4 | 141642 | 1 | Edwd Moore & Co | Tyne Flint Glass Works |
| " | | — | | | South Shields |
| August 5 | √ 3 | 142371 | 1 | Pearce & Compy | 9 Brooke Street, Holborn |
| 21 | 3 | 142814 | 2 | Frederic Lewis | 6 Fleet Street Dublin |
| | | 142815 | | | |
| Decr 12 | √ 5 | 144545 | 1 | Edwin Martin Thornton | 6 Brooke Street Holborn |
| 19 | √ 4 | 144792 | 1 | David H. Lewis | 64 Crown St Finsbury Square |
| 1862 | | — | | | |
| Jan^y 13 | √ 4 | 148562 | 1 | Robert Hennell & Sons | 14 Northumberland Street |
| Feby 12 | √ 5 | 149306 | 1 | Henry Chatwin | 30 Darwin Street Birmingham |
| " 22 | √ 7 | 149521 | 2 | Isaac Barnes | 44 Cambridge Street |
| | | 149522 | | | Birmingham |
| 24 | √ 6 | 149561 | 1 | James Syson Nibbs | Upper Hockley Street Birmingham |
| March 3 | √ 9 | 149776 | 1 | Cross & Blackwell | [illegible] |
| April 7 | √ 10 | 150512 | 2 | Crosse & Blackwell | 20 and 21 Soho Square |
| " | " | 150513 | | | |
| 8 | √ 6 | 150526 | 1 | William Johnston | 49 Mitchell Street, Glasgow |
| 11 | √ 6 | 150809 | 1 | Mercer Hampson Simpson Junior | Birmingham |
| 28 | √ 6 | 151261 | 5 | Dobson & Pearce | 19 St James's Street S.W. |
| " | | to | | | |
| " | | 151265 | | | |
| May 7 | √ 1 | 151468 | | Robinson Donald & Co | Bothwell Lane, West Campbell St |
| Classes III & IV | | — | | | Glasgow |
| 9 | √ 10 | 151570 to 151572 | 3 | R. W. Winfield & Son | Birmingham |

| Date of Deposit | No of Parcel | No. of Design | Name of Proprietor | Address of Proprietor |
|---|---|---|---|---|
| 1862 | | | | |
| May 20 | 5 | 151915 | 1 Dobson & Pearce | 19 St James's Street |
| | 6 | 151916 | 1 Thomas March | Lord Chamberlain's Office St James's Palace |
| June 12 | 6 | 152426 | 1 A W Digby & Co | 8 Church Passage, London Ink Manufacturers |
| 25 | 2 | 152722 | 1 Alfred Dunn of the Firm of Naylor & Co | 7 Princes Street, Cavendish Square. |
| Augst 16 | 6 | 153022 | Messenger & Sons | Birmingham |
| Septr 9 | 6 | 154589 | 1 Robert Woods | 6 Angel & Porter Court Golden Lane Saint Lukes |
| Octr 1 | 3 | 155257 | 1 Elizer Edwards | Birmingham |
| 16 | 5 | 156470 to 156472 | 3 Alfred Dunn of the Firm of Naylor & Co of 7 Princes Street, Cavendish Square | — |
| 23 | 3 | 156712 | 1 Johnston Fraser & Co | 78 Gordon Street Glasgow |
| [illegible] | 9 | 156718 | 1 George Piercy Tye | 107 Gt Charles Street Birmingham |
| Decr 10 | 4 | 158231 | James Hinks & Son | Birmingham |
| 15 | 6 | 158400 / 1 | 2 Defries & Sons | Houndsditch, London |
| " | 7 | 158402 | 1 S. Mordan & Co | 22 City Road London E.C |
| 1863 | | | | |
| March 26 | 5 | 160895 | 1 S. Mordan | Albion Works City Road London |
| April 8 | 7 | 161282 | 1 Napoleon Price | 158 New Bond Street London |
| May 12 | 3 | 162269 | 1 Dobson & Pearce | 19 St James's St S.W |
| June 9 | 2 | 163192 | 1 Isaac Barnes | Birmingham |
| 16 | 5 | 163551 | 1 Dobson & Pearce | 19 St James's Street |
| July 1 | 4 | 163900 | 1 Isaac Barnes | Birmingham |
| 8 | 8 | 164119 | 1 Bewley & Draper | 23 Mary St, Dublin |

| Date of Deposit | No of Parcel | No. of Design | Name of Proprietor | Address of Proprietor |
|---|---|---|---|---|
| 1863 | | | | |
| July 9 | 8 | 164138 | 1 E. Edwards | Birmingham |
| Octobr 16 | 5 | 167365 / 167366 | 2 Alfred Dunn of the Firm of Naylor & Co | 7 Princes Street, Cavendish Square, London. |
| Novr 4 | 8 | 168189 | 1 Nicolas Jacquet | 3 Rue de la Paix Paris |
| 5 | 5 | 168202 | 1 Hodd & Linley | 31 Hatton Garden |
| 25 | 6 | 169480 | 1 Hodd & Linley | 31 Hatton Garden |
| Decr 8 | 6 | 169986 | 1 Septimus [illegible] | 2 New Bond Street |
| 24 | 6 | 170523 / 4 | 2 I. Defries & Sons | 147 Houndsditch |
| 26 | 1 | 170526 | 1 I. Defries & Sons | 147 Houndsditch |
| 1864 | | | | |
| Jany 11 | 11 | 170914 | 1 The Tutbury Glass Company | Tutbury, Staffordshire & 190 High Holborn, London |
| Feby 6 | 6 | 171561 / 2 | 2 Alfred Dunn of the Firm of Naylor & Co | 7 Princes Street Cavendish Square London |
| March 8 | 1 | 172348 / 9 / 172350 / 1 / 2 | 5 Dobson & Pearce | 19 St James's Street, Piccadilly |
| 10 | 11 | 172601 | 1 James Lewis | 6 Bartlett's Buildings Holborn London |
| May 11 | 6 | 174479 | 1 Frederic Lewis | 6 Fleet Street Dublin |
| Classes III & IV 25 | 4 | 174857 | 1 Emily Temple | 104 Regent Street |
| June 8 | 5 | 175314 | 1 Swan & Co | 4 Skinner Place Sise Lane London |
| 14 | 4 | 175421 | 1 James Derbyshire & Bro. | Hulme, Manchester. |
| 15 | 3 | 175494 | 1 Samuel & Charles Bishop | Flint Glass Works St Helens Lancashire |

| Date of Deposit | No. of Parcel | No. of Design | | Name of Proprietor | Address of Proprietor |
|---|---|---|---|---|---|
| 1864 | | | | | |
| June 1[illegible] | 7 | 175749 / 175750 | 2 | Dobson & Pearce | 19 St James's Street, Piccadilly. S.W. |
| " 21 | 8 | 175803 | 1 | Dobson & Pearce | 19 St James's St. ~~Piccadilly~~, S.W. |
| July 2 | 5 | 175901 | | Johnston Fraser & Co. | Glasgow. |
| 6 | 3 | 175994 | | [illegible] & Co. | [illegible] Street, Birmingham |
| 9 | 4 | 176103 | | Johnston, Fraser & Co. | Glasgow. |
| 13 | 5 | 176308 | 1 | John Burgess & Son | 107 Strand London |
| August 17 | 6 | 177744 | 1 | George Robinson | Parkfield Glass Works near Stourbridge |
| 27 | 4 | 178045 / 178046 | 2 | Molineux & Webb | Manchester. |
| Octr 1[illegible] | 3 | 17[illegible] | 1 | Boulton & Mills | Audnam Glass Works, Stourbridge |
| 24 | 7 | 180385 | 1 | [illegible] Davies & Son | 147 [illegible] |
| Novr 2 | 1 | 180696 | 1 | Andrew Smith | 132 [illegible], Glasgow. |
| [illegible] | 4 | 180999 | 1 | James Derbyshire & Brother | Hulme, Manchester. |
| 8 | 2 | 181208 | | Richard Hunt | [illegible] Road. |
| 10 | 2 | 181514 | | James Lewis | [illegible] Buildings [illegible] |
| Dec. 10 | 7 | 182248 | 1 | James Derbyshire & Brother | Hulme, Manchester. |
| 22 | 6 | 1824[illegible] | | Molineux, Webb & Co. | Manchester |

| Date of Deposit | No. of Parcel | No. of Design | | Name of Proprietor | Address of Proprietor |
|---|---|---|---|---|---|
| 1865 | | | | | |
| Jany 18 | 1 | 18335[illegible] / 18335[illegible] | 2 | Percival, Yates and Vickers. | British & Foreign Flint Glass Works, Manchester |
| February 14 | 8 | 183953 | 1 | Alfred Edmund Edwardes | Alma Cottage, Twickenham Green, Middlesex. |
| Classes I & IV also | | — | | | |
| March [illegible] | [illegible] | [illegible] / [illegible] | 2 | [illegible] & Co. | [illegible] Baker St. W. and [illegible] |
| 21 | 6 | 185330 | 1 | Percival, Yates & Vickers | [illegible] Street, Manchester |
| 31 | 2 | [illegible] | 1 | [illegible] | [illegible] Street, [illegible] |
| April [illegible] | 8 | [illegible] | 1 | [illegible] & Co. | Regent Street, London. |
| 24 | 5 | [illegible] | 1 | [illegible] Bishop & Co. | St Helens Lancashire |
| May 1 | 7 | 186461 | 1 | Alderson Higginbottom and Company | Cockhedge Glass Works Warrington, Lancashire |
| | 8 | [illegible] / [illegible] | 2 | Molineux Webb & Co. | Manchester |
| 3 | 1 | 186478 | 1 | Hodgetts, Richardson & Pargeter | Wordsley Nr Stourbridge |
| 12 | 6 | 180808 | 1 | Molineux & Webb | Manchester. Glass Manufacturers |
| 16 | 4 | 186847 | 1 | Jas. Derbyshire & Brother. | Hulme, Manchester |
| 29 | 8 | 187182 / 187183 | 2 | Molineux, Webb & Co. | Manchester. |
| 30 | 4 | 187204 | 1 | James Hinks and Son | Great Hampton Street Birmingham |
| June 14 | 3 | 187536 | 1 | Robinson & Bolton | Warrington |
| 23 | 3 | 187749 | 1 | Dobson & Pearce | 19 St James's Street S.W. |
| 25 | 6 | 188496 | 1 | James Walker | 5&6 Raven Row, Spitalfields |
| August 15 | 4 | 189066 | 1 | James Derbyshire & Brother | Hulme. Manchester |
| 18 | 4 | 189121 / 189122 | 2 | Percival, Yates & Vickers | Manchester |
| 25 | 6 | 189321 | 1 | Jas. Derbyshire & Brother | Hulme Manchester |

| Date of Deposit | Parcel | Design | Name of Proprietor | Address of Proprietor |
|---|---|---|---|---|
| 1865 | | | | |
| September 5 | 1 | 189511 to 189513 | 3 George Burt | 33 Lower Temple Street Birmingham |
| 7 | 3 | 189534 | 1 Mohr & Smith | Birmingham |
| 11 | 1 | 189615, 189616 | 2 Robinson & Bolton | Orford Lane Glass Works Warrington Lancashire |
| 12 | 2 | 189705 | 1 James Derbyshire and Brother | Hulme Manchester Glass Manufacturers |
| 21 | 10 | 189948 | 1 David Jacobs | 33 Haymarket London |
| 29 | 5 | 190325 | 1 John Henry Weston | 65 Kennington Road Lambeth |
| Octr 4 | 4 | 190755, 190756, 190757, 190758 | 4 Molineaux, Webb & Co | Manchester |
| 23 | 4 | 191244 | 1 Richard Gent | 27 Oval Hackney Road |
| 31 | 8 | 191555 | 1 Molineaux Webb & Co | Manchester |
| Novr 4 | 4 | 191995 | 1 Franz Steigerwald & Co | 1 Godliman Street & 19 Great Carter Lane Saint Pauls |
| 6 | 3 | 192008 | 1 Richard Gent | 27 Oval Hackney Road |
| 23 | 8 | 192790, 192791 | 2 Hall & Dulson | St Pauls Square Birmingham |
| " | 9 | 192792 | 1 David Henry Jacobs | 64 Crown Street Finsbury |
| 29 | 10 | 192966 | 1 Thomas Norman | 14 Little Britain City |
| December 6 | 4 | 193264 | 1 Crosse & Blackwell | Soho Square |
| 14 | 5 | 193419 | 1 James Derbyshire & Brother | Hulme Manchester |
| " | 6 | 193420 | 1 James Couper & Sons | The City Flint Glass Works Glasgow |

| Date of Deposit | No of Parcel | No. of Design | Name of Proprietor | Address of Proprietor |
|---|---|---|---|---|
| 1866 | | | | |
| Jany 18 | 6 | 194616 to 194618 | 3 Molineaux Webb & Co | Manchester |
| 20 | 2 | 194685 | 1 Molineaux Webb & Co | Manchester |
| 30 | 7 | 194825 | 1 Molineaux Webb & Co | Manchester |
| 31 | 8 | 194844 | 1 William Brooke | Leeds Yorkshire, Glass Manufacturer |
| Feby 1 | 9 | 194871 | 1 W. B. Tate | 47 Seward Street EC |
| 2 | 6 | 194948 | 1 D. Hulett & Co | 55 High Holborn WC |
| 15 | 2 | 195262 | 1 Molineaux Webb & Co | Manchester |
| 17 | 1 | 195272 | 1 Robinson & Bolton | Orford Lane Glass Works Warrington Lancashire |
| March 1 | 5 | 195623 | 1 Kenny & Brown | [illegible] Street Glasgow |
| " | 10 | 195639 | 1 Dobson & Pearce | 19 St James's Street |
| 16 | 6 | 195936 | 1 J & C Bishop & Co | St Helens Lancashire |
| 27 | 1 | 196244 | 1 James Green | 35 & 36 Upper Thames Street London |
| April 6 | 4 | 196366 to 196368 | 3 James Hayward Mackay | 6 Motcomb Street, Belgrave Square London |
| 7 | 6 | 196419, 196420 | 2 Alfred Arculus | Birmingham |
| 21 | 5 | 196684 | 1 Richard Gent | 27 Oval Hackney Road |
| May 2 | 2 | 197022 | 1 Richard Gent | 27 Oval Hackney Road London |
| 4 | 6 | 197096 | 1 Thomas Charles March | Ambassador's Court St James's Palace |
| 8 | 2 | 197154 | 1 Eliezer Edwards | 49 St Paul's Square Birmingham |
| 10 | 4 | 197298 | 1 McDermott Connolly & Co | Pipewellgate Gateshead-on-Tyne |
| 22 | 17 | 197656, 197657 | 2 Thomas Charles March | Ambassador's Court St James's Palace |
| 24 | 1 | 197703, 197704 | 2 Angus & Greener | Wear Flint Glass Works Sunderland |

| Date of Deposit | No of Parcel | No. of Design | Name of Proprietor | Address of Proprietor |
|---|---|---|---|---|
| 1866 | | | | |
| June 16 | 4 | 198277 | 1. James Derbyshire & Brother | Bridgewater Flint-Glass Works, Hulme, Manchester |
| " | 5 | 198278 | 1 Woodall Tern & Woodall | Birmingham |
| August 15 | 8 | 199959 | 1. Joseph Perkins Teagle & Edwin Martin | 3 John Street, Cornwall Road, Lambeth S |
| 25 | 6 | 200233 | 1. Angus & Greener | Wear Flint Glass Works, Sunderland |
| Septr 22 | 5 | 201546 | 1. Eugene Rimmel | 96 Strand |
| 26 | 5 | 201705 | 1. George Fisher | 87 Murray Street New North Road London |
| Octr 12 | 1 | 202372 | 1 Eugene Rimmel | 96 Strand |
| Novr 10 | 6 | 203523 | 1. S & C Bishop & Co | St Helens Lancashire |
| 28 | 5 | 204182 | 1. Michael & Lewis Beck | 7 [illegible] Street Bishopsgate [illegible] |
| Dec 2[illegible] | 3 | 215210 | 1. Hodgetts, Richardson & Pargeter | Wordsley near Stourbridge |
| 29 | 1 | 205228 | 1. Pellatt & Co | 25 Baker Street Portman Square |
| 1867 | | | | |
| Jany 5 | 6 | 205330 | 1. Pellatt & Co | 25 Baker Street |
| 11 | 8 | 205511 | 1. James Green | 35 and 36 Upper Thames Street, London |
| 26 | 4 | 205812 | 1. Angus & Greener | Wear Flint Glass Works Sunderland |
| Feby 1 | 1 | 205852<br>205853 | 2. Pellatt & Co | 25 Baker Street Portman Square |
| 8 | 7 | 205997 | 1. John Dobson | 19 St James's Street |
| 23 | 9 | 206280 | 1. H. P. Downing | Phoenix Glass Works Helena Street, Birmingham |
| 25 | 5 | 206304 | 1. James Derbyshire & Brother | British Union and Bridgewater Flint Glass Works Hulme Manchester |

| Date of Deposit | No of Parcel | No. of Design | Name of Proprietor | Address of Proprietor |
|---|---|---|---|---|
| 1867 | | | | |
| March 14 | 9 | 206745 | 1. Sidney Brown | 5 Blackfriars Road S. |
| 16 | 3 | 206845 | 1. Thomas Charles March | St James's Palace |
| April 4 | 10 | 207202 | 1 Sidney Brown | 5 Blackfriars Road S. |
| 11 | 5 | 207427 | 1. Mohr & Smith | Birmingham |
| 16 | 7 | 207561 | 1. James Lewis | Bartlett's Buildings, Holborn London |
| ~~May 21~~ | ~~7~~ | ~~208421~~ | ~~1. Richard Gent~~ | ~~[illegible] Hackney Road~~ |
| May 1 | 2 | 208419<br>208420 | 2. James Hinks & Son | Birmingham |
| " | 3 | 208421 | 1. Richard Gent | 27 [illegible] Hackney Road |
| 22 | 10 | 208455 | 1 S & C. Bishop & Co | St Helens Lancashire |
| 28 | 5 | 208519 | 1 James Hinks & Son | Birmingham |
| June 7 | 7 | 208779 | 1 Samuel Chandler & Son | 110 Brook Street Lambeth |
| 24 | 3 | 209086 | 1. Molineaux Webb & Co | Kirby Street Manchester |
| 26 | 8 | 209161 | 1. Angus & Greener | The Wear Flint Glass Works Sunderland |
| 29 | 4 | 209222 | 1 John Whitehouse & Sons | 87 Birchall Street Birmingham |
| July 2 | 4 | 209332 | 1. J M Johnson & Sons | 3 Castle Street Holborn and 56 Hatton Garden London |
| 16 | 2 | 209574<br>209575 | 2. Percival Vickers & Co (Limited) | Manchester |
| August 10 | 3 | 210199 | 1. Molineaux Webb & Co | Manchester |
| 16 | 5 | 210325 | 1. William Blamire Tate | 47 Seward Street Goswell Street London |
| 26 | 5 | 210484 | 1. Molineaux Webb & Co | Manchester |
| 30 | 3 | 210619 | 1. Napoleon Montanari | 12 Langford Road, Kentish Town N.W. and Batignolles, Paris. |
| Septr 10 | 4 | 210941<br>210942 | 2 Molineaux Webb & Co | Manchester |
| Octr 18 | 4 | 212432 | 1. Peter Robinson & Bolton | Warrington |

| Date of Deposit | No. of Parcel | No. of Design | Name of Proprietor | Address of Proprietor |
|---|---|---|---|---|
| 1867 | | | | |
| Octr 19 | 4 | 212674 to 212677 | 4. Thomas Webb & Sons | Stourbridge Glass Works Stourbridge |
| Novr 14 | 5 | 213851 | 1. Richardson & Smith | Stourbridge |
| 25 | 6 | 214321 | 1. Frederick Cadby | Newhall Street Birmingham |
| 26 | 9 | 214357 / 214358 | 2. Angus & Greener | Wear Flint Glass Works Sunderland |
| Decr 2 | 4 | 214597 | 1. Edward Webb | Wordsley Stourbridge |
| 21 | 6 | 215150 | 1. Edward Jackson Hollidge | Symond's Inn, Chancery Lane London |
| 1868 | | | | |
| Jany 13 | 1 | 215734 | 1. Molineaux Webb & Co | Manchester |
| 17 | 11 | 215917 | 1. Frances Mordan | Albion Works, City Road London |
| 31 | 9 | 216348 | 1. Molineaux Webb & Co | Manchester |
| " | 13 | 216361 / 216362 | 2. S&C Bishop & Co | St Helens Lancashire |
| Feby 8 | 4 | 216632 | 1. Molineaux Webb & Co | Manchester |
| 21 | 4 | 216996 / 216997 | 2. S. Defries & Sons | Houndsditch London |
| 27 | 6 | 217101 | 1. Gustav Böhm | Offenbach Germany & 3 & 4 Aldermanbury London |
| 28 | 4 | 217107 to 217109 | 3. The Tutbury Glass Company | Tutbury Staffordshire |
| March 5 | 11 | 217207 | 1. Edward Moore & Co | Tyne Flint Glass Works, South Shields |
| 6 | 7 | 217227 | 1. Percival, Vickers & Co (Limited) | Manchester |

| Date of Deposit | No. of Parcel | No. of Design | Name of Proprietor | Address of Proprietor |
|---|---|---|---|---|
| 1868 | | | | |
| March 27 | 6 | 217676 | 1. Phillips & Pearce | 155 New Bond Street, London |
| 30 | 7 | 217715 | 1. [illegible] Rappolt & Co | 1A Savoy Street, Strand, London |
| April 1 | 7 | 217724 | 1. Angus & Greener | Wear Flint Glass Works, Sunderland |
| 29 | 7 | 218486 | 1. Ker, Webb & Co | Prussia Street Flint Glass Works Manchester |
| May 4 | 6 | 218561 | 1. Angus and Greener | Wear Flint Glass Works. Sunderland |
| May 21 | 11 | 218866 | 1. Berman and Wild | 53 and 54 Aldermanbury E.C. |
| 29 | 8 | 218984 | 1. Frederick Cadby | Newhall Street, Birmingham |
| " | 11 | 218988 | 1. James Derbyshire & Brothers | British Union & Flint Glass Works, Hulme Manchester |
| June 6 | 2 | 219163 to 219165 | 3. Berman & Wild | 53 & 54 Aldermanbury London |
| 11 | 6 | 219303 | 1. S & C Bishop & Co | St Helens Lancashire |
| July 11 | 4 | 219769 | 1. Molineaux Webb & Co | Kirby Street, Ancoats, Manchester |
| 20 | 1 | 220059 | 1. Henry Durandu | 27 Dale Street Liverpool |
| August 1 | 1 | 220230 | 1. Edward Tombs | 35 St Helena Street Goswell Road |
| 6 | 8 | 220317 | 1. Richard Gent | 27 Oval, Hackney Road London |
| 20 | 6 | 220098 to 220900 | 3. Molineaux Webb & Co | Kirby Street Manchester |
| Sept 4 | 7 | 221205 | 1. Frederick Travis | Liverpool in the County of Lancaster, Oil Merchant |
| 5 | 7 | 221220 | 1. S&C Bishop & Co | St Helens, Lancashire |
| 10 | 8 | 221497 | 1. Kerr, Webb & Co | Prussia Street Glass Works Manchester |
| " | 9 | 221498 | 1. Boulton & Mills | Audnam Glass Works Stourbridge |

| Date of Deposit | No of Parcel | No. of Design | Name of Proprietor | Address of Proprietor |
|---|---|---|---|---|
| 1868 | | | | |
| Septr 12 | 2 | 221520 | 1 E Edwards | 49 St Paul's Square Birmingham |
| 15 | 5 | 221563 | 1 Isidore Leveaux & Co | 7 Crutched Friars City |
| 17 | 5 | 221689 | 1 Angus & Greener | Wear Flint Glass Works, Sunderland |
| " | " | — | | |
| 19 | 5 | 221795 | 1 Percival Vickers & Co Limited | Jersey Street Manchester |
| " | " | — | | |
| Octr 13 | 5 | 222546 | 1 H W & L Dee | 8 Sherwood Street |
| 21 | 7 | 223307 | 1 S Defries & Sons | Houndsditch |
| 23 | 4 | 223322 | 1 Percival Vickers & Co Limited | Jersey Street Manchester |
| " | " | — | | |
| Novr 6 | 11 | 224027 | 1 James Lewis | Bartlett's Buildings, Holborn London |
| " | — | | | |
| Decr 2 | 7 | 225010 | 1 S Maw & Son | 11 and 12 Aldersgate Street |
| 4 | 16 | 225286 | 1 McMaster Hodgson & Co | 121-2 Capel Street Dublin |
| 14 | 6 | 225440 | 1 Percival Vickers & Co (Limited) | Jersey Street Manchester |
| " | " | — | | |
| 21 | 4 | 225673 | 1 Percival Vickers & Co (Limited) | Jersey Street Manchester |
| " | " | — | | |
| 30 | 4 | 225972 | 1 Elijah Atkins | Birmingham |
| 1869 | | | | |
| Jany 1 | 9 | 226052 | 1 S & C Bishop & Co | St Helens Lancashire |
| 20 | 5 | 226509 | 2 Elijah Atkins | 48 Great Hampton Street Birmingham |
| " | " | 226510 | | |
| 28 | 8 | 226743 | 1 Thomas Padmore & Sons | Birmingham |
| Feby 1 | 12 | 226916 | 2 Molineaux Webb & Co | Kirby Street Manchester |
| " | " | 226917 | | |
| 11 | 1 | 227266 | 1 Charles Joseph King | 14 Queenhithe, Upper Thames Street E.C |
| " | " | — | | |
| " | 8 | 227274 | 1 Thomas Wesley | 56 Inge Street, Birmingham |
| " | " | — | | |

| Date of Deposit | No of Parcel | No. of Design | Name of Proprietor | Address of Proprietor |
|---|---|---|---|---|
| 1869 | | | | |
| Feby 22 | 12 | 227410 | 1 James Derbyshire & Brother | Hulme, Manchester |
| 24 | 4 | 227429 | 2 Elijah Atkins | 48 Great Hampton Street Birmingham |
| " | " | 227430 | | |
| March 24 | 7 | 228147 | 2 S & C Bishop & Co | St Helens, Lancashire |
| " | " | 8 | | |
| 27 | 1 | 228202 | 1 Molineaux Webb & Co | Kirby Street Manchester |
| 31 | 2 | 228286 | 2 H W & L Dee | 8 Sherwood Street |
| " | " | 228287 | | |
| April 5 | 3 | 228427 | 1 John Sharp | [illegible] |
| 13 | 7 | 228612 | 1 James Derbyshire & Brother | Hulme Manchester |
| 20 | 9 | 228782 | 1 Angus & Greener | The Wear Flint Glass Works Sunderland |
| " | " | — | | |
| 26 | 5 | 228889 | 1 Percival Vickers & Co | Jersey Street Manchester |
| May 20 | 7 | 229522 | 1 C A & E Speyer & Co | 35 Monkwell Street City E C |
| June 8 | 6 | 229958 | 1 W. P. & G Phillips & Pearce | 155 New Bond Street, London |
| " | " | — | | |
| July 1 | 6 | 230596 | 1 Ker Webb & Co | Prussia Street Glass Works, Manchester |
| 2 | 6 | 230631 | 1 Loewenthal & Hesse | 110 Portland Street Manchester |
| 5 | 3 | 230716 | 1 Edward Bolton | Orford Lane Glass Works Warrington |
| 6 | 9 | 230802 | 1 William Thomas Tongue | Wolverhampton Factor in the County of Stafford |
| " | " | — | | |
| 31 | 8 | 231430 | 1 Henry Greener | The Wear Flint Glass Works Sunderland |
| " | " | — | | |
| August 12 | 8 | 231927 | 1 Henry Greener | The Wear Flint Glass Works Sunderland |
| " | " | — | | |
| 26 | 5 | 232473 | 1 Sidney Brown | 8 Blackfriars Road S E |
| Septr 9 | 6 | 232893 | 1 Insell & Baker | Birmingham |
| 13 | 8 | 233022 to 233024 | 3 Henry Brauerrichter & Co | 12 Allen Street Goswell Street E.C |

| Date of Deposit | No. of Parcel | No. of Design | Name of Proprietor | Address of Proprietor |
|---|---|---|---|---|
| 1869 | | | | |
| Sept 15 | 5 | 233092 | 1 Sidney Brown | 8 Blackfriars Road SE |
| 27 | 6 | 233716 | 1 Henry Bauerrichter & Co | 12 Allen Street Goswell Street E.C |
| Octr 16 | 3 | 234517 | 1 Percival Vickers & Co Limited | Jersey Street Manchester |
| 19 | 8 | 234789 | 1 Eugene Rimmel | 96 Strand London |
| 28 | 1 | 235182 | 1 F Fletcher | 6 Charles Street Commercial Road Peckham |
| Novr 2 | 1 | 235568 | 1 Richard Gent | 27 Oval Hackney Road |
| 3 | 11 | 235690 | 1 A Kenyon | Holt Town Glass Works Every Street Manchester |
| 4 | 9 | 235710<br>235711 | 2 James Lewis | Bartletts Buildings Holborn |
| 6 | 3 | 235821 | 1 Percival Vickers & Co Limited | Manchester |
| 10 | 6 | 236001 | 1 R. Gent | 27 Oval, Hackney Road Hackney |
| " | 7 | 236002 | 1 Ker Webb & Co | Prussia Street Glass Works Manchester |
| 16 | 13 | 236235 | 1 Sidney Brown | 8 Blackfriars Road S.E |
| Decr 7 | 7 | 236921 | 1 Henry Greener | Wear Flint Glass Works Sunderland |
| 14 | 3 | 237141 | 1 James Couper & Sons | City Flint Glass Works Glasgow |
| 15 | 4 | 237158 | 1 Lloyd & Summerfield | Birmingham |
| 18 | 1 | 237228 | 1 Johnston Fraser & Co | 78 Gordon Street Glasgow |
| 23 | 8 | 237550 | 1 Percival Vickers & Co Limited | Manchester |
| 1870 | | | | |
| Jany 3 | 3 | 237741 | 1 Molineaux Webb & Co | Kirby Street Ancoats Manchester |
| 7 | 4 | 237893 | 1 E. H. Downes | 13 Smithy Door Manchester |
| 12 | 8 | 238052 | 1 Hodgetts, Richardson & Pargeter | Wordsley Glass Works Stourbridge |

| Date of Deposit | No. of Parcel | No. of Design | Name of Proprietor | Address of Proprietor |
|---|---|---|---|---|
| 1870 | | | | |
| Jany 14 | 11 | 238105 | 1 Henry Greener | Wear Flint Glass Works Sunderland |
| 15 | 10 | 238115 | 1 Edward Bolton | Warrington Lancashire Glass Manufacturer |
| " | 11 | 238131 | 1 J. J. Hicks | 8 Hatton Garden London |
| 28 | 6 | 238431 | 1 Edward Bolton | Warrington Glass Manufacturer |
| Feby 3 | 12 | 238593<br>238594 | 2 Boulton & Mills | Audnam Glass Works Stourbridge |
| 7 | 11 | 238637 | 1 William Thomas Standish | [illegible] Baker Street London |
| 8 | 9 | 238658 | 1 Leon Pyke | 4 Great Russell Street E |
| 16 | 7 | 238916 | 1 James Hateley | Birmingham |
| 21 | 7 | 239056 | 1 Jones Petre & Co | 34 Charlotte Street Fitzroy Square |
| 22 | 4 | 239084 | 1 Molineaux Webb & Co | [illegible] Manchester |
| 24 | 9 | 239136 | 1 Burtles Tate & Co | [illegible] Manchester |
| 28 | 8 | 239241<br>239242 | 2 Hodgetts, Richardson & Pargeter | Wordsley Glass Works Stourbridge |
| March 22 | 3 | 239748 | 1 Joseph Ratcliff & Sons | [illegible] Birmingham |
| 26 | 8 | 240010 | 1 Percival Vickers & Co Limited | Jersey Street Manchester |
| April 2 | 4 | 240217 | 1 Molineaux Webb & Co | Kirby Street Manchester |
| 29 | 7 | 241052 | 1 William Henry Gretton | 3½ Holland Street Blackfriars Road S.E |
| ~~[illegible]~~ | ~~8~~ | ~~241053~~ | ~~1 Sandbach & Co~~ | ~~64 Deansgate Manchester~~ |
| May 5 | 11 | 241259 | 1 Alfred Arculus | Birmingham |
| 19 | 11 | 241590 | 1 Peter Bicker Caarton | 30 Northumberland Place, Bayswater |
| 26 | 6 | 241961 | 1 Molineaux Webb & Co | Kirby Street Ancoats Manchester |
| " | 8 | 241963<br>241964 | 2 Gustav Boehm | 3 & 4 Aldermanbury London |
| 27 | 10 | 242010 | 1 Gustav Boehm | 3 & 4 Aldermanbury London |

| Date of Deposit | No. of Parcel | No. of Design | Name of Proprietor | Address of Proprietor |
|---|---|---|---|---|
| 1870 | | | | |
| June 10 | 4 | 242418 | 1 Frederick Cadby | 65A Mitchall Street Birmingham |
| 21 | 3 | 242570 | 1 J J & T Derbyshire | Hulme Manchester |
| 23 | 2 | 242642 | 1 James Hickifson | 75 Southgate Road, London |
| July 6 | 2 | 242968 to 242970 | 3 Molineaux Webb & Co | Kirby Street, Manchester |
| 18 | 4 | 243267 | 1 James Bond | 75 Southgate Road London |
| August 1 | 1 | 243554 | 1 Percival Vickers & Co Limited | Jersey Street Manchester |
| 29 | 7 | 244354 | 1 Loewenthal & Hesse | [illegible] Manchester |
| Septr 1 | 6 | 244491 | 1 W Gammon & Co | Belmont Glass Works Birmingham |
| 13 | 8 | 244871 | 1 Allen & Baker | Speaking Stile Walk Birmingham |
| 22 | 7 | 245051 to 245052 | 2 Edward Hand Jefferys | Havelock Works Sheffield |
| Octr 6 | 1 | 245563 | 1 Frederick Kingston Gurney, John Henry Gurney | 13 Woodstock Street Bond Street W |
| 12 | 5 | 245730 | 1 S. Barnett | 23 Fasten Street Hoxton London N. |
| 22 | 6 | 246153 | 1 Hodgetts Richardson & Pargeter | Wordsley Glass Works Stourbridge |
| 27 | 8 | 246394 | 1 Richard Gene | 27 Oval Hackney Road |
| Novr 1 | 5 | 246500 | 1 Chance & Malin | [illegible] Birmingham |
| 4 | 7 | 246924 | 1 F W & E Lee | 8 Sherwood Street London |
| 10 | 11 | 247081 | 1 Henry Greener | The Wear Flint Glass Works Sunderland |
| 14 | 10 | 247322 | 1 James Lewis | 6 Bartlett's Buildings Holborn |
| 18 | 2 | 247463 to 247464 | 2 Molineaux Webb & Co | Kirby Street Manchester |
| 22 | 4 | 247945 | 1 Henry Thacker & Co | New Street Square EC |
| 23 | 6 | 247983 | 1 Walter Thornhill | 144 New Bond Street |
| Dec 9 | 9 | 248459 | 1 Saml C. Bishop & Co | St Helens Lancashire |

| Date of Deposit | No. of Parcel | No. of Design | Name of Proprietor | Address of Proprietor |
|---|---|---|---|---|
| 1870 | | | | |
| Dec 23 | 1 | 249039 | 1 Felix Sultana | 17 Poultry EC |
| 24 | 10 | 249099 | 1 S. & C. Bishop and Co | Flint Glass Works St Helens Lancashire |
| 1871 | | | | |
| Jany 17 | 7 | 249600 | 1 Molineaux Webb & Co | Kirby Street Manchester |
| 24 | 3 | 249808 to 249810 | 3 Molineaux Webb & Co | Kirby Street Manchester |
| 25 | 8 | 249882 | 1 Boulton & Mills | Audnam Glass Works, Stourbridge |
| 26 | 4 | 249890 to 249893 | 4 Grégoir Antoin Humanian | 15 Greenwood Street & Corporation Street Manchester |
| 28 | 11 | 249969 | 1 Boulton & Mills | Audnam Glass Works Stourbridge |
| Feby 16 | 5 | 250430 | 1 Blackwood & Co | 18 Bread Street Hill, City EC |
| 24 | 8 | 250600 | 1 Blackwood & Co | [illegible] |
| March 1 | 4 | 250678 | 1 Boulton & Mills | Audnam Glass Works Stourbridge |
| 2 | 8 | 250723 | 1 Henry Greener | [illegible] |
| 8 | 5 | 250835 | 1 Boulton & Mills | Audnam Glass Works Stourbridge |
| 15 | 9 | 251012 | 1 [illegible] | [illegible] |
| 16 | 8 | 251034 | 1 John Bimes & Phillip Pargeter | [illegible] |
| 22 | 3 | 251131 to 251133 | 3 Stuart & Mills | Stourbridge |
| April 29 | 9 | 252159 | 1 Edward Bolton | Orford Lane Glass Works Warrington |
| May 25 | 12 | 252823 | 1 John Henry Wood | 25 Baker Street Portman Square W |
| Annex I, III & IV | | | | |

| Date of Deposit | No. of Parcel | No. of Design | Name of Proprietor | Address of Proprietor |
|---|---|---|---|---|
| 1871 | | | | |
| June 7 | 5 | 253067 | 1 Percival Vickers & Co Limited | Manchester |
| 21 | 6 | 253471 | 1 N Dingwall | 32 Brooke Street Holborn |
| July 17 | 1 | 254050 | 1 Boulton & Mills | Audnam Glass Works Stourbridge |
| 18 | 3 | 254058 | 1 Phillips & Pearce | 155 New Bond Street W |
| August 3 | 7 | 254641 | 1 Henry White Wickins | 6 Gutter Lane Cheapside |
| 17 | 4 | 254864 | 1 Philip Pargeter | Red House Glass Works Stourbridge |
| 22 | 4 | 254993 | 1 William Henry Hewitt | Birmingham |
| Septr 2 | 2 | 255351 | 1 Chance & Malins | Tyndall Works, Camden Street Birmingham |
| " " | | — | | |
| 6 | 7 | 255383 | 1 Ker, Webb & Co | [illegible] Street Glass Works, Manchester |
| 8 | 8 | 255459 | 1 Michael Alexander Dietz trading as Dietz & Co | 17, 19 & 21 Carter Lane in the City of London |
| " " | | – | | |
| 30 | 10 | 256264 | 1 Percival Vickers & Co (Limited) | Jersey Street Manchester |
| Octr 3 | 4 | 256336 | 1 Burtles Tate & Co | Poland Street Manchester |
| 13 | 9 | 256680 | 1 [illegible] Barnes | Birmingham |
| Novr 6 | 9 | 257538 | 1 Loewenthal & Hesse | [illegible] London EC |
| 24 | 10 | 257909 | 1 H. Bock Binko | 3 City Gardens City Road London |
| Decr 7 | 5 | 258445 | 1 Percival Vickers & Co Limited | Jersey Street Manchester |
| 1872 | | | | |
| Jany 5 | 6 | 259270 | 1 James Lewis | Bartletts Buildings Holborn London |
| " " | | — | — | |
| 10 | 8 | 259391 | 1 James Bucklen | 9 Hingeston Street Birmingham |
| " " | | – | | |
| 27 | 12 | 260051 | 1 M Kuhn | 3 Rue Scribe Paris |
| 29 | 11 | 260064 | 1 Akerman, Worrall & Phillips | 6 Chapel Street Pentonville N |
| " " " | | — | | |
| Feby 2 | 1 | 260183 to 260186 | 4. Sowerby & Co | Ellison Glass Works Gateshead-on-Tyne |

| Date of Deposit | No. of Parcel | No. of Design | Name of Proprietor | Address of Proprietor |
|---|---|---|---|---|
| 1872 | | | | |
| Feby 12 | 1 | 260397 | 1 Woodall Keen & Woodall | Birmingham |
| " " | | — | | |
| " | 6 | 260404, 260405 | 2. Sowerby & Co | Ellison Glass Works Gateshead-on-Tyne |
| 15 | 8 | 260472 | 1 Gustav Boehm | 3 & 4 Aldermanbury London |
| 22 | 6 | 260648 to 260650 | 3. Hodgetts, Richardson & Son | Wordsley Glass Works, Stourbridge |
| 29 | 5 | 260802 | 1 Sowerby & Co | Ellison Glass Works Gateshead-on-Tyne |
| " | | — | | |
| March 2 | 12 | 260851 | 1 The Crown Perfumery Company | [illegible] |
| " " | | — | | |
| 14 | 2 | 261125 to 26112[illegible] | 3 Hodgetts, Richardson & Son | Wordsley Glass Works Stourbridge |
| 15 | 8 | 261182 | 1 Akerman, Worrall & Phillips | 6 Chapel Street Pentonville N. |
| " " | | — | | |
| 19 | 6 | 261264 | 1 H. W. Wickins | 6 Gutter Lane Cheapside |
| 25 | 5 | 261445 | 1 J J & T Derbyshire | Bridgewater and Britesh Union Glass Works, Manchester |
| " " | | — | | |
| 28 | 7 | 261532 | 1 W T Copeland & Sons | 160 New Bond Street |
| April 16 | 8 | 261950 | 1 John Frederic Cooke | 105 Cannon Street London |
| 19 | 3 | 262010 | 1 Norton & White | 91 Great Charles Street Birmingham |
| " " | | — | | |
| 23 | 5 | 262193 | 1 Burtles, Tate & Co | Poland Street Oldham Road Manchester |
| " " | | | | |
| May 2 | 7 | 262405 | 1 Percival Vickers & Co Limited | Manchester |
| 11 | 9 | 262680 | 1 J J & T Derbyshire | Bridgewater Glass Works Hulme Manchester |
| " | | — | | |

| Date of Deposit | No. of Parcel | No. of Design | Name of Proprietor | Address of Proprietor |
|---|---|---|---|---|
| 1872 | | | | |
| May 30 | 7 | 263032 | 1. Percival Vickers & Co Limited | Manchester |
| June 11 | 4 | 263314 | 1. Percival Vickers & Co Limited | Manchester |
| 13 | 3 | 263362 | 1. Ker Webb & Co | Prussia Street Glass Works Manchester |
| [illegible] 18 | 2 | 263495 | 1. James Alfred Fussell | 45 Woodcock Street Birmingham |
| 21 | 6 | 263540 | 1. Jane Webb & Joseph Hammond trading as the Executors of the late Joseph Webb | Stourbridge |
| 22 | 1 | 263543 | 1. E A Rippingille | Holborn Hill London |
| July 3 | 7 | 263929 | 1. F S Cleaver & Sons | 32 & 33 Red Lion Street Holborn WC |
| 18 | 6 | 264288 | 1. Robert Sallmann | 69 Liverpool Road London |
| August 28 | 2 | 265528 | 1. John Hanbury | 30 Ladywood Road Birmingham |
| Oct 2 | 8 | 266734 | 1. S Mordan & Co | 41 City Road London |
| Nov 6 | 11 | 267727 | 1. J J & T Derbyshire | Hulme Manchester |
| 7 | 7 | 267742 to 267743 | 2. Sowerby & Co | Gateshead-on-Tyne |
| 19 | 5 | 267990 | 1. Boissière & Ch. Auquenille | La Verrerie du Gast (Orne) France |
| 21 | 12 | 268074 to 268076 | 3. William Singleton | 10 Bakers Hill Sheffield |
| Dec 2 | 7 | 268325 | 1. Akerman Worrall & Phillips | 6 Chapel Street Pentonville |
| 10 | 7 | 268734 | 1. Henry Greener | Wear Flint Glass Works Sunderland |
| 11 | 4 | 268739 | 1. J J & T Derbyshire | Hulme Manchester |
| 13 | 7 | 268786 | 1. Mappin & Webb | 76 & 78 Oxford Street & Royal Cutlery Works Sheffield |

| Date of Deposit | No. of Parcel | No. of Design | Name of Proprietor | Address of Proprietor |
|---|---|---|---|---|
| 1872 | | | | |
| Decr 14 | 8 | 268810 | 1. J J & T Derbyshire & Co | Hulme Manchester |
| 19 | 3 | 268883 to 268884 | 2. Jane Webb and Joseph Hammond trading as the Executors of the late Joseph Webb of Stourbridge. Glass manufacturers | |
| 23 | 3 | 269194 | 1. Percival Vickers & Co Limited | Manchester |
| 1873 | | | | |
| Jany 3 | 4 | 269476 | 1. Ker, Webb & Co | Prussia Street Glass Works Manchester |
| 10 | 3 | 269593 | 1. Charles Joseph King | 7 Holborn Bars E.C. |
| 15 | 4 | 269694 | 1. Percival Vickers & Co Limited | Jersey Street Manchester |
| Feby 1 | 10 | 270083 | 1. William Burrows | Derby |
| 12 | 1 | 270351 | 1. Daniel Pearce | North End Hammersmith |
| 17 | 8 | 270525 | 1. Henry Herbert | 2 Charterhouse Buildings London EC |
| March 5 | 7 | 271027 | 1. Akerman & Worrall | 6 Chapel Street Pentonville |
| 7 | 6 | 271070 to 271072 | 3. D Beck & Co | 12 Hall Street Birmingham |
| 12 | 1 | 271146 | 1. W & T. Mortlock | 19 St James Street London |
| April 5 | 2 | 271867 | 1. Isaac Barnes | 44 [illegible] Street Birmingham |
| 10 | 15 | 272048 | 1. Akerman & Worrall | 6 Chapel Street Pentonville |
| 16 | 14 | 272132 | 1. Jane Webb & Joseph Hammond trading as the Executors of the late Joseph Webb of Stourbridge | |
| 29 | 1 | 272381 to 272382 | 2. Percival Jones | 13 Westmoreland Street Dublin |
| " | 7 | 272424 | 1. Daniel Pearce | North End Works North End Hammersmith |
| May 3 | 9 | 272649 | 1. F.H. Atkins & Co | 62 Fleet Street London WC |

| Date of Deposit | No. of Parcel | No. of Design | Name of Proprietor | Address of Proprietor |
|---|---|---|---|---|
| 1873 | | | | |
| May 7 | 2 | 272685 to 272688 | Percival Vickers & Co Limited | Manchester |
| 16 | 4 | 272981 | Philip Pargeter | Red House Glass Works, Wordsley near Stourbridge |
| 26 | 12 | 273170 | Edward Bolton | Orford Lane Glass Works, Warrington |
| 27 | 5 | 273177 | Boulton & Mills | Audnam Glass Works, Stourbridge |
| " | 6 | 273178 | Ker, Webb & Co | Prussia Street Glass Works, Manchester |
| June 14 | 5 | 273730 | Lloyd & Summerfield | Park Glass Works, Birmingham [illegible] |
| 20 | 13 | 273866 | Sowerby & Co | Ellison Glass Works, Gateshead on Tyne |
| July 31 | 5 | 274743 | Sowerby & Co | Ellison Glass Works, Gateshead on Tyne |
| August 6 | 10 | 274906 to 274910 | H. Barrett | 2 Brecknock Road Camden Road |
| 8 | 7 | 274961 to 274963 | John Derbyshire | Regent Road Flint Glass Works Salford Manchester |
| " | 9 | 274965 | Howes & Burley | Birmingham |
| Sept 2 | 9 | 275756 | John Derbyshire | Regent Road Flint Glass Works Salford Manchester |
| 6 | 2 | 275856 | Hodgetts Richardson & Son | Wordsley Flint Glass Works Stourbridge |
| 25 | 12 | 276524 276525 | James Bromwich | 8 Victoria Buildings Pimlico |

| Date of Deposit | No. of Parcel | No. of Design | Name of Proprietor | Address of Proprietor |
|---|---|---|---|---|
| 1873 | | | | |
| Octr 13 | 1 | 277150 | J. Defries & Sons | 147 Houndsditch City EC |
| 14 | 5 | 277158 | Thomas Riddell | 11 London Place, London Fields Hackney |
| 21 | 8 | 277328 | George Busby | Aston near Birmingham |
| 28 | 5 | 277629 | Thomas Riddell | 11 London Place, London Fields Hackney |
| " | 4 | 277630 | | |
| 31 | 12 | 277834 | Daniel Pearce | North End Villa, Hammersmith [illegible] |
| Novr 3 | 13 | 277869 | Akerman & Rorrall | 6 Chapel Street Pentonville |
| 13 | 8 | 278266 | Percival Vickers & Co Limited | Jersey Street Manchester |
| 14 | 5 | 278292 | E. H. Downs | 13 [illegible] |
| 20 | 9 | 278481 | Benjamin Hastwell | 19 Bennett Street Stamford Street Blackfriars Road |
| 29 | 6 | 278712 | Edward Berman & Co | 30 Addle Street EC |
| Decr 10 | 11 | 279179 | Jane Webb and Joseph Hammond Executors of the late Joseph Webb of Stourbridge | |
| 15 | 7 | 279245 | La Baronne Gabrielle de Falckersahn | 25 Percy Street Bedford Square London |
| 20 | 5 | 279324 | Edward Berman & Co | 30 Addle Street EC |
| 1874 | | | | |
| Jany 6 | 6 | 279532 | John Derbyshire | Regent Road, Flint Glass Works Salford |
| " | 9 | 279535 | Ernest Henry Beck | 42 Bishopsgate Street |
| 15 | 6 | 279876 | Sowerby & Co | Ellison Glass Works Gateshead-on-Tyne |
| 20 | 5 | 279940 | Douglas Coates Crawford | Guildford Street Chertsey Surrey |
| Feby 3 | 5 | 280197 | John Derbyshire | Regent Road Glass Works Salford Manchester |

| Date of Deposit | No. of Parcel | No. of Design | Name of Proprietor | Address of Proprietor |
|---|---|---|---|---|
| 1874 | | | | |
| Feby 14. | 10 | 280193 to 280195 | 3. Molineaux Webb & Co | Kirby Street Manchester |
| 18. | 2 | 280566 | 1. Henry Manton Junior | 108 Great Charles Street Birmingham |
| 23. | 2 | 280660 | 1. Thomas Seago & Benjamin John Jo[illegible] | [illegible] Street Birmingham |
| March 13. | 1 | 281092 | 1 Maw Son & Thompson | Aldersgate Street |
| " | 10 | 281119 | 1 Isaac Barnes | 58 Broad Street Birmingham |
| 28. | 8 | 281435 281436 | 2 Pellatt & Wood | 25 Baker Street, Portman Square W. |
| April 9. | 3 | 281670 to 281675 | 6. Samuel Evans | West Bromwich near Birmingham |
| 11. | 6 | 281767 | 1. Franz Eisert | 25 South Audley Street Grosvenor Square W |
| 13. | 3 | 281771 | 1 A. Aronsberg of and W. H. Gretton of | 8 Parish Street Southwark S.E. 7 Holland Street Blackfriars S.E. |
| 17. | 3 | 281842 | 1. Ker, Webb & Co | Prussia Street Glass Works Manchester |
| 22. | 8 | 281933 | 1. Sowerby & Co | Ellison Glass Works Gateshead-on-Tyne |
| May 12. | 6 | 282260 | 1. John Derbyshire | Regent Road Flint Glass Works Manchester |
| 15. | 10 | 282371 | 1 Ellis Pearson | Malden Surrey |
| 20. | 10 | 282496 | 1. Philip Pargeter of Stourbridge Glass Manufr & Percival Jones of 15 Westmoreland Street Dublin China & Glass Merchant | |
| 26. | 10 | 282505 | 1 Daniel Judson & Sons | Southwark Street S.E. |
| 29. | 2 | 282648 | 1 John Hanbury | 30 Ladywood Road Birmingham, Warwickshire |

| Date of Deposit | No. of Parcel | No. of Design | Name of Proprietor | Address of Proprietor |
|---|---|---|---|---|
| 1874 | | | | |
| June 1. | 8 | 282663 - 4 | 2 Sowerby & Co | Ellison Glass Works Gateshead on Tyne |
| 10. | 4 | 282882 | 1. Toy & Jones | 38 Howard Street Birmingham |
| 15. | 1 | 282961 | 1. Jane Webb & Joseph Hammond Executor of the late Joseph Webb of Coalbourn Hill Glass Works Stourbridge | |
| 24. | 4 | 283214 | 1. George Treble & Son | 42 Gloucester Street Hoxton London |
| July 3. | 4 | 283406 | 1 John Derbyshire | Regent Road Glass Works Manchester |
| 13. | 3 | 283567 | 1. Toy & Jones | 38 Howard Street Birmingham |
| 29. | 8 | 284031 | 1 Percival Vickers & Co Limited | Jersey Street Manchester |
| Augt 10. | 8 | 284291 | 1 Percival Jones | 15 Westmoreland Street Dublin |
| 17. | 5 | 284431 | 1 Sowerby & Co | Ellison Glass Works Gateshead on Tyne |
| 25. | 4 | 284581 | 1 John Short Downing | Crown Works, 104 Irving Street Birmingham |
| 26. | 5 | 284672 | William Henry Heppell & Co | Newcastle Flint Glass Works, Forth Street Newcastle upon Tyne |
| 2[illegible]. | 9 | 284695 | 1 Henry Greener | Wear Flint Glass Works Sunderland |
| Sept 11. | 8 | 284903 | 1 Dietz & Co | 19 Carter Lane, London E.C. |
| 10. | 6 | 285016 | 1 Sowerby & Co | Ellison Glass Works Gateshead on Tyne |
| 11. | 5 | 285175 | 1 John Derbyshire | Regent Road Flint Glass Works, Manchester |
| " | 9 | 285179 | Franke Lyon | 13 Lorrimore Road Walworth London |
| ~~24.~~ | ~~6~~ | ~~28563?~~ | | |
| 24. | 6 | 285632 | 1. Walter C. Stone | Exeter. Chemist |
| Octr 2. | 8 | 285831 to 285834 | 4. R & J Beck | 31 Cornhill EC |

| Date of Deposit | No. of Parcel | No. of Design | Name of Proprietor | Address of Proprietor |
|---|---|---|---|---|
| 1874 Octr 3 | 9 | 285851 | 1. R & J Beck | 31 Cornhill EC |
| " | " | — | | |
| 12 | 3 | 286172 | 1 Thomas & Harding | 157 Piccadilly SW |
| 23 | 12 | 286478 | 1 John Dawson Liddell | 18 Mark Lane London |
| 26 | 5 | 286525 | 1 Hodgetts Richardson & Son | Wordsley, Stourbridge |
| 28 | 7 | 286561 | 1. Edward Bolton | Orford Lane Glass Works |
| " | " | — | | Warrington |
| 26 | 3 | 287474 | 1. Charles Joseph Adie | 136 Hagstone Lane Birmingham |
| " | 5 | 287495 | 1. John Derbyshire | Regent Road Flint Glass Works |
| " | " | — | | Salford |
| Decr 2 | 15 | 287613 | 1. W G Parkin & Co | Sheffield |
| 21 | 1 | 288011 | 1 A Dittrich | 4 Coleman Street |
| " | " | — | | Bunhill Row Finsbury EC |
| " | 4 | 288015 | 1 Jane Webb & Joseph Hammond | Stourbridge Glass Manufacturers |
| " | " | — | trading as the Executors of the late | |
| " | " | — | Joseph Webb | |
| 1875 Jany 1 | 2 | 288210 | 1 Sowerby & Co | Ellison Glass Works Gateshead |
| " | " | — | | on Tyne |
| 7 | 8 | 288295 | 1 Thomas Lane & Son | Birmingham |
| 16 | 7 | 288498 | 3. | |
| " | " | to | Seago Johnson & Co | 23 George Street Birmingham |
| " | " | 288500 | | |
| 28 | 11 | 288858 | 1. Robinson Son | Mersey Glass Works |
| " | " | — | & Skinner | Warrington |
| 29 | 2 | 288863 | 1. John Short Downing | Crown Works 104 Irving Street |
| " | " | — | | Birmingham |
| " | 9 | 288889 | 1. J J Hicks | 8 Hatton Garden |

| Date of Deposit | No. of Parcel | No. of Design | Name of Proprietor | Address of Proprietor |
|---|---|---|---|---|
| 1875 Feby 4 | 9 | 289067 | 2. C J Padgett | 21 Brewer Street |
| " | " | 289068 | | Golden Square W |
| 6 | 10 | 289098 | 2. Thomas & Harding | 157 Piccadilly SW |
| " | " | 289099 | | |
| 8 | 11 | 289165 | 1. Judson & Son | Southwark Street EC |
| 12 | 9 | 289283 | 1. Molineaux Webb & Co | Kirby Street Manchester |
| 15 | 16 | 289314 | 1. James Lewis | Bartlett's Buildings Holborn |
| 22 | 6 | 289493 | 1 James Crichton Kinmond | Kenilworth Street |
| " | " | — | trading as Kinmond & Co | Leamington |
| 26 | 4 | 289645 | 3. | |
| " | " | to | Molineaux, Webb & Co | Kirby Street Manchester |
| " | " | 289647 | | |
| March 1 | 8 | 289713 | 1. Henry Defries | 147 Houndsditch London |
| 8 | 1 | 289799 | 1 John Short Downing | Crown Works, 104 Irving Street |
| " | " | — | | Birmingham |
| 9 | 12 | 289821 | 1. Seago Johnson & Co | George Street Birmingham |
| 13 | 5 | 289894 | 1. Thomas Lane & Son | Birmingham |
| 24 | 5 | 289145 | 1. Frank Lyon | 52 Aldersgate Street London |
| 30 | 4 | 290191 | 2 John Short Downing | Crown Works, Irving |
| " | " | 290192 | | Street Birmingham |
| April 3 | 10 | 290263 | 2 G V de Luca | 43 Wigmore Street |
| " | " | 290264 | | London |
| 19 | 5 | 290778 | 1. Sowerby & Co | Ellison Glass Works |
| " | " | — | | Gateshead-on-Tyne |
| 23 | 14 | 290890 | 1. Hodgetts, Richardson | Wordsley Glass Works |
| " | " | — | & Son | Stourbridge |
| 26 | 14 | 290913 | 1. Beater Bros & Co | 7 Lilypot Lane London EC |
| May 14 | 9 | 291347 | 1. Daniel Pearce | North End Villa, North End Road |
| " | " | — | | Hammersmith |

| Date of Deposit | No. of Parcel | No. of Design | Name of Proprietor | Address of Proprietor |
|---|---|---|---|---|
| 1875 | | | | |
| May 24 | 5 | 291499 to 291501 | 3. D. Beck & Co. | Hall Street, Birmingham |
| 27 | 14 | 291532 | 1. Daniel Pearce | North End Villa Hammersmith |
| June 5 | 9 | 291873 291874 | 2. Sowerby & Co. | Ellison Glass Works, Gateshead-on-Tyne |
| 12 | 9 | 292040 292041 | 2. Hodgetts Richardson & Son | Wordsley Glass Works, Stourbridge |
| 16 | 6 | 292113 | 1. Thomas Gray & Co | Gateshead-on-Tyne |
| 21 | 7 | 292201 | 1. Ortner & Houle | 3 St. James's Street SW |
| July 13 | 7 | 292783 | 1. Woodall & Son | 10 Great Hampton Street, Birmingham |
| 19 | 2 | 292980 | 1. Benjamin Newham & Company | 9 Castle Hill Sheffield |
| 26 | 3 | 293100 | 1. Molineaux, Webb & Co. | Kirby Street, Manchester |
| August 5 | 8 | 293356 | 1 John Derbyshire & Co | Regent Road Salford |
| 23 | 5 | 293890 | 1. James Scott | West Bromwich |
| " | 5 | ~~293940 293941~~ | ~~2. John Bennett & Son~~ | ~~[illegible] Manchester~~ |
| 24 | 6 | 293942 | 1. Hyde & Co | Saint Bride Street London |
| September 8 | 4 | 294315 to 294318 | 4 William Richards & Son | 38 Tenby Street North, Birmingham |
| 10 | 6 | 294376 to 294379 | 4 Sowerby & Co | Ellison Glass Works Gateshead-on-Tyne |
| 14 | 16 | 294522 | 1 Joseph Polak | 59 Francis Road Edgbaston Birmingham |
| 15 | 1 | 294523 | 1 Charles Harris & Frederick Jones | 38 Howard Street, Birmingham |
| 18 | 4 | 294575 | 1. Hodgetts, Richardson & Son | Wordsley Glass Works, Stourbridge |
| 23 | 6 | 294653 294654 | 2. Edward Bolton | Orford Lane Glass Works, Warrington |
| Octr 16 | 10 | 295133 | 1 Molineaux, Webb & Co | Kirby Street Manchester |

| Date of Deposit | No. of Parcel | No. of Design | Name of Proprietor | Address of Proprietor |
|---|---|---|---|---|
| 1875 | | | | |
| Octr 23 | 3 | 295362 | 1. William Henry Heppell | Newcastle-on-Tyne |
| 28 | 4 | 295444 | 1. Sowerby & Co | Ellison Glass Works Gateshead-on-Tyne |
| Novr 13 | 4 | 295919 | 1. William Henry Heppell & Co. | Newcastle-upon-Tyne |
| 15 Class I & III | 7 | 295973 | 1. W. J. Bishop | 3 Northumberland Street, Strand |
| 25 | 7 | 296342 | 1. John Perkins | 23 East Lamartine Street, off Robin Hood Street, Nottingham |
| Decr 3 | 15 | 296556 | 1. Edward Cette and John Louis Guanziroli | 11 & 31 Brooke Street Holborn WC |
| 6 | 5 | 296641 | 1. Thomas Webb & Sons | Stourbridge |
| " | 7 | 296643 | 1. John Derbyshire & Co. | Salford, Manchester |
| 17 | 16 | 297041 297042 | 2 Sowerby & Co | Ellison Glass Works Gateshead on Tyne |
| 22 | 5 | 297157 | 1. Thomas Webb & Sons | Oldham Road Flint Glass Works, Varley Street, Manchester |
| 1876 | | | | |
| Jany 14 | 5 | 297633 | 1. Seago & Co | 23 George Street Parade Birmingham |
| " | 6 | 297634 | 1 Thomas Webb & Sons | Stourbridge & Charterhouse Street, Holborn Circus London |
| Feb 2 | 1 | 298055 to 298057 | 3 G. V. De Luca | 5 Guildhall Chambers Basinghall Street London EC |
| 11 | 1 | 298309 | 1 James Lewis | 6 Bartlett's Buildings Holborn Circus London EC |
| 19 | 1 | 298446 | 1 Whittingham & Percival | Flint Glass Works Pendleton, near Manchester |
| 25 | 8 | 298609 | 1 William Ford trading under the name of John Ford | Holyrood Glass Works Edinburgh |

114

| Date of Deposit | No. of Parcel | No. of Design | Name of Proprietor | Address of Proprietor |
|---|---|---|---|---|
| 1876 | | | | |
| Feb 26 | 9 | 298626 | 2 Thomas Webb & Sons | Stourbridge and Charterhouse Street Holborn Circus Lond |
| " " | | 298627 | — | |
| March 6 | 3 | 298870 to 298876 | 7 Sowerby & Co | Ellison Glass Works Gateshead-on-Tyne |
| 9 | 4 | 299022 | 2 John Derbyshire & Co | Regent Road Manchester |
| " | " | 299023 | | |
| " | 7 | 299050 to 299054 | 5 Sowerby & Co | Ellison Glass Works Gateshead-on-Tyne |
| 11 | 10 | 299158 | 1 Hodgetts Richardson & Son | Stourbridge |
| " | " | — | | |
| 18 | 7 | 299251 | 2 F & C Osler | 45 Oxford Street London W |
| " | " | 299252 | | |
| 22 | 3 | 299305 | 1 Oswald Thiel | 42 Augusta Street Birmingham |
| 27 | 13 | 299424 to 299426 | 3 Sowerby & Co | Ellison Glass Works, Gateshead on Tyne |
| 28 | 1 | 299427 | 1 Hodgetts, Richardson & Son | Wordsley near Stourbridge |
| " | " | — | | |
| " | 7 | 299473 | 1 Sowerby & Co | Ellison Glass Works Gateshead on Tyne |
| " | " | — | | |
| April 4 | 7 | 299697 | 1 Joseph Benson | Cut Glass Works Charles Street Sheffield |
| " | " | — | | |
| 11 | 10 | 299826 | 1 Daniel Pearce | North End Works, North End Road Hammersmith |
| " | " | — | | |
| 28 | 2 | 300300 | 1 John Derbyshire & Co | Regent Road Flint Glass Works Manchester |
| " | " | — | | |
| May 3 | 11 | 300371 | 1 Boulton & Mills | Audnam Glass Works Stourbridge |
| " | " | — | | |

| Date of Deposit | No. of Parcel | No. of Design | Name of Proprietor | Address of Proprietor |
|---|---|---|---|---|
| 1876 | | | | |
| May 8 | 6 | 300419 | 2 Sowerby & Co | Ellison Glass Works Gateshead-on-Tyne |
| " | " | 300420 | | |
| 9 | 10 | 300456 | 1 F H Atkins & Co | 62 Fleet Street London EC |
| 11 | 6 | 300487 | 1 Henry Manton junior | 10 Great Charles Street Birmingham |
| 13 | 3 | 300619 | 1 Charles Harris | [illegible] Street Hockley Birmingham |
| 17 | 9 | 300655 | 1 John Derbyshire & Co | Regent Road Flint Glass Works Salford Manchester |
| " | " | — | | |
| 20 | 2 | 300672 | 1 Sykes Macvay & Co | Albion Glass Works Castleford Yorkshire |
| " | " | — | | |
| 24 | 5 | 300748 | 1 Sowerby & Co | Ellison Glass Works Gateshead-on-Tyne |
| " | " | — | | |
| 29 | 19 | 300940 | 1 Sowerby & Co | Ellison Glass Works Gateshead-on-Tyne |
| June 6 | 2 | 301058 to 301067 | 10 Whittingham & Percival | Pendleton Flint Glass Works Pendleton Manchester |
| 14 | 2 | 301236 to 301238 | 3 Whittingham & Percival | Whit Lane, Pendleton Manchester |
| 15 | 8 | 301266 | 1 John Short Downing | Crown Works Commercial Street Birmingham |
| 17 | 3 | 301298 | 1 Boulton & Mills | Audnam Glass Works Stourbridge |
| " | " | — | | |
| 20 | 1 | 301312 | 1 Sowerby & Co | Ellison Glass Works Gateshead on Tyne |
| " | " | — | | |
| 21 | 1 | 301326 | 2 Sowerby & Co | Ellison Glass Works Gateshead on Tyne |
| " | " | 301327 | | |
| " | 5 | 301331 | 1 Henry Pether | 25 Stockwell Green London |
| 30 | 7 | 301579 | 1 Percival Vickers & Co Limited | Jersey Street, Ancoats Manchester |
| July 14 | 8 | 301951 | 1 Wittman & Roth | 42 Great Marlborough Street Regent Street W |
| Classes III & IV | | — | | |

| Date of Deposit | No of Parcel | No. of Design | Name of Proprietor | Address of Proprietor |
|---|---|---|---|---|
| 1876 | | | | |
| July 19 | 6 | 301999 | 1. E Cetti & Co | 11 & 31 Brooke Street Holborn and Pratt Street Lambeth London |
| " | " | ——— | | |
| 24 | 13 | 302114 | 2 Sowerby & Co | Ellison Glass Works Gateshead-on-Tyne |
| " | " | 302115 | | |
| 29 | 6 | 302199 | 1. Henry Greener | Wear Flint Glass Works Sunderland |
| " | " | ——— | | |
| " | 8 | 302201 | 1. Gustave Marquot | Bayel near Bar-sur-Aube France |
| " | " | ——— | | |
| Augt 16 | 7 | 302625 | 1. Barrow & Co | Glass Works, Icknield Square Birmingham |
| " | " | ——— | | |
| 18 | 10 | 302804 | 2. Sowerby & Co | Ellison Glass Works Gateshead-on-Tyne |
| " | " | 302805 | | |
| 26 | 4 | 302912 | 1. Joseph Kidd | Holt Town Flint Glass Works Manchester |
| | | ——— | | |
| Apr 1 | 3 | 303199 | 1. Albert Bradbrook | 39 Jewin Street London E.C. |
| 7 | 9 | 303379 | 1. Sykes Macvay & Co | Castleford Yorkshire |
| 25 | 1 | 303830 | 1. Barrow & Co | Glass Works, Icknield Square, Birmingham |
| " | " | ——— | | |
| Oct 2 | 2 | 303996 | 1. Seago & Co | 23 George Street, Parade, Birmingham |
| 11 | 5 | 304306 | 1. Louis Henry Beck | [illegible] |
| 16 | 8 | 304363 to 304366 | 4 Sowerby & Co | Ellison Glass Works Gateshead-on-Tyne |
| 17 | 6 | 304378 to 304380 | 3 Benjamin Needham & Co | Sheffield |
| Novr 15 | 4 | 305209 | 1. Sowerby & Co | Ellison Glass Works Gateshead-on-Tyne |
| " | " | ——— | | |
| 17 | 7 | 305227 | 1. Isaac Barnes & Co | 311 Broad Street Birmingham |
| 28 | 10 | 305541 | 1. James Derbyshire & Sons | Trentham Street, Chester Road, Hulme Manchester |

| Date of Deposit | No of Parcel | No. of Design | Name of Proprietor | Address of Proprietor |
|---|---|---|---|---|
| 1876 | | | | |
| Nov 30 | 8 | 305579 | 1. Aston & Marlow | 19 & 20 Newtown Row Birmingham |
| " | " | ——— | | |
| Decr 5 | 9 | 305705 | 1. William Ramsey | 83 & 84 Farringdon Street London E.C. |
| 8 | 3 | 305778 | 1. James Aston | New Town Row, Birmingham |
| 11 | 4 | 305832 | 1. Frederick Vanstan | 19 Bridport Street, Blandford Square. N.W. |
| " | " | ——— | | |
| 18 | 2 | 306083 | 1. Sykes, Macvay & Co | Albion Glass Works, Castleford Yorkshire |
| " | " | ——— | | |
| 19 | 16 | 306149 | 1. Andrew Ker | The Prussia Street Glass Works Oldham Road Manchester |
| " | " | ——— | | |
| 20 | 8 | 306185 | 1. Lloyd & Summerfield | Birmingham |
| 1877 Janr 1 | [illegible] | 306884 | 1. George Davidson & Co | Teams Flint Glass Works Gateshead-on-Tyne |
| " | " | ——— | | |
| " | 11 | 306887 | 1. Sowerby & Co | Ellison Glass Works Gateshead-on-Tyne |
| " | " | ——— | | |
| 22 | 7 | 307126 | 1. Thomas Rule | Beaconsfield Terrace, Harringay |
| 31 | 11 | 307426 | 1. Henry Brett & Co | 26 High Holborn [illegible] |
| 1 | 7 | 307433 | 1. Warren, Stokes & Co | 4 Beresford Place, Dublin |
| 12 | 9 | 307671 | 1. Slack & Brownlow | Canning Works, Hulme Manchester |
| " | " | ——— | | |
| 13 | 8 | 307686 to 307696 | 11. Sowerby & Co | Ellison Glass Works Gateshead-on-Tyne |
| 17 | 1 | 307869 | 1. James Aston | New Town Row Birmingham |
| 21 | 10 | 307910 | 1. J. T. Crawford | 3 Albion Street, Stoke Newington N. |
| 23 | 8 | 307957 | 2 Sowerby & Co | Ellison Glass Works Gateshead-on-Tyne |
| " | " | 307958 | | |
| 28 | 15 | 308104 | 1. George Davidson & Co | Teams Flint Glass Works, Gateshead on Tyne |
| " | " | ——— | | |

| Date of Deposit | No of Parcel | No. of Design | Name of Proprietor | Address of Proprietor |
|---|---|---|---|---|
| 1877 | | | | |
| March 1 | 5 | 308192 | 2. Sowerby & Co | Ellison Glass Works Gateshead on Tyne |
| " | " | 308193 | | |
| 7 | 11 | 308257 | 2. F. & C. Osler | Birmingham |
| " | " | 308258 | | |
| 8 | 13 | 308328 | 1. S. Maw Son & Thompson | 11 Aldersgate Street London EC |
| " | " | — | | |
| 13 | 10 | 308414 | 1. Sowerby & Co | Ellison Glass Works Gateshead-on-Tyne |
| 15 | 1 | 308495 | 1. Sowerby & Co | Ellison Glass Works Gateshead on Tyne |
| 19 | 5 | 308644 | 1. Sowerby & Co | Ellison Glass Works Gateshead on Tyne |
| 21 | 4 | 308667 | 1. The Regent Flint Glass Co. | Regent Road Manchester |
| 22 | 12 | 308713 | 3 Sowerby & Co | Ellison Glass Works Gateshead-on-Tyne |
| | | 308714 | | |
| | | 308715 | | |
| 23 | 7 | 308776 | 1 Sowerby & Co | Ellison Glass Works Gateshead on Tyne |
| 29 | 4 | 308876 | 1 Sowerby & Co | Ellison Glass Works Gateshead on Tyne |
| April 18 | 3 | 309484 | 2. Seago & Co | 23 George Street Birmingham |
| | | 309485 | | |
| 19 | 5 | 309542 | 1. John Davis & Co | Dial Glass Works Stourbridge |
| " | 6 | 309543 | 1. Boulton & Mills | Audnam Glass Works Stourbridge |
| 23 | 7 | 309621 | 1. Crosse & Blackwell | 21 Soho Square W |
| 26 | 6 | 309695 | 1. Max Sugar | 75 Blackfriars Road SE |
| 28 | 12 | 309765 | 1. Max Sugar | 75 Blackfriars Road SE |
| May 4 | 4 | 309902 | 1. The Regent Flint Glass Co. | Regent Road, Manchester |
| ~~12~~ | ~~10~~ | ~~310037~~ | ~~1. Charles Jesson~~ | ~~Gibraltar Street, Sheffield~~ |
| 22 | 4 | 310358 | 1. Ellis Allan & Co | Forth Glass Works Firhill Road Glasgow |
| " | " | — | | |
| 24 | 6 | 310446 | 1. W. Lester | 48 Crown Street Soho |

| Date of Deposit | No of Parcel | No. of Design | Name of Proprietor | Address of Proprietor |
|---|---|---|---|---|
| 1877 | | | | |
| May 24 | 10 | 310450 | 2. G. V. De Luca | 5 Guildhall Chambers Basinghall Street London EC |
| " | " | 310451 | | |
| 31 | 9 | 310595 | 3 Sowerby & Co | Ellison Glass Works Gateshead-on-Tyne |
| " | " | 310596 | | |
| " | " | 310597 | | |
| June 4 | 14 | 310657 | 1. Bolton, Son & Wood | Oxford Lane Glass Works Warrington |
| 21 | 10 | 311138 | 1. James Lewis | 6 Bartlett's Buildings, Holborn |
| July 20 | 6 | 312061 | 1. Emil August Thomson | Moreton Street, Strangeways Manchester |
| " | " | — | | |
| " | 12 | 312070 | 2. Sheldon & Passey | Back of 83 New John Street West, Birmingham |
| " | " | 312071 | | |
| 21 | 2 | 312121 | 1. Eugenie Valade | 12 Rue Lavoisier Paris |
| August 2 | 6 | 312457 | 1. William Lester | 48 Crown Street Soho |
| 9 | 1 | 312701 | 1. Jehoiada A. Rhodes | Britain Works Howard Street Sheffield |
| | | — | | |
| Septr 4 | 3 | 313707 | 1. James Henry Stone | 4 St Paul's Square Birmingham |
| 17 | 2 | 314156 | 2. Willmann & Roth | 42 Great Marlborough Street |
| " | " | 314157 | | |
| 18 | 7 | 314265 to 314285 | 21 Sowerby & Co | Ellison Glass Works Gateshead on Tyne |
| 21 | 1 | 314482 | 1. Samuel Heath | 116 Leopold Street, Birmingham |
| Oct 4 | 12 | 314938 | 1. Samuel H. Martin & Co | 16 Great Marlborough Street W |
| 13 | 12 | 315269 | 1. G. V. de Luca | Guildhall Chambers Basinghall Street, London EC |
| 17 | 2 | 315429 | 1. Molineaux, Webb & Co | Manchester |
| 29 | 6 | 315664 to 315674 | 11. Sowerby & Co | Ellison Glass Works Gateshead-on-Tyne |
| 30 | 6 | 315683 | 1. The Spirit Ageing Company | 67 Garngad Road Glasgow |

| Date of Deposit | No. of Parcel | No. of Design | Name of Proprietor | Address of Proprietor |
|---|---|---|---|---|
| 1877 | | | | |
| Novr 15 | 5 | 316299 | 1. Jehoida A. Rhodes | Britannia Works, Howard Street Sheffield |
| " | | — | | |
| 20 | 4 | 316490 | 3 Sowerby & Co | Ellison Glass Works Gateshead-on-Tyne |
| | " | 316491 | | |
| | " | 316492 | | — |
| 24 | 10 | 316623 | 1. R. Hedges | 279 High Street, Camden Town N.W. |
| Decr 3 | 2 | 316776 | 1. Molineaux Webb & Co | Kirby Street Manchester |
| 6 | 3 | 316862 | 1. Molineaux Webb & Co | Kirby Street Manchester. |
| 17 | 12 | 317233 | 2. Sowerby & Co | Ellison Glass Works Gateshead-on-Tyne |
| | — | 317234 | | |
| 19 | 1 | 317277 | 4. Sowerby & Co | Ellison Glass Works Gateshead on Tyne |
| | | 317278 | | |
| | | 317279 | | |
| | | 317280 | 8 | |
| 1878 | | | | |
| Jany 5 | 1 | 317583 | 2. Archibald Hodge & Co | 5 Bishop Street Port Dundas Glasgow |
| | " | 317584 | | |
| 18 | 2 | 317822 | 1. Frederick William Brownlow | Canning Works Hulme Manchester |
| | | — | | |
| Feby 2 | 14 | 318371 | 1. Eugene Bon-Rougier | Angoulême France |
| 9 | 4 | 318467 | 1 Widmore Hyatt | 5 Newhall Street Dudley |
| " | 5 | 318468 | 1. James Henry Stone | 4 & 5 St. Paul's Square Birmingham |
| 20 | 3 | 318789 | 7 Sowerby & Co | Ellison Glass Works Gateshead-on-Tyne |
| " | " | 318790 | " | |
| " | " | 318791 | " | |
| " | " | 318792 | " | |
| " | " | 318793 | " | |
| " | " | 318794 | " | |
| " | " | 318795 | " | |

| Date of Deposit | No. of Parcel | No. of Design | Name of Proprietor | Address of Proprietor |
|---|---|---|---|---|
| 1878 | | | | |
| Mar 1 | 8 | 319096 | 1. Percival Vickers & Co | Jersey Street, Manchester |
| 14 | 10 | 319413 | 1. H & J Milne | 126 Princes Street Edinburgh |
| 16 | [illegible] | 319533 | 1. E Remy Martin & Co | Château de Ligneres, Rouillac Charente |
| | | — | | |
| 19 | 6 | 319555 | 1. Samuel Roodhouse | London Pickle Works, Ventnor Street, Kirkstall Road Leeds |
| | | — | | |
| 20 | 7 | 319585 | 5. Sowerley & Co | Ellison Glass Works Gateshead-on-Tyne |
| | | 319586 | | |
| | | 319587 | | |
| | | 319588 | | |
| | | 319589 | | — |
| 21 | 6 | 319599 | 1. H W & L Dee | 8 Sherwood Street |
| 22 | 8 | 319619 | 2. Sowerby & Co | Ellison Glass Works Gateshead on Tyne |
| " | " | 319620 | 12 | |
| April 9 | 10 | 320276 | 1. J. Defries & Sons | 147 Houndsditch, City, London |
| 12 | 1 | 320330 | 1. William Frederick Williams | 3, 4 & 5 Little Windmill Street, Golden Square |
| | | — | | |
| May 11 | 8 | 321308 | 1. Samuel Jones | Beech Road Tranmere in the County of Chester |
| | | — | | |
| Classes III, V, XI, XIII 13 | 3 | 321340 | 1. Jane Tyzack | Wood Lodge, Abbeydale Sheffield |
| 14 | 9 | 321368 | 12 Sowerby & Co | Ellison Glass Works Gateshead on Tyne |
| | | 321369 | | |
| | | 321370 | | |
| | | 321371 | | |
| | | 321372 | | |
| | | 321373 | | |
| | | 321374 | | |
| | | 321375 to 321378 | | |
| | | 321379 | 14 | |

| Date of Deposit | No. of Parcel | No. of Design | Name of Proprietor | Address of Proprietor |
|---|---|---|---|---|
| 1878 | | | | |
| Mar 27 | 22 | 322009 | 1. Vve Sardin Roux Bazin & Co | [illegible] |
| " 30 | 16 | 322080 | 1. Hooker's Cream Milk Co. Limited | [illegible] Midland Railway Station [illegible] |
| June 8 | 11 | 322393 | 1. Henry Greener | Wear Flint Glass Works, Sunderland |
| " 25 | 10 | 322819 322820 322821 322822 322823 322824 322825 | Sowerby & Co | Ellison Glass Works Gateshead on Tyne |
| " 2[illegible] | 10 | 322947 | 1 H[illegible] & Lee | 8 [illegible] Street |
| July 8 | 9 | 323400 | 1. Sowerby & Co | Ellison Glass Works Gateshead on Tyne |
| " [illegible] | 5 | 323711 | 1. W. H. Britton | 7 Holland [illegible] |
| " 2[illegible] | 15 | 324317 | 1 [illegible] | Birmingham |
| 29 | 4 | 324321 324322 | 2. Sowerby & Co | Ellison Glass Works Gateshead-on-Tyne |
| Augt 2 | 12 | 324501 | 1. J Barnes & Co | [illegible] Birmingham |
| " 12 | 6 | 324929 324930 324931 324932 | 4 Sowerby & Co | Ellison Glass Works, Gateshead on Tyne |
| " 16 | 11 | 325096 to 325101 | 6. Sowerby & Co | Ellison Glass Works, Gateshead on Tyne |
| " 28 | 4 | 325439 | 1 Joseph Wilson Hodges | Birmingham |
| " 30 | 16 | 325534 | 1 Sowerby & Co | Ellison Glass Works Gateshead on Tyne |

| Date of Deposit | No. of Parcel | No. of Design | Name of Proprietor | Address of Proprietor |
|---|---|---|---|---|
| 1878 | | | | |
| August 31 | 8 | 325347 | 1 Henry Greener | Wear Flint Glass Works Sunderland |
| Septr 5 | 14 | 325782 | 1 F & C. Osler | Birmingham |
| " 7 | 2 | 325876 | 1 Robert Gourlay | Bishopbriggs near Glasgow |
| " 23 | 6 | 326775 326776 | 2. George Davidson & Co | Teams Glass Works Gateshead on Tyne |
| Oct 15 | 4 | 327641 327642 | 2. Jane Webb, Joseph Hammond & Henry Fitzroy Webb trading as the Executors of the late Joseph Webb of Stourbridge | |
| " 19 | 3 | 327771 | 1. J Gill & E. Rawlinson | 2 Dunn Street, Every Street Ancoats Manchester |
| " 26 | 12 | 328347 | 1. William Boyd & Co | Blythswood Foundry Glasgow |
| | 14 | 328349 | 1. Oscar [illegible] | [illegible] |
| Nov 4 | 10 | 328740/12 328741 328742 328743 328744 328745 328746 328747 328748 328749 328750 328751 | Sowerby & Co | Ellison Glass Works Gateshead on Tyne |
| " 7 | 17 | 328919 | 1. Sowerby & Co | Ellison Glass Works Gateshead-on-Tyne |
| " 12 | 6 | 329010 | 1. Francis Thomas Bond M.D. | Barton Lyon in the City of Gloucester |
| " 20 | 11 | 329376 | 1. Sowerby & Co | Ellison Glass Works, Gateshead-on-Tyne |

| Date of Deposit | No. of Parcel | No. of Design | Name of Proprietor | Address of Proprietor |
|---|---|---|---|---|
| 1878 | | | | |
| Nov 21 | 12 | 329408 | 1 Henry Doo Rawlings | Nassau Street Charles Street Berners Street London |
| " | " | — | | |
| " 26 | 12 | 329941 | 1 [illegible] & Co | [illegible] |
| Dec 10 | 13 | 330210 | 1 William [illegible] | Brierley Hill |
| " 12 | 9 | 330326 | 1 [illegible] Cooke | [illegible] Manchester |
| 13 | 10 | 330348 to 330352 | 5 Sowerby & Co | Ellison Glass Works Sunderland |
| 18 | 10 | 3304[illegible] | 1 Henry Greener | Wear Flint Glass Works Sunderland |
| [illegible] | [illegible] | [illegible] | Sowerby & Co | Ellison Glass Works Gateshead |
| 1879 | | | | |
| Jany 2 | 3 | 330816 | 1 Edward Green & Edward Unsworth Green of Ay Champagne in the Republic of France and 63 Great Tower Street in the City of London | |
| " 8 | 10 | 330964 | 1 Sowerby & Co | Ellison Glass Works, Gateshead-on-Tyne |
| 13 | 3 | 331138 | 1 William Boyd | [illegible] Glasgow |
| " 17 | 11 | 331370 | 1 Daniel Pearce | [illegible] Hammersmith |
| " 21 | 1 | 331421 | 1 James Burwell, [illegible] | [illegible] Works [illegible] Street Birmingham |
| " | 8 | 331450 | 1 William Ramsay | [illegible] London E.C. |
| Feby 8 | 8 | 332051 to 332054 | 4 Sowerby & Co | Ellison Glass Works Gateshead-on-Tyne |
| " | 9 | 332055 | 1 William McKinlay Percy | 124 & 128 Trongate Glasgow |

| Date of Deposit | No. of Parcel | No. of Design | Name of Proprietor | Address of Proprietor |
|---|---|---|---|---|
| 1879 | | | | |
| Feb 4 12 | 17 | 332195 | 1 Sowerby & Co | Ellison Glass Works Gateshead on Tyne |
| March 8 | 8 | 333128, 333129 | 2 Hodgetts Richardson & Son | Wordsley Flint Glass Works, Stourbridge |
| " 10 | 9 | 333167 to 333173 | 7 Sowerby & Co | Ellison Glass Works Gateshead-on-Tyne |
| " 17 | 11 | 3334[illegible] to 3334[illegible] | 6 Sowerby & Co | Ellison Glass Works Gateshead on Tyne |
| [illegible] 20 | 9 | 333557 | 1 Ernest Unger | 31 Watling Street London E.C. |
| " | 10 | 333558, 333559, 333560 | 3 [illegible] & [illegible] Osler | Birmingham |
| " 27 | 4 | 333762, 333763 | 2 H. J. Humphreys & Co | 240 Buchanan Street Glasgow |
| April 1 | 13 | 333955 | 1 Mountain, [illegible] | 24 Southwark Bridge, Borough |
| [illegible] | 7 | 334634 to 334643 | 10 Sowerby & Co | Ellison Glass Works Gateshead on Tyne |
| Class VIII & IX May 15 | 9 | 334930 | 1 James Wilson | 29 Orchard Street London |
| " | 10, 12 | 335118 | 1 W. Groves of the firm of Groves & Co | 5 Mark Lane |

| Date of Deposit | No. of Parcel | No. of Design | Name of Proprietor | Address of Proprietor |
|---|---|---|---|---|
| 1879 | | | | |
| May 14 | 3 | 335175 | 1. H W & L Doo | 8 Sherwood Street |
| June 4 | 1 | 335845 | 1. The Rochester Tumbler Co | Pittsburgh, Pennsylvania U.S.A. |
| " 6 | 10 | 335969, 335970, 335971, 335972 | 4. Sowerby & Co | Ellison Glass Works Gateshead on Tyne |
| " 24 | 2 | 336135 | Jane Webb, Joseph Hammond and Henry Fitzroy Webb trading as the Executors of the late Joseph Webb of ~~Stourbridge~~ Coalbourn Hill Glass Works Stourbridge | |
| " 25 | 16 | 336445 | 1. Dalby & Pearson | 24 Summer Road, Birmingham |
| " 30 | 4 | 336594, 336595 | 2. Sowerby & Co | Ellison Glass Works Gateshead on Tyne |
| July 3 | 6 | 336725 | 1. John Shaw & Sons | Latimer Glass Works, Eyre Lane Sheffield |
| " 4 | 5 | 336759, 336760, 336761 | 3. Pellisson Père & Co | Cognac (Charente) France |
| " | " | 3370[illegible] | 1. Thomas Webb & Sons | Dennis, Stourbridge |
| " | 3 | 337072 | 1. William Thomas [illegible] | [illegible] Westminster |
| " 17 | 1 | 337178 | 1. Dalby & Pearson | Summer Road Birmingham |
| " 21 | 2 | 337344 | 1. Jane Webb, Joseph Hammond & Henry Fitzroy Webb trading as Executors to late Joseph Webb of Coalbourn Hill Glass Works Stourbridge | |
| " 22 | 6 | 337409 to 337415 | 7. Sowerby & Co | Ellison Glass Works Gateshead-on-Tyne |
| " | 7 | 337416 | 1. Henry Greener | Millfield Sunderland |
| " 24 | 16 | 337492 | 1. Wheeler & Banks | 54 to 56 Townsend Street Dublin |

| Date of Deposit | No. of Parcel | No. of Design | Name of Proprietor | Address of Proprietor |
|---|---|---|---|---|
| 1879 | | | | |
| July 29 | 7 | 337572 | 1. Jane Webb, Joseph Hammond & Henry Fitzroy Webb of Coalbourn Hill Glass Works | Stourbridge |
| " | 13 | 337623 to 337627 | 5. Sowerby & Co | Ellison Glass Works Gateshead-on-Tyne |
| Augt 1 | 13 | 337775 | 1. E Mordan & Co | Albion Works, City Road London |
| " 8 | 12 | 338015 | 1. Henry Greener | Wear Flint Glass Works, Millfield Sunderland |
| " 11 | 7 | 338093 | 1. Matthew Turnbull | Cornhill Glass Works Southwick Sunderland |
| " 11 | 12 | 338286, 338287 | 2. W. H. Heppell & Co | Forth Street, Newcastle-on-Tyne |
| " | 15 | 338294, 338295, 338296, 338297, 338298 | 5. Sowerby & Co | Ellison Glass Works Gateshead-on-Tyne |
| " 26 | 14 | 338734 | 1. Frederick Siemens | Dresden Saxony |
| Sept 4 | 7 | 339194, 339195, 339196, 339197, 339198, 339199, 339200 | 7. Sowerby & Co | Ellison Glass Works Gateshead-on-Tyne |
| " 12 | 9 | 339494 | 1. John Jackson Wheeler | 189 Fulham Road in the County of Middlesex |

| Date of Deposit | No of Parcel | No. of Design | Name of Proprietor | Address of Proprietor |
|---|---|---|---|---|
| 1879 | | | | |
| Septr 12 | 13 | 339498 | Sowerby & Co. | Ellison Glass Works, Gateshead-on-Tyne. |
| " | " | 339499 | | |
| " | " | 339500 | | |
| " | " | 339501 | | |
| " | " | 339502 | | |
| " 18 | 13 | 340002 | Sowerby & Co. | Ellison Glass Works Gateshead on Tyne |
| " | " | 6 | | |
| " | " | 340006 | | |
| " 19 | 19 | 340104 | 1 Henry Greener | Wear Flint Glass Works Sunderland |
| " | " | " | | |
| " 23 | 2 | 340206 | 1 Molineaux, Webb & Co | Kirby Street, Manchester |
| " | 13 | 340254 | 1 Sowerby & Co | Ellison Glass Works Gateshead on Tyne |
| " | " | " | | |
| " 24 | 15 | 340369 | 1 George W. W. Edwards | Wolverhampton |
| Novr 17 | 9 | 342741 | 1 H W & L Dee | [illegible]wood Street. |
| Decr 2 | 21 | 343724 | Sowerby & Co | Ellison Glass Works, Gateshead-on-Tyne. |
| " | " | 343725 | | |
| " | " | 343726 | | |
| " | " | 343727 | | |
| " | " | 343728 | | |
| " | " | 343729 | | |
| " | " | 343730 | | |
| " | " | 343731 | | |
| " 15 | 9 | 344257 | 1 G. V. De Luca | 21 Jewin Crescent, Aldersgate Street, E.C. |
| " | " | " | | |
| 1880 | | | | |
| Jany 5 | 2 | 344911 | 1 Molineaux Webb & Co | Kirby Street, Manchester |
| " 7 | 2 | 344960 | 1 Molineaux Webb & Co | Kirby Street, Manchester |

| Date of Deposit | No of Parcel | No. of Design | Name of Proprietor | Address of Proprietor |
|---|---|---|---|---|
| 1880 | | | | |
| Jany 9 | 11 | 345042 | Sowerby & Co | Ellison Glass Works Gateshead on Tyne |
| " | " | 345043 | | |
| " | " | 345044 | | |
| " 12 | 3 | 345071 | 1 W. Foster Smith | Barr Street, Birmingham |
| " 14 | 2 | 345166 | Molineaux Webb & Co | Kirby Street Manchester |
| " | " | 345167 | | |
| " | " | 345168 | | |
| " 20 | 14 | 345451 | 1 Abraham Fitton | 3 Robin Hood St, Cheetham Hill, Manchester |
| Feby 4 | 13 | 346020 | 2 The Rochester Tumbler Co | Pittsburgh Penna. U.S. of A. |
| " | " | 346021 | | |
| " 13 | 3 | 346369 | 1 The Rochester Tumbler Co | Pittsburgh Penna. U.S.A. |
| " 16 | 12 | 346505 | 1 Mina Beresch | 85 Charlotte Street, Fitzroy Square, W.C. |
| " 17 | 9 | 346[illegible] | 1 W. H. Heppell & Co | Newcastle on Tyne |
| March 11 | 9 | 347465 | 1 [illegible] Bush & Co | [illegible] 23 [illegible] Lane [illegible] London E. |
| " 20 | 2 | 347[illegible] | 1 John Shaw & Sons | [illegible] Works [illegible] Lane Sheffield |
| " 23 | 12 | 347895 | 1 G V de Luca | 21 Jewin Crescent, Aldersgate Street E.C. |
| " 31 | 13 | 348165 | 1 [illegible] Winfield & Co | [illegible] |
| April 1 | 9 | 348189 | M. L. Verhoeleren junior | 5 and [illegible] Street E.C. |
| " | " | " | | |
| " | " | 348191 | | |
| May 5 | 2 | 349527 | 1 C. B. [illegible] | [illegible] London E.C. |
| " 10 | 16 | 349740 | 1 [illegible] Wellcome | [illegible] City of London |
| " 11 | 13 | 349789 | 1 William Hall | 234 [illegible] Street Birmingham |
| " 14 | 5 | 349879 | 1 [illegible] Tonkinson | [illegible] Foundry, Sunderland |
| " 21 | 3 | 350028 | 1 William Twigg & Co | Birmingham |
| " 22 | 1 | 350065 | 1 Daniel Pearce | North End Hammersmith |

| Date of Deposit | No. of Parcel | No. of Design | Name of Proprietor | Address of Proprietor |
| --- | --- | --- | --- | --- |
| 1880 | | | | |
| May 24 | 8 | 350083 | 11 Sowerby & Co | Ellison Glass Works Gateshead on Tyne |
| | | 350084 | | |
| | | 350085 | | |
| | | 350086 | | |
| | | 350087 | | |
| | | 350088 | | |
| | | 350089 | | |
| | | 350090 | | |
| | | 350091 | | |
| | | 350092 | | |
| | | 350093 | | |
| " 29 | 11 | 350211 | 1. Sykes Macvay & Co. | Albion Glass Works Castleford Yorkshire |
| " | 15 | 350218 | 1. C. H. Kieling M.D. | 1 [illegible] Street, W. |
| " 31 | 15 | 350246 | 1. S. Williamson & Sons | 490 Caledonian Road Holloway |
| June 8 | 6 | 350486 | 1. Ferdinand Mulhens trading as Francis Maria Farina of 4711 Glockengasse | Cologne |
| " 14 | 3 | 351024 | 1. Percival Vickers & Co | Jersey Street Manchester |
| " | 19 | 351052 | 1. Burtles Tate & Co Limited | [illegible] Manchester |
| " 10 | 16 | 351191 | 1. W. H. Heppell & Co | Newcastle on Tyne |
| " 23 | 5 | 351354 | 1. Edmund William Boulding | 22 Great Crosshall Street, Liverpool in the County of Lancaster |
| " | 12 | 351455 | 1. Roland Bourne | [illegible] Birmingham |
| July 1 | 8 | 351728 | 1. Alfred Arculus | Eliza Works, 295 Broad Street Birmingham |
| " (Class I. 11.11.5) | 11 | 351866 | 1. Westwood & Moore | Brierley Hill Staffordshire |
| " " | 12 | 351867 | 1. E. W. Watson | 4 Pall Mall |

| Date of Deposit | No. of Parcel | No. of Design | Name of Proprietor | Address of Proprietor |
| --- | --- | --- | --- | --- |
| 1880 | | | | |
| July 13 | 11 | 352133 | 5. Sowerby & Co | Ellison Glass Works Gateshead on Tyne |
| | | " | | |
| | | 352137 | | |
| " 20 | 11 | 352408 | 1. William Kavanagh (?) Percy | 124 Trongate Glasgow |
| " 21 | 14 | 352519 | 1. Johnson (?) Sadler & Morris | 14 Water Lane Great Tower Street in the City of London |
| " 26 | 10 | 352840 | 6. Sowerby & Co | Ellison Glass Works Gateshead on Tyne |
| | | " | | |
| | | 352845 | | |
| " 27 | [illegible] | 352870 | 1. Percival, Vickers & Co Limited | Jersey Street Manchester |
| August 14 | 14 | 353716 | 1. R. M. Brundige | 880 Broadway, New York City U S A |
| " 23 | 14 | 354071 | 1. Barwell Son & Fisher | Worcester Works, Clement Street Birmingham |
| September 7 | 1 | 354935 | 1. W. H. Heppell & Co | Newcastle on Tyne |
| " 14 | 1 | 355154 | 5. Sowerby & Co | Ellison Glass Works, Gateshead-on-Tyne |
| | | " | | |
| | | 355158 | | |
| " 24 | 9 | 355627 | 3 Sowerby & Co | Ellison Glass Works Gateshead on Tyne |
| " | " | 355628 | | |
| " | " | 355629 | | |
| " 29 | 16 | 355979 | 1. Young's Paraffin Light and Mineral Oil Co L | Birmingham |
| October 5 | 1 | 356111 | 1. Thomas Pargeter Richardson | Wordsley Staffordshire |
| " 12 | 5 | 356515 | 1. Caroline Amelia Elizabeth Swallow | 9 Duvell (?) Place Lower Broughton Road Manchester |
| " 18 | 14 | 356807 | 1. John Ralph Walsh | Soho & Vesta Glass Works, Birmingham |

| Date of Deposit | No. of Parcel | No. of Design | Name of Proprietor | Address of Proprietor |
|---|---|---|---|---|
| 1880 Nov 3 | 1 | 357668? | 1. [illegible] Walsh | [illegible] Glass Works Birmingham |
| " [illegible] | [illegible] | [illegible] | 1. [illegible] | [illegible] |
| " 9 | 1 | 357951 | 1. James Bird | Britannia Works, Oxford Street Bilston |
| " " | 2 | 357953 | 1. Julius Ungar trading as Ungar & Co | 52 Commercial [illegible] |
| " 20 | 2 | 358659 | 1. Pembrook & Dingley | Hall Street Birmingham |
| " 23 | 10 | [illegible] | 1. Jeffries & Sons | [illegible] |
| " 26 | 14 | [illegible] | 1. Jeffries & Sons | 145 Houndsditch |
| Dec 1 | 17 | 359134 | 1. Young's Paraffin Light & Mineral Oil Co | Birmingham |
| " 3 | 15 | 3592[illegible] to 359239 | 3 Jeffries & Sons | 145 Houndsditch |
| 8 | 14 | [illegible] | 1. Henry Greener | Wear Flint Glass Works Sunderland |
| 10 | 7 | 359464 | 1. Watkins Brothers | 29 Hinckley [illegible] |
| " 15 | 15 | 3593[illegible] | [illegible] | |
| " 21 | 4 | 359877 | 1. Obed Charles Hawkes | Bromsgrove Street Birmingham |
| " 22 | 13 | 359928 | 1. Burroughs, Wellcome & Co | Snow Hill, London E.C. |
| 1881 Jany 5 | 3 | 360315 | 2. Obed Charles Hawkes | Bromsgrove Street Birmingham |
| | " | 360316 | | |
| " 7 | 15 | 360486 | 2. Jeffries & Sons | 145 Houndsditch |
| | | 360487 | | |
| " 12 | 16 | 360656 | 1. Edward Berman & Co | 30 [illegible] |
| " 31 | 9 | 361355 | 1. B. Temple | 1 St Thomas' Square Hackney |

| Date of Deposit | No. of Parcel | No. of Design | Name of Proprietor | Address of Proprietor |
|---|---|---|---|---|
| 1881 Feby 8 | 4 | 361535 | 2 John Shaw & Sons | Latimer Works, 52 Eyre Lane, Sheffield |
| " | " | 361536 | | |
| " 16 | 14 | 361810 | 1. Jeffries & Sons | 145 Houndsditch |
| " 28 | 10 | 362043 | 1. George William Hughes | 7 [illegible] Street Birmingham |
| March 1 | 8 | 362318 | 1. Max Sugar | 64 [illegible] Holborn |
| " | 12 | 362328 | 1. Henry Greener | Wear Flint Glass Works Sunderland |
| " 4 | 4 | 362453 | 1. Hodgetts Richardson & Son | Stourbridge |
| " 11 | 2 | 362734 | 11 Sowerby & Co | Ellison Glass Works Gateshead-on-Tyne |
| | | 362735 | | |
| | | 362736 | | |
| | | 362737 | | |
| | | 362738 | | |
| | | 362739 | | |
| | | 362740 | | |
| | | 362741 | | |
| | | 362742 | | |
| | | 362743 | | |
| | | 362744 | | |
| 19 | 11 | 363048 | 2. Sowerby & Co | Ellison Glass Works Gateshead on Tyne |
| " | " | 363049 | | |
| 23 | 9 | 363194 | 10. Young's Paraffin Light & Mineral Oil Co Limited | Birmingham |
| " | " | to | | |
| " | " | 363203 | | |
| " 30 | 8 | 363454 | 5 William Thomas Sugg | Vincent Street Westminster |
| " | " | to | | |
| " | " | 363458 | | |
| April 4 | 6 | 363648 | 1. William Pratt | 234 [illegible] Street Birmingham |
| " 9 | 9 | 363798 | 1. John Gough | 12, Parade, Birmingham |
| " 20 | 9 | 364167 | 1. Sowerby & Co. | Ellison Glass Works, Gateshead on Tyne |

| Date of Deposit | No of Parcel | No. of Design | Name of Proprietor | Address of Proprietor |
|---|---|---|---|---|
| 1881 | | | | |
| April 21 | 13 | 364187 | 1. Henry Greener | Wear Flint Glass Works Sunderland |
| 30 | 17 | 364574 | 1. Samuel Elijah Culver | 2 Rydon Crescent, Clerkenwell |
| May 19 | 9 | 365,165 | 1. Sowerby & Co. | Ellison Glass Works, Gateshead-on-Tyne |
| 31 | 6 | 365634 | 1. Thomas Wimpenny | 72 Bellevue Road Leeds |
| June 14 | 9 | 366,032 | 1. Henry Greener | Millfield, Sunderland |
| 22 | 16 | 366273 | 1. R.A.C. Wilson | 17 Wilson Street, Gray's Inn Road |
| 24 | 10 | 366408 | 1 Henry Greener | Wear Flint Glass Works, Sunderland. |
| July 16 | 9 | 367237 | 1. Crichton & Curry | 45 Rathbone Place W. |
| August 19 | 15 | 368638 | 1. J. Defries & Sons | 147 Houndsditch |
| September 2 | 23 | 369483 | 1. Robert Gardner Bird & Co | 8 Brooke Street, Holborn |
| 19 | 9 | 370198 | 2. Alfred Augustus Hely | 6 Lansdowne Gardens, South Lambeth S.E. |
| " | " | 370199 | | |
| 21 | 16 | 370370 to 370379 | 10 Sowerby & Co | Ellison Glass Works Gateshead on Tyne |
| 23 | 20 | 370469 | 1 J. Defries & Sons | 147 Houndsditch |
| 26 | 1 | 370524 | 1. W. H. Heppell & Co | Newcastle on Tyne |
| 28 | 3 | 370618 | 2 Molineaux Webb & Co | Manchester |
| " | " | 370619 | | |
| Oct 12 | 5 | 371262 | 1. Molineaux Webb & Co | Kirby Street Manchester |
| 14 | 2 | 371343 | 1. William Bartleet & Sons | Abbey Mills, Redditch |
| 22 | 15 | 372018 | 1. Percival Vickers & Co Limited | Jersey Street Manchester |
| Nov 7 | 3 | 372860 | 1 W. H. Heppell & Co | Newcastle on Tyne |
| 8 | 10 | 372967 | 1. Max Sugar | 6 Thavies Inn Holborn. London E.C |
| 15 | 15 | 373268 | 2. A. Dollmann | 37 Monkwell Street E.C |
| " | " | 373269 | | |

| Date of Deposit | No of Parcel | No. of Design | Name of Proprietor | Address of Proprietor |
|---|---|---|---|---|
| 1881 | | | | |
| November 26 | 6 | 373918 | 1. William Sugg & Co Limited | Vincent Works, Westminster |
| December 6 | 8 | 374432 | 1. J. Defries & Sons | 147 Houndsditch |
| " | 13 | 374437 | 1 W. H. Heppell & Co | Newcastle on Tyne |
| 7 | 17 | 374475 | 1. Henry Greener | Wear Flint Glass Works, Sunderland |
| 8 | 8 | 374497 | 1 Harwood Son & Harrison | 187 Newhall Street, Birmingham |
| 12 | 13 | 374629 to 374631 | 3. Messrs Hawkes | Bromsgrove Street Birmingham and |
| 14 | 6 | 374682 to 374686 | 5 Sowerby & Co | Ellison Glass Works Gateshead-on-Tyne |
| 15 | 9 | 374773 | 1. J. Defries & Sons | 147 Houndsditch |
| " | 10 | 374774 | 5. Sowerby & Co. | Ellison Glass Works, Gateshead-on-Tyne |
| " | " | 374775 | | |
| " | " | 374776 | | |
| " | " | 374777 | | |
| " | " | 374778 | | |
| 23 | 1 | 375013 | 2. Hawkesford & Booth | 7 Bath Street, & 23 Great Hampton Row Birmingham |
| " | " | 375014 | | |
| 28 | 7 | 375151 to 375155 | 5 B. Verity & Sons | 31 King Street, Covent Garden W.C. |
| 1882 | | | | |
| January 2 | 1 | 375281 | 1. Molineaux Webb & Co | Kirby Street, Ancoats, Manchester |
| 24 | 7 | 375360 | 1. George Whybrow | 48 & 49 Wellclose Square E London. E. |
| 26 | 8 | 376428 | 1. Hodgetts Richardson & Son | Stourbridge |
| February 9 | 20 | 376905 | 1. Sowerby's Ellison Glass Works Limited | Gateshead-on-Tyne |
| 16 | 19 | 377222 | 1. R. W. Winfield & Co | Birmingham |

| Date of Deposit | No. of Parcel | No. of Design | | Name of Proprietor | Address of Proprietor |
|---|---|---|---|---|---|
| 1882. | | | | | |
| March 4 | 10 | 378022 | 2 | Henry Greener | Wear Flint Glass Works, Sunderland |
| " | " | 378023 | | | |
| 7 | 15 | 378013 | 3 | Samuel Gratrix Jnr. & Brother | Alport Town, Manchester |
| " | " | to | | | |
| " | " | 378015 | | | |
| 17 | 4 | 378495 | 1 | Percival Vickers & Co Limited | Jersey Street, Manchester |
| " | 8 | 378506 | 1 | Phillip M Beck | [illegible] Bishopsgate [illegible] |
| 28 | 19 | 378997 | 2 | J Defries & Sons | 147 Houndsditch |
| " | " | 378998 | | | |
| April 8 | 10 | 379366 | 1 | John William Webb & Robert Richard Sinclair | 75 Sinclair Market, West Ham E |
| 12 | 7 | 379463 | 1 | Henry Gething Richardson | Wordsley, Stourbridge |
| 24 | 2 | 379826 | 1 | John Short Downing | Crown Works, Commercial Street Birmingham |
| 28 | 1 | 380077 | 1 | James Dixon & Sons | Cornish Place, Sheffield |
| " | 13 | 380132 | 3 | Sowerby's Ellison Glass Works Limited | Gateshead-on-Tyne. |
| " | " | 380133 | | | |
| " | " | 380134 | | | |
| May 23 Classes 3 & 4 | 9 | 381317 | 1 | Edward Edwards | Buddle Road, Wollaston, near Stourbridge. |
| 25 | 1 | 381436 | 1 | Percival Vickers & Co Limited | Jersey Street, Manchester |
| " | 12 | 381481 | 1 | Henry Greener | Wear Flint Glass Works, Sunderland |
| 30 | 11 | 381676 | 3 | William Sugg & Co Limited | Vincent Street Westminster |
| " | " | 381678 | | | |
| " | " | 381677 | | | |
| July 1 Class I II III & IV | 10 | 382831 | 1 | Sidney Brown | 8 Blackfriars Road S.E. |
| " | 12 | 382838 | 1 | J Defries & Sons | 147 Houndsditch |

| Date of Deposit | No. of Parcel | No. of Design | | Name of Proprietor | Address of Proprietor |
|---|---|---|---|---|---|
| 1882 | | | | | |
| July 5 | 18 | 383007 | 1 | J. Defries & Sons | 147 Houndsditch |
| 19 | 6 | 383640 | 1 | Henry Greener | Wear Flint Glass Works, Sunderland |
| 31 | 1 | 384159 | 1 | Walton & Co | Earlstown |
| Aug 9 | 14 | 384453 | 3 | Sowerby's Ellison Glass Works Limited | Gateshead on Tyne |
| " | " | 384454 | | | |
| " | " | 384455 | | | |
| 18 | 16 | 384778 | 1 | Hodge & Butler | [illegible] Regent Street London |
| 24 | 13 | 385624 | 2 | Sowerby's Ellison Glass Works Limited | Gateshead on Tyne |
| " | " | 385625 | | | |
| 31 | 16 | 385736 | 1 | E. R. Durkee & Co | Water Street, New York U.S.A |
| Septr 7 | 2 | 386038 | 1 | William Symes | 201 Broad Street Birmingham |
| 22 | 3 | 386878 | 1 | Derby & Pearson | Albert Works, Graham Street Birmingham |
| 25 | 8 | 387036 | 1 | Henry Howe | 46 Queen Street Hammersmith |
| 26 | 9 | 387075 | 3 | J Defries & Sons | 147 Houndsditch |
| " | " | 387076 | | | |
| " | " | 387077 | | | |
| Octr 3 | 4 | 387378 | 1 | Charles Ward & Son | 2 West Chapel Street Mayfair London |
| 23 | 16 | 388896 | 1 | Sowerby's Ellison Glass Works Limited | Gateshead-on-Tyne |
| 31 | 11 | 389157 | 2 | John Walsh Walsh | Soho & Vesta Glass Works, Birmingham |
| " | " | 389158 | | | |
| November 1 | 3 | 389169 | 1 | Deykin & Sons | Jennens Row Birmingham |
| 15 | 11 | 390018 | 1 | Henry Churchman | Horsham |
| 17 | 3 | 390103 | 2 | Thomas Webb & Sons | Stourbridge |
| " | " | 390104 | | | |

| Date of Deposit | No. of Parcel | No. of Design | | Name of Proprietor | Address of Proprietor |
|---|---|---|---|---|---|
| 1882 | | | 4 | | |
| Nov 24 | 17 | 390584 | 3 | W. H. Heppell & Co | Newcastle on Tyne |
| RW. " | " | to | | | |
| " | " | 390586 | | | |
| " 27 | 1 | 390615 | 1 | Percival Vickers & Co Limited | Jersey Street, Manchester |
| " | " | — | | | |
| " " | 2 | 390616 | 1 | Dalby & Pearson | Albert Works, Graham Street, Birmingham |
| " | | — | | | |
| " 29 | 11 | 390709 | 2 | Joseph Shaw | Park Street, Walsall |
| " | " | 390710 | | | |
| December 1 | 13 | 390833 | 3 | W James | 201 Broad Street, Birmingham |
| " | " | to | | | |
| " | " | 390835 | | | |
| Class [illegible] 9 | 18 | 391302 | 1 | H Vanden [illegible] | Regent Street [illegible] |
| AK 19 | 15 | 391669 | 1 | Walton & Co | West Lancashire Flint Glass Works, Newton-le-Willows |
| Class [illegible] | [illegible] | 18 | 2 | Walter Thornhill & Co | 144 & 145 New Bond Street London |
| [illegible] | | 392019 | | | |
| 1883 | | | | | |
| January 6 | 5 | 392521 | 3 | William James | 201 Broad Street Birmingham |
| " | " | to | | | |
| " | " | 392523 | | | |
| " 25 | 20 | 393243 | 2 | John Walsh Walsh | Soho & Vesta Glass Works, Birmingham |
| " | " | 393244 | | | |
| February 3 | 11 | 393638 | 6 | Sowerby's Ellison Glass Works Limited | Gateshead-on-Tyne |
| " | " | 393639 | | | |
| " | " | 393640 | | | |
| " | " | 393641 | | | |
| " | " | 393642 | | | |
| " | " | 393643 | 6 | | |

| Date of Deposit | No. of Parcel | No. of Design | | Name of Proprietor | Address of Proprietor |
|---|---|---|---|---|---|
| 1883 | | | 6 | | |
| February 12 | 9 | 394098 | 1 | Henry Greener | Wear Flint Glass Works Sunderland |
| " 14 | 11 | 394205 | 1 | Percival Vickers & Co Limited | Jersey Street Manchester |
| " 16 | 10 | 394320 | 1 | Jonas & Jules Lang | 13 Charterhouse Buildings |
| " 24 | 15 | 394680 | 1 | Henry Morrell | 149 Fleet Street London |
| March 12 | 1 | 395417 | 2 | Young's Paraffin Light & Mineral Oil Co Limited | Clifford Lamp Works Birmingham |
| " | " | 395418 | | | |
| " 17 | 6 | 395786 | 1 | Henry G Richardson | Wordsley Flint Glass Works Stourbridge |
| " 27 | 5 | 396091 | 1 | Boulton & Mills | Audnam Glass Works, Stourbridge |
| " 31 | 9 | 396305 | 1 | Henry Greener | Flint Glass Works Sunderland |
| April 6 | 1 | 396530 | 1 | Stuckley & Co | Stourbridge |
| " 12 | 22 | 396835 | 1 | Rudolf Edward Frank | Red Cross Street in the City of London |
| " 17 | 3 | 397022 | 1 | Percival Vickers & Co Limited | Jersey Street, Manchester |
| " 27 | 5 | 397473 | 1 | Josiah Lane | 41 to 43 Hampton Street Glass Works, Birmingham |
| May 1 | 16 | 397604 | 1 | Henry Greener | Wear Flint Glass Works, Sunderland |
| " 8 | 4 | 397827 | 1 | John Castle | 87 Edward Street, Parade, Birmingham |
| " | 5 | 397828 | 1 | Henry Gething Richardson | Wordsley Flint Glass Works near Stourbridge |
| " 16 | 2 | 398241 | 1 | Edmund Fowle | Amesbury House, Bickley, Kent |

| Date of Deposit | No. of Parcel | No. of Design | Name of Proprietor | Address of Proprietor |
|---|---|---|---|---|
| 1883 | | | | |
| May 23 | 6 | 398435 | 1 Hopgood & Co | 43 Union Street, Ryde, Isle of Wight |
| " | " | — | | |
| 28 | 18 | 398610 | 1 Allen & Hanburys | Plough Court, Lombard Street E.C. |
| " | " | — | | |
| June 1 | 11 | 398825 | 1 Henry Adolph Wetzel | [illegible] London E C |
| 6 | 10 | 398981 | 1 G V de Luca | 64/7 Long Lane, Aldersgate Street E.C. |
| " | " | — | | |
| 7 | 20 | 399063 | 1 Jefferies & Sons | 147 Houndsditch |
| " | 22 | 399065 | 1 Wittmann & Roth | 47 Great Marlborough Street W |
| " | " | — | | |
| 9 | 7 | 399114 | 1 [illegible] & Company | 111 City Road, London E.C. |
| 12 | 14 | 399313 | 1 Bertles, Tate & Co | Poland Street, Manchester |
| 15 | 3 | 399455 | 1 J Forrest & Son | 219 Argyle Street Glasgow |
| " | " | — | | |
| 29 | 14 | 400089 | 2 Hermann Schulder | Solingen Germany |
| " | " | 400090 | | |
| August 2 | 4 | 401665 | 1 Hames Batchelor & Co | 110 Cannon Street, London E.C. |
| " | " | — | | |
| 11 | 9 | 402039 | 1 Allen & Hanburys | Plough Court Lombard Street E C |
| " | " | — | | |
| 17 | 11 | 402370 | 1 William Ramsay Jamieson & Co | 254 Argyle Street Glasgow |
| 24 | 2 | 402690 | 1 Percival Vickers & Co Limited | Manchester |
| " | " | — | | |
| 31 | 5 | 403109 | 1 Brinbrook & Dingley | Hall Street Birmingham |
| September 13 | 8 | 403804 | 1 Thomas Webb & Sons | Dennis Glass Works Stourbridge |
| " | " | | | |
| 15 | 1 | 403905 | 1 Richard Dendy Sadler | 14, Water Lane in the city of London |
| 24 | 13 | 404322 | 1 M. B. Simmons & Co | 80-82 Kings Cross Road W.C |
| | | — | | |

| Date of Deposit | No. of Parcel | No. of Design | Name of Proprietor | Address of Proprietor |
|---|---|---|---|---|
| 1883 | | | | |
| October 2 | 19 | 404649 | 1 W. Reynolds & Sons | 31 Fort Street, Brushfield Street, Bishopsgate |
| " | " | — | | |
| 6 | 10 | 404899 | 1 James Lewis & Arthur Lewis | 6 Bartlett's Buildings, Holborn Circus London E C |
| | | — | | |
| 12 | 15 | 405338 | 1 William Barker and Son | 48 and 49 Bishopsgate Street Without London E C |
| | | — | | |
| 13 | 14 | 405367 | 1 George Robert Cheshire | Pottery Warehouse 6 York Road City Road E C |
| | | — | | |
| 15 | 8 | 405382 | 2 Richard Dendy Sadler and William Bagley | 14 Water Lane, Tower Street in the City of London |
| " | " | 405383 | | |
| November 2 | 12 | 406456 | 1 Percival Vickers & Co Limited | Jersey Street, Manchester |
| | | — | | |
| 9 | 16 | 406731 | 1 John J Wheeler | 189 Fulham Road, London S W |
| " | " | — | | |
| 13 | 15 | 406880 | 2 Richard Dendy Sadler & William Bagley | 14 Water Lane, Tower Street in the City of London |
| " | " | 406881 | | |
| 14 | 11 | 406942 | 2 Thomas Webb & Sons | Stourbridge |
| " | " | 406943 | | |
| " | 12 | 406944 | 1 Henry Greener | Wear Flint Glass Works Sunderland |
| " | " | — | | |
| 17 | 11 | 407253 | 2 Innes & Grieve | [illegible] Waterloo Place Edinburgh |
| " | " | 407254 | | |
| 28 | 2 | 407766 | 1 Khoosh Bitters Co Ld | 12 Goree Piazzas Liverpool |
| Decr 12 | 11 | 408221 | 1 Cuthbert Britton Slee, & Herbert Hutton Slee trading as Batty & Co | 123 & 125, Finsbury Pavement, London E.C. |
| " | " | — | | |
| " | " | — | | — |

## GLASS REGISTER 1884 — 1908

First number of each year

| | | |
|---|---|---|
| 675 | 23rd January | 1884 |
| 19937 | 6th January | 1885 |
| 40484 | 1st January | 1886 |
| 64590 | 1st January | 1887 |
| 90649 | 4th January | 1888 |
| 116710 | 1st January | 1889 |
| 141333 | 1st January | 1890 |
| 163914 | 1st January | 1891 |
| 185803 | 4th January | 1892 |
| 205280 | 3rd January | 1893 |
| 224765 | 1st January | 1894 |
| 247064 | 2nd January | 1895 |
| 268508 | 2nd January | 1896 |
| 291360 | 4th January | 1897 |
| 311691 | 1st January | 1898 |
| 331808 | 4th January | 1899 |
| 351372 | 5th January | 1900 |
| 368272 | 3rd January | 1901 |
| 385541 | 10th January | 1902 |
| 403012 | 3rd January | 1903 |
| 424157 | 4th January | 1904 |
| 447615 | 3rd January | 1905 |
| 471617 | 3rd January | 1906 |
| 493532 | 2nd January | 1907 |
| 518475 | 2nd January | 1908 |

The descriptions against the registrations are as in the registers of 1842—1883 and 1884—1908, or as written on the drawing submitted to the Design Registration office. When the description is within brackets it is taken from looking at the drawing of the original object registered, and is observation.

On pieces of glass prior to 1884, the date of the glass, when it was registered, can be worked out from the diamond shaped registration mark. In the registers, a number was given alongside the date and this number has been included in the lists to provide as much information as possible. However, during and after 1884 articles were stamped with the number that was given at the time of registration, so the number of the pressed glass then coincides with the number given in the register and the date is ascertained by looking up that number in the register. It must be emphasised that this number was only used after the diamond registration mark was disbanded.

The glass register from 1842 to 1884 is as complete as possible. The 1884 onwards register has been edited, due to the large numbers of registered items. It must be made clear that the firms left out are mainly those that are not likely to be encountered in the study of household glass, such as that of 30th January 1885, registered by Thorsten Nordenfelt, Civil Engineer. "Design for bottle with moulded ridge for scraping off excess liquid".

Despite this pruning the list of registrations is more full than any lists hitherto published and includes all types of glass.

| *Registration* No. | *Date* | *Year* | *Registered* Party | *Design* |
|---|---|---|---|---|
| 675 | 23 January | 1884 | Kemp and Taylor, Manchester. Stationers | Improved shape of ink bottle with recess at upper part of bottle to hold pen |
| 1113 | 31 January | | Lawrence Brothers, London. Merchants | Shape of bottle |
| 1415 | 7 February | | Percival, Vickers & Co. Ltd., Manchester. Glass Makers | Pattern for pressed glassware |
| 1627 | 9 February | | Barnes and Company, Birmingham. Glass Maker | Shape of sugar or cream basin; oblong, taper, eight sides |
| 1628 | | | Barnes and Company (see prior) | Shape of a flint jelly dish; oblong, rounded sides |
| 1815 | 13 February | | William Barker & Son, London. Wine Merchant | Shape of bottle |
| 1909 | 14 February | | John Walsh Walsh, (The Soho & Vesta Glass Works), Birmingham. Glass Maker | Arch-topped, rolled over pillar known as the "Queen Anne" and applied to glass |
| 2339 | 22 February | | Edwin William Streeter, London. Diamond Merchant | Shape of claret jug with stopper beneath the lid |
| 2659 | 29 February | | Henry Gething Richardson, Stourbridge. Glass Maker | New design for glass globe to be used with comet fitting |
| 3613/4 | 14 March | | Burtles, Tate & Co., Manchester. Glass Makers | Ornamental design applicable for patterns |
| 3658 | 15 March | | Reuben Jackson, Sheffield, York. Cut Glass Manufacturer | Shape of a circular glass cruet |
| 4242 | 27 March | | Alfred & James Davies, Stourbridge. Glass Makers | Pattern and shape |
| 4406 | 29 March | | T. L. Willis, Winder & Co., London. Wine Merchant | Shape of bottle |
| 4489 | 2 April | | John Walsh Walsh (see prior) | Shape of the acorn |
| 4546 | | | James Dixon & Sons, Sheffield. Merchant | Shape |
| 4589 | | | Edward Webb, Wordsley, Stourbridge. Glass Maker | Pattern and shape |
| 4833 | 7 April | | Sowerby's Ellison Glass Works Ltd., Gateshead. Glass Maker. | Pattern |
| 5418 | 18 April | | Henry Johnson, Holborn. Glass Maker Agent | Pressed glass flower stand; pattern and shape |
| 5442 | 19 April | | Edward Webb (see prior) | Shape — crimping and decoration of flower stand |
| 5849 | 29 April | | Sowerby's Ellison Glass Works Ltd. (see prior) | Pattern and shape |
| 6481 | 8 May | | Sowerby's Ellison Glass Works Ltd. (see prior) | Pattern and shape of flower vase |
| 6658 | 10 May | | Percival, Vickers & Co. Ltd., (see prior) | Design for round platter in moulded glass |
| 7978/9 | 5 June | | Sowerby's Ellison Glass Works Ltd. (see prior) | Butter dish and cover; shape and pattern |
| 8013 | 7 June | | John Walsh Walsh (see prior) | Shape |
| 8824 | 24 June | | G. Murray Wilson, Hawick, Scotland. Manufacturer | Conical or pear-shaped ink bottle |
| 9213 | 3 July | | John Fuller Spong, Clapham, Surrey. Gentleman | Design for neck and stopper of glass bottle |
| 9805-8 | 15 July | | Alfred and James Davies (see prior) | Pattern and shape |
| 10038 | 19 July | | A. J. Smith, Birmingham. Manufacturing Jeweller | Ornamental glass case for scarf pins |
| 10277 | 25 July | | Thomas Webb & Sons, Stourbridge. Glass Maker | Shape of valence edge glass |
| 10422 | 29 July | | Thomas Rule, Leeds. Commercial Traveller | Shape of stopper |

| *Registration* No. | *Date* | *Year* | *Registered* Party | *Design* |
|---|---|---|---|---|
| 10594 | 2 August | 1884 | Philip Schuyler Malcolm, London. Gentleman | Design for glass bottle |
| 10595 | | | Max Sugar, London. Manufacturer | Shape |
| 10966 | 11 August | | Sowerby's Ellison Glass Works Ltd., Gateshead. Glass Maker | Pattern and shape |
| 10967 | | | Sowerby's Ellison Glass Works Ltd. (see prior) | Sugar basin, shape and ornamentation |
| 11109 | 12 August | | Thomas Webb & Sons, Stourbridge. Glass Maker | Scent bottle |
| 11344 | 15 August | | Max Sugar & Co. (see prior) | Shape of boat flower vase |
| 12723 | 10 September | | Silber and Fleming, London. Foreign & Fancy goods dealers | Pattern and shape |
| 12758/9 | 11 September | | Thomas Webb & Sons (see prior) | Shape of bottle |
| 12839/40 | 12 September | | Thomas Webb & Sons (see prior) | Shape and decoration |
| 13563 | 19 September | | Sowerby's Ellison Glass Works Ltd. (see prior) | Handle of jug made at the side instead of at back opposite the lip. |
| 13792 | 24 September | | Sowerby's Ellison Glass Works Ltd. (see prior) | Shape of glass post pillar money box manufactured in one piece |
| 13870 | 25 September | | Groves and Company, London. Wine Merchant | Shape of Greek amphora-shaped bottle with foot added |
| 14057 | 27 September | | W. W. Harrison & Co., Montgomery Works, Sheffield. Electro Plate Manufacturer | Shape for biscuit or sugar basket |
| 14390 | 3 October | | Henry Greener, Wear Flint Glass Works, Sunderland and London. Glass Maker | Ornamental design for glasses for pavement lights, floor lights, etc. |
| 15256 | 16 October | | Henry Gething Richardson, Wordsley Flint Glass Works, Stourbridge. Glass Maker | Ornamental design for glass decoration |
| 15332 | 18 October | | Percival, Vickers & Co. Ltd., Manchester. Glass Makers | Shape and pattern in pressed glass |
| 15352 | | | Johnson, Sons & Edmonds, Bedford Row. Silversmiths | Pattern and shape of bottle |
| 15353 | | | Stevens & Williams, Brierley Hill Glass Works,Stafford. Glass Makers | Design for glass ornament to be used for decorating bowls, vases, etc. |
| 16235 | 3 November | | Selinger & Emanuel, London. Merchants | Design for an ornamental tray representing the Nile expedition |
| 16475 | 7 November | | Boulton & Mills, Audnam Glass Works, Stourbridge. Glass Maker | Shape of glass candlestick & flower-holder combined |
| 16828/9 | 13 November | | Thomas Webb & Sons (see prior) | Shape of scent bottle |
| 16835 | | | William Henry Wood, Jr., Birmingham. Manufacturer Iron, Tin & Zinc Goods | Glass cover for floral and artificial decoration; novel-shaped glass cover |
| 17102/3 | 17 November | | George Cole, London. Merchant | Pattern and shape of moulded and blown glass |
| 17721 | 27 November | | George Cole (see prior) | Pattern and shape of cruet set |
| 18069 | 3 December | | Joseph Lucas & Son, Birmingham. Lamp Manufacturer | Shape |
| 18108/9 | 3 December | | Sampson Mordan & Co., London. Manufacturer | Shape of perfume bottle |
| 18749 | 10 December | | Percival, Vickers & Co. Ltd. (see prior) | Railway and other lamps — pressed scolloped band on glass. |

| *Registration* No. | *Date* | *Year* | *Registered* Party | *Design* |
|---|---|---|---|---|
| 18806 | 12 December | 1884 | Sampson Mordan & Co., London. Manufacturer | Shape of a perfume or salts bottle |
| 18827 | 13 December | | Francis Dixon Nuttal, Ravenhead Glass Bottle Works, St. Helens, Lancashire. Glass Bottle Manufacturer | Glass jars of novel shape, with straight sides internally and a projecting external flange or rim at the top. |
| 19238 | 18 December | | Edmond Rocher, Clichy, France. Glass Maker | Protection for bottle having internal lozenges, facets or prisms |
| 19704 | 20 December | | George Cole, London. Merchant | Shape for glass or china vase |
| 19733 | 21 December | | Lampereur & Bernard, Liege, Belgium. Manufacturer | Chimney for mineral oil and gas lamps |
| 19740 | 23 December | | Mills, Walker & Co., Glass Works, Stourbridge. Table Glass Manufacturer | Acorn and leaf running round article made in glass |
| 19741 | | | Mills, Walker & Co. (see prior) | Acorn and oak leaf supporting article made in glass |
| 19742 | | | Mills, Walker & Co. (see prior) | Acorn and oak leaf |
| 19744 | 31 December | | J. Dunlop Mitchell & Co., Glasgow. Merchant | Shape of combination bottle and top |
| 19937 | 6 January | 1885 | Sowerby's Ellison Glass Works Ltd., Gateshead. Glass Maker | Pattern of sugar basin |
| 20079 | 8 January | | George Cole (see prior) | Shape and pattern of blown or moulded vase |
| 20085 | | | Burtles, Tate & Co., Poland Street Glass Works, Manchester. Glass Makers | Design for glass flower holder or bracket |
| 20086 | | | Burtles, Tate & Co. (see prior) | Design for glass flower holder |
| 20355 | 14 January | | Percival, Vickers & Co. Ltd., Manchester. Glass Maker | Pattern for pressed butter trencher |
| 20634 | 19 January | | Selinger & Emanuel, London. Merchants | Design for a bottle |
| 20775 | 21 January | | Sowerby's Ellison Glass Works Ltd. (see prior) | Pattern of water jug |
| 20860 | | | Jane Webb & Henry Fitzroy Webb, Coalbourn Hill Glass Works, Stourbridge. Glass Makers. | Embossed pine decoration for cutting and moulding in glass |
| 20861 | | | Jane Webb & Henry Fitzroy Webb (see prior) | Glass perfume bottle formed as a shell |
| 20862 | | | Jane Webb & Henry Fitzroy Webb (see prior) | Glass perfume bottle formed as a horn |
| 20930 | 22 January | | Edward Edwards, The Novelty Glass Works, Stourbridge. Glass Maker. | Shape for relief ornament for vases |
| 20936 | | | Percival, Vickers & Co. Ltd. (see prior) | Design for pressed glass marmalade |
| 20972 | 24 January | | Burtles, Tate & Co. (see prior) | Shape and pattern of flower stand |
| 21108-10 | 28 January | | Burtles, Tate & Co. (see prior) | Pattern and shape of flower stand |
| 21284 | 31 January | | Sowerby's Ellison Glass Works Ltd. (see prior) | Pattern of glass dish |
| 21326/7 | 2 February | | Burtles, Tate & Co. (see prior) | Shape and pattern of flower stand |
| 21328/9 | | | Burtles, Tate & Co. (see prior) | Shape and pattern of flower stand |
| 21616 | 5 February | | Boulton & Mills, Audnam Glass Works, Stourbridge. Glass Maker | Pattern of glass decoration |
| 21620 | 6 February | | James Hateley, Birmingham. Flint Glass Manufacturer | Pattern and shape |
| 22179 | 17 February | | Boulton & Mills (see prior) | Maiden Hair fern decoration on glass |
| 22506 | 24 February | | Thomas Edward Bladon, Birmingham. Tin & Iron Plate Worker | Pattern and shape of the glass |

| *Registration* No. | *Date* | *Year* | *Registered* Party | *Design* |
|---|---|---|---|---|
| 22614 | 25 February | 1885 | C. George, Islington. Chemist | Pattern and shape of tumbler |
| 22928 | 3 March | | Heine Bros. & Co., London. Importers | Shape of glass globe, ornamental design |
| 23040/1 | 5 March | | Molineaux, Webb & Co., Manchester. Glass Maker | Pattern and shape |
| 23184 | | | Yeatman & Co., London. Manufacturer | Shape of the bottle |
| 23333-8 | 10 March | | Molineaux, Webb & Co. (see prior) | Pattern and shape |
| 23378 | 11 March | | Molineaux, Webb & Co. (see prior) | Pattern and shape |
| 24100 | 20 March | | Burtles, Tate & Co., Poland Street Glass Works, Manchester. Glass Makers | Shape and pattern of flower stand |
| 24139 | 21 March | | Joseph Braham, Soho. Silversmith | Shape of bottle for toilet or scent bottle representing a grenade |
| 24953 | 13 April | | Sowerby's Ellison Glass Works Ltd., Gateshead. Glass Maker | Shape of butter dish |
| 25435 | 20 April | | Thomas Webb & Sons, Stourbridge. Glass Maker | Pattern of decoration |
| 25863-5 | 27 April | | Thomas Webb & Sons (see prior) | Shape of bottle |
| 26170 | 2 May | | George Watts, Jr. Middlesex. Jeweller's Pattern Maker | Perfume bottle in the shape of a "walnut shell" |
| 26173 | 4 May | | Max Sugar & Co., London. Manufacturer | Pattern and shape |
| 26480 | 7 May | | Burtles, Tate & Co. (see prior) | Shape of glass shell |
| 27072 | 16 May | | Lotz, Abbot & Co., Middlesex. Merchant | Shape |
| 27553 | 28 May | | Percival, Vickers & Co. Ltd., Manchester. Glass Makers | Pattern for moulded marmalade |
| 27624 | 1 June | | Hardcastle & Co., London. East India Merchant | Shape |
| 27642 | | | Lotz, Abbot & Co. (see prior) | Shape |
| 27985-90 | 5 June | | William Oppenheim, London. Importer | Shape of lamp ornament or stick top |
| 28338 | 12 June | | J. Dunlop Mitchell & Co., Glasgow. Merchant | Shape and pattern of gas shade |
| 28709 | 20 June | | Sampson Mordan & Co. London. Manufacturer | Design for a scent bottle |
| 28770 | 22 June | | Miles Williams, Liverpool. Varnish Manufacturer | Glass bottle, three sides plain and one plain having a wide neck |
| 29106 | 29 June | | Burtles, Tate & Co. (see prior) | Pattern of flower boat |
| 29145 | 1 July | | Percival, Vickers & Co. Ltd. (see prior) | Design for pressed glass butter |
| 29260 | 2 July | | Sampson Mordan & Co. (see prior) | Design for scent bottle |
| 29677 | 10 July | | J. Shaw & Sons, Sheffield. Cut Glass Manufacturer | Pattern shown on the paper not the shape of bottle |
| 29780/1 | 14 July | | Molineaux, Webb & Co. (see prior) | Pattern and shape |
| 30244 | 22 July | | Sowerby's Ellison Glass Works Ltd. (see prior) | Pattern of a sugar |
| 30345 | 24 July | | Henry Johnson, Holborn. Glass Maker | Moulded glass horseshoe photograph frame |
| 30704 | 1 August | | Henry Johnson (see prior) | Moulded glass bowl attached to moulded glass stand |
| 31844 | 21 August | | Molineaux, Webb & Co. (see prior) | Shape and pattern |

| *Registration* No. | *Date* | *Year* | *Registered* Party | *Design* |
|---|---|---|---|---|
| 32125/6 | 25 August | 1885 | George Seibdrat, Finsbury. Agent | Shape and pattern of cruet |
| 32253 | 27 August | | Sowerby's Ellison Glass Works Ltd., Gateshead. Glass Maker | Pattern of dish |
| 33714/5 | 19 September | | John Walsh Walsh, The Soho & Vesta Glass Works, Birmingham. Glass Maker. | Shape |
| 34196 | 26 September | | Burtles, Tate & Co., Poland Street Glass Works, Manchester. Glass Makers | Pattern and shape of glass flower vase |
| 35063 | 7 October | | Prince & Symmons, Lion Lamp Works, Shoreditch. Lamp Manufacturer | Pattern of a parrot to be used as a lamp |
| 35064 | | | Prince & Symmons (see prior) | Pattern of bulldog to be used as a lamp |
| 35293 | 10 October | | Percival, Vickers & Co. Ltd., Manchester. Glass Maker | Design for pressed glass cruets |
| 35660 | 15 October | | Thomas Seage, Heeley. Glass Mixer. | New form of glass jelly dish for mounting in silver electro plate metal |
| 35709 | 18 October | | Alfred Arculus, Birmingham. Glass Maker | Ornamentation on the shade |
| 36184 | 22 October | | John Walsh Walsh (see prior) | Honeysuckle made in glass and used as a decoration on glass |
| 36477/8 | 26 October | | M. Davis & Co., London. Lamp & Glass Manufacturer | Pattern on globes to be applied to lamps |
| 36536 | 27 October | | Guiseppe Vincenzo De Luca, London. Agent | Pattern |
| 36846 | 30 October | | Guiseppe Vincenzo De Luca (see prior) | Pattern of bottle |
| 37026 | 2 November | | Prince & Symmons (see prior) | Pattern and design of a bear to be used as a lamp |
| 37027 | | | Prince & Symmons (see prior) | Pattern and design of a dog to be used as a lamp |
| 37110 | 4 November | | Sowerby's Ellison Glass Works Ltd. (see prior) | Shape of sugar |
| 37111 | | | Sowerby's Ellison Glass Works Ltd. (see prior) | Pattern of sugar |
| 37300 | 6 November | | Julius Faulkner, Birmingham. General Brassfounder | Finger plate |
| 37487 | 7 November | | Saunders & Shepherd, London. Manufacturing Goldsmiths & Jewellers | Human hand holding egg adapted to scent bottles |
| 38431 | 19 November | | William James Green, Sudbury. Suffolk. Builder | Shape of round glass honey bell or jar |
| 38486 | 21 November | | Walter Edwards, London. Commercial Traveller | Pattern and shape of lamp representing tiger lily |
| 38487 | | | Walter Edwards (see prior) | Pattern and shape of lamp representing heartsease |
| 38488 | | | Walter Edwards (see prior) | Pattern and shape of lamp representing dog rose |
| 38582 | 23 November | | Greener & Co., Wear Flint Glass Works Sunderland & London. Glass Maker | Shape for glass mould |
| 38983 | 1 December | | Stevens & Williams, Brierley Hill Glass Works, Stafford. Glass Makers | Pattern for the ornamentation of flint glass table ware |
| 39062-4 | 3 December | | Sowerby's Ellison Glass Works Ltd. (see prior) | Pattern of sugar |
| 39086 | 30 November | | Sidney Wittmann, Wittmann & Roth, London. Glass & China Manufacturer | Raised pattern on glass surface to imitate hammered metal |
| 39328 | 10 December | | Robinson, Son & Skinner, Mersey Glass Works | Ornamental design for glass frame |
| 39414 | 11 December | | Edward Bolton, Orford Lane Glass Works, Warrington. Glass Maker | Pattern of glass boat |

| *Registration* No. | *Date* | *Year* | *Registered* Party | *Design* |
|---|---|---|---|---|
| 39415 | 11 December | 1885 | Edward Bolton, Orford Lane Glass Works, Warrington. Glass Maker | Pattern of a flower trough |
| 39626 | 15 December | | Miles Bros. & W. Claridge, Hackney Road. Manufacturer of Coloured Glass | Scent bottle in the shape of a lemon |
| 39648 | 16 December | | Joseph Benson, Sheffield. Cut Glass Manufacturer | Glass marmalade dish |
| 39807 | 18 December | | Burtles, Tate & Co., Poland Street Glass Works, Manchester. Glass Maker | Pattern and shape of flower bracket |
| 39984 | 21 December | | Saunders & Shepherd, London. Manufacturing Goldsmiths & Jewellers | Pattern and shape of ornamental vessel |
| 40484 | 1 January | 1886 | Percival, Vickers & Co. Ltd., Manchester. Glass Maker | Pressed glass cruet |
| 40927 | 7 January | | Batty & Company, London. Wholesale Italian Warehousemen | Pattern of bottle |
| 41919 | 25 January | | Saunders & Shepherd (see prior) | Elephant head as scent bottles |
| 41925 | 26 January | | Wittmann & Roth, London. Glass & China Manufacturer | Pattern worked on body of the glass to represent fish scales |
| 42041 | 28 January | | A. & R. Cochran, St. Rollox Flint Glass Works, Glasgow. Flint Glass Manufacturer | Pattern to be applied to gas and lamp globes |
| 42538 | 3 February | | Arthur Abraham, London. Glass Cutter | Pattern of mirror frame |
| 42716 | 29 January | | John Walsh Walsh, The Soho & Vesta Glass Works, Birmingham. Glass Maker | Shape of biscuit jar pushed in at four sides |
| 42726 | 6 February | | Meigh, Forester & Co., Longton. | Pattern |
| 42947 | 10 February | | Sowerby's Ellison Glass Works Ltd., Gateshead. Glass Maker | Pattern of dish |
| 43069 | 11 February | | Saunders & Shepherd (see prior) | Lighthouse as a design for scents, etc. |
| 43165 | 10 February | | Martin, Hall & Co. Ltd., Shrewsbury Works, Sheffield. Manufacturer of Silver and Electro Plated Goods | Pattern and shape |
| 43197/8 | 15 February | | W. H. Dixon & Co., Hull. Lamp Manufacturer | Shape of lamp chimneys |
| 43501 | 19 February | | Elkington & Co., London. Silversmiths | Ornamental group |
| 43502 | | | Blumberg & Co., London. Fancy Goods Merchant | Pattern and shape of flower bowl |
| 43536 | 20 February | | Gebhardt Rottmann & Co., Cheapside. Fancy Goods Warehouseman | Shape of combined inkstand, calendar and memorandum tablet |
| 43650 | 22 February | | James Testro & John Richard, Chandos Glass Works, London. Glass Maker | Shape of a bottle having a likeness to the Right Honorable W. E. Gladstone, M.P. |
| 43749 | 24 February | | James Aston, Birmingham. Designer on glass | Glass show card |
| 43867 | 25 February | | Henry Sarsons & Son, Chester Street Glass Works, Birmingham. Glass Maker | Shape of the glass vessel forming the inner part of the glass mustard pot |
| 43869 | | | James Testro & John Richard (see prior) | Shape of a bottle having a likeness to the late Right Honorable, the Earl of Beaconsfield. |
| 44219 | 4 March | | W. H. Dixon & Co. (see prior) | Fluted shape pine lamp glass |

| *Registration* No. | *Date* | *Year* | *Registered* Party | *Design* |
|---|---|---|---|---|
| 44220 | 4 March | 1886 | W. H. Dixon & Co., Hull. Lamp Manufacturer | Serrated top fluted shape pine lamp glass |
| 44408 | | | J. H. Roger, Glasgow. Wine Merchant | Shape and pattern of jug |
| 44445 | 8 March | | Burtles, Tate & Company, Poland Street Glass Works, Manchester. Glass Maker | Pattern and shape of flower boat |
| 44546 | 9 March | | Blumberg & Co. Ltd., London. Fancy Goods Merchant | Pattern and shape of flower bowl |
| 44659 | 11 March | | Sowerby's Ellison Glass Works Ltd., Gateshead. Glass Maker | Shape of dish |
| 45759 | 25 March | | Sowerby's Ellison Glass Works Ltd. (see prior) | Pattern of sugar |
| 45768 | | | Henry Gething Richardson, Wordsley Flint Glass Works, Stourbridge. Glass Maker | Shape of improved "Ice Drainer" |
| 45942 | 26 March | | Percival, Vickers & Co. Ltd., Manchester. Glass Maker | Moulded glass marmalade or biscuit jar |
| 46252 | 24 March | | Edward Webb, Stourbridge. Glass Maker | Shape of bowl |
| 46253 | 30 March | | Jonas & Jules Lang, London. Glass & China Merchants | Shape of jug |
| 46294/5 | 24 March | | Hempton & Son (Kempton & Son), Lambeth. Glass Maker | Pattern of table lamp |
| 46498 | 1 April | | Henry G. Richardson, Stourbridge. Glass Maker | Combination of threads of glass of different shades of colour, arranged as to form a plaid, to be used for glass decoration |
| 46897/8 | 9 April | | Hempton & Son (see prior) | Shape of whole as a lampshade |
| 47381-6 | 16 April | | Alfred Arculus, Birmingham. Glass Maker | Shape |
| 47514 | 21 April | | Sowerby's Ellison Glass Works Ltd. (see prior) | Pattern and shape of pressed glass fan picture frame |
| 47696 | 22 April | | Moses Davis & Co., London. Lamp & Glass Manufacturer | Shape of a bottle having a likeness to H.R.H. The Prince of Wales |
| 47698 | | | Moses Davis & Co. (see prior) | Shape of bottle having a likeness to her Gracious Majesty Queen Victoria |
| 47900 | 20 April | | Mills, Walker & Co., Stourbridge. Table Glass Manufacturer | Design of flower dish |
| 48008 | 28 April | | Stead, Simpson & Nephews, Leicester. Boot & Shoe Manufacturer | Shape of an ash tray representing various kinds of boots and shoes in relief |
| 48212 | | | Mills, Walker & Co. (see prior) | Shape of glass fairy light |
| 48228 | 4 May | | Sowerby's Ellison Glass Works Ltd. (see prior) | Pattern and shape of butter |
| 48352 | 5 May | | Greener & Co., Wear Flint Glass Works, Sunderland & London. Glass Maker | Shape of glass dish |
| 48909 | 11 May | | Sowerby's Ellison Glass Works Ltd. (see prior) | Shape of celery |
| 48910 | | | Sowerby's Ellison Glass Works Ltd. (see prior) | Shape of sweetmeat |
| 50071 | 1 June | | Sowerby's Ellison Glass Works Ltd. (see prior) | Pattern of butter |
| 50165 | 2 June | | Alfred Arculus (see prior) | Shape |
| 50422 | 3 June | | Francis Paine Hill, Surrey. Glass Embosser | Pattern and shape |
| 50425 | 5 June | | Ward & Holloway, Birmingham. Glass Tablets Manufacturer | Spill box with glass front |

| *Registration* No. | *Date* | *Year* | *Registered* Party | *Design* |
|---|---|---|---|---|
| 50594 | 8 June | 1886 | Mappin & Webb, London. Silversmiths | Pattern and shape of salad bowl |
| 50725/6 | 10 June | | Boulton & Mills, Audnam Glass Works, Stourbridge. Glass Maker | Pattern |
| 50859 | 12 June | | Alfred Arculus, Birmingham. Glass Maker | Shape |
| 51026 | 16 June | | Sampson Mordan & Co., London. Manufacturer | Design for a toilet bottle |
| 51047 | 15 June | | Thomas Webb & Sons, Stourbridge. Glass Maker | Pattern — hexagonal configuration with raised and sunk surfaces |
| 51423 | 25 June | | Max Emanuel, London. Foreign Agent | Shape of a card tray |
| 51812 | 3 July | | Baxendale & Co., Manchester. Manufacturer | Pattern |
| 52218 | 9 July | | Baxendale & Co. (see prior) | Pattern |
| 52434 | 13 July | | Sowerby's Ellison Glass Works Ltd., Gateshead. Glass Maker | Pattern and shape of boat stand |
| 53013 | 23 July | | William Cutler, Birmingham. Glass Maker | Shape and configuration of a show glass |
| 53466 | 3 August | | Percival Jones, Dublin. Glass & China Merchant | Shape of a handle for glass jugs |
| 53468 | | | Percival, Vickers & Co. Ltd., Manchester. Glass Maker | Moulded glass tumbler |
| 53483 | 30 July | | H. G. Richardson, Wordsley Flint Glass Works, Stourbridge. Glass Maker | Design for a Hyacinth glass made with two projections on the upper or cup part and having an indentation on the upper part of the body to carry and keep in position a stick or other support to the plant |
| 53732 | 3 August | | Stuart & Sons, Stourbridge, Glass Maker. | Pattern of a flower bowl for use with fairy lamps |
| 53733 | 7 August | | Stuart & Sons (see prior) | Pattern of a fairy lamp shade |
| 53734 | | | Stuart & Sons (see prior) | Pattern of a flower stand with fairy light on top |
| 54040 | 13 August | | A. & R. Cochran, St. Rollox Flint Glass Works, Glasgow. Flint Glass Manufacturer | Design for ornamenting glass globes, etc. |
| 54098 | 14 August | | Kempton & Sons (Hempton & Sons), Lambeth. Glass Maker | Pattern and shape |
| 54314 | 18 August | | Sowerby's Ellison Glass Works Ltd. (see prior) | Shape and design of moulded glass sugar basin |
| 54315/6 | | | Sowerby's Ellison Glass Works Ltd. (see prior) | Shape of moulded glass jelly dish |
| 54702 | 19 August | | Hauptman Albert & Co., Edinburgh. Glass Maker | Design of vase |
| 55113 | 27 August | | Stone, Fawdry & Stone, Birmingham. Glass Maker | Pattern of glass jelly dish |
| 55162 | 28 August | | Baxendale & Co. (see prior) | Pattern |
| 55235 | 26 August | | John Shaw & Sons, Latimer Glass Works, Sheffield. Cut Glass Manufacturer. | Shape of glass bottle |
| 55272 | 30 August | | Guiseppe Vincenzo De Luca, London. Agent | Shape |
| 55275 | 27 August | | Josiah Lane, Birmingham. Glass Maker | Pattern |
| 55693 | 6 September | | Stevens & Williams, Brierley Hill Glass Works, Stafford. Glass Maker | Pattern for the ornamentation of glassware |
| 55773 | 7 September | | Edward Webb, Stourbridge. Glass Maker | Design for configuration |

| *Registration* No. | *Date* | *Year* | *Registered* Party | *Design* |
|---|---|---|---|---|
| 55865 | 8 September | 1886 | Atkin Brothers, London & Truro Works, Sheffield. Silversmiths | Shape of glass body to represent boar's tusk |
| 55866 | | | Atkin Brothers (see prior) | Shape of glass body to represent elephant's tusk |
| 56047 | 11 September | | Percival, Vickers & Co. Ltd., Manchester. Glass Maker | Pattern for pressed glass dish |
| 56942/3 | 22 September | | Sampson Mordan & Co., London. Manufacturer | Design and shape of scent bottle |
| 56961-6 | 23 September | | Sowerby's Ellison Glass Works Ltd., Gateshead. Glass Maker | Shape and pattern of sugar |
| 57070 | 27 September | | Henry Titterton Brockwell, London. Manufacturer | Design and shape of pear for scent bottle |
| 57071 | | | Henry Titterton Brockwell (see prior) | Design and shape of a lobster claw for scent bottle |
| 57072 | | | Henry Titterton Brockwell (see prior) | Design and shape of a shell for scent bottle |
| 57073 | | | Henry Titterton Brockwell (see prior) | Design and shape of a stone for scent bottle |
| 58092 | 6 October | | Saunders & Shepherd, London. Manufacturing Goldsmiths & Jewellers | Shape and pattern of a canoe for personal use or ornament |
| 58103 | | | Sampson Mordan & Company, London. Manufacturer | Shape and pattern of a scent bottle |
| 58275 | 7 October | | Edward Moore, Tyne Flint Glass Works, South Shields. Glass Maker | Pattern |
| 58374 | 8 October | | Thomas Webb & Sons, Stourbridge. Glass Maker | Diaper of semi-circular lines forming a decorative pattern |
| 58375 | | | Thomas Webb & Sons (see prior) | Diaper of irregular lines forming a watery or wavy pattern on the surface of glass |
| 59136 | 19 October | | Boulton and Mills, Audnam Glass Works, Stourbridge. Glass Maker | Pattern |
| 59777 | 26 October | | Henry Holcroft, London. Agent | Shape of lamp vase or fountain with legs |
| 59794 | | | Hayward Bros. & Eckstein, London. Manufacturing Ironmongers | Shape of glass tile |
| 60108 | 29 October | | Percival, Vickers & Co. Ltd., (see prior) | Design for a pressed glass pillar or lamp stand |
| 60270 | | | Carl Quitmann, London. Merchant | Pattern of a glass globe with the National Emblem |
| 60351 | 1 November | | Edward Webb, Stourbridge. Glass Maker | Pattern of chamber lamp |
| 60872 | 8 November | | Edward Webb (see prior) | Shape of plate |
| 61091/2 | 11 November | | Powell, Bishop & Stonier, Hanley, Staffordshire. Manufacturer | Design for a shape |
| 61211 | 12 November | | Sampson Mordan & Co. (see prior) | Shape of a scent bottle |
| 61357 | 15 November | | Stevens & Williams, Brierley Hill Glass Works, Stafford. Glass Maker | Pattern for the ornamentation of glass |
| 61922 | 22 November | | Johnstone Sadler & Co., London. Wine Merchant | A pentagonal bottle |
| 61923 | | | Johnstone Sadler & Co. (see prior) | A hexagonal bottle |

| *Registration* No. | *Date* | *Year* | *Registered* Party | *Design* |
|---|---|---|---|---|
| 61924 | 22 November | 1886 | Johnstone Sadler & Co. London. Wine Merchant | A heptagonal bottle |
| 62029 | 23 November | | Thomas Webb & Sons, Stourbridge. Glass Maker | For the form cylindrical, tapering, having six rows of arched corrugations |
| 62325 | 19 November | | Charles Kempton & Sons (Charles Hempton & Sons), Lambeth. Glass Maker | Shape of a combined flower stand and lamp |
| 62584 | 1 December | | Frederick Augustus Heepe & Co., London. Importer and Agent | Pattern and shape of cruet stand |
| 62925 | 6 December | | Hayward Brothers & Eckstein, London. Manufacturing Ironmongers | Shape of glass tile |
| 63008 | | | B. Cars, Lion Lamp Works, London. | Combination of flower stand mounted on plush base with fixed or loose lamps |
| 63267 | 10 December | | F. & C. Osler, Birmingham. Flint Glass Manufacturer | Shade for electric light |
| 63473 | 14 December | | John Mortlock & Co., London. | Magpies with landscape as applied to decoration of china and glass services |
| 63474 | | | Stevens & Williams, Brierley Hill Glass Works, Stafford. Glass Maker | Design for cameo glass lamp |
| 63533-5 | 15 December | | W. P. Phillips & G. Phillips, London. China and Glass Merchants | Shades for fairy lamps made in the shape of a cactus flower, of a dahlia and of a carnation |
| 63543 | 15 December | | Edward Moore, Tyne Flint Glass Works, South Shields. Glass Makers | Shape and pattern of a gas moon or shade |
| 63665 | 17 December | | Guiseppe Vincenzo De Luca, London. Agent | Pattern |
| 63937 | 21 December | | Guiseppe Vincenzo De Luca (see prior) | Pattern of glass bottle |
| 64086 | 22 December | | Sowerby's Ellison Glass Works Ltd., Gateshead. Glass Maker | Pattern of sugar |
| 64087/8 | | | Scotney & Earnshaw, London. Merchant | Pattern for the decoration of glass ware |
| 64106 | 23 December | | Sowerby's Ellison Glass Works Ltd. (see prior) | Pattern of butter |
| 64234 | 28 December | | Burtles, Tate & Co., Poland Street Glass Works, Manchester. Glass Maker | Pattern and shape of flower holder |
| 64517 | | | Powell, Bishop & Stonier, Hanley, Staffordshire. Manufacturer | Shape |
| 64590 | 1 January | 1887 | C. Kempton & Sons (see prior) | Shape of glass stand or mount for lamp, etc. |
| 64641 | 4 January | | Mills, Walker & Co., Glass Works, Stourbridge. Table Glass Manufacturer | Shape of lamp |
| 64766 | 6 January | | Prince & Symmons, Lion Lamp Works, Shoreditch. Lamp Manufacturer | Pattern and shape of lamp shade |
| 64920/1 | 7 January | | Powell, Bishop & Stonier (see prior) | Pattern |
| 64967-9 | 11 January | | S. Falk, London. Merchant | Shape of globe |
| 65229 | | | Stevens & Williams (see prior) | Decoration of ornamental glass in colours and relief |
| 65339 | 14 January | | Edward Moore & Co. (see prior) | Shape and pattern of pressed gas shade |
| 65455 | 17 January | | Burtles, Tate & Co. (see prior) | Pattern and shape of new flower holder |
| 65468 | 8 January | | James Carpenter, Clapham Common, Surrey. Merchant | Design for the commemoration of the Jubilee of Queen Victoria |

| *Registration* No. | *Date* | *Year* | *Registered* Party | *Design* |
|---|---|---|---|---|
| 65495 | 17 January | 1887 | Charles Kempton & Sons (Charles Hempton & Sons), Lambeth. Glass Maker | Shape of stand for holding lamp, etc. |
| 65543 | 15 January | | John Walsh Walsh, The Soho & Vesta Glass Works, Birmingham. Glass Maker | Shape |
| 66273 | 25 January | | C. Kempton & Sons (see prior) | Shape of stand for a lamp or flower vase |
| 66450 | 27 January | | C. Kempton & Sons (see prior) | Shape of a flower stand |
| 66813 | 26 January | | Alfred Arculus, Birmingham. Glass Maker | Ornamental design for use on gas, paraffin or other globes consisting of rose, shamrock and thistle wreath |
| 67040 | 2 February | | Wittmann & Roth, London. China & Glass Manufacturer | Pattern of lampshade |
| 67113 | 3 February | | James Buchanan & Co., London. Spirit Merchant | Shape and pattern of spirit jar |
| 67124 | 4 February | | C. Kempton & Sons (see prior) | Shape of a stand for flowers |
| 67262 | 5 February | | C. Kempton & Sons (see prior) | Shape of a dish or stand for flowers |
| 67263 | | | Stevens & Williams, Brierley Hill Glass Works, Stafford. Glass Maker | Design in glass lamp |
| 67425 | 7 February | | Edward Moore, Tyne Flint Glass Works, South Shields. Glass Maker | Shape and pattern of pressed glass gas shade |
| 67646 | 9 February | | John Grinsell & Sons, Birmingham. Silver & Art Metal Smiths | Water bottle |
| 67941 | 10 February | | Sampson Mordan & Co., London. Manufacturer | Pattern of decoration for a scent bottle |
| 68066 | 16 February | | William Leuchars, London. Silversmith | Pattern and shape of a tray with metal rim and glass bottom |
| 68249 | 18 February | | Edward Moore (see prior) | Shape and pattern of a pressed glass lampshade |
| 68327 | 21 February | | H. G. Richardson, Wordsley Flint Glass Works, Stourbridge. Glass Maker | Shape of a flower or lamp bowl with sides turned down or lapped over, shewing (sic) from side view a crescent shape |
| 68633/4 | 24 February | | William Leuchars (see prior) | Pattern and shape |
| 68746 | 26 February | | C. Kempton & Sons (see prior) | Shape of a bucket or lamp suitable for illumination |
| 68806 | 28 February | | Stevens & Williams (see prior) | Shape in glass for table ornament |
| 68846 | 1 March | | Sowerby's Ellison Glass Works Ltd., Gateshead. Glass Maker | Pattern of dish |
| 68984 | | | Fisher Brown & Co., Lion Works, Birmingham. Manufacturer of brass and iron bedsteads | Glass rose for ornamentation of bed |
| 69362 | 8 March | | William Oppenheim, London. Importer | Shape for lamp |
| 69699 | 15 March | | Wittman (sic) & Roth (see prior) | Pattern of lamp shade |
| 69969 | 17 March | | C. Kempton & Sons (see prior) | Shape of lamp |
| 70422 | 23 March | | Molineaux, Webb & Co., Manchester. Glass Maker | Shape |
| 70868 | 29 March | | Sampson Mordan & Co. (see prior) | Design to be applied for the decoration of circular smelling bottles, etc. |
| 70872 | | | J. Hayes | Pattern and shape |
| 71216 | 1 April | | J. Hayes | Pattern and shape of ornamental pincushion |
| 71528 | 6 April | | Molineaux, Webb & Co. (see prior) | Pattern |
| 71534/5 | | | J. Hayes | Shape of ornamental pincushion |
| 71736 | 9 April | | Greener & Co., Wear Flint Glass Works, Sunderland & London. Glass Maker | Design for the ornamentation of glass |

| *Registration* No. | *Date* | *Year* | *Registered* Party | *Design* |
|---|---|---|---|---|
| 71753 | 12 April | 1887 | Edward Moore, Tyne Flint Glass Works, South Shields. Glass Maker | Shape and pattern of an oval covered dish |
| 71816 | 13 April | | Edward Moore (see prior) | Shape and pattern of a gas shade |
| 71869 | 14 April | | Percival, Vickers & Co. Ltd., Manchester. Flint Glass Manufacturers | Pattern of a moulded cruet |
| 72071 | 16 April | | J. Hayes | Pattern and shape of pincushion |
| 72169 | 15 April | | Saunders & Shepherd, London. Manufacturing Goldsmiths & Jewellers | Group of nuts as ornamental cruet stand |
| 72345 | 25 April | | Victoria Hansom Cab Co., Ltd., London. Cab Proprietors | Pattern, shape and ornament |
| 72453 | 5 April | | Daniel Judson & Son Ltd., Surrey. Manufacturer | Shape and pattern of scent bottles and vinaigrettes |
| 72790 | 28 April | | Philip M. Beck, London. Glass Maker | Design for glass tumbler |
| 72815 | | | Edward Moore (see prior) | Pattern for a pressed glass shade |
| 72884 | 29 April | | Edward Moore (see prior) | Pattern for pressed glass shade |
| 73319 | 6 May | | Guiseppe V. De Luca, London. Agent | Shape of bottle |
| 73351 | 7 May | | Sir Robert Burnett & Co., Vauxhall. Distillers | Shape and pattern of bottle |
| 73836 | 17 May | | Scotney & Earnshaw, London. Merchant | Pattern for decoration of table glass ware |
| 74164 | 21 May | | C. Kempton & Sons, Lambeth. Glass Maker | Shape of an illumination lamp can also be used as a flower vase |
| 74556 | 26 May | | John Walsh Walsh, The Soho & Vesta Glass Works, Birmingham. Glass Maker | Flower holder in the form of a tree trunk |
| 74878 | 4 June | | J. Hayes | Shape and pattern of pincushion |
| 74879 | | | J. Hayes | Shape and pattern of thimble case |
| 75015/6 | 8 June | | Edward Moore (see prior) | Pattern |
| 75091/2 | 9 June | | Edward Moore (see prior) | Pattern |
| 75175 | | | W. P. & G. Philips (sic), London. Glass Maker | Shape of a jug in glass or china |
| 75843 | 25 June | | Wittmann & Roth, London. China & Glass Manufacturer | Pattern |
| 75942 | 29 June | | Percival, Vickers & Co. Ltd., Manchester. Glass Maker | Pattern for moulded glass marmalade |
| 76057 | 1 July | | Wittmann & Roth (see prior) | Pattern |
| 76682 | 11 July | | Alfred & James Davies, Stourbridge. Glass Maker | Pattern and shape of flower stand |
| 76759 | 9 July | | J. H. & A. Hawkesford, Birmingham. Fancy tin plate workers | Shape and ornament of a money box |
| 76762-5 | 12 July | | Alfred & James Davies (see prior) | Pattern and shape of flower stand |
| 76878-80 | 13 July | | Edward Moore (see prior) | Shape |
| 76935 | 14 July | | Edward Moore (see prior) | Pattern |
| 77116 | 20 July | | J. H. & A. Hawkesford (see prior) | Shape and ornament of spill box |
| 77341 | 25 July | | Edward Moore (see prior) | Pattern |
| 77881 | 2 August | | Sowerby's Ellison Glass Works Ltd., Gateshead. Glass Maker | Pattern and shape of butter |
| 77967 | 3 August | | Sowerby's Ellison Glass Works Ltd. (see prior) | Pattern and shape of biscuit |

| *Registration No.* | *Date* | *Year* | *Registered Party* | *Design* |
|---|---|---|---|---|
| 78084 | 3 August | 1887 | Sowerby's Ellison Glass Works Ltd., Gateshead. Glass Maker | Pattern and shape of sugar and cover |
| 78233 | 5 August | | Guiseppe V. De Luca London. Agent | Shape and pattern |
| 78551 | 11 August | | Sowerby's Ellison Glass Works Ltd. (see prior) | Pattern of sugar |
| 78688 | 12 August | | Mills, Walker & Co., Stourbridge. Table Glass Manufacturer | Shape of lamp |
| 78704 | 13 August | | Sowerby's Ellison Glass Works Ltd. (see prior) | Pattern of sugar |
| 78754 | | | Woodall & Son, Birmingham. Glass Maker | Squat shaped globe with crimped and threaded top |
| 78795/6 | 15 August | | Mills, Walker & Co. (see prior) | Shape of lamp |
| 80012 | 1 September | | Edward Moore, Tyne Flint Glass Works, South Shields. Glass Maker | Shape and pattern |
| 80013 | | | Edward Moore (see prior) | Shape and pattern |
| 80153 | 3 September | | Guiseppe V. De Luca (see prior) | Shape of menthol stand |
| 80167 | 5 September | | Thomas Webb & Sons, Stourbridge. Glass Maker | Shape for particular form of edge |
| 80260 | 6 September | | Saunders & Shepherd, London. Manufacturing Goldsmiths & Jewellers | Shape of scent bottle |
| 80530 | 10 September | | Sowerby's Ellison Glass Works Ltd. (see prior) | Pattern of sugar basin in glass |
| 80632 | 12 September | | Percival, Vickers & Co. Ltd., Manchester. Glass Maker | Pattern of pressed glass celery vase |
| 80687 | | | Guiseppe V. De Luca (see prior) | Shape and pattern of menthol stand |
| 81051 | 15 September | | Stevens & Williams, Brierley Hill Glass Works, Stafford. Glass Maker | Pattern of ornamental glass |
| 81158 | | | S. Mordan & Co., London. Manufacturer | Design for scent bottle |
| 81159 | | | S. Mordan & Co. (see prior) | Pattern and shape of pencil case |
| 81160 | | | Greener & Co., Wear Flint Glass Works, Sunderland & London. Glass Maker | Pattern of table glass |
| 81959 | 24 September | | Edward Moore (see prior) | Shape and pattern |
| 82606 | 30 September | | Edward Moore (see prior) | Shape and pattern |
| 82776/7 | 3 October | | William Blenko, Clapton Park. Glass Maker | Pattern of stained glass window pane |
| 83773 | 12 October | | Edward Moore (see prior) | Shape |
| 83777 | 7 October | | Sowerby's Ellison Glass Works Ltd. (see prior) | Pattern and shape of a advertising plate in pressed glass |
| 84001 | 15 October | | Sowerby's Ellison Glass Works Ltd. (see prior) | Pattern of sugar |
| 84218 | 18 October | | Sowerby's Ellison Glass Works Ltd. (see prior) | Pattern of dish |
| 84495 | 17 October | | W. P. & G. Phillips, London. Glass Maker | Shape of drinking glass |
| 84747 | 21 October | | Sowerby's Ellison Glass Works Ltd. (see prior) | Pattern of butter |
| 85870 | 1 November | | Sowerby's Ellison Glass Works Ltd. (see prior) | Shape of comportier and dish |
| 85913 | 1 November | | Samuel Clarke, London. Night Light Manufacturer. | Shape and ornament of fairy lamps |

| *Registration* No. | *Date* | *Year* | *Registered* Party | *Design* |
|---|---|---|---|---|
| 86044 | 3 November | 1887 | T. Stapleton & Son, London. Silversmiths | Pattern and shape of glass bottle — the novelty being the concave depression in one side of the bottle for the hand |
| 86246 | 5 November | | Thomas Webb & Sons Ltd., Stourbridge. Glass Maker | Shape — a particular form of edging |
| 87058 | 15 November | | Sowerby's Ellison Glass Works Ltd., Gateshead. Glass Maker | Pattern and shape of shoe |
| 87082 | | | J. Hayes | Pattern and shape of boot pincushion |
| 87083 | | | J. Hayes | Pattern and shape of shoe pincushion |
| 87259 | 18 November | | Johnson & Company | Pattern and shape of a lemon squeezer |
| 87776 | 24 November | | Sowerby's Ellison Glass Works Ltd. (see prior) | Pattern of sugar |
| 87777 | | | Sowerby's Ellison Glass Works Ltd. (see prior) | Pattern of salt |
| 88120 | 26 November | | Greener & Co., Wear Flint Glass Works, Sunderland & London. Glass Maker | Pattern or shape of a dish |
| 88124 | 29 November | | Edward Moore, Tyne Flint Glass Works, South Shields. Glass Maker | Shape |
| 88125 | | | Edward Moore (see prior) | Pattern |
| 88254 | 30 November | | S. Mordan & Co., London. Manufacturer | Shape of scent bottle |
| 88730 | 5 December | | Edward Moore (see prior) | Shape |
| 88940 | 7 December | | Richard Morgan, Masbro. Glass Blower | Shape of bottle |
| 89209 | 9 December | | Wilson Salamon & Co., London. Agent | Shape of bottle |
| 89920 | 20 December | | Saunders & Shepherd, London. Manufacturing Goldsmiths & Jewellers | Filbert for a scent bottle with neck for stopper |
| 90268 | 28 December | | Samuel Clarke, London. Night Light Manufacturer | Pattern of a fairy lamp |
| 91241 | 11 January | 1888 | Samuel Clarke (see prior) | Shape of a cup for food warmers |
| 91359 | 13 January | | Henry John Manton, Birmingham. Glass Maker | Shape |
| 91431 | 14 January | | Sowerby's Ellison Glass Works Ltd. (see prior) | Pattern of dish |
| 91432 | | | Sowerby's Ellison Glass Works Ltd. (see prior) | Pattern of sugar |
| 91449 | 11 January | | Greener & Company (see prior) | Pattern of a plate |
| 91857 | 20 January | | J. Hayes | Pattern and shape of a ladies companion |
| 92045 | 23 January | | Edward Moore (see prior) | Shape |
| 92226 | 26 January | | W. P. & G. Phillips, London. Glass Maker | Fairy or any other lamp shade in the form of a plum |
| 92229 | | | W. P. & G. Phillips (see prior) | Lamp shade in the form of a fir cone |
| 92230 | | | W. P. & G. Phillips (see prior) | Lamp shade in the shape of an orange |
| 92231 | | | W. P. & G. Phillips (see prior) | Lamp shade in the form of an apple |
| 92571 | 30 January | | J. Stembridge & Co., Holborn. Importers | Pattern table decoration — lamp |
| 92631-3 | 31 January | | W. P. & G. Phillips (see prior) | Lamp shades in the forms of a raspberry, a cabbage and a strawberry |
| 93225 | 9 February | | Charles Edward Hill, Brighton. Importer | Shape |
| 93320 | 11 February | | Samuel Clarke (see prior) | Shape of a fairy lamp |
| 93450 | | | Guiseppe Vincenzo De Luca, London. Agent | Shape of bottle |

| Registration No. | Date | Year | Registered Party |
|---|---|---|---|
| 93905 | 18 February | 1888 | Percival, Vickers & Co. Ltd., Manchester. Glass Makers |
| 94025 | 17 February | | Stevens & Williams, Brierley Hill Glass Works, Stafford. Glass Maker |
| 94100/1 | 18 February | | Mills, Walker & Co., Stourbridge. Table Glass Manufacturer |
| 94181 | 22 February | | Frederick Watson Bach, London. Manufacturer |
| 94543 | 25 February | | Greener & Company, Wear Flint Glass Works, Sunderland & London. Glass Maker |
| 94775 | 1 March | | W. P. & G. Phillips, London. Glass Maker |
| 94820 | | | Edward Moore, Tyne Flint Glass Works, South Shields. Glass Maker |
| 95106 | 2 March | | W. P. & G. Phillips (see prior) |
| 95114 | 5 March | | Samuel Clarke, London. Night Light Manufacturer |
| 95300 | 7 March | | Sowerby's Ellison Glass Works Ltd., Gateshead. Glass Maker |
| 95382/3 | 8 March | | The Glasgow Plate Glass Co., Glasgow. Glass Maker |
| 95461 | 9 March | | Guiseppe Vincenzo De Luca, London. Agent |
| 95482 | | | Samuel Clarke (see prior) |
| 95625 | 12 March | | Edward Moore (see prior) |
| 95676 | 13 March | | Falk, Stadlemann & Co. |
| 95775 | 14 March | | Edward Moore (see prior) |
| 95894 | 16 March | | Sowerby's Ellison Glass Works Ltd. (see prior) |
| 95935 | | | Greener & Company (see prior) |
| 96679 | 27 March | | Powell, Bishop & Stonier, Hanley, Staffordshire. Manufacturer |
| 96775/6 | | | Greener & Co. (see prior) |
| 96813 | 29 March | | Charles E. Hill, Brighton. Importer |
| 96945 | 31 March | | Thomas Davidson, Teams Glass Works, Gateshead on Tyne. Glass Maker |
| 97198 | 5 April | | George Watts & Co. |
| 97380 | 29 March | | James A. Cox, London. China & Glass Manufacturer |
| 97697 | 12 April | | W. P. & G. Phillips (see prior) |
| 98215/6 | 18 April | | Sowerby's Ellison Glass Works Ltd. (see prior) |
| 98242 | | | Frederick Leslie Jeyes, The Chandos Glass Works, Bermondsey. Glass Maker |
| 98551 | 21 April | | Greener & Co. (see prior) |
| 98578 | 23 April | | Burtles, Tate & Co., Poland Street Glass Works, Manchester. Glass Maker |
| 98658 | 24 April | | W. P. & G. Phillips (see prior) |

| Registration No. | Date | Year | Registered Party |
|---|---|---|---|
| 98744 | 25 April | 1888 | A. & R. Cochran, Glasgow. Flint Glass Manufacturer |
| 99487 | 7 May | | W. P. & G. Phillips (see prior) |
| 99489 | | | W. P. & G. Phillips (see prior) |
| 99490 | | | J. Stembridge & Co., Holborn. Importers |
| 99715 | 9 May | | Sowerby's Ellison Glass Works Ltd. (see prior) |
| 99911 | 10 May | | H. G. Richardson, Wordsley Flint Glass Works, Stourbridge. Glass Maker |
| 99928-39 | 9 May | | Samuel Clarke (see prior) |
| 100004 | 12 May | | John Walsh Walsh, Birmingham. Glass Maker |
| 100207/8 | 14 May | | J. Stembridge & Co. (see prior) |
| 100404 | 18 May | | Guiseppe V. De Luca (see prior) |
| 100456 | 19 May | | Thomas Webb & Sons, Stourbridge. Glass Maker |
| 100724 | 25 May | | Warrick Bros, London. Wholesale Perfumers |
| 101007 | 31 May | | Wittman (sic) & Roth, London. Glass & China Manufacturer |
| 101008 | | | Hinrichs & Co., New York, U.S.A. Glass & China Merchant |
| 101809 | 13 June | | George Watts & Company |
| 101901 | 12 June | | Wade & Co., Burslem, Staffordshire. Jet & Rockingham Manufacturer |
| 101985 | 15 June | | The Glasgow Plate Glass Co., Glasgow. Glass Maker |
| 102405 | 22 June | | Powell, Bishop & Stonier (see prior) |
| 102902 | 28 June | | Boulton & Mills, Audnam Glass Works, Stourbridge. Glass Makers |
| 102939 | 2 July | | W. P. & G. Phillips (see prior) |
| 102977 | 3 July | | John Tams, Longton. Manufacturer |
| 103434 | 11 July | | Greener & Co. (see prior) |
| 103532 | 12 July | | Wittmann & Roth (see prior) |
| 103703/4 | 16 July | | Charles E. Hill, Brighton. Importer |
| 103949 | 18 July | | John Walsh Walsh (see prior) |
| 103954 | | | Charles E. Hill (see prior) |
| 103975 | 17 July | | Greener & Co. (see prior) |
| 104051 | 19 July | | W. P. & G. Phillips (see prior) |
| 104241/2 | 23 July | | Charles E. Hill (see prior) |
| 104759 | 31 July | | Duncan Webb, Manchester. Glass Maker |
| 104890 | 2 August | | Boulton & Mills (see prior) |
| 105233 | 9 August | | W. P. & G. Phillips (see prior) |
| 105464 | 11 August | | Edward Bolton & Sons, Orford Lane Glass Works, Warrington. Glass Maker |
| 105558 | 13 August | | Samuel Clarke (see prior) |

| *Registration* No. | *Date* | *Year* | *Registered* Party |
|---|---|---|---|
| 105713/4 | 13 August | 1888 | Charles E. Hill, Brighton. Importer |
| 105830 | 14 August | | Thomas Webb & Sons, Stourbridge. Glass Maker |
| 106892 | 30 August | | Sowerby's Ellison Glass Works Ltd., Gateshead. Glass Maker |
| 106938 | 31 August | | Sowerby's Ellison Glass Works Ltd. (see prior) |
| 106954/5 | | | Charles E. Hill (see prior) |
| 107316 | 5 September | | Edward Moore, Tyne Flint Glass Works, South Shields. Glass Maker |
| 107409 | 6 September | | Duncan Webb, Manchester. Glass Maker |
| 107697 | 10 September | | Wittmann & Roth, London. Glass & China Manufacturer |
| 107808/9 | 12 September | | John Walsh Walsh, The Soho & Vesta Glass Works, Birmingham. Glass Maker |
| 108018/9 | 14 September | | Greener & Co., Wear Flint Glass Works Sunderland & London. Glass Makers |
| 108129 | 15 September | | Mills, Walker & Co., Stourbridge. Table Glass Manufacturer |
| 108271 | 18 September | | W. P. & G. Phillips, London. China & Glass Merchants |
| 108469 | | | Wittmann & Roth (see prior) |
| 108470 | 19 September | | Caspar & Co., London. Manufacturer of Crystallized Glass |
| 109330/1 | 28 September | | Wittmann & Roth (see prior) |
| 109338 | 26 September | | Wittmann & Roth (see prior |
| 109461/2 | 29 September | | Greener & Co. (see prior) |
| 109531 | 1 October | | Burtles, Tate & Co., Poland Street Glass Works, Manchester. Glass Makers |
| 109568 | 2 October | | The Glasgow Plate Glass Co., Glasgow |
| 109612 | | | Edward Moore (see prior) |
| 109926 | 5 October | | Guiseppe V. De Luca, London. Agent |
| 110458/9 | 11 October | | Robert E. Finley, Birmingham. Cut Glass Manufacturer |
| 110914 | 12 October | | Wittmann & Roth (see prior) |
| 110916 | 10 October | | Cartier & Amez Droz, Geneve, Suisse. Watchmakers |
| 111269/70 | 17 October | | Sowerby's Ellison Glass Works Ltd. (see prior) |
| 111289/90 | | | Duncan Webb (see prior) |
| 111295 | 16 October | | Max Emanuel, London. Foreign Agent |
| 111661 | 19 October | | Matthew Turnbull, Cornhill Glass Works, Sunderland. Flint Glass Manufacturer |

| *Registration* No. | *Date* | *Year* | *Registered* Party |
|---|---|---|---|
| 112468 | 1 November | 1888 | John T. Creasy & James Dingwall, Blackfriars. Glass Maker |
| 112730/1 | 1 November | | Robert Emmett Finley (see prior) |
| 113389 | 10 November | | Wittmann & Roth (see prior) |
| 113560 | 13 November | | Sowerby's Ellison Glass Works Ltd. (see prior) |
| 113746 | 15 November | | Wade & Co., Burslem, Staffordshire. Jet & Rockingham Manufacturer |
| 113896 | | | Greener & Co. (see prior) |
| 113915-7 | | | Samuel Clarke, London. Night Light Manufacturer |
| 113989 | 16 November | | Thomas Goode & Co. |
| 114006 | 14 November | | Boulton & Mills, Audnam Glass Works, Stourbridge. Glass Maker |
| 114044 | 17 November | | Sowerby's Ellison Glass Works Ltd. (see prior) |
| 114297 | 21 November | | E. Ackroyd & J. Ridgway, Bedford Works, Stoke-on-Trent. Manufacturer |
| 114667 | 27 November | | Charles E. Hill (see prior) |
| 115000 | 1 December | | Thomas Goode & Co. |
| 115077 | 28 November | | Percival, Vickers & Co. Ltd., Manchester. Glass Makers |
| 115156 | 5 December | | The Army & Navy Cooperative Society Ltd., London. Manufacturer |
| 115743 | 14 December | | Greener & Co. (see prior) |
| 115748 | 12 December | | Stone, Fawdry & Stone Union Glass Works, Birmingham. Glass Maker |
| 115910 | 17 December | | John Shaw & Sons, Latimer Glass Works, Sheffield, Cut Glass Manufacturer |
| 116148-50 | 20 December | | Thomas Goode & Co. |
| 116158-61 | 19 December | | Georges Dreyfus, Paris. Merchant |
| 116254 | | | Charles Horner, Halifax. Jeweller |
| 116983 | 8 January | 1889 | The Army & Navy Cooperative Society Ltd. (see prior) |
| 117086 | 9 January | | John Walsh Walsh (see prior) |
| 117556/7 | 14 January | | Burtles, Tate & Co (see prior) |
| 117569 | 17 January | | Sowerby's Ellison Glass Works Ltd. (see prior) |
| 117815 | 21 January | | Matthew Turnbull (see prior) |
| 118152 | 24 January | | J. Stembridge & Co., London. Importer |
| 118285 | 26 January | | A. & R. Cochran, St. Rollox Flint Glass Works, Glasgow. Flint Glass Manufacturer |
| 118358/9 | 26 January | | Chance Bros. & Co. Ltd., West Smethwick. Glass Maker |

| *Registration No.* | *Date* | *Year* | *Registered Party* |
|---|---|---|---|
| 118485 | 28 January | 1889 | Max Emanuel, London. Foreign Agent |
| 118864 | 2 February | | Boulton & Mills, Audnam Glass Works, Stourbridge. Glass Maker |
| 119318 | 9 February | | Matthew Turnbull, Cornhill Glass Works, Sunderland. Flint Glass Manufacturer |
| 119981 | 18 February | | John Mortlock & Co., London. Glass & China Dealer |
| 120229 | 23 February | | Sowerby's Ellison Glass Works Ltd., Gateshead. Glass Maker |
| 120374 | 26 February | | Falk, Stadelmann & Co. Ltd. |
| 120437 | | | Edward Moore, Tyne Flint Glass Works, South Shields. Glass Maker |
| 120451 | 27 February | | Henry G. Richardson, Wordsley Flint Glass Works, Stourbridge. Glass Maker |
| 120547 | 25 February | | Frederick S. Balls, Cambridge. Glass & China Merchant |
| 120760 | 2 March | | Monot & Stump, Pantin, France. Glass Maker |
| 120808 | 4 March | | Burtles, Tate & Co., Poland Street Glass Works, Manchester. Glass Makers |
| 121729-31 | 19 March | | James Couper & Sons, City Glass Works, Glasgow. Glass Maker |
| 121760 | 20 March | | Russell, Jones & Price, London. Wholesale Glass & China Merchant |
| 121841 | 22 March | | Charles E. Hill, Brighton. Importer |
| 121891/2 | 21 March | | George (sic) Dreyfus, Paris. Merchant |
| 121894 | 22 March | | William Brown, London. China & Glass Warehouseman |
| 121927 | 23 March | | Arthur W. Pennington, Birmingham. Silversmith |
| 121984 | | | C. & G. E. Asprey, London. Dressing Case Makers |
| 121985 | | | Greener & Co., Wear Flint Glass Works, Sunderland & London. Glass Makers |
| 122046 | 20 March | | Russell, Jones & Price (see prior) |
| 122047 | 25 March | | Russell, Jones & Price (see prior) |
| 122093/4 | 26 March | | Guiseppe V. De Luca, London. Agent |
| 122096 | | | Boulton & Mills (see prior) |
| 122274 | 28 March | | F. & C. Osler, Birmingham. Flint Glass Manufacturer |
| 122393 | 30 March | | Sowerby's Ellison Glass Works Ltd. (see prior) |
| 122519 | 2 April | | Sowerby's Ellison Glass Works Ltd. (see prior) |
| 122521 | 2 April | 1889 | J. Hulls & A. Griffiths, Birmingham. Glass Beveller |
| 122581 | | | Pilkington Bros., Lancaster. Glass Maker. |
| 122583 | | | T. Stapleton & Son, London. Silversmiths |
| 122790 | 5 April | | John Henry Downing, Birmingham. Glass Merchant |
| 123030 | 8 April | | Charles H. Reynolds, Stoke-on-Trent. Engraver |
| 123198 | 10 April | | G. Davidson & Co., Teams Flint Glass Works, Gateshead-on-Tyne. Glass Maker |
| 123702/3 | 20 April | | W. P. & G. Phillips, London. China & Glass Merchants |
| 124116 | 25 April | | Pilkington Bros (see prior) |
| 124771 | 8 May | | The Glasgow Plate Glass Co., Glasgow. Glass Maker |
| 124835 | | | Richard Vann, Birmingham. Glass Toy Manufacturer |
| 125024 | 10 May | | C. Stolzles Sohne, Vienna, Manufacturer |
| 125028 | 11 May | | W. P. & G. Phillips (see prior) |
| 125490 | 16 May | | W. P. & G. Phillips (see prior) |
| 125847 | 22 May | | Charles Kempton & Sons, Lambeth. Glass Maker |
| 126244 | 30 May | | Charles E. Hill (see prior) |
| 126315 | 31 May | | F. & C. Osler (see prior) |
| 126688 | 1 June | | Boulton & Mills (see prior) |
| 126694 | 5 June | | G. Davidson & Co. (see prior) |
| 126869 | 8 June | | Percival, Vickers & Co. Ltd., Manchester. Glass Makers |
| 126940 | 11 June | | Sowerby's Ellison Glass Works Ltd. (see prior) |
| 126941 | | | Wittmann & Roth, London. Glass & China Manufacturer |
| 127512 | 21 June | | W. P. & G. Phillips (see prior) |
| 127515/6 | 22 June | | Matthew Turnbull (see prior) |
| 127704-6 | 26 June | | Charles E. Hill (see prior) |
| 128472 | 10 July | | Charles Kempton & Sons (see prior) |
| 128665 | 13 July | | C. Stolzles Sohne (see prior) |
| 128763 | 16 July | | Wittmann & Roth (see prior) |
| 128882-4 | 17 July | | Greener & Co., (see prior) |
| 129295/6 | 29 July | | Alfred Arculus, Birmingham. Glass Maker |
| 129933 | 31 July | | Edward Moore (see prior) |
| 130641 | 13 August | | G. Davidson & Co. (see prior) |
| 130643 | | | G. Davidson & Co. (see prior) |
| 130648 | 14 August | | Horton & Allday, Birmingham. Manufacturing Jeweller |
| 131653 | 23 August | | Stuart & Sons, Red House Glass Works, Stourbridge. Glass Maker |
| 132189 | 31 August | | Edward Moore (see prior) |

| *Registration* No. | *Date* | *Year* | *Registered* Party |
|---|---|---|---|
| 132777 | 7 September | 1889 | Charles E. Hill, Brighton. Importer |
| 132789/90 | 9 September | | James Abraham Cox, London. Glass & China Manufacturer |
| 133053 | 11 September | | Sowerby's Ellison Glass Works Ltd., Gateshead. Glass Makers |
| 133560 | 18 September | | Edward Moore, Tyne Flint Glass Works, South Shields. Glass Maker |
| 133643/4 | 20 September | | Charles E. Hill (see prior) |
| 133909 | 24 September | | Sowerby's Ellison Glass Works Ltd. (see prior) |
| 134350 | 1 October | | William J. Blenko, London. Glass Maker |
| 134907 | 5 October | | Percival, Vickers & Co. Ltd., Manchester. Glass Makers |
| 134908 | | | Molineaux, Webb & Co., Manchester. Glass Makers |
| 135780 | 16 October | | Henry Dreydel, London. China & Glass Manufacturer |
| 135946 | 18 October | | Elkington & Co. Ltd., London. Silversmiths |
| 136053 | 21 October | | Saunders & Shepherd, London. Manufacturing Goldsmiths & Jewellers |
| 136495 | 25 October | | Johnson, Sons & Edmonds, London. Silversmiths |
| 136980 | 28 October | | Stevens & Williams, Brierley Hill Glass Works, Stafford. Glass Makers |
| 137288 | 4 November | | Stevens & Williams (see prior) |
| 138051 | 14 November | | Greener & Co., Wear Flint Glass Works, Sunderland & London. Glass Makers |
| 138055 | | | W. Thornhill & Co., London. Silversmiths |
| 138523 | 19 November | | Henry Dreydel (see prior) |
| 139101 | 26 November | | Pilkington Brothers, Lancaster. Glass Maker |
| 139589 | 4 December | | Edward Moore (see prior) |
| 139808 | 6 December | | Sowerby's Ellison Glass Works Ltd. (see prior) |
| 140021 | 10 December | | Falk, Stadelmann & Co. |
| 140225 | 12 December | | Haynes & Fisher, London. Glass Merchant |
| 141068 | 24 December | | Edward Moore (see prior) |
| 141080 | 27 December | | Sowerby's Ellison Glass Works Ltd. (see prior) |
| 141128 | 27 December | | F. & C. Osler, Birmingham. Flint Glass Manufacturer |
| 141892/3 | 6 January | 1890 | Edward J. Shaw & Co., Astral Works, Walsall. Lamp Manufacturer |
| 141980 | 11 January | | Haynes & Fisher (see prior) |
| 142179 | 15 January | | Phillips (sic), London. China & Glass Merchants |

| *Registration* No. | *Date* | *Year* | *Registered* Party |
|---|---|---|---|
| 142433 | 18 January | 1890 | Boulton & Mills, Audnam Glass Works, Stourbridge. Glass Makers |
| 142675 | 22 January | | Sowerby's Ellison Glass Works Ltd. (see prior) |
| 142755/6 | 23 January | | Siebdrat & Schmidt, London. Manufacturer |
| 142985 | 28 January | | Burtles, Tate & Co., Poland Street Glass Works, Manchester. Glass Makers |
| 143135 | 30 January | | Guiseppe V. De Luca, London. Agent |
| 143153 | 28 January | | Molineaux, Webb & Co. Ltd. (see prior) |
| 143884 | 11 February | | Matthew Turnbull, Cornhill Glass Works, Sunderland. Flint Glass Manufacturer |
| 144725 | 24 February | | James Dixon & Sons, Sheffield. Silver Plate Manufacturer |
| 144779 | 25 February | | Molineaux, Webb & Co. Ltd. (see prior) |
| 144848 | 26 February | | George Jackson & Sons, London. Interior Decorator |
| 145000 | 28 February | | Phillips (sic) (see prior) |
| 145008 | | | Matthew Turnbull (see prior) |
| 145668 | 12 March | | Samuel Clarke, London. Night Light Manufacturer |
| 145813 | 14 March | | A. & R. Cochran, St. Rollox Flint Glass Works, Glasgow. Flint Glass Manufacturer |
| 145999 | | | Frederick S. Balls, Cambridge. Glass & China Manufacturer |
| 146042 | 18 March | | Mappin & Webb, London. Silversmiths |
| 146125 | 19 March | | Wittmann & Roth, London. Glass & China Manufacturer |
| 146736 | 28 March | | Samuel Clarke (see prior) |
| 147123 | 3 April | | Samuel Clarke (see prior) |
| 147194/5 | 5 April | | Charles E. Hill (see prior) |
| 147747 | 16 April | | Samuel Clarke (see prior) |
| 147915 | 15 April | | The General Electric Co. Ltd., London. Manufacturing Electricians |
| 148640 | 30 April | | Phillips (sic) (see prior) |
| 148661 | | | Burtles, Tate & Co. (see prior) |
| 148740 | | | C. & G. E. Asprey, London. Silversmiths |
| 149002 | 5 May | | Charles Kempton & Sons, Lambeth. Glass Maker |
| 149468 | 14 May | | John Walsh Walsh, The Soho & Vesta Glass Works, Birmingham. Glass Maker |
| 149470 | | | Schindler & Co., London. Glass Maker |
| 149959 | 22 May | | James Bridger, Upper Edmonton. Glass Merchant |
| 150045/6 | 24 May | | Charles Kempton & Sons (see prior) |

| Registration No. | Date | Year | Registered Party |
|---|---|---|---|
| 150063 | 27 May | 1890 | Charles E. Hill, Brighton. Importer |
| 150087 | 28 May | | Henry Mayer & Co., London. Glass & China Exporters |
| 150166/7 | 31 May | | Wittmann & Roth, London. Glass & China Manufacturer |
| 150277 | 3 June | | Greener & Co., Wear Flint Glass Works, Sunderland & London. Glass Makers |
| 150401 | 5 June | | Greener & Co. (see prior) |
| 150532 | 7 June | | Chance Bros. & Co. Ltd., Birmingham. Glass Maker |
| 150552 | 4 June | | Rowland Ward & Co., London. Naturalist |
| 150597 | 10 June | | Chance Bros. & Co. Ltd. (see prior) |
| 150662 | 11 June | | Charles E. Hill (see prior) |
| 151046 | 18 June | | Siebdrat & Schmidt, London. Manufacturers |
| 151548 | 27 June | | Phillips (sic), London. Glass & China Manufacturer |
| 151657 | 1 July | | Stevens & Williams, Brierley Hill Glass Works, Stafford. Glass Makers |
| 151745 | 2 July | | Falk, Stadelmann & Co. |
| 152059 | 8 July | | M. J. Reynolds, Stoke-on-Trent. Engraver |
| 152135 | 10 July | | Charles E. Hill (see prior) |
| 152257 | | | Samuel Clarke, London. Night Light Manufacturer |
| 152546 | 9 July | | M. J. Reynolds (see prior) |
| 152906-8 | 21 July | | Franz Aut Mehlem, Bonn, Germany. China & Glass Manufacturer |
| 153858 | 2 August | | George Davidson & Co., Teams Flint Glass Works, Gateshead-on-Tyne. Glass Makers |
| 153901/2 | 5 August | | Phillips (sic) (see prior) |
| 154104 | 7 August | | Louis Hats-chek & Co., Vienna & London. Importers |
| 154350 | 1 August | | John Tams, Longton, Staffordshire. Manufacturer |
| 154486 | 15 August | | William S. Thomson, London. Perfumer |
| 154679 | 19 August | | Edward John Shaw, Astral Works, Walsall. Lamp Manufacturer |
| 154744/5 | 20 August | | F. H. Davy & Co., Upper Edmonton. Glass Merchants |
| 154849 | 19 August | | The Pendleton Flint Glass Co. Ltd., Lancaster. Flint Glass Manufacturer |
| 155744 | 2 September | | John Walsh Walsh, The Soho & Vesta Glass Works, Birmingham. Glass Maker |
| 155890 | 4 September | | William Walker |
| 156218-20 | 8 September | | Louis Sepulchre, Herstal les Liege, Belgium. Manufacturer |

| Registration No. | Date | Year | Registered Party |
|---|---|---|---|
| 156417 | 10 September | 1890 | F. H. Davy & Co. (see prior) |
| 156626 | | | Saunders & Shepherd, London. Manufacturing Goldsmiths & Jewellers |
| 157103 | 19 September | | William Walker |
| 157164 | 20 September | | Samuel Clarke (see prior) |
| 157979 | 30 September | | Siebdrat & Schmidt (see prior) |
| 158283 | 4 October | | Saunders & Shepherd (see prior) |
| 158327/8 | 6 October | | L. Straus & Sons, New York. Merchants |
| 158336 | | | Samuel Clarke (see prior) |
| 158804 | 9 October | | Schindler & Co., London. Glass Maker |
| 158841 | | | Schindler & Co. (see prior) |
| 158948 | 15 October | | Molineaux, Webb & Co. Ltd., The Manchester Flint Glass Works, Manchester. Glass Maker |
| 158967 | | | Schindler & Co. (see prior) |
| 159189 | 18 October | | Percival, Vickers & Co. Ltd., Manchester. Flint Glass Manufacturer |
| 160244 | 3 November | | Greener & Company (see prior) |
| 162057 | 29 November | | M. J. Reynolds (see prior) |
| 163075 | 16 December | | Greener & Co. (see prior) |
| 163179 | 17 December | | James Marshall, Novelty Glass Works, Stourbridge. Glass Manufacturer |
| 163914 | 1 January | 1891 | Martin Gray, London. China & Glass Merchant |
| 164521 | 12 January | | Molineaux, Webb & Co. Ltd. (see prior) |
| 164606/7 | 13 January | | Stone, Fawdry & Stone, The Union Glass Works, Birmingham. Flint Glass Manufacturers |
| 164670 | 14 January | | John Walsh Walsh (see prior) |
| 165012 | 20 January | | John Walsh Walsh (see prior) |
| 165559 | 30 January | | Sowerby's Ellison Glass Works Ltd., Gateshead-on-Tyne. Glass Maker |
| 166178 | 10 February | | Burtles, Tate & Co., Poland Street Glass Works, Manchester. Glass Makers |
| 166347 | 12 February | | A. & R. Cochran, St. Rollox Flint Glass Works, Glasgow. Flint Glass Manufacturer |
| 166359/60 | | | Max Emanuel, London. Merchant |
| 166650/1 | 18 February | | The Glass & Metal Engraving Co. Ltd., Glasgow. Engravers |
| 166677 | | | Mappin & Brothers, Queens Cutlery Works, Sheffield. Silversmiths & Cutlers |
| 166680 | | | James Deakin & Sons, London. Silversmiths |

| *Registration* No. | *Date* | *Year* | *Registered* Party |
|---|---|---|---|
| 166960 | 24 February | 1891 | John Grinsell & Sons, Birmingham. Silversmiths |
| 167269 | 2 March | | Francis A. Coles, Birmingham. Silversmiths |
| 167516 | 5 March | | Thomas Webb & Sons, Stourbridge. Glass Maker |
| 168065 | 12 March | | Edward J. Shaw, Astral Works, Walsall. Lamp Manufacturer |
| 168130 | 13 March | | Percival, Vickers & Co. Ltd., Manchester. Glass Makers |
| 168132 | | | Samuel Clarke, London. Night Light Manufacturer |
| 168237 | 14 March | | Henry C. Stephens, London. Ink Manufacturer |
| 168686 | 24 March | | James Hateley & Co., Aston Glass Works, Birmingham. Glass Maker |
| 169054 | 2 April | | Alfred Arculus, Birmingham. Glass Maker |
| 169069 | | | Wittmann & Roth, London. Glass & China Manufacturer |
| 169292 | 8 April | | Wittmann & Roth (see prior) |
| 169406-9 | 9 April | | Wittmann & Roth (see prior) |
| 169410 | | | Matthew Turnbull, Sunderland. Flint Glass Manufactuer |
| 170269/70 | 24 April | | Wittmann & Roth (see prior) |
| 170363 | 25 April | | A. & R. Cochran, St. Rollox Flint Glass Works, Glasgow. Flint Glass Manufacturer |
| 170658 | 30 April | | Stevens & Williams, Brierley Hill Glass Works, Stafford. Glass Makers |
| 170909 | 6 May | | Wittmann & Roth (see prior) |
| 171058 | 7 May | | Saunders & Shepherd, London. Manufacturing Goldsmith & Jeweller |
| 171377 | 13 May | | Guiseppe V. De Luca, London. Agent |
| 171770-2 | 20 May | | Charles E. Hill, Brighton. Importer |
| 171774 | | | Charles E. Hill (see prior) |
| 171819/20 | 22 May | | Charles E. Hill (see prior) |
| 172125 | 29 May | | John Walsh Walsh, The Soho & Vesta Glass Works, Birmingham. Glass Maker |
| 172810 | 11 June | | John Walsh Walsh (see prior) |
| 173044 | 18 June | | Percival, Vickers & Co. Ltd. (see prior) |
| 173059 | | | Sowerby & Co., Lemington Glass Works, Newcastle-on-Tyne. Glass Maker |
| 173528 | 26 June | | S. Mordan & Co., London. Manufacturer |
| 173566 | 27 June | | M. J. Reynolds, Stoke-on-Trent. Engraver |
| 173968 | 3 July | | Charles E. Hill (see prior) |
| 173976 | | | Guiseppe V. De Luca (see prior) |
| 174527 | 14 July | | Guiseppe V. De Luca (see prior) |
| 174850/1 | 18 July | 1891 | Edward J. Shaw & Co. (see prior) |
| 174913 | 20 July | | John Line & Sons, Reading & London. Paperhanging & Glass Merchant |
| 175031 | 23 July | | Boulton & Mills, Stourbridge. Glass Makers |
| 175420 | 29 July | | Wittmann & Roth (see prior) |
| 175802 | 4 August | | Thomas Webb & Sons (see prior) |
| 175894 | 6 August | | Schindler & Co., London. Importers |
| 176239 | 10 August | | Greener & Co., Wear Flint Glass Works, Sunderland. Glass Makers |
| 176566 | 15 August | | George Davidson & Co., Teams Flint Glass Works, Gateshead-on-Tyne. Glass Maker |
| 176642 | 17 August | | Hukin & Heath, Imperial Works, Birmingham. Silversmiths |
| 176677 | | | Edward Coppin, London. China, Glass & Bottle Contractors |
| 176723 | 18 August | | Hukin & Heath (see prior) |
| 176764 | 19 August | | The Glasgow Plate Glass Co., Glasgow. Glass Maker |
| 177399 | 28 August | | Boulton & Mills (see prior) |
| 177733 | 2 September | | John Walsh Walsh (see prior) |
| 178065/6 | 7 September | | Thomas Goode & Co., London. Glass & China Merchant |
| 178133 | 8 September | | Hukin & Heath (see prior) |
| 178135/6 | | | Weiss & Biheller, London. Importers |
| 178174 | 9 September | | Thomas Webb & Sons Ltd. (see prior) |
| 178653 | 16 September | | Thomas Webb & Sons Ltd. (see prior) |
| 179709 | 29 September | | J. & W. B. Smith, London. Glass Maker |
| 179726 | | | Henry J. Latham, New York City. Manufacturer |
| 181040 | 16 October | | Hukin & Heath (see prior) |
| 181041-3 | | | Army and Navy Cooperative Society Ltd., London. Manufacturer |
| 181057 | | | G. Heath & Co., London. Silversmith |
| 181326-9 | 22 October | | Richard Schmidt, Finsbury. Agent |
| 181572 | 27 October | | Stevens & Williams (see prior) |
| 181922 | 29 October | | John Walsh Walsh (see prior) |
| 182002 | 30 October | | Greener & Co. (see prior) |
| 182180/1 | 3 November | | Webb Shaw & Co. Ltd., Stourbridge, Glass Maker |
| 183187 | 17 November | | Hukin & Heath (see prior) |
| 183264 | 18 November | | S. Mordan & Co. (see prior) |

| Registration No. | Date | Year | Registered Party |
|---|---|---|---|
| 183415-7 | 20 November | 1891 | John Walsh Walsh, The Soho & Vesta Glass Works, Birmingham. Glass Maker |
| 183637 | 23 November | | Richard Schmidt, Finsbury. Agent |
| 183799 | 26 November | | Joseph Holdcroft, Longton, Staffordshire. Manufacturer |
| 184359 | 4 December | | Stone, Fawdry & Stone, Birmingham. Glass Maker |
| 184501 | 7 December | | John Walsh Walsh (see prior) |
| 184548 | 8 December | | John Walsh Walsh (see prior) |
| 184582 | 9 December | | Falk, Stadelmann & Co. Ltd. |
| 184619 | | | Richard Thomas Grocott, Whitehall Works, Longport, Staffordshire. Manufacturer |
| 185045 | 17 December | | Hukin & Heath, Imperial Works, Birmingham. Silversmiths |
| 185803 | 4 January | 1892 | Stuart & Sons, Red House Glass Works, Stourbridge, Glass Maker |
| 185823/4 | 5 January | | Falk, Stadelmann & Co. |
| 185847 | | | Henry J. Latham, New York City. Manufacturer |
| 185911 | 7 January | | Thomas Webb & Sons Ltd. Stourbridge, Glass Maker |
| 186137 | 12 January | | John Walsh Walsh (see prior) |
| 186286 | 14 January | | Richard Wilkes, Cross Glass Works, Dudley. Glass Maker |
| 186335 | | | John Henry Downing, Birmingham. Glass Merchant |
| 186382 | 15 January | | Boulton & Mills, Audnam Glass Works, Stourbridge, Glass Maker. |
| 186546 | 21 January | | John Walsh Walsh (see prior) |
| 186567 | | | John Walsh Walsh (see prior) |
| 186770 | 25 January | | Thomas Webb & Sons Ltd. (see prior) |
| 187037 | 29 January | | Saunders & Shepherd, London. Manufacturing Goldsmiths & Jewellers |
| 187105 | 30 January | | Francis Fether, London. Glass Blower |
| 187145 | 1 February | | Hukin & Heath (see prior) |
| 187169 | 2 February | | Schindler & Co., London. Glass Maker |
| 187222 | 3 February | | Price's Patent Candle Co., Battersea. Manufacturer |
| 187759 | 15 February | | Hukin & Heath (see prior) |
| 187891 | 17 February | | Edward John Shaw, Astral Works, Walsall. Lamp Manufacturer |
| 188148 | 22 February | | Hukin & Heath (see prior) |
| 188440 | 27 February | | Charles E. Hill, Brighton. Importer |
| 188489 | 29 February | | Edward John Shaw (see prior) |
| 188944/5 | 10 March | | Alfred Arculus & Co., Birmingham. Glass Maker |

| Registration No. | Date | Year | Registered Party |
|---|---|---|---|
| 189247 | 15 March | 1892 | Percival, Vickers & Co. Ltd., Manchester. Glass Makers |
| 189324 | 16 March | | Sowerby's Ellison Glass Works Ltd., Gateshead-on-Tyne. Glass Maker |
| 189344 | 16 March | | Percival, Vickers & Co. Ltd. (see prior) |
| 190428 | 2 April | | Boulton & Mills (see prior) |
| 190543 | 5 April | | J. & J. Price, Birmingham. Glass Maker |
| 190696 | 7 April | | Saunders & Shepherd (see prior) |
| 191042 | 14 April | | Frederick Hewitt, North Shields. Glass and China Merchant |
| 191191 | 20 April | | Mrs. Marcus Stone, London. Gentlewoman |
| 191254 | 21 April | | Pilkington Bros., Lancaster. Glass Maker |
| 191384 | 22 April | | Guiseppe V. De Luca, London. Agent |
| 191886 | 3 May | | Webb, Shaw & Co. Ltd., Stourbridge. Glass Maker |
| 191932 | 4 May | | Boulton & Mills (see prior) |
| 192298 | 10 May | | Robinson, Skinner & Co., Warrington. Glass Maker |
| 192350 | 11 May | | The Lamp Manufacturing Co. Ltd. |
| 192553 | 14 May | | Saunders & Shepherd (see prior) |
| 192595 | 16 May | | Thomas Webb & Sons Ltd. (see prior) |
| 192602-4 | | | Charles E. Hill (see prior) |
| 192807 | 20 May | | Thomas Webb & Sons Ltd. (see prior) |
| 192876 | 21 May | | Percival, Vickers & Co. Ltd. (see prior) |
| 193196 | 28 May | | Zeno & Company, London. Perfumers |
| 193365 | 1 June | | George Davidson & Co., Teams Flint Glass Works, Gateshead-on-Tyne. Glass Maker |
| 193492/3 | 3 June | | M. J. Reynolds, Stoke-on-Trent. Engraver |
| 193624 | 4 June | | Schindler & Co. (see prior) |
| 193626 | | | Schindler & Co. (see prior) |
| 193691 | 8 June | | Soane & Smith, London. China & Glass Merchant |
| 193694/5 | 9 June | | Percival, Vickers & Co. Ltd. (see prior) |
| 193821 | 14 June | | Percival, Vickers & Co. Ltd. (see prior) |
| 193826/7 | | | Krausse & Auerbach, London. Foreign Agents |
| 193917 | 15 June | | Saunders & Shepherd (see prior) |
| 194040/1 | 17 June | | Schindler & Co. (see prior) |

| *Registration* No. | *Date* | *Year* | *Registered* Party |
|---|---|---|---|
| 194188 | 21 June | 1892 | George Betjemann & Sons, London. Dressing Case Manufacturer |
| 194189 | 21 June | | Charles E. Hill, Brighton. Importer |
| 194562 | 24 June | | John Grinsell & Sons, Birmingham. Art Metal Smiths |
| 194616 | 25 June | | Chance Brothers & Co. Ltd., West Smethwick. Glass Manufacturers |
| 194638 | 27 June | | Percival, Vickers & Co. Ltd., Manchester. Glass Makers |
| 194696 | 28 June | | Mappin & Webb, London. Silversmiths |
| 194813 | 30 June | | Soane & Smith, London. China & Glass Merchant |
| 195324 | 12 July | | William Ault, Swadlincote. Manufacturer |
| 195482 | 15 July | | I. & W. B. Smith, London. Glass Makers and Importers |
| 195689 | 21 July | | M. J. Reynolds, Stoke-on-Trent. Engraver |
| 196009 | 26 July | | S. Reich & Co., London. Glass Maker |
| 196342 | 3 August | | Mappin & Webb (see prior) |
| 196639 | 10 August | | Percival, Vickers & Co. Ltd. (see prior) |
| 196641 | | | Greener & Co., Wear Flint Glass Works, Sunderland. Glass Makers |
| 196748/9 | 12 August | | Pilkington Brothers, St. Helens. Glass Maker |
| 196953/4 | 17 August | | Herbert Price & Co., London. Wholesale China and Glass Merchant |
| 197221 | 20 August | | Charles E. Hill (see prior) |
| 198233 | 8 September | | Guiseppe V. De Luca, London. Agent |
| 198248 | | | William Ault (see prior) |
| 198959 | 17 September | | Wittmann & Roth, London. Glass & China Manufacturer |
| 199109 | 20 September | | Henry G. Richardson, Wordsley Flint Glass Works, Stourbridge. Glass Maker |
| 199110 | | | Woodall & Son, London. Glass Maker |
| 199284 | 23 September | | Woodall & Son (see prior) |
| 199590 | 28 September | | Francis A. Coles, Birmingham. Silversmith |
| 200502 | 11 October | | Stone, Fawdry & Stone, Birmingham. Glass Maker |
| 200505 | | | Boulton & Mills, Audnam Glass Works, Stourbridge. Glass Makers |
| 201102 | 19 October | | Richard Schmidt, Finsbury. Agent |
| 201139 | 20 October | | Herbert Price & Co. (see prior) |

| *Registration* No. | *Date* | *Year* | *Registered* Party |
|---|---|---|---|
| 201225 | 21 October | 1892 | Molineaux, Webb & Co. Ltd., The Manchester Flint Glass Works. Manchester. Glass Makers |
| 201392 | 25 October | | John Shaw & Sons, Latimer Glass Works, Sheffield. Cut Glass Manufacturer |
| 201648 | 31 October | | Walter Thornhill & Co., London. Silversmiths |
| 201902 | 3 November | | Wittmann & Roth (see prior) |
| 202200/1 | 8 November | | John Stewart, Glasgow. Glass Stainer and Embosser |
| 202625-9 | 15 November | | Walter Thornhill & Co. (see prior) |
| 202675 | 16 November | | Saunders & Shepherd, London. Manufacturing Goldsmiths & Jewellers |
| 203135 | 25 November | | John Walsh Walsh, The Soho & Vesta Glass Works, Birmingham. Glass Maker |
| 203159 | | | Weiss & Biheller, London. Importers |
| 203235-7 | 28 November | | Hukin & Heath, Imperial Works, Birmingham. Silversmiths |
| 203327 | 30 November | | Max Emanuel & Co., London. Merchant |
| 204089-91 | 12 December | | William Ault (see prior) |
| 204189 | 14 December | | Josiah Lane, Birmingham. Glass Maker |
| 204438 | 17 December | | Henry Mayer & Co., London. China & Glass Merchants |
| 204629 | 21 December | | Phillips's, London. Glass & China Manufacturer |
| 205238 | 31 December | | Schindler & Co., London. Glass Maker |
| 205280/1 | 3 January | 1893 | Zimmermann & Co., London. Lamp Manufacturer |
| 205884 | 14 January | | Schindler & Co. (see prior) |
| 205994 | 17 January | | Boulton & Mills (see prior) |
| 206025/6 | 18 January | | Webb Brothers Ltd., Manchester. Flint Glass Manufacturer |
| 206204 | 2 February | | Phillips's (see prior) |
| 206612 | 27 January | | Thomas Webb & Sons Ltd., Stourbridge. Glass Maker |
| 206623/4 | | | Guiseppe V. De Luca (see prior) |
| 207004 | 3 February | | Edward John Shaw, Astral Works, Walsall. Lamp Manufacturer |
| 207065 | 4 February | | Webb, Shaw & Co. Ltd., Stourbridge. Glass Maker |
| 207120 | 7 February | | Wood Brothers & Co., Borough Flint Glass Works, Barnsley. Glass Maker |
| 207243 | 9 February | | Guiseppe V. De Luca (see prior) |

| Registration No. | Date | Year | Registered Party |
|---|---|---|---|
| 207909 | 20 February | 1893 | G. Davidson & Co., Teams Flint Glass Works, Gateshead-on-Tyne. Glass Maker |
| 208112 | 24 February | | Schindler & Co., London. Glass Maker |
| 208367 | 1 March | | Matthew Turnbull, Cornhill Glass Works, Sunderland. Flint Glass Manufacturer |
| 208600 | 6 March | | Saunders & Shepherd, London. Manufacturing Goldsmiths & Jewellers |
| 208658 | 7 March | | Saunders & Shepherd (see prior) |
| 209222 | 15 March | | William Ault, Derby. Manufacturer |
| 209414 | 17 March | | Molineaux, Webb & Co. Ltd., The Manchester Flint Glass Works, Manchester. Glass Maker |
| 209465 | 18 March | | Herbert Price & Co., London. Wholesale China and Glass Merchant |
| 209493 | 20 March | | Stevens & Williams, Brierley Hill Glass Works, Stafford. Glass Makers |
| 210371 | 10 April | | Greener & Company, Wear Flint Glass Works, Sunderland. Glass Makers |
| 210373 | | | M. J. Reynolds, Stoke-on-Trent. Engraver |
| 210704 | 15 April | | Stone, Fawdry & Stone, Birmingham. Glass Maker |
| 210719 | | | Stone, Fawdry & Stone (see prior) |
| 210755 | 17 April | | Thomas Webb & Sons Ltd., Stourbridge. Glass Maker |
| 211129 | 24 April | | Guiseppe V. De Luca, London. Agent |
| 211352 | 28 April | | Max Emanuel & Co., London. Merchant |
| 211616 | 3 May | | M. J. Reynolds (see prior) |
| 211617 | | | Percival, Vickers & Co. Ltd., Manchester. Glass Makers |
| 211778 | 6 May | | John Walsh Walsh, The Soho & Vesta Glass Works, Birmingham. Glass Maker |
| 211800 | 8 May | | M. J. Reynolds (see prior) |
| 212166 | 15 May | | Max Emanuel & Co. (see prior) |
| 212315 | 17 May | | Pilkington Brothers, Lancaster. Glass Maker |
| 212319 | | | John Mortlock & Co., London. China and Glass Dealer |
| 212459 | 19 May | | Thomas Goode & Co., London. China & Glass Merchant |
| 212679 | 25 May | | De Grelle, Houdret & Co., London. Manufacturer |
| 212684 | 25 May | 1893 | George Davidson & Co. (see prior) |
| 212730 | 29 May | | Thomas Webb & Sons Ltd. (see prior) |
| 212735 | | | Guiseppe V. De Luca (see prior) |
| 212950 | 1 June | | Richard Schmidt, Finsbury. Agent |
| 212983 | 2 June | | Francis A. Coles, Birmingham. Silversmith |
| 213282 | 8 June | | The Army & Navy Cooperative Soc. Ltd., London. Manufacturer |
| 213324 | 9 June | | Pilkington Brothers (see prior) |
| 213374 | 10 June | | Matthew Turnbull (see prior) |
| 213381 | | | Percival, Vickers & Co. Ltd. (see prior) |
| 213455 | 13 June | | Oppenheimer Son & Co. Ltd., London. Merchant |
| 213768 | 21 June | | Stone, Fawdry & Stone (see prior) |
| 214578 | 5 July | | William Ault (see prior) |
| 215082 | 15 July | | Sowerby's Ellison Glass Works Ltd., Gateshead-on-Tyne. Glass Maker |
| 215154 | 18 July | | Greener & Co. (see prior) |
| 215774/5 | 28 July | | Max Emanuel & Co. (see prior) |
| 216088 | 3 August | | Burtles, Tate & Co., Poland Street Glass Works, Manchester. Glass Makers |
| 216157 | | | Henry G. Richardson & Sons, Wordsley Flint Glass Works, Stourbridge. Glass Maker |
| 216255/6 | 4 August | | T. Wilkinson & Sons, Pelican Works, Birmingham. Electro Plate Manufacturer |
| 216578 | 10 August | | G. V. De Luca, Hill & Co. (see prior) |
| 216626 | 11 August | | Schindler & Co., London. Glass Maker |
| 216627 | | | Wittmann & Roth, London. Glass & China Manufacturer |
| 216711 | 15 August | | Arthur Mortimer, London. Glass Merchant |
| 216779/80 | 16 August | | Henry G. Richardson & Sons (see prior) |
| 217198 | 25 August | | M. J. Reynolds (see prior) |
| 217199 | | | Sowerby's Ellison Glass Works Ltd. (see prior) |
| 217202 | | | Henry G. Richardson & Sons (see prior) |
| 217204 | | | Saunders & Shepherd, London. Manufacturing Goldsmiths & Jewellers |
| 217327 | 28 August | | George Jackson & Sons, London. Manufacturer |
| 217405 | 29 August | | Saunders & Shepherd (see prior) |

| Registration No. | Date | Year | Registered Party |
|---|---|---|---|
| 217448 | 30 August | 1893 | Phillips's, London. Glass & China Manufacturer |
| 217651 | 4 September | | Molineaux, Webb & Co. Ltd., The Manchester Flint Glass Works, Manchester. Glass Maker |
| 217660 | | | Saunders & Shepherd, London. Manufacturing Goldsmiths & Jewellers |
| 217749 | 6 September | | Greener & Co., Wear Flint Glass Works, Sunderland. Glass Makers |
| 217752 | | | G. Davidson & Co., Teams Flint Glass Works, Gateshead-on-Tyne. Glass Maker |
| 217831/2 | 7 September | | J. Defries & Son |
| 217900 | 9 September | | Henry G. Richardson & Sons, Wordsley Flint Glass Works, Stourbridge. Glass Maker |
| 218085 | 11 September | | Thomas Webb & Sons Ltd., Stourbridge. Glass Maker |
| 218103 | 12 September | | Stevens & Williams, Brierley Hill Glass Works, Stafford. Glass Makers |
| 218417/8 | 18 September | | De Grelle, Houdret & Co., London. Manufacturer |
| 218710 | 20 September | | Greener & Co. (see prior) |
| 219465 | 2 October | | M. J. Reynolds, Stoke-on-Trent. Engraver |
| 219565 | 3 October | | John Ford & Co., Holyrood Glass Works, Edinburgh. Manufacturer |
| 219638 | 4 October | | Matthew Turnbull, Cornhill Glass Works, Sunderland, Durham. Flint Glass Manufacturer |
| 220471-3 | 14 October | | Molineaux, Webb & Co. Ltd. (see prior) |
| 220863 | 19 October | | Stevens & Williams (see prior) |
| 221006 | 21 October | | James A. Cox, London. Glass & China Merchant |
| 221175 | 25 October | | Hukin & Heath, Imperial Works, Birmingham. Silversmiths |
| 221354 | 27 October | | Boulton & Mills, Audnam Glass Works, Stourbridge. Flint Glass Makers |
| 221480 | 30 October | | M. J. Reynolds, Stoke-on-Trent. Engraver |
| 221684 | 2 November | | M. J. Reynolds (see prior) |
| 221728 | 3 November | | Harold Faraday, London. Electric Light Fitting Manufacturer |
| 222032/3 | 8 November | | J. & J. Price, Birmingham. Glass Maker |
| 222389 | 15 November | | William Ault, Derby. Manufacturer |
| 222451 | 16 November | | Guiseppe V. De Luca, Hill & Co., London. Merchant |

| Registration No. | Date | Year | Registered Party |
|---|---|---|---|
| 223294 | 4 December | 1893 | Saunders & Shepherd (see prior) |
| 223362 | 5 December | | John Ford & Co., (see prior) |
| 223645 | 8 December | | William Ault (see prior) |
| 223742 | 11 December | | Greener & Co. (see prior) |
| 223873/4 | 13 December | | G. V. De Luca, Hill & Co. (see prior) |
| 224171 | 19 December | | G. Davidson & Co. (see prior) |
| 224229 | 20 December | | J. Defries & Sons Ltd. |
| 224362 | 22 December | | Andrew Murray Malloch, Glasgow. Glass Maker |
| 224603 | 28 December | | Stevens & Williams (see prior) |
| 224713 | 30 December | | Saunders & Shepherd (see prior) |
| 224765 | 1 January | 1894 | G. V. De Luca, Hill & Co. (see prior) |
| 225794 | 20 January | | Schindler & Co., London. Glass Maker |
| 226750 | 3 February | | Stevens & Williams (see prior) |
| 226959 | 7 February | | William Hutton & Sons Ltd., London. Manufacturing Silversmiths |
| 226976 | 8 February | | Schindler & Co. (see prior) |
| 227177 | 10 February | | Hukin & Heath (see prior) |
| 227396 | 14 February | | Wittmann and Roth, London. Glass & China Manufacturer |
| 227564 | 15 February | | Hukin & Heath (see prior) |
| 227966 | 23 February | | Hukin & Heath (see prior) |
| 228608 | 6 March | | Hukin & Heath (see prior) |
| 228636 | 7 March | | William Hutton & Sons Ltd. (see prior) |
| 229738 | 24 March | | William Hutton & Sons Ltd. (see prior) |
| 230031 | 3 April | | Jules Lang & Co., London. Glass and China Merchant |
| 230286 | 7 April | | John Ford & Co. (see prior) |
| 230336 | 9 April | | Falk, Stadelmann & Co. Ltd. |
| 230704 | 14 April | | Henry Briggs & Co., Hood Street Glass Works, Manchester. Glass Workers |
| 230817 | 17 April | | Falk, Stadelmann & Co. Ltd. |
| 230818 | | | Saunders & Shepherd (see prior) |
| 231039 | 20 April | | G. V. De Luca, Hill & Co. (see prior) |
| 231387 | 26 April | | Thomas Webb & Sons Ltd. (see prior) |
| 231490 | 28 April | | Henry Salsbury, London. Lamp Manufacturer |
| 232529 | 22 May | | Jules Lang & Co. (see prior) |
| 232959-61 | 28 May | | J. Defries & Sons Ltd. |
| 233062 | 30 May | | Matthew Turnbull (see prior) |
| 233135 | 31 May | | Hukin & Heath (see prior) |
| 233181 | 1 June | | Max Emanuel & Co., London. Merchant |

| Registration No. | Date | Year | Registered Party |
|---|---|---|---|
| 233256-60 | 2 June | 1894 | Max Emanuel & Co., London. Merchant |
| 233564 | 8 June | | Leuchars & Son, London. Dressing Case Makers |
| 233571 | | | M. J. Reynolds, Stoke-on-Trent. Engraver |
| 233766 | 11 June | | Percival, Vickers & Co. Ltd., Manchester. Glass Makers |
| 233768 | | | Molineaux, Webb & Co. Ltd., The Manchester Flint Glass Works, Manchester. Glass Maker |
| 233777 | | | Henry Turner, London. Glass and China Manufacturer |
| 233948 | 13 June | | Richard Schmidt, Finsbury. Agent |
| 234231 | 14 June | | Greener & Co., Wear Flint Glass Works. Sunderland. Glass Makers |
| 234288 | 15 June | | Max Emanuel & Co (see prior) |
| 234561/2 | 20 June | | M. J. Reynolds (see prior) |
| 235217 | 28 June | | Phillips's, London. Glass & China Manufacturer |
| 235230 | | | Max Emanuel & Co. (see prior) |
| 235824 | 12 July | | Boulton & Mills, Audnam Glass Works, Stourbridge. Flint Glass Makers |
| 237038 | 1 August | | G. Davidson & Co., Teams Flint Glass Works, Gateshead-on-Tyne. Glass Maker |
| 237567 | 10 August | | J. Defries & Sons Ltd. |
| 237641 | 13 August | | M. J. Reynolds (see prior) |
| 237720 | 14 August | | A. Ruch & Co., London. Glass Bottle Manufacturer |
| 238352 | 23 August | | Sowerby's Ellison Glass Works Ltd., Gateshead-on-Tyne. Glass Maker |
| 238623 | 27 August | | Hukin & Heath, Imperial Works, Birmingham. Silversmiths |
| 238687-90 | 28 August | | Jules Lang & Co., London. Glass & China Merchant |
| 238856 | 30 August | | Jules Lang & Co. (see prior) |
| 239188 | 4 September | | Charles Parsons, Lancaster. Glass Merchant |
| 239655 | 11 September | | A. Ruch & Co. (see prior) |
| 239938 | 15 September | | Max Emanuel & Co (see prior) |
| 240048 | 18 September | | William Brown, London. Glass & China Warehouseman |
| 240049 | | | Hukin & Heath (see prior) |
| 240703 | 25 September | | C. H. Moody, London. Glass Bottle Manufacturer |
| 240865 | 27 September | | A. & R. Cochran, St. Rollox Flint Glass Works, Glasgow. Flint Glass Manufacturer |
| 241122 | 28 September | | Max Emanuel & Co (see prior) |
| 241304/5 | 2 October | | William Ault, Derby. Manufacturer |
| 241570 | 4 October | | Max Emanuel & Co (see prior) |
| 241788 | 9 October | 1894 | Max Emanuel & Co (see prior) |
| 241930 | 10 October | | Greener & Co. (see prior) |
| 242610 | 19 October | | Hukin & Heath (see prior) |
| 242706 | 22 October | | M. J. Reynolds (see prior) |
| 243177 | 27 October | | Edward J. Shaw & Co., Astral Works, Walsall. Lamp Manufacturer |
| 243452 | 1 November | | Chance Brothers & Co. Ltd., Birmingham. Glass Maker |
| 243946 | 9 November | | M. J. Reynolds (see prior) |
| 244076 | 12 November | | Max Emanuel & Co (see prior) |
| 244118/9 | 13 November | | A. Ruch & Co. (see prior) |
| 244245 | 14 November | | C. Depinoix, Paris. Bottle Manufacturer |
| 245039 | 27 November | | M. J. Reynolds (see prior) |
| 245044 | | | Jules Lang & Co. (see prior) |
| 245141 | 28 November | | John Walsh Walsh, The Soho & Vesta Glass Works, Birmingham. Glass Maker |
| 245520 | 5 December | | Falk, Stadelmann & Co. Ltd. |
| 245720 | 10 December | | Matthew Turnbull, Cornhill Glass Works, Sunderland. Flint Glass Manufacturer |
| 246383 | 18 December | | A. Ruch & Co. (see prior) |
| 246507 | 20 December | | Zeno & Co., London. Perfumers |
| 247064 | 2 January | 1895 | Alfred Arculus & Co., Birmingham. Glass Maker |
| 247225 | 4 January | | Alfred Arculus & Co (see prior) |
| 247617 | 12 January | | Alfred Arculus & Co (see prior) |
| 247777 | 15 January | | G. V. De Luca, Hill & Co., London. Merchant |
| 247921 | 17 January | | De Grelle, Houdret & Co., London. Manufacturer |
| 248011 | 18 January | | Roberts & Belk, Furnival Works, Sheffield. Silversmiths |
| 248169-72 | 22 January | | Max Emanuel & Co (see prior) |
| 248507 | 26 January | | Roberts & Belk (see prior) |
| 248671 | 30 January | | Thomas Webb & Sons Ltd., Stourbridge. Glass Maker |
| 249009 | 5 February | | G. V. De Luca, Hill & Co. (see prior) |
| 249104 | 7 February | | John Shaw, Latimer Glass Works, Sheffield. Cut Glass Manufacturer |
| 249121/2 | | | Max Emanuel & Co (see prior) |
| 249450/1 | 14 February | | Boulton & Mills (see prior) |
| 249824 | 20 February | | Schindler & Co., London. Glass Maker |
| 249976 | 22 February | | M. J. Reynolds (see prior) |
| 250254 | 27 February | | Webb, Shaw & Co., Stourbridge. Glass Maker |
| 250515 | 2 March | | Matthew Turnbull (see prior) |
| 250842 | 7 March | | Henry Turner, The Crown Pottery, London. Glass & China Manufacturer |
| 251098-101 | 11 March | | Gustav Doring, London. Glass Bottle Manufacturer |

| *Registration* No. | *Date* | *Year* | *Registered* Party |
|---|---|---|---|
| 251168 | 12 March | 1895 | Alfred Arculus, Birmingham. Glass Maker |
| 251393 | 15 March | | Molineaux, Webb & Co. Ltd., The Manchester Flint Glass Works, Manchester. Glass Maker |
| 251816 | 23 March | | John Walsh Walsh. The Soho & Vesta Glass Works, Birmingham. Glass Maker |
| 251997 | 27 March | | A. Ruch & Co., London. Glass Bottle Manufacturer |
| 252416 | 4 April | | Oppenheimer Brothers & Co., London. Merchant |
| 252587 | 5 April | | Hukin & Heath, Imperial Works, Birmingham. Silversmiths |
| 252957 | 10 April | | Saunders & Shepherd, London. Manufacturing Goldsmiths & Jewellers |
| 252968 | | | Mills, Walker & Co. Ltd., London. Glass and China Manufacturer |
| 253219 | 16 April | | The Acme Patents China, Glass & Earthenware Co., London. Dealers |
| 253348 | 18 April | | Hukin & Heath (see prior) |
| 253531 | 22 April | | James Keiller & Sons Ltd., Dundee & London. Confectioners |
| 253737 | 25 April | | John Grinsell & Sons, Victoria Works, Birmingham. Silvermsith |
| 253744 | | | John Grinsell & Sons (see prior) |
| 253880-3 | 27 April | | Max Emanuel & Co., London. Merchant |
| 253934/5 | 29 April | | John Walsh Walsh (see prior) |
| 254027 | 1 May | | G. Davidson & Co., Teams Flint Glass Works, Gateshead-on-Tyne, Glass Maker |
| 254070/1 | 2 May | | M. J. Reynolds, Stoke-on-Trent. Engraver |
| 254406 | 7 May | | Percival, Vickers & Co. Ltd., Manchester. Glass Makers |
| 254496/7 | 8 May | | G. V. De Luca, Hill & Co., The French Flint Glass Bottle Co., London. Manufacturer |
| 255279 | 23 May | | William Hutton & Sons Ltd., London. Silversmiths |
| 255999 | 8 June | | Saunders & Shepherd (see prior) |
| 256117 | 11 June | | De Grelle, Houdret & Co., London. Manufacturer |
| 256561 | 20 June | | B. Peacock & Sons, Venetian & Industry Glass Works, Castleford. Glass Bottle Manufacturer |
| 256562-5 | | | Jules Lang & Co., London. Glass & China Merchant |
| 256710 | 21 June | | J. Dunlop Mitchell & Co., Glasgow. Bottle & Glassware Manufacturer |

| *Registration* No. | *Date* | *Year* | *Registered* Party |
|---|---|---|---|
| 257024 | 27 June | 1895 | G. V. De Luca, Hill & Co. (see prior) |
| 257357 | 2 July | | Gustav Doring, London. Glass Bottle Manufacturer |
| 257632 | 6 July | | Joseph Hawkes, Birmingham. Silversmith |
| 258032-4 | 12 July | | Gustav Doring (see prior) |
| 258147 | 15 July | | John Walsh Walsh (see prior) |
| 258156 | | | Greener & Co., Wear Flint Glass Works, Sunderland. Glass Makers |
| 259153 | 3 August | | Herbert Price & Co., London. Wholesale China & Glass Merchant |
| 259467 | 12 August | | The Albion Lamp Co., Birmingham. Lamp Manufacturer |
| 260128 | 20 August | | Saunders & Shepherd (see prior) |
| 260279 | 22 August | | Max Emanuel & Co (see prior) |
| 260538 | 26 August | | Max Emanuel & Co (see prior) |
| 260968 | 3 September | | G. V. De Luca, Hill & Co. (see prior) |
| 261065/6 | 4 September | | Henry G. Richardson & Sons, Wordsley Flint Glass Works, Stourbridge. Glass Maker |
| 261274 | 6 September | | Allen & Hanbury's Ltd., London. Chemists |
| 261292 | 7 September | | Schindler & Co., London. Glass Maker |
| 262018 | 16 September | | Greener & Co. (see prior) |
| 262255 | 19 September | | G. V. De Luca, Hill & Co. (see prior) |
| 263133/4 | 4 October | | Max Emanuel & Co (see prior) |
| 263426 | 10 October | | Herbert Price & Co (see prior) |
| 263675 | 12 October | | A. Ruch & Co., London. Glass Bottle Manufacturer |
| 264396/7 | 23 October | | Herbert Price & Co (see prior) |
| 264444 | 24 October | | Max Emanuel & Co (see prior) |
| 264500 | 25 October | | Jules Lang & Co. (see prior) |
| 264751 | 29 October | | John Walsh Walsh (see prior) |
| 264997 | 1 November | | John Walsh Walsh (see prior) |
| 265003 | | | Jules Lang & Co. (see prior) |
| 265102 | 4 November | | Henry Salsbury, London. Lamp Manufacturer |
| 265305 | 7 November | | G. V. De Luca, Hill & Co. (see prior) |
| 265365 | 8 November | | A. Ruch & Co. (see prior) |
| 265549 | 12 November | | I. & E. Atkinson, London. Perfumers |
| 265716 | 14 November | | George C. Fowler & Morris B. Fowler, Brockley, Kent. Night Light Manufacturer |
| 265925 | 19 November | | Henry Salsbury (see prior) |
| 266768 | 2 December | | Eunson & Scurr, Sunderland. Glass Maker |
| 266897 | 4 December | | Pilkington Brothers Ltd., St. Helens. Glass Maker |

| *Registration* No. | *Date* | *Year* | *Registered* Party |
|---|---|---|---|
| 267079 | 6 December | 1895 | Max Emanuel & Co. London. Merchant |
| 267156 | 7 December | | Saunders & Shepherd, London. Manufacturing Goldsmiths & Jewellers |
| 267857 | 19 December | | Max Emanuel & Co (see prior) |
| 267930 | 20 December | | Hukin & Heath, Imperial Works, Birmingham. Silversmiths |
| 267931/2 | | | Eunson & Scurr, Sunderland. Glass Maker |
| 268126 | 27 December | | Jules Lang & Co., London. Glass & China Merchant |
| 268576-8 | 3 January | 1896 | Jules Lang & Co. (see prior) |
| 268869 | 10 January | | G. V. De Luca, Hill & Co. The French Flint Glass Bottle Co., London. Manufacturer |
| 268968 | 13 January | | Percival, Vickers & Co. Ltd., Manchester. Glass Makers |
| 269113 | 15 January | | Molineaux, Webb & Co. Ltd., The Manchester Flint Glass Works, Manchester. Glass Makers |
| 269118 | | | Tomlinson & Co. Ltd., Manor Flint Glass Works, Barnsley. Glass Blower |
| 269203 | 16 January | | Jules Lang & Co. (see prior) |
| 269927-9 | 27 January | | Thomas Webb & Sons Ltd., Stourbridge. Glass Maker |
| 270110 | 30 January | | E. H. Cutler & Co., Boston, U.S.A. Perfume Manufacturer |
| 270546 | 7 February | | Jules Lang & Co. (see prior) |
| 270756 | 10 February | | A. Ruch & Co., London. Glass Bottle Manufacturer |
| 270831 | 12 February | | Jules Lang & Co. (see prior) |
| 270832 | | | Max Emanuel & Co (see prior) |
| 271344 | 20 February | | Weiss & Biheller, London. Importers |
| 271422 | 21 February | | John Walsh Walsh, The Soho & Vesta Glass Works, Birmingham. Glass Maker |
| 271500 | 22 February | | John Grinsell & Sons, Victoria Works, Birmingham. Silversmiths |
| 271534/5 | 24 February | | McDougall & Sons, Glasgow. Glass & China Merchant |
| 271700 | 26 February | | Molineaux, Webb & Co. Ltd. (see prior) |
| 271766 | 27 February | | Wittmann & Co., London. Glass & China Merchant |
| 272192 | 5 March | | M. J. Reynolds, Stoke-on-Trent. Engraver |
| 272238 | 6 March | | Mappin & Webb, London. Silversmiths |
| 272672 | 13 March | | E. Coaney & Co., Birmingham. Glass Maker |
| 273414 | 25 March | | John Walsh Walsh (see prior) |
| 273503 | 26 March | | Hukin & Heath (see prior) |
| 273702 | 30 March | 1896 | A. Ruch & Co (see prior) |
| 273840 | 1 April | | Davies & Stewart, Tower Glass Works, Birmingham. Manufacturer |
| 274253 | 11 April | | Edward J. Shaw, Astral Works, Walsall. Lamp Manufacturer |
| 274427 | 15 April | | C. H. Moody & Co., London. Glass Bottle Merchant |
| 274732 | 21 April | | Jules Lang & Co. (see prior) |
| 274885 | 24 April | | McDougall & Sons (see prior) |
| 274887-9 | | | John Walsh Walsh (see prior) |
| 274897/8 | | | William Ault, Derby. Manufacturer |
| 275000-3 | 27 April | | Edward J. Shaw (see prior) |
| 275639 | 5 May | | James Lewis, London. Wholesale & Export Perfumers |
| 275802 | 7 May | | Percival, Vickers & Co. Ltd. (see prior) |
| 275897 | 8 May | | G. V. De Luca, Hill & Co. (see prior) |
| 275954 | 9 May | | James L. Shepherd, Birmingham. Glass Merchant |
| 276415-8 | 18 May | | Edward J. Shaw (see prior) |
| 276909 | 29 May | | John Grinsell & Sons, Victoria Works, Birmingham. Silversmiths |
| 276977 | 1 June | | Greener & Co., Wear Flint Glass Works, Sunderland. Glass Makers |
| 277168 | 4 June | | Jules Lang & Co. (see prior) |
| 277412 | 8 June | | James Buchanan & Co., London. Whiskey Merchant |
| 277775/6 | 15 June | | A. Ruch & Co. (see prior) |
| 277837-9 | 16 June | | William Whiston, Birmingham. Lamp Manufacturer |
| 278033/4 | 18 June | | Phillips's, London. Glass & China Manufacturer |
| 278141 | 20 June | | Gustav G. Doring, London. Glass Bottle Manufacturer |
| 278273 | 23 June | | Arthur T. Woodhall, London. Glass Maker |
| 278699 | 29 June | | McDougall & Sons (see prior) |
| 278782 | 30 June | | M. J. Reynolds (see prior) |
| 279511 | 13 July | | James Buchanan & Co. (see prior) |
| 279782 | 16 July | | Falk, Stadelmann & Co. Ltd. |
| 280388 | 28 July | | Henry Mayer & Co., London, Glass & China Merchant |
| 280525 | 30 July | | Eunson & Scurr Ltd., Sunderland. Glass Maker |
| 282113/4 | 25 August | | Schindler & Co., London. Glass Maker |
| 282607/8 | 31 August | | John Walsh Walsh (see prior) |
| 282614 | | | John L. Grossmith, London. Manufacturer of Perfumery |

| *Registration* No. | *Date* | *Year* | *Registered* Party |
|---|---|---|---|
| 282775 | 2 September | 1896 | Richter & Kuttner, London. Glass Bottle Manufacturer |
| 283227 | 5 September | | Henry Defries |
| 283577 | 10 September | | Thomas Webb & Sons Ltd., Stourbridge, Glass Maker |
| 284403 | 19 September | | Charles Melin, London. Glass Merchant |
| 284639 | 23 September | | Greener & Co., Wear Flint Glass Works, Sunderland. Glass Makers |
| 284640 | | | The Baccarat Glass Co., London. Glass Manufacturer |
| 284895 | 26 September | | Wittmann & Co., London. Glass & China Manufacturer |
| 285342 | 2 October | | G. Davidson & Co., Teams Flint Glass Works, Gateshead-on-Tyne. Glass Maker |
| 286107 | 13 October | | Hukin & Heath, Imperial Works, Birmingham. Silversmiths |
| 286391 | 15 October | | Soane & Smith, London. China & Glass Merchant |
| 287135 | 27 October | | Lea & Perrins, Midlands Works, Birmingham. Chandelier Manufacturer |
| 287267 | 29 October | | Hukin & Heath (see prior) |
| 287472 | 2 November | | Henry G. Richardson & Sons, Wordsley Flint Glass Works, Stourbridge. Glass Maker |
| 287653 | 4 November | | Percival, Vickers & Co. Ltd., Manchester. Glass Makers |
| 287927 | 9 November | | Wittmann & Co. (see prior) |
| 288044 | 11 November | | Mappin & Webb, London. Silversmiths |
| 288049 | | | Frederick W. Neuburger & Co., London. China & Glass Merchant |
| 288442 | 17 November | | James Cox, London. Glass Merchant |
| 288785/6 | 20 November | | A. Ruch & Co., London. Glass Bottle Manufacturer |
| 288969 | 24 November | | Phillips's, London. Glass & China Manufacturer |
| 289233 | 27 November | | G. V. De Luca, Hill & Co., The French Flint Glass Bottle Co., London. Manufacturer |
| 290039 | 11 December | | Jules Lang & Co., London. Glass & China Merchant |
| 290299 | 15 December | | William Ramsey, London. Glass Maker |
| 290483 | 18 December | | James Cox (see prior) |
| 291659 | 8 January | 1897 | Henry G. Richardson & Sons (see prior) |
| 291662 | | | Eunson & Scurr, Sunderland. Glass Maker |
| 291928/9 | 14 January | | John Grinsell & Sons, Victoria Works, Birmingham. Silversmiths |
| 291933 | 14 January | 1897 | Henry G. Aldridge, Marylebone. China & Glass Dealer |
| 292005 | 15 January | | Schindler & Co., London. Glass Maker |
| 292506 | 23 January | | Percival, Vickers & Co. Ltd. (see prior) |
| 292744 | 27 January | | John Grinsell & Sons (see prior) |
| 292752 | | | E. Coaney & Co., Birmingham. Glass & Earthenware Merchant |
| 292875 | 28 January | | Gustav Doring, London. Glass Bottle Manufacturer |
| 292934 | 29 January | | G. V. De Luca, Hill & Co. (see prior) |
| 293046 | 1 February | | M. J. Reynolds, Stoke-on-Trent. Engraver |
| 293052 | | | A. Ruch & Co. (see prior) |
| 293210-3 | 3 February | | John Walsh Walsh, The Soho & Vesta Glass Works, Birmingham. Glass Maker |
| 293416 | 5 February | | Briedenbach & Co., London. Perfumer |
| 293484 | 6 February | | John Grinsell & Sons (see prior) |
| 293696/7 | 9 February | | M. J. Reynolds (see prior) |
| 295198 | 5 March | | James Green & Nephew, London. China & Glass Merchant |
| 295260 | 6 March | | Wood Brothers & Co., Borough Flint Glass Works, Barnsley. Glass Maker |
| 295653 | 15 March | | John Walsh Walsh (see prior) |
| 296025 | 22 March | | John L. Grossmith, London. Manufacturer of Perfumery |
| 296071 | 23 March | | F. & C. Osler, Birmingham. Flint Glass Manufacturer |
| 296134 | 24 March | | James Green & Nephew (see prior) |
| 296418-20 | 27 March | | Alfred Arculus & Co., Birmingham. Glass Maker |
| 297352 | 14 April | | John Ford & Co., Holyrood Glass Works, Edinburgh. Manufacturer |
| 297500 | 15 April | | G. V. De Luca, Hill & Co. (see prior) |
| 297595 | 17 April | | Chance Brothers & Co. Ltd., Birmingham. Glass Maker |
| 297675 | 21 April | | Chance Brothers & Co. Ltd. (see prior) |
| 297791 | 23 April | | A. Ruch & Co. (see prior) |
| 298560-3 | 8 May | | William E. Barras, Middlesex. Glass Blower |
| 299123/4 | 19 May | | Charles Kempton, Sen., Lambeth. Glass Maker |
| 299383 | 22 May | | Schindler & Co. (see prior) |

| *Registration* No. | *Date* | *Year* | *Registered* Party |
|---|---|---|---|
| 299464 | 22 May | 1897 | Alfred W. Levee, Manchester. Glass & China Merchant |
| 299712 | 28 May | | John Walsh Walsh, The Soho & Vesta Glass Works, Birmingham. Glass Maker |
| 299974 | 3 June | | A. Ruch & Co., London. Glass Bottle Manufacturer |
| 300319 | 14 June | | M. J. Reynolds, Stoke-on-Trent. Engraver |
| 300657 | 23 June | | Holophane Ltd., London. Manufacturer of Glass Globes & Shades |
| 300950 | 1 July | | H. Labern & Son, Stoke Newington. Wholesale Perfumers |
| 301224 | 8 July | | Schindler & Co., London. Glass Maker |
| 301324 | 10 July | | Charles Kempton, Sen., Lambeth. Glass Maker |
| 301443 | 13 July | | Jules Lang & Co., London. Glass & China Merchant |
| 302034 | 23 July | | Jules Lang & Co. (see prior) |
| 302035 | | | Richard Wittmann, London. Glass & China Manufacturer |
| 302085 | 24 July | | Richard Wittmann (see prior) |
| 302165-9 | 27 July | | The Glasgow Plate Glass Co., Glasgow. Glass Maker |
| 302340 | 30 July | | William Ault, Derby. Manufacturer |
| 303344/5 | 16 August | | Richard Wittmann (see prior) |
| 303519 | 18 August | | G. Davidson & Co., Teams Flint Glass Works, Gateshead-on-Tyne. Glass Maker |
| 304097 | 30 August | | Jules Lang & Co. (see prior) |
| 304505 | 3 September | | Greener & Co., Wear Flint Glass Works, Sunderland. Glass Makers |
| 305840 | 20 September | | Percival, Vickers & Co. Ltd., Manchester. Glass Makers |
| 306459 | 4 October | | M. J. Reynolds (see prior) |
| 307899 | 23 October | | Max & Jacques Guggenheim, London. Glass & China Importers |
| 307946-8 | 25 October | | G. V. De Luca, Hill & Co., The French Flint Glass Bottle Co., London. Manufacturer |
| 308830 | 9 November | | A. Ruch & Co. (see prior) |
| 310593 | 10 December | | Gustav G. Doring, London. Glass Bottle Manufacturer |
| 310924/5 | 16 December | | Scotney & Earnshaw, London. Glass Maker |
| 311070-2 | 18 December | | Herbert Price & Co., London. Wholesale China & Glass Merchant |
| 311867 | 5 January | 1898 | Edward J. Shaw, Astral Works, Walsall. Lamp Manufacturer |

| *Registration* No. | *Date* | *Year* | *Registered* Party |
|---|---|---|---|
| 312304 | 13 January | 1898 | G. V. De Luca, Hill & Co. (see prior) |
| 314494 | 18 February | | Percival, Vickers & Co. Ltd. (see prior) |
| 314569 | 19 February | | G. V. De Luca, Hill & Co. (see prior) |
| 314989 | 26 February | | James A. Cox, London. Glass & China Merchant |
| 315340 | 4 March | | John Walsh Walsh (see prior) |
| 315841/2 | 15 March | | Haswell J. Twiner, London. Glass & China Merchant |
| 316068 | 18 March | | Pilkington Brothers Ltd., Lancaster. Glass Maker |
| 316351 | 23 March | | The Lamp Manufacturing Co. Ltd., London. Lamp Manufacturer |
| 316413 | 24 March | | Burtles, Tate & Co., Poland Street Glass Works, Manchester. Glass Makers |
| 316997 | 5 April | | Hukin & Heath, Imperial Works, Birmingham. Silversmiths |
| 317331 | 15 April | | Jules Lang & Co. (see prior) |
| 317448 | 18 April | | Henry G. Richardson & Sons, Wordsley Flint Glass Works, Stourbridge. Glass Maker |
| 317720 | 23 April | | Antony Rueckl, Bienenthal, Bohemia, Austria. Glass Maker |
| 317767 | 25 April | | William Breffit, York. Glass Maker |
| 318345 | 6 May | | Henry G. Richardson & Sons (see prior) |
| 319082 | 18 May | | Jules Lang & Co. (see prior) |
| 319151 | 19 May | | Percival, Vickers & Co. Ltd. (see prior) |
| 319400 | 24 May | | Alfred Arculus & Co., Birmingham. Glass Maker |
| 319604/5 | 27 May | | James Stevens & Son |
| 320124 | 10 June | | G. Davidson & Co. (see prior) |
| 320494/5 | 18 June | | Schindler & Co. (see prior) |
| 321093 | 29 June | | The British & Foreign Bottle Co., London. Glass Maker |
| 321637 | 7 July | | G. V. De Luca, Hill & Co. (see prior) |
| 321667 | 8 July | | Alfred Arculus & Co. (see prior) |
| 322001 | 15 July | | Alfred Arculus & Co. (see prior) |
| 322177 | 20 July | | John Walsh Walsh (see prior) |
| 323035 | 4 August | | The Improved Electric Glow Lamp Co. Ltd., London. Lamp Manufacturer |
| 323220 | 8 August | | M. J. Reynolds (see prior) |
| 323288/9 | 9 August | | John Walsh Walsh (see prior) |

| Registration No. | Date | Year | Registered Party |
|---|---|---|---|
| 323997 | 20 August | 1898 | Percival, Vickers & Co. Ltd., Manchester. Glass Makers |
| 324169 | 23 August | | Alfred Arculus & Co., Birmingham. Glass Maker |
| 324870 | 2 September | | James Green & Nephew, London. China & Glass Merchant |
| 325071 | 7 September | | Jules Lang & Co., London. Glass & China Merchant |
| 325194 | 9 September | | Greener & Co., Wear Flint Glass Works, Sunderland. Glass Maker |
| 325497 | 14 September | | The Improved Electric Glow Lamp Co. Ltd., London. Lamp Manufacturer |
| 325539 | 15 September | | Greener & Co. (see prior) |
| 325615 | 16 September | | Alfred Arculus & Co. (see prior) |
| 327603 | 18 October | | Schindler & Co., London. Glass Maker |
| 328530/1 | 3 November | | James Stevens & Son |
| 328630-2 | 4 November | | Webb, Shaw & Co. Ltd., The Dial Glass Works, Stourbridge. Glass Maker |
| 328770-4 | 7 November | | Laurie & Lazarus, London. Art Ware Merchant |
| 330042 | 30 November | | Josef R. Sohne, Dux, Bohemia. Glass Maker |
| 330700 | 12 December | | M. J. Reynolds, Stoke-on-Trent. Engraver |
| 331189 | 19 December | | Henry G. Richardson & Sons, Wordsley Flint Glass Works, Stourbridge. Glass Maker |
| 332356-9 | 16 January | 1899 | M. J. Reynolds (see prior) |
| 332563 | 21 January | | Alfred Arculus & Co. (see prior) |
| 332564/5 | | | John Walsh Walsh, The Soho & Vesta Glass Works, Birmingham. Glass Maker |
| 332798 | 25 January | | Hukin & Heath, Imperial Works, Birmingham. Silversmiths |
| 333004 | 28 January | | Johnsen & Jorgensen, London. Commission Merchant |
| 333324 | 4 February | | Thomas Webb & Sons Ltd., Stourbridge. Glass Maker |
| 333367 | 6 February | | Johnsen & Jorgensen (see prior) |
| 333665 | 13 February | | G. V. De Luca, Hill & Co., The French Flint Glass Bottle Co., London. Manufacturer |
| 333753 | 14 February | | J. & R. Craw, London. Glass Merchant |
| 333851/2 | 16 February | | John Walsh Walsh (see prior) |
| 333944 | 18 February | | John Walsh Walsh (see prior) |
| 334085 | 21 February | | Weiss & Biheller, London. Importers |

| Registration No. | Date | Year | Registered Party |
|---|---|---|---|
| 334241 | 23 February | 1899 | Johnsen & Jorgensen (see prior) |
| 334242 | | | Weiss & Biheller (see prior) |
| 334596 | 1 March | | Johnsen & Jorgensen (see prior) |
| 334659 | 2 March | | The York Glass Co., Ltd., York. Glass Maker |
| 334962 | 9 March | | Jules Lang & Co. (see prior) |
| 334976 | | | Weiss & Biheller (see prior) |
| 335468 | 18 March | | G. V. De Luca, Hill & Co. (see prior) |
| 335478 | 20 March | | M. J. Reynolds (see prior) |
| 335479 | | | Johnsen & Jorgensen (see prior) |
| 335692 | 23 March | | A. Ruch & Co., London. Glass Bottle Manufacturer |
| 335854 | 27 March | | La Societe Anonyme des Glaces de Charleroi, Roux, Belgium. Glass Makers |
| 336112 | 1 April | | Schindler & Co. (see prior) |
| 336261 | 6 April | | Burtles, Tate & Co., Poland Street Glass Works, Manchester. Glass Makers |
| 336510 | 12 April | | Percival, Vickers & Co. Ltd. (see prior) |
| 336752 | 18 April | | John Walsh Walsh (see prior) |
| 336967/8 | 22 April | | Jules Lang & Co. (see prior) |
| 337349-53 | 28 April | | Johnsen & Jorgensen (see prior) |
| 337607/8 | 2 May | | Jules Lang & Co. (see prior) |
| 337930 | 9 May | | Johnsen & Jorgensen (see prior) |
| 338590 | 20 May | | Molineaux, Webb & Co. Ltd., The Manchester Flint Glass Works, Manchester. Glass Makers |
| 339015 | 2 June | | Laurie & Lazarus (see prior) |
| 339343 | 8 June | | Burtles, Tate & Co. (see prior) |
| 339350 | | | S. Reich & Co., London. Austrian Glass Manufacturer |
| 339402/3 | 9 June | | Webb, Shaw & Co. Ltd., The Dial Glass Works, Stourbridge. Glass Maker |
| 340647/8 | 3 July | | Johnsen & Jorgensen (see prior) |
| 340825 | 5 July | | G. Davidson & Co., Teams Flint Glass Works, Gateshead-on-Tyne. Glass Maker |
| 341077 | 10 July | | The British & Foreign Bottle Co., London. Glass Maker |
| 341684 | 17 July | | The Crown Perfumery Co., London. Manufacturing Perfumery |
| 342692 | 4 August | | Laurie & Lazarus (see prior) |
| 342852 | 8 August | | James A. Cox, London. Glass & China Merchant |
| 343063 | 11 August | | Greener & Co. (see prior) |

| Registration No. | Date | Year | Registered Party |
|---|---|---|---|
| 344484 | 4 September | 1899 | Federick (sic) E. Payton, Birmingham. Glass Merchant |
| 345228 | 15 September | | Thomas Shorter & Sons, London. Glass, China & Earthenware Merchant |
| 345789 | 23 September | | Laurie & Lazarus, London. Art Ware Merchant |
| 346764 | 9 October | | The Lamp Manufacturing Co. Ltd., London. Lamp Manufacturer |
| 346841 | 10 October | | Mappin & Webb Ltd., London. Silversmiths |
| 347446 | 19 October | | Henry Salsbury, London. Lamp Manufacturer |
| 349043 | 11 November | | G. V. De Luca, Hill & Co., The French Flint Glass Bottle Co. Ltd., London. Manufacturer |
| 349881 | 27 November | | M. & J. Guggenheim, London. Glass & China Importers |
| 350115 | 4 December | | Thomas Webb & Corbett Ltd., The White House Glass Works, Stourbridge. Glass Maker |
| 350676 | 14 December | | Scotney & Earnshaw, London. Merchants & Glass Manufacturers |
| 351372 | 5 January | 1900 | Burtles, Tate & Co., Poland Street Glass Works, Manchester. Glass Makers |
| 352198 | 20 January | | Molineaux, Webb & Co. Ltd., The Manchester Flint Glass Works, Manchester. Glass Makers |
| 352530 | 27 January | | Johnsen & Jorgensen, London. Commission Merchant |
| 353374 | 16 February | | John Walsh Walsh, The Soho & Vesta Glass Works, Birmingham. Glass Maker |
| 355149 | 24 March | | F. & C. Osler, Birmingham. Glass Maker |
| 355232 | 26 March | | John Ford & Co., Holyrood Glass Works, Edinburgh. Manufacturer |
| 355424 | 29 March | | Harry Salsbury (see prior) |
| 356046 | 12 April | | James Green & Nephew, London. China & Glass Merchant |
| 358727 | 13 June | | George Sowerby Ltd., Lemington Glass Works, Newcastle in (sic) Tyne. Glass Maker |
| 359416 | 27 June | | Charles E. Hill, Brighton. Importer |
| 360167 | 13 July | | G. Davidson & Co., Teams Flint Glass Works, Gateshead-on-tyne. Glass Maker |
| 360332 | 14 July | 1900 | Greener & Co., Wear Flint Glass Works, Sunderland. Glass Maker |
| 361366 | 3 August | | Percival, Vickers & Co. Ltd., Manchester. Glass Makers |
| 361580 | 8 August | | Jules Lang & Co., London. Glass & China Merchant |
| 362212 | 22 August | | Schindler & Co., London. Glass Maker |
| 362643 | 31 August | | Jules Lang & Co. (see prior) |
| 363130 | 8 September | | George Sowerby Ltd. (see prior) |
| 363606-8 | 18 September | | Jules Lang & Co. (see prior) |
| 364576/7 | 10 October | | The Glasgow Plate Glass Co., Glasgow. Glass Maker |
| 366190 | 13 November | | Schindler & Co. (see prior) |
| 366297 | 14 November | | Henry Salsbury (see prior) |
| 366502 | 20 November | | Stevens & Williams, Brierley Hill Glass Works, Stafford. Glass Makers |
| 367054 | 3 December | | Thomas Webb & Sons Ltd., Stourbridge. Glass Maker |
| 367883 | 20 December | | Weiss & Biheller, London. Importers |
| 368149 | 31 December | | Jules Lang & Co. (see prior) |
| 368272/3 | 3 January | 1901 | A. Ruch & Co., London. Glass Bottle Manufacturer |
| 368460/1 | 9 January | | J. Grossmith Son & Co., London. Wholesale Perfumer |
| 369254-6 | 28 January | | Hateleys Ltd., Aston. Glass & Chandelier Manufacturer |
| 369858 | 9 February | | Weiss & Biheller (see prior) |
| 370017 | 13 February | | Alfred Arculus & Co., Birmingham. Glass Maker |
| 370273 | 19 February | | Alfred Arculus & Co. (see prior) |
| 370320 | 20 February | | Jules Lang & Co. (see prior) |
| 370835 | 1 March | | Weiss & Biheller (see prior) |
| 371401 | 9 March | | Johnsen & Jorgensen Ltd. (see prior) |
| 371438/9 | 11 March | | Edward J. Shaw, Astral Works, Walsall. Lamp Manufacturer |
| 371480 | 12 March | | The Improved Electric Glow Lamp Co. Ltd., London. Lamp Manufacturer |
| 371553 | 14 March | | Alfred Arculus & Co. (see prior) |
| 371639 | 16 March | | Alfred Arculus & Co. (see prior) |
| 371733 | 19 March | | Weiss & Biheller (see prior) |
| 371885 | 22 March | | A. Ruch & Co. (see prior) |
| 372309 | 3 April | | G. V. De Luca (see prior) |
| 373032/3 | 20 April | | Schott & Gen, Jena, Germany. Glass Maker |
| 373598-600 | 3 May | | S. Reich & Co., London. Glass Maker |

| Registration No. | Date | Year | Registered Party |
|---|---|---|---|
| 373634 | 4 May | 1901 | Jules Lang & Co., London. Glass & China Merchant |
| 374215 | 16 May | | Weiss & Biheller, London. Importers |
| 374792 | 1 June | | George Sowerby Ltd., Lemington Glass Works, Newcastle-on-Tyne. Glass Maker |
| 375464 | 17 June | | Johnsen & Jorgensen Ltd., London. Commission Merchant |
| 375533 | 18 June | | Thomas Webb & Son Ltd., Stourbridge. Glass Maker |
| 375896 | 25 June | | John Walsh Walsh, The Soho & Vesta Glass Works, Birmingham. Glass Maker |
| 375977 | 26 June | | The Glasgow Plate Glass Co., Glasgow. Glass Maker |
| 376659 | 9 July | | Phillips's Ltd., London. Glass & China Dealers |
| 376708 | 10 July | | Johnsen & Jorgensen Ltd. (see prior) |
| 377055/6 | 18 July | | Robinson. King & Co. |
| 377126 | 20 July | | Wood Brothers & Co., Borough Flint Glass Works, Barnsley. Glass Maker |
| 377322 | 25 July | | Johnsen & Jorgensen Ltd. (see prior) |
| 377323 | | | Chance Brothers & Co. Ltd., Birmingham. Glass Maker |
| 377726/7 | 1 August | | Johnsen & Jorgensen Ltd. (see prior) |
| 378198 | 14 August | | Johnsen & Jorgensen Ltd. (see prior) |
| 378648/9 | 23 August | | John Walsh Walsh (see prior) |
| 378765 | 27 August | | Greener & Co., Wear Flint Glass Works, Sunderland. Glass Makers |
| 378861 | 28 August | | Jules Lang & Co. (see prior) |
| 379455 | 9 September | | Schindler & Co., London. Glass Maker |
| 381210 | 8 October | | Schindler & Co. (see prior) |
| 381646/7 | 18 October | | John Walsh Walsh (see prior) |
| 381704/5 | 19 October | | John Walsh Walsh (see prior) |
| 381854-7 | 22 October | | Weiss & Biheller (see prior) |
| 382225 | 28 October | | Messenger & Sons, Birmingham. Lamp & Chandelier Manufacturer |
| 382298 | 29 October | | Federick (sic) E. Payton, Staffordshire. Glass & China Merchant |
| 383623 | 25 November | | Johnsen & Jorgensen Ltd. (see prior) |
| 384633 | 14 December | | Schindler & Co. (see prior) |
| 385754 | 15 January | 1902 | Johnsen & Jorgensen Ltd. (see prior) |
| 385793 | 16 January | | Johnsen & Jorgensen Ltd. (see prior) |
| 385795-8 | 16 January | 1902 | Chance Brothers & Co. Ltd. (see prior) |
| 386121/2 | 23 January | | John Walsh Walsh (see prior) |
| 386174 | 24 January | | Phillips's Ltd. (see prior) |
| 386488 | 30 January | | John Walsh Walsh (see prior) |
| 386616/7 | 3 February | | Burtles, Tate & Co., Poland Street Glass Works, Manchester. Glass Makers |
| 387680 | 24 February | | James G. James, London. Glass Letter Manufacturer |
| 387780 | 26 February | | James Hateley & Co., Birmingham. Flint Glass Manufacturer |
| 388142 | 5 March | | Johnsen & Jorgensen Ltd. (see prior) |
| 388143 | | | Mortlocks Ltd., London. Glass & China Merchant |
| 388197 | 6 March | | Greener & Co. (see prior) |
| 388595 | 15 March | | Molineaux, Webb & Co. Ltd., The Manchester Flint Glass Works, Manchester. Glass Makers |
| 388857 | 20 March | | Burtles, Tate & Co. (see prior) |
| 389019 | 24 March | | Thomas Dukes, Stourbridge. Glass Maker |
| 389876 | 17 April | | G. V. De Luca, London. Merchant |
| 390019 | 22 April | | Percival, Vickers & Co. Ltd., Manchester. Glass Makers |
| 390020/1 | | | Thomas Dukes (see prior) |
| 391285 | 21 May | | Molineaux, Webb & Co. Ltd. (see prior) |
| 391513 | 27 May | | Johnsen & Jorgensen Ltd. (see prior) |
| 391761 | 2 June | | Schott & Gen., Jena, Germany. Glass Maker |
| 391814 | 3 June | | Burtles, Tate & Co. (see prior) |
| 392571 | 17 June | | G. V. De Luca (see prior) |
| 393177/8 | 2 July | | Falk, Stadelmann & Co. Ltd. |
| 393328 | 4 July | | Federick (sic) E. Payton (see prior) |
| 394152 | 21 July | | The Union Plate Glass Co. Ltd. |
| 394747/8 | 1 August | | Schott & Gen. (see prior) |
| 394758 | 1 August | | Jonas Lang & Co., London. Glass Merchant |
| 396001/2 | 26 August | | Falk, Stadelmann & Co. Ltd. |
| 396074 | 27 August | | T. (sic) Reich & Co. London. Glass Maker |
| 397605 | 19 September | | Johnsen & Jorgensen Ltd. (see prior) |
| 398503 | 7 October | | John Walsh Walsh (see prior) |
| 399983 | 31 October | | George Farmiloe & Sons Ltd., London. Lead & Glass Merchant |

| *Registration* No. | *Date* | *Year* | *Registered* Party |
|---|---|---|---|
| 400075 | 3 November | 1902 | M. J. Reynolds, Stoke-on-Trent. Engraver |
| 400564 | 11 November | | M. & J. Guggenheim, London. Glass & China Importers |
| 401196 | 25 November | | Weiss & Biheller, London. Importers |
| 401278-80 | 26 November | | Oesterreichische Glaskutten-Geselkschaft, Austria. Glass Maker |
| 402635/6 | 23 December | | Johnsen & Jorgensen Ltd. London. Commission Merchant |
| 402712/3 | 24 December | | Falk, Stadelmann & Co. Ltd. |
| 403012 | 3 January | 1903 | John Walsh Walsh, The Soho & Vesta Glass Works, Birmingham. Glass Maker |
| 403015 | | | Weiss & Biheller (see prior) |
| 403028 | 5 January | | Thomas Webb & Sons Ltd., Stourbridge. Glass Maker |
| 403073 | 6 January | | Weiss & Biheller (see prior) |
| 403075 | | | Weiss & Biheller (see prior) |
| 403657 | 17 January | | Burtles, Tate & Co., Poland Street Glass Works, Manchester. Glass Makers |
| 404248 | 29 January | | Jules Lang & Co., London. Glass & China Merchant |
| 404514 | 4 February | | Guiseppe V. De Luca, The French Flint Glass Bottle Co., London. Glass Maker |
| 404676 | 6 February | | Schindler & Co., London. Glass Maker |
| 404678 | | | Wood Brothers & Co., Borough Flint Glass Works, Barnsley. Glass Maker |
| 404686 | | | Johnsen & Jorgensen Ltd. (see prior) |
| 405034-6 | 11 February | | Liberty & Co. Ltd., London. Merchant |
| 405100-3 | 12 February | | The Societe Anonyme des Manufactures des Glaces et Produits Chimiques de St. Gobain, Paris. Manufacturer |
| 405139 | 13 February | | William Dow, Aberdeen. Glass Merchant |
| 405727 | 25 February | | Sir Hiram Maxim Electrical & Engineering Co. Ltd., London. Manufacturers of Electrical Lamps |
| 406300 | 5 March | | Burtles, Tate & Co. (see prior) |
| 407269 | 23 March | | Sir Hiram Maxim Electrical & Engineering Co. Ltd. (see prior) |
| 407375 | 25 March | | Jules Lang & Co. (see prior) |
| 407480 | 27 March | | Sir Hiram Maxim Electrical & Engineering Co. Ltd. (see prior) |
| 408211 | 8 April | | Richard F. Isherwood, Manchester. Glass Maker |
| 408379 | 11 April | 1903 | Jules Lang & Co. (see prior) |
| 408782-6 | 21 April | | S. Reich & Co., London. Glass Maker |
| 409057 | 27 April | | A. Riess & Co., London. Importers of Foreign Glass & China |
| 409145 | 28 April | | S. Reich & Co. (see prior) |
| 409508-13 | 5 May | | S. Reich & Co. (see prior) |
| 409768 | 9 May | | Stevens & Williams, Brierley Hill Glass Works, Stafford. Glass Makers |
| 409769 | | | John Walsh Walsh (see prior) |
| 409876 | 12 May | | William Ritchie, Glasgow. Glass Merchant |
| 410290-8 | 19 May | | S. Reich & Co. (see prior) |
| 410468 | 21 May | | Federick (sic) E. Payton, Handsworth. Glass & China Merchant |
| 410529 | 22 May | | Stafford Hill, The Eclipse Glass Works, London. Glass Bottle Manufacturer |
| 411103 | 3 June | | The British & Foreign Bottle Co., London. Glass Maker |
| 411733-41 | 16 June | | William Ritchie (see prior) |
| 413200 | 7 July | | J. Harrison & Co., Stafford. Glass Merchant |
| 413692 | 14 July | | The Glasgow Plate Glass Co., Glasgow. Glass Maker |
| 413701 | | | G. Davidson & Co., Teams Flint Glass Works, Gateshead-on-Tyne. Glass Maker |
| 414327 | 23 July | | Weiss & Biheller (see prior) |
| 414362-67 | 24 July | | Schott & Gen, Jena, Germany. Glass Maker |
| 414496 | 27 July | | S. Reich & Co. (see prior) |
| 415219 | 10 August | | The British & Foreign Bottle Co. (see prior) |
| 415221 | | | Johnsen & Jorgensen Ltd. (see prior) |
| 415661 | 18 August | | John Southerst, Manchester. Glass Maker |
| 415705-7 | 19 August | | Johnsen & Jorgensen Ltd. (see prior) |
| 415804 | 20 August | | William A. Bailey, London. Potter & Glass Manufacturer |
| 415969 | 24 August | | William Ritchie (see prior) |
| 416126/7 | 26 August | | Johnsen & Jorgensen Ltd. (see prior) |
| 416157-67 | 27 August | | William Ritchie (see prior) |
| 416239 | 28 August | | Chance Brothers & Co. Ltd., Birmingham. Glass Maker |
| 416507/8 | 3 September | | Chance Brothers & Co. (see prior) |
| 416512-9 | | | S. Reich & Co. (see prior) |
| 416529 | 4 September | | Schindler & Co. (see prior) |
| 417253 | 11 September | | The Eclipse Glass Works Ltd. (see prior) |

| Registration No. | Date | Year | Registered Party |
|---|---|---|---|
| 417598/9 | 19 September | 1903 | Johnsen & Jorgensen Ltd., London. Commission Merchant |
| 417965 | 25 September | | John Walsh Walsh, The Soho & Vesta Glass Works, Birmingham. Glass Maker |
| 418052 | 28 September | | John Southerst, Flint Glass Bottle Works, Manchester. Bottle Manufacturer |
| 419077 | 8 October | | Johnsen & Jorgensen Ltd. (see prior) |
| 419358 | 13 October | | James Green & Nephew, London. China & Glass Merchant |
| 419488 | 15 October | | The British & Foreign Bottle Co., London. Glass Maker |
| 420155-60 | 27 October | | Matthew Tytler & Sons, Greenock. Glass Makers |
| 421474 | 14 November | | The French Flint Glass Bottle Co. Ltd., London. Manufacturer |
| 421546 | 17 November | | The French Flint Glass Bottle Co. Ltd. (see prior) |
| 422146/7 | 25 November | | The British & Foreign Bottle Co. (see prior) |
| 423257/8 | 14 December | | Johnsen & Jorgensen Ltd. (see prior) |
| 423313 | 15 December | | Jules Lang & Co., London. Glass & China Merchant |
| 423693-9 | 23 December | | S. Reich & Co., London. Glass Maker |
| 424157/8 | 4 January | 1904 | Weiss & Biheller, London. Importers |
| 424198-201 | 5 January | | S. Reich & Co. (see prior) |
| 424247 | 6 January | | Jules Lang & Co. (see prior) |
| 424618 | 13 January | | Jules Lang & Co. (see prior) |
| 424756/7 | 15 January | | Messenger & Sons, Birmingham. Lamp & Chandelier Manufacturer |
| 425609 | 29 January | | S. Reich & Co. (see prior) |
| 426067 | 5 February | | A. Ruch & Co., London. Glass Bottle Manufacturer |
| 426322 | 9 February | | Jules Lang & Co. (see prior) |
| 426846-8 | 17 February | | Jules Lang & Co. (see prior) |
| 427017 | 19 February | | Schindler & Co., London. Glass Maker |
| 427029-33 | 19 February | | Weiss & Biheller (see prior) |
| 427524 | 25 February | | Burtles, Tate & Co., Poland Street Glass Works, Manchester. Glass Makers |
| 427847 | 1 March | | M. J. Reynolds, Stoke-on-Trent. Engraver |
| 427894 | 2 March | | Schindler & Co. (see prior) |
| 427905 | | | Weiss & Biheller (see prior) |
| 427995 | 3 March | | William A. Bailey, London. Potter & Glass Manufacturer |
| 428875 | 16 March | | William A. Bailey (see prior) |
| 429277/8 | 22 March | | Schindler & Co. (see prior) |
| 429743 | 29 March | 1904 | J. Grossmith, Son & Co., London. Perfumer |
| 430325 | 12 April | | Harry Peck & Co., London. Manufacturer |
| 430630 | 16 April | | Johnsen & Jorgensen Ltd. (see prior) |
| 430944 | 21 April | | Pilkington Brothers Ltd., Lancaster. Glass Maker |
| 431162-4 | 25 April | | Johnsen & Jorgensen Ltd. (see prior) |
| 431293-6 | 27 April | | Johnsen & Jorgensen Ltd. (see prior) |
| 431365 | 28 April | | The British & Foreign Bottle Co. (see prior) |
| 431862 | 6 May | | Jules Lang & Co. (see prior) |
| 431924 | 7 May | | John Southerst (see prior) |
| 432256 | 12 May | | Johnsen & Jorgensen Ltd. (see prior) |
| 432431 | 14 May | | Salsbury & Son Ltd., London. Lamp Manufacturer |
| 432703 | 17 May | | Chance Brothers & Co. Ltd., Birmingham. Glass Maker |
| 432755 | 18 May | | Jules Lang & Co. (see prior) |
| 433624 | 31 May | | Jules Lang & Son (see prior) |
| 433625 | | | William Ritchie, Glasgow. Glass Merchant |
| 433867 | 2 June | | Frederick Payton, Birmingham. Glass Dealer |
| 434662-70 | 15 June | | William Ritchie (see prior) |
| 435141 | 22 June | | Jules Lang & Son (see prior) |
| 435651/2 | 28 June | | John Walsh Walsh (see prior) |
| 435959 | 1 July | | John Walsh Walsh (see prior) |
| 435962 | | | Johnsen & Jorgensen Ltd. (see prior) |
| 436260 | 5 July | | Chance Brothers & Co. Ltd. (see prior) |
| 436719 | 11 July | | Salsbury & Son Ltd. (see prior) |
| 436804 | 12 July | | G. Davidson & Co., Teams Flint Glass Works, Gateshead-on-Tyne. Glass Maker |
| 436862/3 | 13 July | | John Walsh Walsh (see prior) |
| 436876 | | | The Improved Electric Glow Lamp Co. Ltd., London. Manufacturer |
| 436943 | 14 July | | Jules Lang & Son (see prior) |
| 437164 | 18 July | | Schott & Gen., Jena, Germany. Glass Maker |
| 437349/50 | 21 July | | Alfred Arculus & Co., Birmingham. Glass Maker |
| 437570 | 23 July | | Jules Lang & Son (see prior) |
| 437601 | 25 July | | Jules Lang & Son (see prior) |
| 437654 | 26 July | | Breidenbach & Co., London. Manufacturing Perfumer |
| 438209 | 4 August | | Harry Peck & Co., London. Manufacturer |

| *Registration* No. | *Date* | *Year* | *Registered* Party |
|---|---|---|---|
| 438542 | 9 August | 1904 | R. Wittmann, London. China & Glass Manufacturer |
| 438787 | 12 August | | Johnsen & Jorgensen Ltd., London. Commission Merchant |
| 439007 | 17 August | | Glashutte Vormals Gebruder Siegwart and Cie Actien Gesellschaft, Rheinland, Germany. Glass Manufacturer |
| 439199 | 19 August | | Johnsen & Jorgensen Ltd. (see prior) |
| 439537 | 24 August | | Falk, Stadelmann & Co. Ltd. |
| 439965 | 29 August | | Jules Lang & Son, London. Glass Merchant & Bottle Manufacturer |
| 440645-51 | 7 September | | S. Reich & Co., London. Glass Maker |
| 440767 | 9 September | | John Walsh Walsh, The Soho & Vesta Glass Works, Birmingham. Glass Maker |
| 441530 | 17 September | | Schindler & Co., London. Glass Maker |
| 441666 | 20 September | | John Walsh Walsh (see prior) |
| 441788-92 | 22 September | | Jules Lang & Son (see prior) |
| 441804/5 | | | Johnsen & Jorgensen Ltd. (see prior) |
| 442961 | 8 October | | Jules Lang & Son (see prior) |
| 443151 | 12 October | | Thomas Webb & Corbett Ltd., White House Glass Works, Wordsley. Glass Maker |
| 444212 | 29 October | | S. Reich & Co. (see prior) |
| 444370 | 1 November | | The Eclipse Glass Works Ltd., London. Glass Bottle Manufacturer |
| 444417 | 2 November | | Jules Lang & Son (see prior) |
| 444419/20 | | | Alfred Arculus & Co., Birmingham. Glass Maker |
| 444601-3 | 5 November | | S. Reich & Co. (see prior) |
| 444604 | | | G. Davidson & Co., Teams Flint Glass Works, Gateshead-on-Tyne. Glass Maker |
| 444605 | | | Johnsen & Jorgensen Ltd. (see prior) |
| 444681 | 7 November | | William A. Bailey, London. Potter & Glass Manufacturer |
| 444744 | 8 November | | Alfred Arculus & Co. (see prior) |
| 445181 | 16 November | | Falk, Stadelmann & Co. Ltd. |
| 445653 | 24 November | | Jules Lang & Son (see prior) |
| 446067 | 2 December | | Jules Lang & Son (see prior) |
| 446079-81 | | | Falk, Stadelmann & Co. Ltd. |
| 446594 | 12 December | | M. & J. Guggenheim, London. Glass & China Importers |
| 446747 | 14 December | | The French Flint Glass Bottle Co. Ltd., London. Manufacturer |
| 446924 | 17 December | 1904 | Weiss & Biheller, London. Importers |
| 447006 | 20 December | | John Walsh Walsh (see prior) |
| 447316 | 27 December | | Chance Brothers & Co. Ltd., Birmingham. Glass Makers |
| 447543-5 | 31 December | | S. Reich & Co. (see prior) |
| 447615/6 | 3 January | 1905 | M. & J. Guggenheim (see prior) |
| 448090 | 12 January | | Alfred Arculus & Co. (see prior) |
| 448364/5 | 16 January | | Johnsen & Jorgensen Ltd. (see prior) |
| 448986 | 26 January | | Chance Brothers & Co. Ltd. (see prior) |
| 449885 | 8 February | | The French Flint Glass Bottle Co. Ltd. (see prior) |
| 449988 | 9 February | | The French Flint Glass Bottle Co. Ltd. (see prior) |
| 450630/1 | 21 February | | Schindler & Co. (see prior) |
| 450823 | 23 February | | John Walsh Walsh (see prior) |
| 450838-42 | | | Johnsen & Jorgensen Ltd. (see prior) |
| 451273 | 1 March | | William A. Bailey (see prior) |
| 451544 | 4 March | | Hukin & Heath, Imperial Works, Birmingham. Silversmiths |
| 452043 | 11 March | | Johnsen & Jorgensen Ltd. (see prior) |
| 452189 | 14 March | | Jules Lang & Son (see prior) |
| 452425 | 16 March | | Richard Wittmann (see prior) |
| 452954 | 23 March | | Weiss & Biheller (see prior) |
| 453077/8 | 24 March | | Falk, Stadelmann & Co. Ltd. |
| 453483 | 31 March | | Hukin & Heath (see prior) |
| 454322/3 | 12 April | | S. Reich & Co. (see prior) |
| 454444/5 | 13 April | | Messenger & Son, Birmingham. Lamp & Chandelier Manufacturer |
| 454455/6 | | | William A. Bailey (see prior) |
| 455225 | 27 April | | Schindler & Co. (see prior) |
| 455497/8 | 2 May | | S. Reich & Co. (see prior) |
| 456270 | 13 May | | Thomas G. Webb, Manchester. Glass Maker |
| 456577 | 18 May | | Hukin & Heath (see prior) |
| 456828 | 22 May | | Henry G. Richardson & Son, Wordsley Flint Glass Works. Stourbridge. Glass Maker |
| 457361 | 26 May | | Jules Lang & Son (see prior) |
| 457832 | 1 June | | Jules Lang & Son (see prior) |
| 458014 | 3 June | | The French Flint Glass Bottle Co. Ltd. (see prior) |
| 458218 | 6 June | | Weiss & Biheller (see prior) |
| 458344 | 8 June | | John Walsh Walsh (see prior) |
| 458346 | | | Herbert Price & Co., London. China & Glass Merchant |
| 458785 | 17 June | | William A. Bailey (see prior) |
| 458983 | 21 June | | S. Reich & Co. (see prior) |

| *Registration* No. | *Date* | *Year* | *Registered* Party |
|---|---|---|---|
| 459027 | 22 June | 1905 | Samuel Keeling, Falcon Glass Works, Hanley. Glass Merchant |
| 460510 | 14 July | | Schindler & Co., London. Glass Maker |
| 460944 | 19 July | | The Eclipse Glass Works Ltd., London. Glass Bottle Manufacturer |
| 460949/50 | | | William A. Bailey, London. Potter & Glass Manufacturer |
| 460989 | 20 July | | Jules Lang & Son, London. Glass Merchant & Bottle Manufacturer |
| 462109/10 | 4 August | | S. Reich & Co., London. Glass Maker |
| 462690 | 16 August | | F. W. Neuburger & Co., London. China & Glass Merchant |
| 464073 | 2 September | | James Hateley, Birmingham. Flint Glass Manufacturer |
| 464621 | 11 September | | G. Davidson & Co., Teams Flint Glass Works, Gateshead-on-Tyne. Glass Maker |
| 464696 | 12 September | | John Walsh Walsh, The Soho & Vesta Glass Works, Birmingham. Glass Maker |
| 465540 | 22 September | | Johnsen & Jorgensen Ltd., London. Commission Merchant |
| 465660 | 23 September | | William A. Bailey (see prior) |
| 465892 | 26 September | | Greener & Co., Wear Flint Glass Works, Sunderland. Glass Makers |
| 466431 | 4 October | | Schindler & Co. (see prior) |
| 466544 | 5 October | | Johnsen & Jorgensen Ltd. (see prior) |
| 468077 | 30 October | | Fred Day, Barnsley. Glass Blower |
| 468590-2 | 8 November | | Johnsen & Jorgensen Ltd. (see prior) |
| 468873 | 11 November | | Jules Lang & Son (see prior) |
| 469519/20 | 22 November | | Johnsen & Jorgensen Ltd. (see prior) |
| 470127 | 1 December | | Jules Lang & Son (see prior) |
| 470262 | 4 December | | Pilkington Brothers Ltd., Lancaster. Glass Maker |
| 471692 | 4 January | 1906 | Johnsen & Jorgensen Ltd. (see prior) |
| 471761-70 | 5 January | | S. Reich & Co. (see prior) |
| 472064-76 | 11 January | | S. Reich & Co. (see prior) |
| 472207 | 13 January | | Jules Lang & Son (see prior) |
| 472301 | 16 January | | Johnsen & Jorgensen Ltd. (see prior) |
| 472480 | 19 January | | Falk, Stadelmann & Co. Ltd. |
| 472625 | 22 January | | Reynolds & Sons, Stoke-on-Trent. Engravers |
| 473273 | 31 January | | William A. Bailey (see prior) |

| *Registration* No. | *Date* | *Year* | *Registered* Party |
|---|---|---|---|
| 473435 | 2 February | 1906 | Hukin & Heath, Imperial Works, Birmingham. Silversmiths |
| 473554 | 6 February | | Johnsen & Jorgensen Ltd. (see prior) |
| 474109/10 | 16 February | | Jules Lang & Son (see prior) |
| 474238 | 19 February | | James Green & Nephew, London. China & Glass Merchant |
| 474329 | 20 February | | Burtles, Tate & Co., Poland Street Glass Works, Manchester. Glass Makers |
| 474330 | | | John Walsh Walsh (see prior) |
| 474924 | 28 February | | Falk, Stadelmann & Co. Ltd. |
| 475286 | 7 March | | Burtles, Tate & Co. (see prior) |
| 475366 | 8 March | | Johnsen & Jorgensen Ltd. (see prior) |
| 475648 | 14 March | | Frederick C. Payton, Birmingham. Glass Merchant |
| 476078 | 21 March | | John Walsh Walsh (see prior) |
| 476270 | 24 March | | Jules Lang & Son (see prior) |
| 476366 | 27 March | | Weiss & Biheller, London. Importers |
| 476448 | 29 March | | Henry Mayer & Co., London. Glass & China Importers |
| 476516 | 30 March | | Henry Richardson & Sons, Wordsley Flint Glass Works, Stourbridge. Glass Maker |
| 476881 | 4 April | | The French Flint Glass Bottle Co. Ltd., London. Manufacturer |
| 476986 | 5 April | | Clarke's Pyramid and Fairy Light Co. Ltd., London. Manufacturer |
| 477092 | 6 April | | William Ault, Derby. Manufacturer |
| 478191/2 | 1 May | | S. Reich & Co. (see prior) |
| 478834 | 9 May | | Thomas Goode & Co., London. Glass & China Merchant |
| 478903 | 10 May | | Jules Lang & Son (see prior) |
| 479162 | 12 May | | Jules Lang & Son (see prior) |
| 479368 | 17 May | | Jules Lang & Son (see prior) |
| 479730 | 23 May | | William Ault (see prior) |
| 480105/6 | 30 May | | Ingram & Kemp Ltd., London Works, Birmingham. Chandelier Manufacturer |
| 480125 | | | Clarke's Pyramid & Fairy Light Co. Ltd. (see prior) |
| 480885 | 18 June | | Samuel Eaton & Sons, Birmingham. Chandelier Manufacturer |
| 481519-22 | 27 June | | Liberty & Co. Ltd., London. Merchant |
| 483573 | 23 July | | Schindler & Co. (see prior) |
| 483793 | 26 July | | Johnsen & Jorgensen Ltd. (see prior) |

| Registration No. | Date | Year | Registered Party |
|---|---|---|---|
| 484799 | 11 August | 1906 | John Walsh Walsh, The Soho & Vesta Glass Works, Birmingham. Glass Maker |
| 484918 | 14 August | | Jules Lang & Son, London. Glass Merchant & Bottle Manufacturer |
| 486003 | 28 August | | Jules Lang & Son (see prior) |
| 486198 | 31 August | | Schindler & Co., London. Glass Maker |
| 486298 | 1 September | | George Davidson & Co., Teams Flint Glass Works, Gateshead-on-Tyne. Glass Maker |
| 486381 | 4 September | | John Walsh Walsh (see prior) |
| 486685 | 8 September | | Stuart & Sons, Stourbridge. Glass Maker |
| 486706 | 10 September | | Schindler & Co. (see prior) |
| 486969 | 13 September | | John Walsh Walsh (see prior) |
| 487200 | 15 September | | Schindler & Co. (see prior) |
| 487788 | 25 September | | John Walsh Walsh (see prior) |
| 487789 | | | Schindler & Co. (see prior) |
| 488023 | 27 September | | Jules Lang & Son (see prior) |
| 488368 | 2 October | | Jules Lang & Son (see prior) |
| 488888 | 8 October | | C. & E. Bougard, Manage, Belgium. Glass Maker |
| 489099/100 | 10 October | | The London Sand Blast Decorative Glass Works Ltd., London. Manufacturer of Decorative Glass |
| 489326 | 15 October | | S. Reich & Co., London. Glass Maker |
| 489719 | 22 October | | Schott & Gen., Jena, Germany. Glass Maker |
| 489850 | 23 October | | The British & Foreign Bottle Co., London. Glass Maker |
| 489854 | | | Weiss & Biheller, London. Importers |
| 489947 | 24 October | | Schott & Gen. (see prior) |
| 491329 | 15 November | | Johnsen & Jorgensen Ltd., London. Commission Merchant |
| 491837 | 23 November | | United States Glass Co., London. Glass Maker |
| 492244 | 30 November | | John Walsh Walsh (see prior) |
| 492468-70 | 6 December | | Max Kray & Co., London. Manufacturer |
| 492726-8 | 11 December | | Weiss & Biheller (see prior) |
| 493080 | 18 December | | Thomas Webb & Corbett Ltd., The White House Glass Works, Stourbridge. Glass Maker |
| 493237/8 | 21 December | | F. W. Neuburger & Co., London. China & Glass Merchant |
| 493373 | 28 December | | Jules Lang & Son (see prior) |
| 493475 | 31 December | | Thomas Webb & Corbett Ltd. (see prior) |
| 493485/6 | 31 December | 1906 | Falk, Stadelmann & Co. Ltd. |
| 493532 | 2 January | 1907 | John Walsh Walsh (see prior) |
| 493686 | 5 January | | Max Kray & Co. (see prior) |
| 493785 | 8 January | | A. Ruch & Co., London. Glass Bottle Manufacturer |
| 494747 | 24 January | | M. & J. Guggenheim, London. Glass & China Importers |
| 495273 | 1 February | | Falk, Stadelmann & Co. Ltd. |
| 495408/9 | 5 February | | Schindler & Co. (see prior) |
| 495682 | 8 February | | Falk, Stadelmann & Co. Ltd. |
| 496110 | 14 February | | Schindler & Co. (see prior) |
| 496449 | 19 February | | Gustav Boehm, London. Perfumery Manufacturer |
| 496583/4 | 21 February | | Johnsen & Jorgensen Ltd. (see prior) |
| 497306-11 | 4 March | | S. Reich & Co. (see prior) |
| 497354 | 5 March | | Herbert Mew, Isle of Wight. China & Glass Merchant |
| 497532 | 7 March | | Johnsen & Jorgensen Ltd. (see prior) |
| 497724 | 11 March | | Jules Lang & Son (see prior) |
| 497726 | | | A. Ruch & Co. (see prior) |
| 497872 | 13 March | | Jules Lang & Son (see prior) |
| 498162 | 15 March | | Weiss & Biheller (see prior) |
| 498958 | 26 March | | Jules Lang & Son (see prior) |
| 499022 | 27 March | | Johnsen & Jorgensen Ltd. (see prior) |
| 499334 | 4 April | | Johnsen & Jorgensen Ltd. (see prior) |
| 499445 | 5 April | | Mabel Priem, London. Glass Merchant |
| 499974 | 15 April | | Schindler & Co. (see prior) |
| 500502 | 20 April | | John Walsh Walsh (see prior) |
| 500650 | 23 April | | Schindler & Co. (see prior) |
| 501603 | 8 May | | Schindler & Co. (see prior) |
| 501821/2 | 11 May | | Burtles, Tate & Co., Poland Street Glass Works, Manchester. Glass Makers |
| 502044 | 15 May | | Burtles, Tate & Co. (see prior) |
| 502904/5 | 22 May | | Weiss & Biheller (see prior) |
| 504941/2 | 19 June | | Weiss & Biheller (see prior) |
| 505105-7 | 21 June | | S. Reich & Co. (see prior) |
| 505499 | 26 June | | Johnsen & Jorgensen Ltd. (see prior) |
| 505767 | 29 June | | Johnsen & Jorgensen Ltd. (see prior) |
| 506632/3 | 10 July | | John Walsh Walsh (see prior) |
| 506634 | | | The Army & Navy Cooperative Society Ltd., London. Manufacturer |
| 506873 | 12 July | | Constantin Kopp, Settenz, Bohemia. Glass Maker |
| 507206 | 15 July | | The French Flint Glass Bottle Co. Ltd., London. Manufacturer |
| 507457 | 19 July | | S. Reich & Co. (see prior) |

| *Registration* No. | *Date* | *Year* | *Registered* Party |
|---|---|---|---|
| 507678 | 22 July | 1907 | Schindler & Co., London. Glass Maker |
| 508970 | 9 August | | Schindler & Co. (see prior) |
| 509943 | 23 August | | Weiss & Biheller, London. Importers |
| 510076/7 | 26 August | | The French Flint Glass Bottle Co. Ltd., London. Manufacturer |
| 510395 | 28 August | | Schindler & Co. (see prior) |
| 510403 | | | Guiseppe V. De Luca, Bromley, Kent. Merchant |
| 510504 | 29 August | | Burtles, Tate & Co., Poland Street Glass Works, Manchester. Glass Makers |
| 510978/9 | 6 September | | Thomas Webb & Corbett Ltd., The White House Glass Works, Stourbridge. Glass Maker |
| 511318 | 11 September | | John Walsh Walsh, The Soho & Vesta Glass Works, Birmingham. Glass Maker |
| 511401 | 12 September | | Jules Lang & Son, London. Glass Merchant & Bottle Manufacturer |
| 511845 | 17 September | | John Walsh Walsh (see prior) |
| 511929 | 18 September | | George F. Webb, Manchester. Glass Maker |
| 512195 | 21 September | | Jules Lang & Son (see prior) |
| 512560 | 25 September | | George Davidson & Co., Teams Flint Glass Works, Gateshead-on-Tyne. Glass Maker |
| 512874 | 1 October | | S. Mordan & Co. Ltd., London. Manufacturer |
| 513163 | 4 October | | Thomas Webb & Corbett Ltd. (see prior) |
| 513236 | 5 October | | Pilkington Brothers Ltd., Lancaster. Glass Maker |
| 513721 | 12 October | | Henry G. Richardson & Sons, Wordsley Flint Glass Works, Stourbridge. Glass Maker |
| 514062 | 18 October | 1907 | S. Reich & Co., London. Glass Maker |
| 514133 | 19 October | | James Green & Nephew, London. China & Glass Merchant |
| 514597 | 28 October | | Weiss & Biheller (see prior) |
| 514650 | 29 October | | Schindler & Co. (see prior) |
| 514681 | | | Georges Lemiere, London. Glass Blower |
| 514796 | 31 October | | Greener & Co., Wear Flint Glass Works, Sunderland. Glass Makers |
| 514848 | 1 November | | George Davidson & Co. (see prior) |
| 516674 | 28 November | | William A. Bailey, London. Glass Manufacturer |
| 517385 | 10 December | | Henry Hunt, Manchester. Glass Maker |
| 517677 | 16 December | | Jules Lang & Son (see prior) |
| 517826 | 18 December | | Falk, Stadelmann & Co. Ltd. |
| 518541 | 3 January | 1908 | Weiss & Biheller (see prior) |
| 518739 | 10 January | | Falk, Stadelmann & Co. Ltd. |
| 518867 | 15 January | | Falk, Stadelmann & Co. Ltd. |
| 518913 | 16 January | | John Walsh Walsh (see prior) |
| 519017 | 20 January | | Schindler & Co. (see prior) |
| 519087 | 21 January | | Weiss & Biheller (see prior) |
| 519330 | 28 January | | Weiss & Biheller (see prior) |
| 519389 | 30 January | | Weiss & Biheller (see prior) |
| 519900/1 | 7 February | | Weiss & Biheller (see prior) |
| 519902 | | | The British & Foreign Bottle Co., London. Glass Makers |
| 520168 | 13 February | | The British & Foreign Bottle Co. (see prior) |
| 520225 | 14 February | | John Walsh Walsh (see prior) |
| 520386/7 | 18 February | | S. Reich & Co. (see prior) |
| 520598 | 24 February | | Jules Lang & Son (see prior) |
| 520674 | 25 February | | George Davidson & Co. (see prior) |
| 520878 | 28 February | | Weiss & Biheller (see prior) |